RACE AND NATION IN MODERN LATIN AMERICA

EDITED BY

Nancy P. Appelbaum,

Anne S. Macpherson, and

Karin Alejandra Rosemblatt

RACE&NATION
IN MODERN LATIN AMERICA

WITH A FOREWORD BY

Thomas C. Holt

AND AN AFTERWORD BY

Peter Wade

THE UNIVERSITY OF
NORTH CAROLINA PRESS
Chapel Hill and London

Designed by Heidi Perov
Set in Minion and Kabel
by Keystone Typesetting, Inc.

The paper in this book meets the guidelines for permanence and
durability of the Committee on Production Guidelines for Book
Longevity of the Council on Library Resources.

Some material in this book has been reprinted with permission in revised
form from Sueann Caulfield, "Interracial Courtship in the Rio de Janeiro
Courts, 1918–1940," in *In Defense of Honor: Morality, Modernity, and Nation
in Early-Twentieth-Century Brazil* (Durham: Duke University Press, 2000), and
Sarah C. Chambers, *From Subjects to Citizens: Honor, Gender, and Politics in
Arequipa, Peru, 1780–1854* (University Park: Pennsylvania State University
Press, 1999), copyright 1999 Pennsylvania State University Press.

Library of Congress Cataloging-in-Publication Data

Race and nation in modern Latin America / edited by Nancy P.
Appelbaum, Anne S. Macpherson, and Karin Alejandra Rosemblatt;
with a foreword by Thomas C. Holt and an afterword by Peter Wade.
    p. cm.
  Includes bibliographical references and index.
  ISBN 0-8078-2769-x (cloth : alk. paper)
  ISBN 0-8078-5441-7 (pbk. : alk. paper)
    1. Latin America—History—1830–   .   2. Nationalism—Latin America—
History.   3. Latin America—Race relations.   4. Race discrimination—Latin
America—History.   5. Ethnicity—Latin America—History.   6. Identity
(Psychology)—Latin America.   7. Social classes—Latin America—History.
8. Man-woman relationships—Latin America—History.
I. Appelbaum, Nancy P.   II. Macpherson, Anne S.
III. Rosemblatt, Karin Alejandra.
F1413.R33 2003
323.1′8′09–dc21   2002011044

CLOTH 07 06 05 04 03   5 4 3 2 1
PAPER 07 06 05   5 4 3 2

CONTENTS

THE FIRST
NEW NATIONS

Thomas C. Holt

In the preface to the revised edition of his *Imagined Communities*, Benedict Anderson notes that despite all the attention his book had received his crucial observation on the origins of modern national consciousness among Creoles of European descent in the Americas was strangely ignored.[1] The Eurocentric provincialism "that everything important in the modern world originated in Europe" remained undisturbed. The essays collected here—almost all of them from larger projects—signal the emergence of a formidable archive that will thoroughly challenge such provincial habits of thought. They also challenge Anderson's own provincialism, however, such as his misreading of the complex relations between race and nation—the subject of sustained criticism already— as well as his blindness to the mediating force of gender in shaping both.[2] Attacking this triad of race, nation, and gender from diverse terrains and angles of vision, these essays establish important markers that future inquiries must negotiate. Such inquiries should also be guided by the image of an Atlantic world in which influences moved in both directions across the seas.

Despite the many telling criticisms alluded to above, Anderson's thesis continues to be compelling, indeed, a necessary point of departure even for work that pushes its implications in entirely different directions. By positing that the modern nation is not a historical given, but the product of a social-historical process, Anderson puts the nation on the same conceptual terrain as race and gender. Once it is accepted that a nation-state must be "emotionally plausible" as well as "politically viable,"[3] the nation itself necessarily becomes an object of negotiation and contestation, for nonelite as well as elite groups. Once the sheer novelty of the modern nation-state is evoked, one realizes that the very capacity to think and feel "nation-ness" only became possible through a radical change of consciousness, a changed sense of space and time, and thus of social relations. Separation from king and country required a new consciousness of "we-ness"—one premised quite literally on novel criteria: not ancient lineage and not obeisance and fealty to an aristocratic polity. People must now picture themselves as part of a physical and conceptual abstraction, their loyalties, allegiances, and social ties meditated not in face-to-face interactions or embedded in a political-religious hierarchical order.

Euro-American Creoles are important to Anderson's argument, therefore, because they pioneered this break with past imaginings. They had both means and motive to create a consciousness of separateness that could only be manifested in terms of novel national formations. The means were exemplified by the Spanish administrative and commercial policy that established and reinforced the self-contained character and identity of these proto-nations. Bureaucratic functionaries mapped the terrains of future nations by their movements. As they recorded prices and shipping schedules, printers and gazetteers normalized for their readers the notion that they shared a common space and interests. Together with novels and newspapers, they "provided the technical means for 're-presenting' the *kind* of imagined community that is the nation."[4] With these came the sense of simultaneity through which linkages between people and events took form, structuring senses of place and identity that would lend themselves to national imagining. Discrimination within the colonial bureaucracy against Creoles—who were simultaneously upper class and colonial—provided the motive, as it reinforced a sense of difference, of "a fatal distinction" between themselves and *peninsulares* and of a common fate with fellow Creoles.

Rich and provocative as Anderson's analysis is, there are anomalies and disconnects within it. For example, there seems to be a contradiction between his intriguing commentary on the necessity of the emergence of print language vernaculars to the forms of consciousness underpinning national imaginaries and the fact that the Creoles who formed the first new nations shared the same language as their metropolitan adversaries. It is also curious that while most of his attention to American Creoles focuses on those in the Spanish empire, the first new nation fitting his model in fact arose in North America. More important still are suggestions by Latin American specialists that Anderson's schema actually misses important features of the evolution of Creole nationalism, the most significant being the multiple "bonds of dependence" that modified in practice any notion of "a horizontal comradeship."[5] Hierarchies of gender, race, and class molded both pre- and postrevolutionary communities, which leads us to the troubling and inescapable fact that all of these new American nations were formed in slave societies, with slaveholders prominent among those doing the imagining. The loudest cries of national belonging, to paraphrase Samuel Johnson, came from those who denied it to others.

This last point is perhaps most pertinent to the discussion here. With race sitting like the proverbial 500-pound gorilla at their independence feasts, the founding fathers of the new American nation in the North all but ignored it in their inaugural state documents. Moreover, despite being forced by military necessity to address the slavery question, those in the South did little more to break the profound silence of that founding generation on the problem of race. Simón Bolívar, for example, much like his counterparts to the North, brooded that American racial diversity worked against pure democracy.

The larger issue raised by their silence is not the hypocrisy of the founding generation of nationalists, but the possibility that race and gender might well be fundamental to and even constitutive of the very process of nation-making. Early-nineteenth-century ideologies of national formation were seamlessly linked with classical liberal theory, to its notions of civil society and a public sphere, to the values of individual consent and choice (economic as well as political). Indeed, as the editors of this volume point out in the Introduction, a fundamental premise of liberal theory was a society of "unmarked, raceless, even genderless individual[s]." In contrast to that abstraction, however, actual nations must be fashioned from existing identities that are gendered, racialized, and classified.

It is precisely here that the essays in this volume make decisive interventions into contemporary discussions of national formation. Challenging Anderson's claim that nationality and race occupy different conceptual space—the one thinking about historical destinies, the other, "outside history," dreaming of eternal contaminations[6]—the introductory essay plots instead the complex play of race, gender, and nation. These concepts are mutually constitutive and historically contingent. National identities were sometimes constituted as racial identities, and vice versa, at different historical moments and in response to different social and political needs. Several of the essays that follow demonstrate how race, too, is often transformed in step with the exigencies of nation-making. Most of all, the editors argue, we must recognize that both race and nation are not fixed in conceptual space: they are in motion, their meanings constructed, their natures processual, their significance at any given moment shaped by their historical context.

Thus, to the formative moment to which Anderson attends the editors add three other critical periods when the nature and meaning of race and nation were transformed, shaped by and shaping very different ideological and material determinants. The late nineteenth–early twentieth century witnessed the rise of a virulent scientific racism and, paradoxically, the explosive growth of export economies that demanded the immigration of workers from racially suspect stocks. The interwar years of the 1920s and 1930s saw similar antinomies, with immigration barriers being raised by one hand while the other clasped the racial "other" (mestizo, mulatto, or Indian) as a national emblem.[7]

It is clear, therefore, that only from *within* the national imaginary itself can the nation exist timeless and eternal, "moving calendrically through homogenous, empty time."[8] From any other perspective, nations are not imagined at one moment, once and for all, but must be periodically *reimagined*, even reinvented, often at moments of crises, precipitated by the need to determine who belongs and who does not, who defines the character of the nation and who is its antithesis.

American nations are exemplary of these historical forces because they were explicitly settler societies and therefore necessarily and undeniably multiethnic (multiethnicity being a quality that European societies have sometimes plausibly—if erroneously—denied). Each American nation also passed through similar phases of development with similar demands on its self-constitution: colonial separation, slavery emancipation, and export-driven growth that brought in new populations.

The latter two developments suggest the powerful influences of material forces—offstage but pressing on many of the analyses here—that shaped the antinomies of national destinies. Slavery emancipation brought confrontation—however muted or deflected—with the problem of determining the place of blacks in societies whose very identities were premised on their democratic character. Export-driven growth required workers and thus new population policies and dynamics.[9] Two world wars and a global depression forced to the surface issues of national subordination in international relations abroad and the need to control class relations at home. All of this suggests that discussions of these matters cannot be confined to an intellectual history terrain, a point implied in several of the essays below. The social and economic transformations of the world capitalist system at the dawn of the twentieth century formed a common template for reimagining the nation on both sides of the Atlantic.

The differences in what was imagined are also instructive, however. Undoubtedly, the most striking difference in the Latin American case was the phenomenon of *mestizaje*, the positive inflection given to interracial mixtures that shaped strategies of national imagining in several countries in the early twentieth century. Although manifested in different ways—from embracing Indian-white or black-white mixtures to glorifying the pure Indian—*mestizaje* and *indigenismo* challenged the exclusive association of modernity with whiteness. Although it could form part of a racially conservative agenda—for example, the whitening of the national population stock—it necessarily decoupled racial mixture from the idea of racial degeneration, which was so prevalent in North American and European thought. It always began as an initiative of white intellectual elites, however, and often served to maintain the social status quo. In this regard, Cuba is an interesting counterpoint. There the idea of black-white alliance (rather than biological mixture) was born of revolutionary struggle, thus emerging as a social-military necessity rather than an intellectual conceit. The revolution framed a raceless ideal that—despite betrayals—formed the basis of Afro-Cuban claims to national belonging for decades to come.[10]

Mestizaje had some parallels across the Atlantic, though with different inflections, which could be instructive to comparative analyses. Faced with a declining birthrate, French intellectuals and policymakers encouraged not simply the immigration of workers but their assistance in biologically reproducing the French nation. Not all immigrants were suitable for this role. Italians and Spaniards, being from putatively kindred Latin racial stocks, were favored; Africans and Asians were not. Even so, the goal was not so much a cultural mixture that created a new "cosmic race" as the rejuvenation of a lost French essence through a return to its hardy, virile, peasant origins.[11] In some ways, this mode of thinking was not dissimilar to that of Teddy Roosevelt, who dreamed of recovering America's lost manhood by a selective immigration of Europeans modeled after the earlier frontier generation. As in France, Asians and Africans were explicitly excluded from his national vision.[12] Each of these variants of *mestizaje* also shared a faith in the force of environment, physical, cultural, or moral, to shape a racial and, through it, a national destiny. For French and Latin American intellectuals, this faith accorded with an explicit neo-Lamarckian bias, but this does not account for America, where Mendelian genetics held sway.[13] Further evidence, perhaps, that science (and pseudo-science) was only one of the tools of racial and national imagining, a language for its expression, but not its source.

Gender provided the most powerful language to describe national and racial relations. Whether invoked as metaphor, metonym, or allegory, the very idea of nation and national belonging is more often than not expressed in familial metaphors. This is not surprising, since the essence of national belonging is that one can be called upon to kill or die for the nation. Intimations of fatality and mortality are among the more powerful, if underdeveloped, themes running through Anderson's account of how the nation becomes "emotionally viable." The family is the site where one's sense of mortality is most immediately negotiated. Nations, meanwhile, must be made to seem whole, despite being drawn from disparate elements, with different local identities and roles, and despite the absence of traditional religious or political sanction for that wholeness. Given that the function of a metaphor is to make the emotionally unfamiliar familiar by association with something known, then metaphors of familial relations can mediate the allocation of national roles, rights, responsibilities, and claims. It follows that such reasoning could pave the way for the preservation of male dominance as well—patriarchal power within the family being projected onto the nation.

The family metaphor opens the way to other gendered familial functions. In national narratives, heterosexual desire levels and subverts social and political differences of all kinds, with the processes of the nation's political union often being represented as relations between a man and a woman, often of different class, regional, or political origins. National (re)formation becomes a family romance (a striking example of which is the ending of Thomas Dixon's 1915 film, *Birth of a Nation*, in which sectional reconciliation is achieved through the marriage of a northern woman and a southerner).[14]

The iconographic power of such narratives and images may well reflect the fact that actual, biological reproduction is perceived to be essential to the reproduction of the nation. Mature capitalist economies generate cultures and values inimical to large families and high levels of reproduction. Immigrants augment the national workforce, but at a cost to its racial and/or cultural homogeneity; fissures therefore emerge between the perceived needs of the nation and those of capital. The timing of these difficulties may be instructive. They arose in the late nineteenth and early twentieth centuries, as capitalism matured and extended its global reach, pressing heavily upon the destinies of nations.

Thus, a century after its genesis, the modern nation confronted radically changed historical-material conditions, conditions that required not only different national population policies—French pronatalism, for example—but even a different mode of national imagining. A number of the essays here touch on the amazing national romance that Gilberto Freyre authored for Brazil. In Freyre's historical narrative Brazilian national character emerges out of the cultural and sexual union of master and slave—or, more specifically, out of the consensual embrace of the white male master and his female slave concubine. Sexual union mediated racial difference, binding together and melding a nation of racial opposites, notwithstanding that—as in other gender-mediated national relations—the results are unequal and hierarchical, the gift of citizenship coming from above. However problematic Freyre's image is, however much it may have sprung from his own complex personal and sexual history, however much it served the political ends of the Vargas regime, and however much it was contested by Paulista opponents of that regime who wished for a more respectable national pedigree, it obviously struck deep chords within ordinary as well as elite Brazilians.[15] Indeed, among its fruits is the much-debated but enduring image of Brazil as a racial democracy, the actual contradictions of which—as Sueann Caulfield shows—are lived out in the everyday lives of ordinary Brazilians.

We are brought back, then, to the power of national imagining and its necessary articulation with other, equally powerful identities that suture our sense of social belonging. The essays that follow are powerful testaments to the proposition that the modern nation cannot be imagined separate from racial and gender ideologies and relations.

NOTES

1. Benedict Anderson, *Imagined Communities: Reflections on the Origins and Spread of Nationalism*, rev. ed. (London: Verso, 1991), xiii.

2. For a critique that addresses both race and gender, see Anne McClintock, "No Longer in a Future Heaven: Gender, Racism, and Nationalism," in *Dangerous Liaisons: Gender, Nation, and Postcolonial Perspectives*, ed. Anne McClintock, Aamir Mufti, and Ella Shohat (Minneapolis: University of Minnesota Press, 1997), 89–112. See also Etienne Balibar, "Racism and Nationalism," chap. 3 in *Race, Nation, Class: Ambiguous Identities*, by Etienne Balibar and Immanuel Wallerstein (London: Verso, 1991).

3. Anderson, *Imagined Communities*, 51–52.

4. Ibid., 25.

5. See especially Claudio Lomnitz-Adler, "Nationalism as a Practical System: Benedict

Anderson's Theory of Nationalism from the Vantage Point of Spanish America," in *The Other Mirror: Grand Theory through the Lens of Latin America*, ed. Miguel Angel Centeno and Fernando López-Alves (Princeton: Princeton University Press, 2001), 329–59.

6. Anderson, *Imagined Communities*, 149.

7. The possible resonances between the *mestizaje* phenomena in Latin America and the contemporaneous "Negro vogue" in the United States and France deserve study. The fact that racially inflected immigration restrictions were at their peak in all these countries heightens the puzzle. See Tyler Stovall, *Paris Noir: African Americans in the City of Light* (Boston: Houghton Mifflin, 1996), and Nathan I. Huggins, *The Harlem Renaissance* (New York: Oxford University Press, 1971).

8. Anderson, *Imagined Communities*, 26.

9. This contradiction is explored in Alejandro de la Fuente, *A Nation for All: Race, Inequality, and Politics in Twentieth-Century Cuba* (Chapel Hill: University of North Carolina Press, 2001), chap. 3.

10. Ibid.; Ada Ferrer, *Insurgent Cuba: Race, Nation, and Revolution, 1868–1898* (Chapel Hill: University of North Carolina Press, 1999).

11. Elisa Camiscioli, "Producing Citizens, Reproducing the 'French Race': Immigration, Demography, and Pronatalism in Early Twentieth-Century France," *Gender and History* 13, no. 3 (Fall 2001): 503–621.

12. Gary Gerstle, "Theodore Roosevelt and the Divided Character of American Nationalism," *Journal of American History* 86, no. 3 (Dec. 1999): 1280–1307.

13. Nancy Leys Stepan, *"The Hour of Eugenics": Race, Gender, and Nation in Latin America* (Ithaca: Cornell University Press, 1991); William H. Schneider, *Quality and Quantity: The Quest for Biological Regeneration in Twentieth-Century France* (Cambridge: Cambridge University Press, 1990).

14. See Thomas Cripps, *Slow Fade to Black: The Negro in American Film, 1900–1942* (New York: Oxford University Press, 1977), 41–69.

15. For the influence of Freyre's own biography, see Jeffrey D. Needell, "Identity, Race, Gender, and Modernity in the Origins of Gilberto Freyre's Oeuvre," *American Historical Review* 100, no. 1 (Feb. 1995): 51–77. For regional and political influences, see Barbara Weinstein's article in this volume.

ACKNOWLEDGMENTS

This project began in an upstate New York Latin American history writing group in 1999, when Karin Rosemblatt proposed to Nancy Appelbaum and Anne Macpherson that we produce a volume of new historical research on race and nation in Latin America. In the process of turning this vision into reality, we not only have learned much about how to work with each other but have received valuable assistance from a larger community of colleagues.

We are grateful to all the chapter authors for their participation in the project, and for their painstaking writing and rewriting. We are particularly appreciative of Thomas Holt's and Peter Wade's support and of their incisive commentaries.

All of the contributors to the book read and provided helpful comments on the Introduction, especially Alexandra Stern and Sarah Chambers. In addition, Eileen Suárez Findlay, Thomas Klubock, and George Yúdice provided useful feedback. At a crucial juncture, Roger Kittleson pitched in. We thank them all, while taking ultimate responsibility for any errors contained in the final product. We also thank the two anonymous readers whose reports to the University of North Carolina Press were so valuable in revising the entire manuscript.

We are indebted to Elaine Maisner at the University of North Carolina Press for her patience and professionalism and, above all, for her enthusiasm regarding this project. Thank you also to Paula Wald, our project editor, and Mary Reid, our copyeditor, both of whom were meticulous in the best possible way.

Ken Pennington and the Office of the Vice President for Research and Computing at Syracuse University supplied funds for the preparation of the final manuscript. We thank Feigue Cieplinksi, graduate student in history at Binghamton University, for preparing the bibliography, and we are grateful to Teri Rombaut, secretary of the History Department at SUNY College at Brockport, for her technical expertise in helping to produce the final manuscript.

Our mentors at the University of Wisconsin–Madison—Florencia E. Mallon, Francisco A. Scarano, and Steve J. Stern—deserve special mention. Together they created a provocative learning environment, encouraged our individual development within a strong ethos of collegiality, and provided a model of committed scholarship. This book is the direct outgrowth of their insistence that we engage with, and learn from, each other.

Finally, our deep appreciation to those immediate family members who have made our lives more enjoyable and productive while we put together this project: Amy and Hank Appelbaum, Jamie Spiller, Joyce and Alan Macpherson, Lucy Klecky, Héctor Parada, Iván Rosemblatt, and Mario Rosemblatt.

RACE AND NATION IN MODERN LATIN AMERICA

RACIAL NATIONS

Nancy P. Appelbaum,
Anne S. Macpherson, and
Karin Alejandra Rosemblatt

We want it to be written into the Constitution that we *indígenas* are Mexican but that we have different cultures and traditions. Before 1994, being an *indígena* meant . . . abuse and humiliation, but now, as a result of our struggle, being an *indígena* is raising your head up high, with pride. This great Mexico that we have today is thanks to our forebears.

Queremos que quede escrito en la Constitución que los indígenas somos mexicanos pero tenemos diferencias de cultura y tradiciones. Antes de 1994, ser indígena era . . . maltrato y humillación, pero ahora con nuestra lucha ser indígena es ver con la cara arriba y con orgullo. El gran México que hoy tenemos es gracias a nuestros antepasados.

COMANDANTE MOISÉS, Tzeltal member of the Ejército
Zapatista de Liberación Nacional, 2 December 2000

Ever since eighteenth- and early-nineteenth-century colonial subjects conceived of creating independent republics out of highly stratified and diverse colonial societies, tensions between sameness and difference and between equality and hierarchy have shaped Latin American nation building. Elite and popular classes have argued about whether inclusion in the nation requires homogenization. Does equality among citizens necessitate merging distinct racial identities? Can the assertion of difference be made compatible with equality? When does difference interfere with a common citizenship? When does it reaffirm inequality and hierarchy? When does it overcome humiliation and generate pride? Must discourses of racial mixing always imply the reassertion of a dominant culture that is European or white? Answers to these questions have varied according to who has asked them, when, and why.

This book explores the historical roots of popular and elite expressions of race and national identity in postindependence Latin America. In this introductory essay, we argue that national identities have been constructed in racial terms and that definitions of race have been shaped by processes of nation building. The historical account we provide here rejects a priori definitions of both race and nation and posits that neither construct has been stable or universal. Diverse actors have ignored, expressed, appropriated, and transformed racial difference. Apprehensions of national identity have been equally varied. National or racial difference has sometimes reinforced discrimination and sometimes undermined it. Efforts to transcend difference have likewise functioned ambiguously.

Local, national, and transnational contexts—including North Atlantic imperialism and ingrained hierarchies of gender, class, and region—have patterned the articulations of race and nation. Thus, rather than taking the nation as a given unit of analysis or engaging in teleological accounts of the nation-building process, this essay looks at the transnational and local practices through which national identity has been constructed. We show that race has been central to gendered and sexualized constructions of nationhood and to the inscription of national territories in space.[1]

In order to recognize existing forms of racial identification without reifying them, this essay differentiates between race as a contingent historical phenomenon that has varied over time and space, and race as an analytical category. To minimize slippage between the two uses, we reserve the word "race" to mark phenomena that were identified as such by contemporaries. We define "racialization" as the process of marking human differences according to hierarchical discourses grounded in colonial encounters and their national legacies.[2] The meanings of race over time and space in postcolonial Latin America constitute the subject of our historical analysis; racialization is our conceptual tool.

Differentiating in this way allows us to stress the ubiquity of both race and racialization while highlighting the specific contexts that have shaped racial thinking and practice. We do not assume that race has always and everywhere made reference to biology, heredity, appearance, or intrinsic bodily differences, but instead we look at how historical actors themselves deployed the term. In addition, we acknowledge that systems of racial classification have coexisted and overlapped. Because scholarly understandings of race have been part of racialization, rather than simply descriptions of it, we examine academic debates in tandem with other elite and popular views.[3] As we suggest below, this approach allows us to move beyond still prevalent debates about whether or not racial discrimination exists in Latin America and beyond mechanistic contrasts of U.S. and Latin American racial systems. Instead, we ask how ideas regarding race have changed over time and how racial ideas have constructed dichotomies between North and South (as well as between and within Latin American nations).

Below, we begin by discussing elite racial ideology, which has been the primary focus of existing scholarship on race in Latin America. Next, we highlight the specific contributions of this volume. We discuss the spatial dynamics of race and nation, racial categorization, the formation of national identities, the gendering of nation-building and racial projects, and the relation between elite and popular understandings of race and nation. Further study of these issues will, we hope, allow scholars and activists to overcome simplistic dichotomies and to imagine integration without homogenization, and difference without hierarchy.

ELITE VISIONS OF RACE AND NATION

Elite racial discourse developed in response to metropolitan and local influences. In this section, drawing on conventional periodizations, we trace that development across four relatively distinct periods. Although the section stresses the political and economic contexts in which elites' ideas regarding race took shape, we do not assume that these factors were the only determinants of their racial practices. Nor should our attention to ruling classes and leading intellectuals be taken to imply that popular actors were unimportant. Elite practices developed in dialogue and conflict with popular mobilizations, which are examined at length in the final section of this essay. Moreover, our periodization should not be taken to suggest radical disjuncture. Each of the four periods was marked by continuities in definitions of race and nation, while various and contradictory discourses of racialized nationhood overlapped and blended. The timing and context of change also varied by country and region. The trajectories of Brazil and Cuba diverged especially sharply from regional patterns, since both outlawed slavery and became republics only in the late nineteenth and early twentieth centuries. This periodization should consequently be understood as fluid and the racial discourses of each moment as contested.

During the first moment, early-nineteenth-century liberal patriots faced the challenges of creating citizens out of colonial subjects and forging national communities from colonial societies marked by stark social divisions. Racial boundaries established in the colonial era had reaffirmed the exclusion of non-Europeans from the high spheres of economic and political power. Rural Indians, generally considered to be outside Spanish society, not only were subject to special taxes but also retained a degree of local political autonomy. Especially in the late colonial era, however, racial demarcations were far from rigid, and those outside European circles could ascend the social ladder by adopting European mores and/or acquiring wealth.[4]

Pro-independence elites revamped the racial divisions created under colonial rule, even as they drew on classical liberalism to reject imperial hierarchies and assert sovereignty and democracy. Liberalism presumed an unmarked, raceless, even genderless individual, yet nineteenth-century liberals on both sides of the Atlantic described the ideal qualities of citizens and nations in implicitly racialized and gendered terms.[5] Latin American liberal patriots, most of them members of the white colonial Creole upper class or descended from it, associated the traits of the proper citizen—literacy, property ownership, and individual autonomy—with whiteness and masculinity. Only properly cultured and educated men were deemed to have "civic virtue"; only they were capable of self-government; and only they accrued equal rights. Those men who did not conform to citizen norms—slaves, Indians, and the propertyless—were generally deemed to be dependent and excluded from full citizenship. Women, too, were denied full rights because they presumably lacked autonomy. Yet while certain leaders sought to permanently exclude women and non-elite men from participation in the nation, others insisted that, through training, uncivilized and dependent men could be made into virtuous citizens.[6] Still, when those in subordinate positions pushed too strongly for inclusion—either by seeking individual mobility or by mobilizing collectively—they were often contained through mechanisms of outright exclusion, including the restriction of suffrage.[7]

Liberal independence leader Simón Bolívar saw racial "diversity" as a central impediment to "perfect" democracy. For Bolívar, the lack of virtue of Venezuela's mixed-race population counseled against an overly representative democracy, and he advocated a strong executive and hereditary peerage. Central to his argument was the premise that all people were not in fact equal, and that the long oppressed and racially mixed population needed education before it could enjoy full citizen rights.[8] Twenty years later, Argentine liberal Domingo F. Sarmiento argued more strongly for the intrinsic incapacity of the nation's nonwhite inhabitants. For Sarmiento, the forging of a civilized nation implied the absolute negation of the barbaric colonial past forged by both Spaniard and Indian. To make Argentina anew, he proposed national instruction, the creation of a landowning yeoman farmer class, and European immigration. He also called for the extermination of those who could not be educated, especially indigenous peoples of the pampas. He thus emulated the more "advanced" United States, with its independent farmers and policy of warfare toward native populations.[9]

In contrast to liberals such as Sarmiento, nineteenth-century conservatives harked back to the colonial period, sought to restore the privileges of the Church and landed elites, and affirmed difference and hierarchy. Liberals excoriated conservative caudillos—military strongmen who practiced personalist forms of politics—as being backward, brutal, and barbarous and hence obstacles to the progress of the nation. Recent scholarship has shown that conservative nation-making was often racially inclusive, though not egalitarian. In Argentina, for example, Juan Manuel de Rosas forged ties with mestizo gauchos (cowboys), incorporated Afro-Argentines into the military, and wove aspects of Afro-Argentine culture into patriotic rituals. In Guatemala, Rafael Carrera took power with popular ladino and Mayan support, though he did not articulate a Guatemalan national identity in culturally Mayan terms. Rosas eventually abandoned Afro-Argentines, however, and destroyed the gaucho way of life by helping privatize the pampas. Carrera similarly supported the privatization and sale of indigenous lands in areas with commercial agricultural potential.[10] Yet in contrast to liberals, who saw sameness as a precondition for inclusion within the nation, conservatives created racialized forms of subordinate inclusion, even as they emphasized caste divisions over common citizenship.

During a second moment, as countries emerged out of the economic and political disorder that had characterized the early republics, late-nineteenth-century governments sought to maintain the social and labor order that they considered fundamental to national economic progress. Commodity exports rose dramatically, slavery ended, and proletarianization spread. Elites experimented with various forms of coercion to overcome popular reticence toward wage labor, often arguing that particular races were especially apt for certain types of work.[11] With the expansion of plantations and commercial agriculture, indigenous communal landholdings came under renewed attack.[12] The southern frontiers of Argentina and Chile were finally, and brutally, conquered.

Across Latin America, authorities sought to repopulate their nations by encouraging the immigration of presumably cultured and hardworking Europeans.[13]

Many intellectuals now conceptualized their nations as racially heterogeneous, without abandoning the whitened civilization ideal of nationhood first articulated by liberal leaders of the independence era. National leaders promoted education as well as immigration to turn a racially and culturally mixed population into one that was hardworking, progressive, and cultured in the way posited by the normative whitened definition of citizenship. But though elites advocated a process of cultural homogenization that, given prevalent cultural definitions of race, implied racial whitening, they maintained the racial distinctions that undergirded efforts to stratify and control labor and that justified regional hierarchies within their respective nations.

In addition, national leaders increased their efforts to understand, categorize, and control their populations. Intellectuals borrowed frequently if selectively from the new currents of racial science emerging in Europe, avidly reading Gustave LeBon, Cesare Lombroso, Hippolyte Taine, Count Arthur de Gobineau, and Herbert Spencer.[14] Thus armed with the legitimizing shield of modern science, they used the resources of expanding central states to measure, count, classify—and then improve—national populations. In the neo-Lamarckian version of eugenic science prevalent in Latin America, environmental conditions shaped heredity. As a result, elites sought racial rehabilitation not only through the control of reproduction championed by eugenicists in the United States but also through control of the social milieu. Authorities implemented hygiene and sanitation campaigns, taught housekeeping and puericulture (the science of conception, pregnancy, and childrearing), and sought to fortify citizens' bodies and brains through recreation and education. By uplifting their fellow citizens, they insisted, they would improve their national stock and compete with more advanced nations.[15] Even abolitionist arguments against slavery were often framed in these terms; slavery and blackness were both associated with backward social conditions that had to be overcome to ensure national progress.[16]

In a third moment, increasingly populist national projects emerged. Popular mobilization in the Cuban independence struggles of the late nineteenth century, the Mexican Revolution of 1910–20, and new peasant and urban working-class movements throughout Latin America, along with fledgling feminist movements, pressured elites to formulate more inclusive national projects. In the aftermath of World War I, and more coherently from the beginning of the 1930s depression, the economic doctrine of import-substitution stressed production for the domestic market and national self-sufficiency. As populist politicians of the mid-twentieth century tried to rally capitalists and workers (and sometimes peasants) behind industrialization, they used unifying discourses of racial similarity and national harmony to buttress cross-class and cross-gender alliances.[17] The idea that nations were cohesive races responded to popular pressure by offering a more expansive conception of citizenship. It also countered the pervasive power of the United States by positing a united national community.

Latin American intellectuals embraced an anti-imperialist position that inverted North Atlantic assertions of the inferiority of Latin American populations. In Cuba, José Martí and his generation of Cuban nationalists attempted to mobilize both ex-slaves and former slave masters against Spain by defining the Cuban nation as "raceless" and hence inclusive of all Cubans.[18] Later, the negritude movement inspired an artistic avant-garde to embrace Cuba's black origins as a source of national difference from the United States and Europe.[19] Early-twentieth-century theorists in Brazil, Mexico, Peru, and elsewhere—such as Gilberto Freyre, Manuel Gamio, José Vasconcelos, and Uriel García—repudiated the theory that Latin Americans were degenerate hybrids, articulating discourses of *mestizaje* that instead stressed the benefits of racial mixing. Some even argued for a positive eugenics—a healthy cross-breeding. Vasconcelos maintained that Latin American miscegenation was sparking the creation of a beautiful transnational "Cosmic Race." In casting the mestizo as the modern racial ideal, he and other Mexican intellectuals challenged the prevalent coupling of whiteness with modernity and citizenship. Brazilian intellectuals similarly described their nation in inclusive and explicitly antiracist terms as a "racial democracy." Meanwhile, *indigenistas* (intellectuals who exalted the Indian, or *indígena*) trumpeted the purity and beauty of native peoples, positing indigenous civilizations as the basis of national cultures and arguing that *indígenas'* advancement was crucial to national progress.[20]

The "cult of the mestizo" thus emerged at the same time as *indigenismo*. Some thinkers considered the "pure" Indian to be superior to the mestizo, as in Peru where *indigenistas* urged that indigenous peoples avoid diluting noble Indian blood through racial mixing. Others believed that the Indian would ultimately disappear into the "bronze race." *Indigenismo* was not necessarily incompatible with a discourse of *mestizaje*, and especially in Mexico some prominent "mestizophiles" were also *indigenistas*. But even those who idealized Indians and promoted indigenous rituals and languages still worked within racialized paradigms that ascribed inherent biological and cultural characteristics to each race. Moreover, promoters of both *mestizaje* and *indigenismo* were fundamentally concerned with preparing Indians for citizenship by integrating, educating, and modernizing them.[21]

During the fourth moment of nation building, after World War II and the Holocaust, scientists and politicians largely abandoned the explicit terminology of race. They did not, however, abandon the assumptions that underlay racial thinking. "Ethnicity" became a more acceptable term for what had previously been referred to as race, but the term "ethnic" was used mainly to describe groups—especially Indians—who did not conform to a racialized national norm, generally coded as either mestizo or white.[22] The shift toward ethnicity did not displace the reifying equation of culture, place, and human biology.

Moreover, the doctrines of modernization and development that arose in the 1950s and 1960s replicated the civilizational discourse of earlier eras. Social scholarship on the family patterns and gender mores of urban residents and on the landholding and consumption patterns of rural people promulgated an implicitly white, elite, and North Atlantic norm. Marxist scholars did not escape this developmental paradigm. For instance, Brazil's Florestan Fernandes subsumed Afro-Brazilians in a class project that would supposedly modernize them, erase the dysfunctions caused by the historical legacies of slavery, and promote the progress of Brazil as a whole.[23] The early Cuban Revolution took a similar stance toward Afro-Cubans.

In this fourth period, social movements increasingly questioned assumptions of racial fraternity and democracy and asserted difference. Decolonization in Africa, Asia, and the Caribbean occurred simultaneously with mobilizations in the United States for racial equality and ethnic autonomy, such as the Chicano, American Indian, civil rights, and Black Power movements, which often described their differences as national as well as racial. The pan–Latin American indigenous rights movement burgeoned in the last quarter of the twentieth century, culminating in the 1992 Quincentenary, when Afro–Latin Americans protested alongside indigenous peoples.

Revisionist scholars, too, participated in this demystification. As early as the 1950s, the São Paulo school of Brazilian social scientists, to which Fernandes belonged, documented widespread patterns of racial inequality.[24] Historians of slavery dispelled myths of slaveowner paternalism and magnanimity.[25] Studies of Cuba showed that extreme racial violence against blacks was not limited to the United States.[26] Scholars of ethnicity in Mesoamerica and the Andes emphasized the pernicious effects of the dismemberment of corporate indigenous communities in the name of progress, accentuating the problematic aspects of what Jeffrey Gould referred to in Nicaragua as the "myth of *mestizaje*."[27] Revisionists argued that doctrines of racial democracy, racial fraternity, and *mestizaje* were insidious myths that masked racial discrimination and stymied civil rights movements in Latin America.[28]

The revisionist critiques have aroused the ire of intellectuals who have criticized North American academics for imposing a North American obsession with race over class identity and for applying U.S. racial categories to much more fluid Latin American realities.[29] Important revisionist works by George Reid Andrews and Aline Helg, for example, have been called into question for lumping people of African descent into one racial category and downplaying the significance of the intermediary category of mulatto in Latin American history.[30] A polemic has thus emerged around issues such as whether racial democracy is or is not a myth, whether *mestizaje* is or is not ethnocide, and whether Latin America is less racist or more racist than the United States. These questions have given rise to important research. Such debates, however, reproduce the racial dilemmas that have plagued North Atlantic thinkers and Latin American elites since the time of the independence wars, asking if, how, and why Latin American nations differ from those in Europe and the United States. Like Vasconcelos and Freyre, some scholars promote a nationalist reassertion of Latin American difference. Others emphasize similarities.[31] Neither question the categorization of regions according to their racial characteristics. From this perspective, the United States and Latin America appear as unified wholes.

As we note below, the best new work on race and nation in Latin America moves beyond these debates by advancing a processual and contextual understanding of nation building and race-making. This volume draws on and deepens that scholarship by furthering our understanding of spatialization, racial categorization, nationalism, and gender. It also demonstrates how the elite theories outlined above were constructed through interactions with definitions of race and nation that came "from below." By examining the racial construction of nations and the diversity of racial formations within nations, this volume reframes discussions of racial and national similarities and differences. Our use of the concept of racialization, and our insistence on the variety of meanings that have been attributed to the term "race," allow us to focus on *why* different articulations arose, while noting the continuities that have made race and the racialization of national identities so pervasive.

RACE AND SPACE

Rather than taking boundaries for granted and comparing the racial characteristics of discrete national territories, this book foregrounds how race and nation have been conjointly constructed and projected in spatial terms. Spatial boundaries, we suggest, have been constructed by racialized ideas of progress and modernity.[32] As noted above, Latin American elites often sought to become more like the North, yet at other times they inverted this equation by asserting the superiority of the South's mestizo populations and racial democracies. But whether they accepted or confronted assumptions of the North's superiority, they drew distinctions between the racial order of their own nations and those of allegedly more modern, "whiter" nations. Rather than debate the accuracy of these reified distinctions, this volume attempts to understand how they constructed and naturalized relations of power by embedding them in space.

Aims McGuinness's essay traces how the very term "Latin America" emerged out of racialized transnational encounters. During the California gold rush of the late 1840s and 1850s, New Granada's (present-day Colombia's) province of Panama became an important international transit route. As migrants from the United States flooded the isthmus, they became involved in racially charged conflicts with local residents. Some New Granadan intellectuals countered the disruptive presence of the U.S. "Saxon race" by forging an oppositional "Latin American" racial-cum-geographical identity.

This volume also builds on Latin Americanist writing on the mutually constituting relation between regions, localities, and national states to examine how race relations and racialized idioms have framed discussions of sameness and difference *within* as well as between and among nations. Regional differences, Latin American scholarship has shown, were racialized.[33] Those regions that have been marked off as black and Indian (such as northeastern Brazil, highland Peru, or southern Mexico) have been labeled backward in relation to more modern, whiter regions (such as southern Brazil, coastal Peru, or northern Mexico). Regions identified as black or Indian, such as the Caribbean coast of Central America, have not been considered fully part of the nation.[34]

Barbara Weinstein's essay shows that the São Paulo elite's assertion of regional pride was often couched in the racialized discourse of modernization. Prominent Paulistas presented their region as the motor of the Brazilian economy, asserting that its advanced industrial infrastructure would pull the entire Brazilian nation upward. In their view, São Paulo stood metonymically for the modern whitened nation as a whole and against the "black" Northeast. The

Paulistas' opposition to the regime of Getúlio Vargas, which culminated in a 1932 regionalist uprising, drew on these racialized identities. While Vargas asserted a more populist, Freyrian, racially mixed vision of the nation, Paulista elites envisioned a modern nation that was implicitly whiter. Similarly, the Sonorans described in Gerardo Rénique's essay insisted on the superiority of their northern "*blanco-criollo*" regional type over the mestizo type of Mexico's center-south. In the years following the Mexican Revolution of 1910, these racialized regional identities bolstered Sonorans' successful bids to consolidate their power over the central government.

Though racialized regional differences could provoke conflict and even violence, and though nation-state formation at times involved the imposition of homogeneity, regionalism was not always antithetical to nation building.[35] Especially in the early years of the republics, when national leaders actively attempted to create unity out of geographical difference, intellectuals paradoxically emphasized racial and spatial heterogeneity within the national territory. Mid-nineteenth-century intellectuals, often sponsored by their national governments, explored and mapped their territories and classified peoples and other natural species.[36] The resulting geographical treatises and natural histories, along with *costumbrista* novels and illustrations, produced images of each nation-state as internally divided into separate races, regions, climates, and cultural practices. Intellectuals reified the cultural and geographic boundaries that marked off unified regions within the nation and naturalized hierarchy by embedding it in racially differentiated landscapes. Yet they also projected their nations as the aggregates of regional components.[37] In pointing to these racialized regional dynamics, we follow Peter Wade and others in arguing that nation building was not simply a homogenizing process based on the eradication of difference—though at times it functioned in that way.[38]

Race thus constructed space. At the same time, space constructed race: racial distinctions were created and reinforced through allusions to how place determined or shaped the racial characteristics of individuals and groups. Late-colonial efforts to identify the flora and fauna of the American territories had developed simultaneously with the construction of Creole identities that emphasized the racial differences between denizens of the Americas and peninsular-born Europeans.[39] Nineteenth-century geographical expeditions continued that enterprise and portrayed the environmental characteristics of specific locales as shaping the races that inhabited them. When the term "race" appeared in the resulting treatises, it could indicate the broad human races (Ethiopian/Black, Mongolian/Asian, Caucasian/White, American/Indian, and

Malay) laid out by Enlightenment thinkers or refer to specific nations, subnational regions, localities, or kin groups. Such varied usages, which could express overlapping as well as contradictory forms of identity, would continue in Latin America throughout the postcolonial era.

DEFINING RACE

In the eighteenth century the German naturalist J. F. Blumenbach divided humanity into the five distinct varieties mentioned above. Today, scholars generally reject such biologically determinist theories of human difference and insist that race is a social construct. They have not, however, fully moved beyond Blumenbach's racial typology. Nor have they abandoned the idea that race refers to visible attributes grounded in biological differences. In contrast, we argue here that racial categorization has not operated exclusively through biologically determinist scientific discourses. It is a mistake to assume, based on present understandings of race, that alternative past usages of the word "race" were not actually about race at all.[40] This, then, is the second major contribution of our approach: we provide a historical account of racial categorization, demonstrating how criteria for racial classification have shifted over time. Following authors Robert Young, Marisol de la Cadena, Nancy Stepan, Ann Stoler, and Matthew Jacobsen, among others, we contend that systems of racial classifications have drawn as often on cultural as biological criteria. Racial difference has been defined according to notions such as civilization, honor, and education that have been manifested in dress, language, and religion as well as body type. Moreover, like Jacobsen, we stress how various, sometimes even incompatible definitions of race have coexisted. In Latin America, scientists drew simultaneously on neo-Lamarckian systems of racial classification, premised on the overriding influence of the environment, and on notions of race grounded in immutable bodily differences. In fact, early-twentieth-century scientists confounded environment and heredity by positing that "racial poisons" such as syphilis, tuberculosis, and alcohol could modify the genes and make progeny degenerate.[41]

Alexandra Stern's essay in this book highlights the diverse conceptualizations of race at play in twentieth-century Mexico. Stern chronicles how, during the post–World War II era, "biotypology" eclipsed "mestizophilia" within Mexican scientific circles. With the rise of a version of Mendelian genetics that stressed the randomness of individual inheritance, eugenicists turned to biotypology, a science based on the measurements of physiognomic, mental, and behavioral characteristics. But though they largely discarded race as a scientific category, racialization continued. Biotypologists retained many aspects of prevailing racial theories, including an emphasis on the hereditary bodily manifestations of cultural differences. Their statistical comparisons of norms and averages, moreover, were based on Eurocentric assumptions regarding statistically "normal" body types.

In pointing to the variety of systems of racial categorization, this book shows that race has been more pervasive, resilient, and malleable than recognized by previous scholarship. Clearly, racial thinking in Latin America predated the new scientific racism of the late nineteenth century and persisted after the discrediting of racial science in the postwar era. The new scientific racism of the late nineteenth and early twentieth centuries represented a rearticulation of older ideas and new insights rather than a radical departure from earlier racial thinking. Neo-Lamarckians, for instance, harked back to early republican efforts to typologize and understand the environment in order to specify difference, and biologically determinist eugenicists built on colonial definitions of race based in inheritance, lineage, and bloodlines.

In addition, we show that Latin Americans did not import European racial theories wholesale but instead interpreted those theories through local racial ideologies.[42] Stern examines how Mexican intellectuals appropriated transnational scientific ideas. Rénique suggests that Sonoran migrants to California brought anti-Chinese theories back with them to Mexico and then used them for nationally and regionally specific ends. These insights regarding racial thinking lead us to challenge scholarship that posits hard boundaries between U.S. and Latin American practices of racial differentiation. That scholarship, we believe, has missed how racial conceptions have overlapped and changed over time. It has also focused too much on whether or not Latin American populations conform to U.S. racial classifications, thus failing to take adequate stock of how transnational processes—including scientific and cultural exchange, travel, commerce, migration, and imperialist military incursions—have shaped racialization in both North and South.

NATIONALISMS AND RACIAL DISCOURSE

Similarly, scholarship on nationalism has often missed the historically specific ways in which national communities have been defined and how diverse definitions of the nation have been mobilized by different actors. Our third contribution, then, is to point to the multiple imaginings of national community.

National belonging has often been understood as based in shared cultures rooted in common histories, or in shared lineages. National identity, moreover, has sometimes been seen as the teleological outcome of evolution, as an organic maturation, or as the result of social engineering. The nation has also been conceived of as a community united through a shared racial identification or by the homogenizing influence of a shared territory.[43]

References to national races, such as the "*raza chilena*" or the "New Granadan race," were common in the nineteenth and early twentieth centuries, but the relation of these national races to the presumably distinct races that inhabited each national territory varied.[44] For instance, immigrants, blacks, and Indians were often construed as being outside the nation.[45] As Rénique notes in his contribution to this volume, certain politicians and intellectuals defined the early-twentieth-century Mexican nation as mestizo in opposition to the contaminating influence of Chinese immigrants. The Chilean nation was often defined in opposition to the "barbarous" Mapuche Indians. At the same time, as new scholarship on Chile is showing, experts thought that the survival and reproduction of the Chilean national race depended on assimilating the previously excluded working classes. The nation's poorer inhabitants could implicitly whiten their racial stock and contribute to national progress through education, hard work, proper nutrition, and health care. In other contexts, racialized notions of nationhood worked neither through exclusion nor assimilation but instead accommodated hierarchy and difference. One could be at once a member of the "*raza mexicana*" and of the "*raza sonorense*." Syrian and Lebanese immigrants to Brazil were ultimately, if unevenly, accepted as Arab-Brazilians.[46]

Nationalism was often anti-imperialist yet mimetic, imitating the presumably white and modern nations of the North Atlantic. McGuinness suggests that elite intellectuals, when faced with the U.S. presence in the Isthmus of Panama, employed a discourse of anti-Yankee nationalism and transnational Latin unity to unite elites and popular classes. Still, they excluded Antillean blacks. Lillian Guerra argues in her contribution to this volume that the conservative leaders who headed Cuba's first republican government sought to make Cuba more like the United States by sponsoring European immigration.

As we argue more fully below, ideals of nation were mobilized by different individuals and groups for different ends—as were ideals of transnational and subnational community. As Guerra highlights, not all Cubans shared a whitened vision of the nation. Liberal elites advocated racial fraternity and a race-blind nation. Afro-Cuban veterans and striking workers invoked the same principles as the liberals in their bids to abolish discrimination and improve their social condition. But in Cuba as elsewhere, popular groups sometimes stressed racial difference in their bids for inclusion. It was perhaps because of these insistent popular pressures, as well as because of their own need for a subordinate workforce, that elites developed models of nationhood that permitted a degree of difference and hierarchy even as they sought to create a national community of shared interests. The ambiguities of *mestizaje* and racial democracy—which could at once imply a whitened homogeneity, a true mixture, or a coexistence of difference—are best understood in the context of these plural definitions of nationhood.

GENDERING RACE AND NATION

The fourth main contribution of this volume is to note how gender and sexuality shaped racialized conceptions of nation. As the essays by Rénique, Sueann Caulfield, and Anne Macpherson demonstrate, elites often linked political authority to masculine authority and racial eugenics to the control of sexuality and reproduction. In so doing, they bound private and public realms metaphorically and used that association to justify public regulation of sexual and domestic relations. Central to these regulatory efforts were revamped colonial conceptions of honor, nineteenth-century gender norms, and the sciences of hygiene and eugenics.

Intellectuals and statesmen invoked gender allegorically and metonymically, asserting national belonging or citizenship through familial and sexual metaphors that likened the nation to a family and the bonds of citizenship to the magnetic pull of sexual desire. Three common and overlapping metaphors of the nation were those of heterosexual coupling, racial fraternity, and filial pact. The erotic coupling of lovers from different racial, regional, or class backgrounds in nineteenth-century fiction, as Doris Sommer has shown, legitimated and naturalized the political community of the nation, with desire subverting difference. Still, the metaphor of nation as product of a unifying heterosexual embrace projected the patriarchal power of the family onto the nation. National romances legitimated and promoted race and class hierarchy, portraying subordinate groups as not only racially "other" but also as the feminized dependents of elite patriarchs. Metaphors of nation were thus marked by the tension between the leveling effects of heterosexual desire and the equation of sexual difference with cultural and racial hierarchy.[47] Gilberto Freyre's claim that Brazilian racial democracy emerged out of the affective ties forged in sexual relationships between white men and women of color can be seen as an effort to resolve that tension.[48] But while Freyre focused on how those ties underscored a consensual national order, his national myth could also be read as reinscribing racial hierarchy by equating it with gender hierarchy (and vice versa).

Gendered tropes of nation also referred more explicitly to relations among men. Especially in the nineteenth century, when civil and international wars plagued the region's fledgling nations, national belonging was often portrayed as a brotherhood shaped in the fraternal embrace of battle. For example, the founding trope of Cuban nationality, like the Belizean national myth discussed by Macpherson in this volume, excluded women. Cuban nationality allegedly originated in militarized homosociality among men that transcended race.[49] Middle-class leaders in late-nineteenth-century Belize (at the time the colony of British Honduras) similarly portrayed their embryonic nation as emerging out of slaves' loyalty to their masters in the eighteenth-century battles in which Britain repulsed Spanish attacks on the colony. Yet, given the hierarchies implicit in the military, this gendered construction of nationality structured racial hierarchies among men, turning "fraternity" into something less than horizontal. Moreover, father-and-son metaphors for the nation not only provided a language of mutual obligation but also reinforced paternalistic relations between political leaders cast as father figures and their humble "sons."[50]

Hierarchical relationships among men were partially rooted in differential control over women's labor and sexuality. Men's ability to protect the sexual virtue of their women dependents affected their status vis-à-vis other men and their stature within the polity. The male-headed household, as the basis for men's citizenship, underscored women's roles as objects of contention. Whitened father figures' full citizen rights were affirmed, sons' poverty and difficulties in maintaining family headship were racialized, and elite male experts' public authority over junior men's women was legitimated. Men in subordinate positions did not reject the notion that their stature and citizen rights should be gauged by their sexual control over wives and daughters. Rather, they asserted their masculine propriety, honor, citizen virtue, and implicitly their whiteness, by affirming their ability to control the sexual and reproductive labor of "their" women.[51]

The presumed relation between family and nation led to concrete prescriptions regarding gender and sexuality. Both eugenicists and *indigenistas* sought to restrict interracial sex in order to maintain racial purity and strengthen their nations.[52] The Sonorans described by Rénique alleged that if Chinese immigrant men "mated" with Sonoran women, their degenerate children would precipitate the decline of their region and of Mexico as a whole. Sonoran elites championed chastity on the part of women and portrayed women who associated with Chinese men as promiscuous, uncivilized traitors to the nation.

In other contexts, references to racial purity were more oblique, but the link between women's virtue and the racial regeneration of the nation persisted. Hygienists of the late nineteenth and early twentieth centuries worried about producing sickly, inferior children and advocated premarital chastity and marital fidelity to prevent the spread of the sexually transmitted diseases that would lead to racial decline. In repudiating promiscuity, these medical experts reinforced the assumption that men—whether national leaders or male family members—needed to protect women sexually while also avoiding diseases that threatened the nation's moral integrity, racial vigor, and biological and demographic strength. The teaching of domestic economy and puericulture, both of which drew on Lamarckian eugenics, made women's domestic and childrearing activities crucial to the future of the nation.[53]

Prescriptions for proper sexual and domestic conduct thus persistently associated virtue with whiteness. Politicians and experts cast dissolute, uncultured, and degenerate men who failed to protect their wives and daughters as subordinate citizens with fewer rights. Prostitutes and other presumably promiscuous women were also deemed second- or third-rate citizens and were routinely and sternly policed. And although first-wave feminists contested women's subordinate status, they did not fundamentally challenge these racialized notions of virtuous womanhood and manhood.

POPULAR CONCEPTIONS OF RACE AND NATION

As should be evident from our discussion above, this book contributes to an account of how subordinated peoples have participated in the transnational, national, regional, and local production of race and nation. For conceptual as well as methodological reasons, historians have found it difficult to uncover popular views regarding race. Conceptually, much recent scholarship has viewed race as an elite construct and a tool of domination. For this scholarship, issues of how, why, and if subordinate groups have understood race, or how their actions have contributed to shaping elite racial ideology, have been at best secondary. Methodologically, too, the elite-authored texts with which historians have for the most part worked have made it notoriously difficult for historical scholarship to discern subaltern motivations.[54]

This volume builds upon the recent historiography on "everyday forms of state formation" in Latin America to foreground popular concepts of race and their emergence in dialogue with elite racial constructs. The state formation literature has used Antonio Gramsci's insights regarding the mutually constituting nature of state and civil society and the role of a shared cultural "common sense" in political mobilization to understand how elite and subordinated groups have, in negotiation with one another, built and transformed states and national projects. Historical transformation, from this viewpoint, has come about not as a result of popular mobilization or elite programs but precisely in the interaction of the two. Ideals of citizenship and nationhood have not been simply tools of oppression but negotiated frameworks or contested terrains on which the transformative, dialogic routines and rituals of rule took place.[55] The essays in this book, together with several recently published studies, expand on the state formation approach by showing how contests over the definition of communities, regions, and the nation, including the conflicts over labor, land, and voting that have figured so prominently in the historiography of Latin America, have been racialized.[56] Like recent volumes on the cultural encounters of imperialism, our book brings the international dimension back into play while writing against reified dichotomies like popular/elite and local/foreign.[57]

By illuminating how racial ideology pervaded popular discourse, several of the essays in this collection question the notion that ideals of mestizo, raceless, or even whitened nationhood were simply mystifying, elite-imposed myths that cemented oligarchic domination. The authors show instead how subaltern groups used racial discourse to their own ends. Popular groups could stress difference, and even their own inferiority, but could also cast aside pejorative identities such as *indio* altogether and assume more advantageous identities, such as mestizo or white. Subordinate peoples could also insist on the need for education and the material resources that might allow them to progress and become modern. Popular groups could demand education and material progress to defend particular identities or project their particular identities as part of a universal, shared, national character.

Overall, people of varying status used racial discourse, participating selectively in the institutions and the discursive fields of the state. Sarah Chambers's essay illustrates how members of indigenous groups in and around the provincial capital of Arequipa, Peru, discarded the identity of Indian. During the early republic, when indigenous identity helped guarantee access to land, many Arequipeños adopted the label "Indian." But once the national state overturned the laws protecting indigenous lands, native peoples increasingly adopted the label "Spanish" or "white" to avoid tribute payments. Moreover, as Chambers argues elsewhere, the regional Arequipa elite had long accepted a broad and fluid definition of white in part because it helped incorporate popular classes into an alliance against Lima during the civil wars following independence.[58]

The indigenous communities of Cauca, Colombia, studied by James Sanders, used racist nineteenth-century liberal discourses equating progress and whiteness and contrasted their own civilized industriousness to the ostensible savagery of both Afro-Colombians and lowland Amazon Indians. While sharing a hierarchical racial discourse with the elite, the Cauca Indians neither fused into a homogeneous national culture nor accepted elite ideologies in their entirety. Instead, they affirmed their place as Indians within the nation. Because opposing elite factions of liberals and conservatives sought to forge political alliances with Indians, the latter found it possible to negotiate the meanings of race and citizenship and successfully preserve communal lands and autonomy. While the Indians' strategy did not contest normative ideals, it did destabilize the equation of all Indians with backwardness.[59]

Focusing on domestic relations and everyday life, Sueann Caulfield's contribution to this volume contends that the urban working classes of twentieth-century Rio de Janeiro framed their experiences within the nationalist discourse of racial democracy even as they practiced racial discrimination in their choices of sexual and marital partners. Caulfield analyzes trial documents of sexual crimes in Rio de Janeiro to show that while ordinary Brazilians practiced considerable racial endogamy—a practice at odds with the ideology of racial democracy—they did not explain their desire for or resistance to certain partners in terms of race. Caulfield concludes that working-class Brazilians did value whiteness over blackness, but in a context of social mixing and a shared culture in which people were not explicitly defined primarily by race. Thus, in their daily lives they inhabited and continually reenacted the contradictions of Brazil's presumed racial democracy.[60]

Recent research on late colonial and early republican Cuba, including Guerra's contribution to this book, suggests that the discourse of racial fraternity and a "raceless" Cuba served Afro-Cubans as a potent tool for gaining greater equality. Alejandro de la Fuente has argued that the ideal of racial fraternity was both empowering and disempowering. Black and mulatto Cubans could and did use the discourse of a raceless nation to gain inclusion in the new political system and patronage networks in newly independent Cuba.[61] Guerra shows that popular and elite visions of the nation, even when framed in similar discourses of racial equality, often diverged in their particulars. Popular veterans of the independence wars based their claim to citizenship on their participation and sacrifice in creating a nation that they believed would include them. But while rejecting racial hierarchy and state-sanctioned racial identification in favor of the label "citizen," not all jettisoned racial identities. Rather, they adopted a variety of strategies. Those Afro-Cuban political leaders who feared that Afro-Cuban demands and mobilizations could conjure white fears of a race war used discourses of "racelessness" to discourage autonomous Afro-Cuban organizing. Some Afro-Cuban politicians even trumpeted the superiority of mulattos over whites and suggested that Afro-Cubans could gain equality only by acquiring education and culture. But others insisted both on autonomous Afro-Cuban political and cultural expressions and on Afro-Cubans' rights and responsibilities as citizens.

These insights regarding the diverse popular appropriations of nationalism are supported by studies of popular religiosity. As various authors have pointed out, popular groups' religious manifestations—which combined the recuperated elements of European, African, and/or indigenous traditions—could strengthen popular autonomy, despite their substantial convergence with orthodox practices. In many cases, hybrid popular religions functioned to reaffirm nationalist projects, as in Mexico's Hidalgo revolt, where popular classes marched for independence from Spain under the banner of the Virgin of Guadalupe, who represented Mexico's indigenous *and* Spanish heritage.[62]

As several essays in this collection reveal, the interplay between popular and elite conceptions of race and nation was shaped by U.S. imperialism. McGuinness argues that elite invocations of a Latin race in early-nineteenth-century Panama responded not just to elite concerns, but also to popular classes' vocal rejection of North American racial arrogance, which they experienced on a daily basis. Guerra suggests that allegations regarding the divisiveness and antinational character of Afro-Cuban demands were compounded by the threat of U.S. intervention. Macpherson argues that the Belizean middle class's awareness of the U.S. intervention against popular rebellion in Cuba, along with fears of black working-class mobilization, led them to intensify their adherence to British imperial racial norms and deny their mixed-race heritage. Elite and middle-class racial formulations thus emerged in dialogue with both imperial territorial expansion and popular groups' reaction to that expansion.

These explorations of popular racial discourse inevitably raise the questions of how and if historians can apprehend popular convictions. The petitions and court testimony that historians often use to reconstruct popular attitudes are mediated by legal discourse. These documents likely exaggerate popular convergence with elite ideas and provide an overly instrumental view of popular discourse. Yet to the extent that subaltern actions outside the courtroom and outside the immediate jurisdiction of political elites do not contradict testimony and petition, the insights gleaned from these documents can be used as a point of departure for the investigation of popular views regarding race.[63] Moreover, it may be wrong to see popular actions that take place at a distance from elites and state institutions as authentic while characterizing those that take place in more proximate negotiation as shallow or instrumentally performative.[64] Ultimately, to show how popular understandings of race operated and to see their effects on elite discourse, we need to conceptualize identity in a way that takes seriously the multiple and specific contexts in which it was enacted rather than taking popular resistance and opposition to elites for granted.

In the end, such an understanding of identity and nation formation may also allow us to move beyond the reified categories prevalent in scholarly analyses of the relation between race and nation. Thus, to say that elite formulations, such as the doctrine of racial democracy, were not simply pernicious myths is not to say that they were egalitarian, or that they meant the same thing to all social classes and racial groups, or even that they were similarly interpreted by the same person in different contexts. Doctrines of racial mixing or amalgamation, for instance, could be discourses of heterogeneity but could also devalue African and indigenous cultures and justify the alienation of communal lands. In defining and organizing their nations as composed of distinct regions and races, Latin American elite intellectuals did not overcome their own desires for whitening and homogenization. Efforts by elites to create inclusive nations have often been driven by their desire to maintain their own privilege and undergirded by racialized understanding of citizenship and nationhood. But ultimately, these processes were rent with conflict and negotiation between elite and subaltern actors.

CONCLUSION

In today's world of increasingly globalized neoliberalism, national and racial identities are once again being conjointly reconfigured. Along with pressures to transform the role of the nation-state has come a resurgence of ethnic and racial movements within and across national borders. Like the Zapatista militant quoted at the start of this essay, many Latin Americans of indigenous and African descent are now revalorizing their ethnic and racial identities. Many are putting forward the notion of a multicultural nation, asserting their right to both autonomy and participation in a national community. As this essay has made clear, these ideas have historical antecedents, even if the context in which they are being articulated is novel.

In response to resurgent ethnic and racial movements, scholars in the United States and Latin America have renewed their attention to race. This book is part of a reinvigorated scholarly interest in this topic evident throughout the Americas. Given that intellectual debates regarding race have historically influenced both state policies and social movements, one might ask how current scholarship participates in the reconfiguration of racial politics and identities. The concept of racialization, with its insistence on the connections between discourses of progress and race, might, for instance, reinforce hierarchies and discrimination by emphasizing racial divisions. It might also foreclose alternative narratives of progress by tying notions of development and improvement too firmly to difference and to the history of colonialism and its hierarchies. Ultimately, however, we see this kind of criticism as misguided. As the historical studies in this book demonstrate, the affirmation of race—like the affirmation of nation—may bolster political and economic inequalities and can lead to violence. But racial and national identities may also serve those committed to overturning inequality and injustice.

NOTES

1. On nationalism, gender, and imperialism, see Dipesh Chakrabarty, "Postcoloniality and the Artifice of History: Who Speaks for the 'Indian' Pasts?," *Representations*, no. 37 (Winter 1992): 1–26; Partha Chatterjee, *The Nation and Its Fragments: Colonial and Postcolonial Histories* (Princeton: Princeton University Press, 1993); Pransenjit Duara, *Rescuing History from the Nation: Questioning Narratives of Modern China* (Chicago: University of Chicago Press, 1995); Geoff Eley and Ronald Grigor Suny, eds., *Becoming National: A Reader* (New York: Oxford University Press, 1996); Anne McClintock, *Imperial Leather: Race, Gender, and Sexuality in the Colonial Contest* (New York: Routledge, 1995); Florencia E. Mallon, *Peasant and Nation: The Making of Postcolonial Mexico and Peru* (Berkeley: University of California Press, 1995); Ann Laura Stoler, *Race and the Education of Desire: Foucault's* History of Sexuality *and the Colonial Order of Things* (Durham: Duke University Press, 1995).

2. On "racialization," see Michael Banton, *Racial Theories* (Cambridge: Cambridge University Press, 1987), and Peter Wade, *Music, Race, and Nation: Música Tropical in Colombia* (Chicago: University of Chicago Press, 2000), esp. 14. Our thanks to Brigit Baur for helping us to see the utility of an approach based on the concept of racialization.

3. On the role of anthropology and science in constructing racial systems, see Lee D. Baker, *From Savage to Negro: Anthropology and the Construction of Race, 1896–1954* (Berkeley: University of California Press, 1998); Nancy Leys Stepan, *"The Hour of Eugenics": Race, Gender, and Nation in Latin America* (Ithaca: Cornell University Press, 1991); George W. Stocking Jr., *Race, Culture, and Evolution: Essays in the History of Anthropology* (New York: Free Press, 1968); Robert J. C. Young, *Colonial Desire: Hybridity in Theory, Culture, and Race* (London: Routledge, 1995).

4. On race in the colonial period see, among others, Sarah C. Chambers, *From Subjects to Citizens: Honor, Gender, and Politics in Arequipa, Peru, 1780–1854* (University Park: Pennsylvania State University Press, 1999); R. Douglas Cope, *The Limits of Racial Domination: Plebeian Society in Colonial Mexico City, 1660–1720* (Madison: University of Wisconsin Press, 1994); Ramón A. Gutiérrez, *When Jesus Came, the Corn Mothers Went Away: Marriage, Sexuality, and Power in New Mexico* (Stanford: Stanford University Press, 1991); Lyman L. Johnson and Sonya Lipsett-Rivera, eds., *The Faces of Honor: Sex, Shame, and Violence in Colonial Latin America* (Albuquerque: University of New Mexico Press, 1998); Verena Martínez-Alier, *Marriage, Class, and Colour in Nineteenth-Century Cuba: A Study of Racial Attitudes and Sexual Values in a Slave Society*, 2d ed. (Ann Arbor: University of Michigan Press, 1989); Leslie S. Offutt, *Saltillo, 1770–1810: Town and Region in the Mexican North* (Tucson: University of Arizona Press, 2001); Patricia Seed, *To Love, Honor, and Obey in Colonial Mexico: Conflicts over Marriage Choice, 1524–1821* (Stanford: Stanford University Press, 1998); Steve J. Stern, *The Secret History of Gender: Women, Men, and Power in Late Colonial Mexico* (Chapel Hill: University of North Carolina Press, 1995); Ann Twinam, *Public Lives, Private Secrets: Gender, Honor, Sexuality, and Illegitimacy in Colonial Spanish America* (Stanford: Stanford University Press, 1999).

5. Frederick Cooper, Thomas C. Holt, and Rebecca J. Scott, *Beyond Slavery: Explorations of Race, Labor, and Citizenship in Postemancipation Societies* (Chapel Hill: University of North Carolina Press, 2000); David Theo Goldberg, *Racist Culture: Philosophy and the Politics of Meaning* (Oxford: Blackwell, 1993); Carole Pateman, *The Disorder of Women: Democracy, Feminism, and Political Theory* (Stanford: Stanford University Press, 1989).

6. Chambers, *From Subjects to Citizens*, 161–254; Elizabeth Dore, "One Step Forward, Two Steps Back: Gender and the State in the Long Nineteenth Century," in *Hidden Histories of Gender and the State in Latin America*, ed. Elizabeth Dore and Maxine Molyneux (Durham: Duke University Press, 2000), 3–32.

7. On similar processes in the British Caribbean, see Thomas C. Holt, *The Problem of Freedom: Race, Labor, and Politics in Jamaica and Britain, 1832–1938* (Baltimore: Johns Hopkins University Press, 1992).

8. Vicente Lecuña and H. A. Bierck Jr., eds., *Selected Writings of Bolívar* (New York: Colonial Press, 1951), 173–97; John Lynch, *The Spanish American Revolutions, 1808–1926*, 2d ed. (New York: Norton, 1986), 191–266.

9. Domingo Sarmiento, *Facundo: Civilización y barbarie: Vida de Juan Facundo Quiroga*, ed. Raimundo Lazo (Mexico City: Editorial Porrúa, 1977). On Sarmiento and Argen-

tine liberalism, see Tulio Halperín Donghi, *El espejo de la historia: Problemas argentinos y perspectivas hispanoamericanas* (Buenos Aires: Editorial Sudamericana, 1987); Tulio Halperín Donghi et al., *Sarmiento, Author of a Nation* (Berkeley: University of California Press, 1994); Aline Helg, "Race in Argentina and Cuba, 1880–1930: Theory, Policies, and Popular Reaction," in *The Idea of Race in Latin America, 1870–1940*, ed. Richard Graham (Austin: University of Texas Press, 1990), 39–43; Francine Masiello, *Between Civilization and Barbarism: Women, Nation, and Literary Culture in Modern Argentina* (Lincoln: University of Nebraska Press, 1992).

10. On Argentina, see George Reid Andrews, *The Afro-Argentines of Buenos Aires, 1800– 1900* (Madison: University of Wisconsin Press, 1980), 96–101, 147, 180–81; John Charles Chasteen, "Black Kings, Blackface Carnival, and Nineteenth-Century Origins of the Tango," in *Latin American Popular Culture: An Introduction*, ed. William H. Beezley and Linda Curcio-Nagy (Wilmington, Del.: Scholarly Resources, 2000), 43–59; Mark D. Szuchman and Jonathan C. Brown, eds., *Revolution and Restoration: The Rearrangement of Power in Argentina, 1776–1860* (Lincoln: University of Nebraska Press, 1994).

On Guatemala, see Greg Grandin, *The Blood of Guatemala: A History of Race and Nation* (Durham: Duke University Press, 2000), esp. 99–109; Lowell Gudmundson and Héctor Lindo-Fuentes, *Central America, 1821–1871: Liberalism before Liberal Reform* (Tuscaloosa: University of Alabama Press, 1995); René Rethier Reeves, "Liberals, Conservatives, and Indigenous Peoples: The Subaltern Roots of National Politics in Nineteenth-Century Guatemala" (Ph.D. diss., University of Wisconsin–Madison, 1999), esp. chap. 2.; Arturo Taracena Arriola, *Invención criolla, sueño ladino, pesadilla indígena: Los Altos de Guatemala: De región a Estado, 1740–1850* (Antigua, Guatemala: Centro de Investigaciones Regionales de Mesoamérica, 1997).

11. For example, on the use of Chinese indentured labor as slavery declined in Cuba, see Rebecca J. Scott, *Slave Emancipation in Cuba: The Transition to Free Labor, 1860–1899* (Princeton: Princeton University Press, 1985), and Juan Pérez de la Riva, *Los culíes chinos en Cuba, 1847–1880: Contribución al estudio de la inmigración contratada en el Caribe* (Havana: Editorial de Ciencias Sociales, 2000).

12. Nancy Appelbaum, "Whitening the Region: Caucano Mediation and 'Antioqueño Colonization' in Nineteenth-Century Colombia," *Hispanic American Historical Review* 79, no. 4 (Nov. 1999): 631–67; Jeffrey L. Gould, *To Die in This Way: Nicaraguan Indians and the Myth of Mestizaje, 1880–1965* (Durham: Duke University Press, 1998); Evelyn Hu-DeHart, *Yaqui Resistance and Survival: The Struggle for Land and Autonomy, 1821–1910* (Madison: University of Wisconsin Press, 1984); Gilbert M. Joseph, *Revolution from Without: Yucatán, Mexico, and the United States, 1880–1924* (Durham: Duke University Press, 1988); Reeves, "Liberals, Conservatives."

13. On race, whitening, and immigration, see Helg, "Race in Argentina and Cuba"; Thomas E. Skidmore, "Racial Ideas and Social Policy in Brazil, 1870–1940," in Graham, *The Idea of Race*, 7–36; George Reid Andrews, *Blacks and Whites in São Paulo, Brazil, 1888–1988* (Madison: University of Wisconsin Press, 1991) and *The Afro-Argentines of*

Buenos Aires; Jeffrey Lesser, *Welcoming the Undesirables: Brazil and the Jewish Question* (Berkeley: University of California Press, 1995) and *Negotiating National Identity: Immigrants, Minorities, and the Struggle for Ethnicity in Brazil* (Durham: Duke University Press, 1999).

14. Charles A. Hale, "Political and Social Ideas in Latin America, 1870–1930," in *The Cambridge History of Latin America*, vol. 4, *C. 1870–1930* (Cambridge: Cambridge University Press, 1986), 367–441.

15. Stepan, *"The Hour of Eugenics"*; Eduardo A. Zimmerman, "Racial Ideas and Social Reform: Argentina, 1890–1916," *Hispanic American Historical Review* 72, no. 1 (Feb. 1992): 23–46; Dain Borges, "'Puffy, Ugly, Slothful and Inert': Degeneration in Brazilian Social Thought, 1880–1940," *Journal of Latin American Studies* 25, no. 2 (May 1993): 235–56; Julyan G. Peard, *Race, Place, and Medicine: The Idea of the Tropics in Nineteenth-Century Brazilian Medicine* (Durham: Duke University Press, 1999).

16. Emilia Viotti da Costa, *The Brazilian Empire: Myths and Histories*, rev. ed. (Chapel Hill: University of North Carolina Press, 2000); Thomas E. Skidmore, *Black into White: Race and Nationality in Brazilian Thought* (New York: Oxford University Press, 1974; reprint, with a new preface and bibliography, Durham: Duke University Press, 1993); Hebe Maria Mattos de Castro, *Escravidão e cidadania no Brasil monárquico* (Rio de Janeiro: Jorge Zahar, 2000).

17. See Susan K. Besse, *Restructuring Patriarchy: The Modernization of Gender Inequality in Brazil, 1914–1940* (Chapel Hill: University of North Carolina Press, 1996); John D. French, *The Brazilian Workers' ABC: Class Conflict and Alliances in Modern São Paulo* (Chapel Hill: University of North Carolina Press, 1992); Daniel James, *Resistance and Integration: Peronism and the Argentine Working Class, 1946–1976* (Cambridge: Cambridge University Press, 1988); Thomas Miller Klubock, *Contested Communities: Class, Gender, and Politics in Chile's El Teniente Copper Mine, 1904–1951* (Durham: Duke University Press, 1998); Asunción Lavrin, *Women, Feminism, and Social Change in Argentina, Chile, and Uruguay, 1890–1940* (Lincoln: University of Nebraska Press, 1995); Anne S. Macpherson, "'Those Men Were So Coward': The Gender Politics of Social Movements and State Formation in Belize, 1912–1982" (Ph.D. diss., University of Wisconsin–Madison, 1998); Karin Alejandra Rosemblatt, *Gendered Compromises: Political Cultures and the State in Chile, 1920–1950* (Chapel Hill: University of North Carolina Press, 2000); Mary Kay Vaughan, *Cultural Politics in Revolution: Teachers, Peasants, and Schools in Mexico, 1930–1940* (Tucson: University of Arizona Press, 1997); Barbara Weinstein, *For Social Peace in Brazil: Industrialists and the Remaking of the Working Class in São Paulo, 1920–1964* (Chapel Hill: University of North Carolina Press, 1996), among others.

18. José Martí, "Our America," in *Our America: Writings on Latin America and the Struggle for Cuban Independence*, ed. Philip S. Foner (New York: Monthly Review Press, 1977), 93–94. See also Jeffrey Belnap and Raúl Fernández, eds., *José Martí's "Our America": From National to Hemispheric Cultural Studies* (Durham: Duke University Press, 1998); Ada Ferrer, *Insurgent Cuba: Race, Nation, and Revolution, 1868–1898* (Chapel Hill: Univer-

sity of North Carolina Press, 1999); Lillian Guerra, "Crucibles of Liberation in Cuba: José Martí, Conflicting Nationalisms, and the Search for Social Unity, 1895–1933" (Ph.D. diss., University of Wisconsin–Madison, 2000).

19. See Robin D. Moore, *Nationalizing Blackness: Afrocubanismo and Artistic Revolution in Havana, 1920–1940* (Pittsburgh: University of Pittsburgh Press, 1997), and Alejandra Bronfman, "Reforming Race in Cuba, 1902–1940" (Ph.D. diss., Princeton University, 2000). Examples include Alejo Carpentier, *El reino de este mundo* (Mexico City: Edición y Distribución Ibero Americana de Publicaciones, 1949), and the art of Wifredo Lam.

20. On Mexico, see Gonzalo Aguirre Beltrán, *Obra polémica* (Mexico City: Instituto Nacional de Antropología e Historia, 1976); Agustín Basave Benítez, *México mestizo: Análisis del nacionalismo mexicano en torno a la mestizofilia de Andrés Molina Enríquez* (Mexico City: Fondo de Cultura Económica, 1992); David A. Brading, "Manuel Gamio and Official Indigenismo in Mexico," *Bulletin of Latin American Research* 7, no. 1 (1988): 75–89; Alexander S. Dawson, "Our Noble Race: Remaking the Indian in Revolutionary Mexico" (unpublished manuscript); Manuel Gamio, *Forjando patria*, 4th ed. (Mexico City: Editorial Porrúa, 1992); Alan Knight, "Racism, Revolution, and *Indigenismo*: Mexico, 1910–1940," in Graham, *The Idea of Race*, 71–114; José Vasconcelos, *The Cosmic Race/La raza cósmica*, trans. and with an introduction by Didier T. Jaén (Baltimore: Johns Hopkins University Press, 1997). On Peru, see Marisol de la Cadena, *Indigenous Mestizos: The Politics of Race and Culture in Cuzco, Peru, 1919–1991* (Durham: Duke University Press, 2000). On Brazil, see Gilberto Freyre, *Brazil: An Interpretation* (New York: Alfred A. Knopf, 1945), and Skidmore, *Black into White*.

21. De la Cadena, *Indigenous Mestizos*; Knight, "Racism, Revolution, and *Indigenismo*." As Deborah Poole has recently argued, discourses of *mestizaje* could be discourses of diversity. Deborah Poole, "Cultural Diversity and Racial Unity in Oaxaca: Rethinking Hybridity and the State in Post-Revolutionary Mexico" (paper presented to the New York City Latin American History Workshop, New York University, 26 Jan. 2001).

22. UNESCO, *The Race Concept: Results of an Inquiry* (Paris: UNESCO, 1951); Peter Wade, *Race and Ethnicity in Latin America* (London: Pluto Press, 1997).

23. Florestan Fernandes, *The Negro in Brazilian Society* (New York: Columbia University Press, 1969). On Fernandes and the São Paulo school, see also Costa, *The Brazilian Empire*, 244–46.

24. Important examples of this work available in English include Fernandes, *The Negro in Brazilian Society*, and Octavio Ianni, "Research on Race Relations in Brazil," in *Race and Class in Latin America*, ed. Magnus Mörner (New York: Columbia University Press, 1970), 256–78. See also Roger Bastide and Florestan Fernandes, *Brancos e negros em São Paulo*, 2d ed. (São Paulo: Editora Nacional, 1959).

25. Francisco A. Scarano, *Sugar and Slavery in Puerto Rico: The Plantation Economy of Ponce, 1800–1850* (Madison: University of Wisconsin Press, 1984); Stuart B. Schwartz, *Sugar Plantations in the Formation of Brazilian Society: Bahia, 1500–1835* (Cambridge: Cambridge University Press, 1985); Scott, *Slave Emancipation*.

26. Aline Helg, *Our Rightful Share: The Afro-Cuban Struggle for Equality, 1886–1912* (Chapel Hill: University of North Carolina Press, 1995); Tomás Fernández Robaina, *El negro en Cuba, 1902–1958: Apuntes para la historia de la lucha contra la discriminación racial* (Havana: Editorial de Ciencias Sociales, 1990).

27. Gould, *To Die in This Way*. See also Ronald Stutzman, "*El Mestizaje*: An All-Inclusive Ideology of Exclusion," in *Cultural Transformations and Ethnicity in Modern Ecuador*, ed. Norman E. Whitten Jr. (Urbana: University of Illinois Press, 1981), 45–94, and Tristan Platt, "Liberalism and Ethnocide in the Southern Andes," *History Workshop Journal* 17 (1984): 3–18.

28. On the lack of civil rights movements, see Michael George Hanchard, *Orpheus and Power: The* Movimento Negro *of Rio de Janeiro and São Paulo, Brazil, 1945–1988* (Princeton: Princeton University Press, 1994), and Andrews, *Blacks and Whites*.

29. See especially Pierre Bourdieu and Loïc Wacquant, "On the Cunning of Imperialist Reason," *Theory, Culture, and Society* 16, no. 1 (1999): 41–58. This view was also expressed at panels on Latin American history at the American Historical Association meetings in Washington, D.C., Jan. 1999 ("Racializing Region and Regionalizing Race in Latin America"), Chicago, Jan. 2000, and Boston, Jan. 2001 ("Practices and Narratives of Latin American Social and Cultural History").

30. Helg justifies this tactic by arguing that Cuba has been marked by a division between whites and the Cuban *clase de color* for specific historical reasons. Helg, *Our Rightful Share*. Compare Ferrer, *Insurgent Cuba*, 10–12, and Alejandro de la Fuente, "Myths of Racial Democracy: Cuba, 1900–1912," *Latin American Research Review* 34, no. 3 (1999): 39–73.

31. Classic comparisons of race relations in Latin America and the United States include Carl N. Degler, *Neither Black nor White: Slavery and Race Relations in Brazil and the United States* (Madison: University of Wisconsin Press, 1986), and Marvin Harris, ed., *Patterns of Race in the Americas* (New York: Walker Press, 1964). A more recent work is Anthony W. Marx, *Making Race and Nation: A Comparison of South Africa, the United States, and Brazil* (Cambridge: Cambridge University Press, 1998). For analyses of these debates, see John D. French, "The Missteps of Anti-Imperialist Reason: Bourdieu, Wacquant, and Hanchard's *Orpheus and Power*," *Theory, Culture, and Society* 17, no. 1 (2000): 107–28, and de la Fuente, "Myths of Racial Democracy."

32. For transnational analyses, which we extend by examining race, see Fernando Coronil, "Beyond Occidentalism: Toward Nonimperial Geohistorical Categories," *Cultural Anthropology* 11, no. 1 (Feb. 1996): 51–87; Gilbert M. Joseph, Catherine C. LeGrand, and Ricardo D. Salvatore, eds., *Close Encounters of Empire: Writing the Cultural History of U.S.–Latin American Relations* (Durham: Duke University Press, 1998); Frederick Cooper and Ann Laura Stoler, eds., *Tensions of Empire: Colonial Cultures in a Bourgeois World* (Berkeley: University of California Press, 1997).

33. On the racialized relationship between regions and nations, see Ana María Alonso, *Thread of Blood: Colonialism, Revolution, and Gender on Mexico's Northern Frontier* (Tuc-

son: University of Arizona Press, 1995); Nancy P. Appelbaum, *Muddied Waters: Race, Region, and Local History in Colombia, 1846–1948* (Durham: Duke University Press, forthcoming); de la Cadena, *Indigenous Mestizos*; Claudio Lomnitz-Adler, *Exits from the Labyrinth: Culture and Ideology in the Mexican National Space* (Berkeley: University of California Press, 1992); Benjamin S. Orlove, "Putting Race in Its Place: Order in Colonial and Postcolonial Peruvian Geography," *Social Research* 60, no. 2 (1993): 301–36; Mary Roldán, *Blood and Fire: La Violencia in Antioquia, Colombia, 1946–1953* (Durham: Duke University Press, 2002); Peter Wade, *Blackness and Race Mixture: The Dynamics of Racial Identity in Colombia* (Baltimore: Johns Hopkins University Press, 1993) and *Music, Race, and Nation*.

34. Darío A. Euraque, "The Banana Enclave, Nationalism, and Mestizaje in Honduras, 1910s–1930s," in *Identity and Struggle at the Margins of the Nation-State: Laboring Peoples of Central America and the Hispanic Caribbean*, ed. Aviva Chomsky and Aldo Lauria-Santiago (Durham: Duke University Press, 1998), 151–68; Aviva Chomsky, *West Indian Workers and the United Fruit Company in Costa Rica* (Baton Rouge: Louisiana State University Press, 1996); Edmund T. Gordon, *Disparate Diasporas: Identity and Politics in an African-Nicaraguan Community* (Austin: University of Texas Press, 1998); Steven Paul Palmer, "Racismo intelectual en Costa Rica y Guatemala, 1870–1920," *Mesoamerica* 17, no. 31 (June 1996): 99–121; Charles R. Hale, *Resistance and Contradiction: Miskitu Indians and the Nicaraguan State, 1894–1987* (Stanford: Stanford University Press, 1994).

35. Rather than assume that regions within nations are prenational holdovers that impede the formation of nation-states, some scholars of regionalism in Latin America and elsewhere consider how regions emerged as part of modern nation-state formation. See Celia Applegate, "A Europe of Regions: Reflections on the Historiography of Sub-National Places in Modern Times," *American Historical Review* 104, no. 4 (Oct. 1999): 1157–82, and Appelbaum, *Muddied Waters*.

36. Examples of such texts are cited and discussed in Appelbaum, *Muddied Waters*; Orlove, "Putting Race in Its Place"; Frank Safford, "Race, Integration, and Progress: Elite Attitudes and the Indian in Colombia, 1750–1870," *Hispanic American Historical Review* 71, no. 1 (Feb. 1991): 1–33; Derek Williams, "Indians on the Verge: The 'Otavalo Indian' and the Regional Dynamics of the Ecuadorian 'Indian Problem,' 1830–1940" (paper presented at the Conference on Latin American History, Boston, 4–7 Jan. 2001).

37. In other instances, the indigenous cultures of specific regions were made to represent the diverse racial heritage of the nation, as when Mexicans attempted to showcase their uniqueness at the world's fairs or, more recently, when Mexico has spotlighted its "authentic" tourist attractions. See Mauricio Tenorio-Trillo, *Mexico at the World's Fairs: Crafting a Modern Nation* (Berkeley: University of California Press, 1996), and Poole, "Cultural Diversity and Racial Unity."

38. Wade, *Music, Race, and Nation*, esp. 3–14.

39. On eighteenth-century Spanish American intellectuals and identity, see Jorge Cañizares-Esguerra, *How to Write the History of the New World: Histories, Epistemologies, and Identities in the Eighteenth-Century Atlantic World* (Stanford: Stanford University

Press, 2001); Derek Williams, "Indians on the Verge"; Safford, "Race, Integration, and Progress."

40. Matthew Frye Jacobson makes this point in *Whiteness of a Different Color: European Immigrants and the Alchemy of Race* (Cambridge, Mass.: Harvard University Press, 1998).

41. De la Cadena, *Indigenous Mestizos*; Jacobson, *Whiteness of a Different Color*; Stepan, *"The Hour of Eugenics"*; Stoler, *Race and the Education of Desire*; Young, *Colonial Desire*. See also Mary Weismantle and Stephen F. Eisenman, "Race in the Andes: Global Movements and Popular Ontologies," *Bulletin of Latin American Research* 17, no. 2 (May 1998): 121–42.

42. On Brazilian scientists' participation in racialized international theories of medicine, see Peard, *Race, Place, and Medicine*; Lilia Moritz Schwarcz, *O espetáculo das raças: Cientistas, instituições e questão racial no Brasil, 1870–1930* (São Paulo: Companhia das Letras, 1993); Stepan, *"The Hour of Eugenics."*

43. Benedict Anderson, *Imagined Communities: Reflections on the Origin and Spread of Nationalism*, rev. ed. (London: Verso, 1991); Chatterjee, *The Nation and Its Fragments*; Duara, *Rescuing History*. On the relationship between popular and elite nationalisms, see Mallon, *Peasant and Nation*, and Gilbert M. Joseph and Daniel Nugent, eds., *Everyday Forms of State Formation: Revolution and the Negotiation of Rule in Modern Mexico* (Durham: Duke University Press, 1994).

44. Rosemblatt, *Gendered Compromises*; Safford, "Race, Integration, and Progress."

45. On racial purity and nation, see Paul Gilroy, *"There Ain't No Black in the Union Jack": The Cultural Politics of Race and Nation* (London: Hutchison, 1987). Defining racial groups as outside of the nation can have extremely violent consequences, leading to expulsions and even massacres. On the Cuban massacre of 1912, see Helg, *Our Rightful Share*. On Haitians in the Dominican Republic, see Lauren Derby, "Haitians, Magic, and Money: *Raza* and Society in the Haitian-Dominican Borderlands, 1900 to 1937," *Comparative Studies in Society and History* 36, no. 3 (July 1994): 488–526; Silvio Torres-Saillant, "The Tribulations of Blackness: Stages in Dominican Racial Identity," *Callaloo* 23, no. 3 (Summer 2000): 1086–1111; Richard Lee Turits, "A World Destroyed, a Nation Imposed: The 1937 Haitian Massacre in the Dominican Republic," *Hispanic American Historical Review* 82, no. 3 (Aug. 2002): 585–630.

46. Thomas Miller Klubock, "Nationalism, Race, and the Politics of Imperialism: Workers and North American Capital in the Chilean Copper Industry," in *Reclaiming the Political in Latin American History: Essays from the North*, ed. Gilbert M. Joseph (Durham: Duke University Press, 2001), 231–67; Karin Alejandra Rosemblatt, "Sexuality and Biopower in Chile and Latin America," *Political Power and Social Theory* 15 (2002): 229–62; Lesser, *Welcoming the Undesirables*.

47. Doris Sommer, *Foundational Fictions: The National Romances of Latin America* (Berkeley: University of California Press, 1991).

48. Gilberto Freyre, *Casa grande e senzala*, 14th ed. (Recife: Imprensa Oficial, 1966).

49. Ferrer, *Insurgent Cuba*.

50. For examples, see Patrick J. McNamara, "Sons of the Sierra: Memory, Patriarchy, and Rural Political Culture in Mexico, 1855–1911" (Ph.D. diss., University of Wisconsin–Madison, 1999); Sandra McGee Deutsch, "Gender and Sociopolitical Change in Twentieth-Century Latin America," *Hispanic American Historical Review* 71, no. 2 (May 1991): 259–306; Mallon, *Peasant and Nation*.

51. Alonso, *Thread of Blood*; Sueann Caulfield, *In Defense of Honor: Sexual Morality, Modernity, and Nation in Early-Twentieth-Century Brazil* (Durham: Duke University Press, 2000); Chambers, *From Subjects to Citizens*; Eileen Suárez Findlay, *Imposing Decency: Race and Sexuality in Puerto Rico, 1870–1920* (Durham: Duke University Press, 1999); Rosemblatt, *Gendered Compromises*.

52. On these issues, see also Ann Laura Stoler, "Sexual Affronts and Racial Frontiers: European Identities and the Cultural Politics of Exclusion in Colonial Southeast Asia," in Cooper and Stoler, *Tensions of Empire*, 198–237.

53. Stepan, *"The Hour of Eugenics"*; Barbara Weinstein, "Unskilled Worker, Skilled Housewife: Constructing the Working-Class Housewife in São Paulo, Brazil, 1900–1950," in *The Gendered Worlds of Latin American Women Workers: From the Household and Factory to the Union Hall and Ballot Box*, ed. John D. French and Daniel James (Durham: Duke University Press, 1997), 72–99; Rosemblatt, *Gendered Compromises*; Lavrin, *Women, Feminism, and Social Change*; Findlay, *Imposing Decency*; Donna Guy, *Sex and Danger in Buenos Aires: Prostitution, Family, and Nation in Argentina* (Lincoln: University of Nebraska Press, 1991).

54. For ethnographic research that reveals subaltern racial thought, see Philippe Bourgois, *Ethnicity at Work: Divided Labor on a Central American Banana Plantation* (Baltimore: Johns Hopkins University Press, 1989); Gordon, *Disparate Diasporas*; Roger Lancaster, *Life Is Hard: Machismo, Danger, and the Intimacy of Power in Nicaragua* (Berkeley: University of California Press, 1992); Greg Urban and Joel Sherzer, eds., *Nation-States and Indians in Latin America* (Austin: University of Texas Press, 1991); Wade, *Blackness and Race Mixture*; Norman Whitten and Rachel Corr, "Contesting the Images of Oppression: Indigenous Views of Blackness in the Americas," *NACLA Report on the Americas* 34, no. 6 (May–June 2001): 24–28.

55. Joseph and Nugent, *Everyday Forms of State Formation*; Antonio Gramsci, *Selections from the Prison Notebooks*, ed. and trans. Quintin Hoare and Geoffrey Nowell Smith (London: International Publishers, 1971); Mallon, *Peasant and Nation*; Vaughan, *Cultural Politics in Revolution*.

56. Recent books that incorporate race into analyses of nation-state formation include Chambers, *From Subjects to Citizens*; Alejandro de la Fuente, *A Nation for All: Race, Inequality, and Politics in Twentieth-Century Cuba* (Chapel Hill: University of North Carolina Press, 2001); Ferrer, *Insurgent Cuba*; Findlay, *Imposing Decency*; Gould, *To Die in This Way*; Grandin, *The Blood of Guatemala*; Mark Thurner, *From Two Republics to One Divided: Contradictions of Postcolonial Nationmaking in Andean Peru* (Durham: Duke University Press, 1997).

57. Joseph, LeGrand, and Salvatore, *Close Encounters of Empire*; Cooper and Stoler, *Tensions of Empire*; Gordon, *Disparate Diasporas*; Louis A. Pérez Jr., *On Becoming Cuban: Identity, Nationality, and Culture* (Chapel Hill: University of North Carolina Press, 1999); Lisa Brock and Digna Castañeda Fuentes, eds., *Between Race and Empire: African-Americans and Cubans before the Cuban Revolution* (Philadelphia: Temple University Press, 1998).

58. Chambers, *From Subjects to Citizens*.

59. See also Dawson, "Our Noble Race."

60. On the everyday "making" of race, see Thomas C. Holt, "Marking: Race, Race-making, and the Writing of History," *American Historical Review* 100, no. 1 (Feb. 1995): 1–20.

61. De la Fuente, "Myths of Racial Democracy"; Bronfman, "Reforming Race."

62. Most scholarship on race and popular religiosity has been by anthropologists, for instance, John Burdick, *Blessed Anastácia: Women, Race, and Popular Christianity in Brazil* (New York: Routledge, 1998); Ruth Behar, *Translated Woman: Crossing the Border with Esperanza's Story* (Boston: Beacon Press, 1993); de la Cadena, *Indigenous Mestizos*, 231–71. For a historical account, see Kim D. Butler, *Freedoms Given, Freedoms Won: Afro-Brazilians in Post-Abolition São Paulo and Salvador* (New Brunswick: Rutgers University Press, 1998).

63. On the difficulty of recovering subaltern views, see Eric Van Young, "The New Cultural History Comes to Old Mexico," *Hispanic American Historical Review* 79, no. 2 (May 1999): 211–47.

64. Compare James C. Scott, *Domination and the Arts of Resistance: Hidden Transcripts* (New Haven: Yale University Press, 1990).

CHAPTER ONE

LITTLE MIDDLE GROUND

The Instability of
a Mestizo Identity in
the Andes, Eighteenth
and Nineteenth
Centuries

Sarah C. Chambers

In contrast to Mesoamerican nations, in the Andes positive discourses of *mestizaje* have been relatively weak and received official state sanction only in the middle of the twentieth century, if at all.[1] Instead, for much of the region's colonial and republican history, racial ideologies have recognized diversity but emphasized the division between Spanish and indigenous cultures, usually depicting the latter as uncivilized and backward. Even the elite defenders of Indians similarly highlighted a cultural dichotomy by criticizing racial mixing. This chapter will explore how systems of racial categorization created by the colonial state were negotiated by subalterns during the formative period of nation building in Peru. The distinction between Indians and all others was rooted in the colonial tribute system, which was continued even after independence from Spain in the 1820s. Although elites recognized an intermediate category of mestizos, which they often associated with illegitimacy and deviancy, tax structures and dominant racial ideologies discouraged subalterns from publicly embracing this label until the twentieth century.

This essay, like the others in this volume, begins from the assumption that there are no essential races. Rather, categories based upon both cultural and physical characteristics were defined by state policies and frequently contested by those to whom they were applied. Although colonial officials emphasized the superiority of "pure blood," they considered dress, language, and occupation as well as phenotype when assigning subalterns to racial categories. In the nineteenth century, ideologies of scientific racism became dominant in Latin America, but intellectuals continued to associate essential cultural attributes with various races, such as the assumption that Indians were uneducated. This blending of culture and genealogy is also reflected in the use of the terms "Spanish" and "white." For most of the colonial period, Americans of European descent were simply referred to as "Spaniards"; beginning in the late eighteenth century, the term "*blanco*" (white) came into increasing but not exclusive use. Even those of presumably mixed ancestry may have felt justified in claiming to be Spanish (and later white) if they participated in the dominant culture by, for example, speaking Spanish and wearing European clothing.

Of course, determining self-identification in the past is difficult. Especially for the illiterate majority, there remains a record only of how they defined themselves to state or ecclesiastical officials. Nonetheless, it would be difficult to maintain a cohesive shared identity without some public manifestations, so we can safely assume that the virtual absence of claims to *mestizaje* was not merely a screen. Since the emphasis was on tax-paying status, most of the examples from the documents used for this study are men; the racial identity of women came into question only when establishing one's genealogy. Following the lead of the editors' Introduction, ascriptive labels based upon presumed genealogy, such as "mestizo," will be referred to as racial categories; the term "ethnicity," by contrast, implies a shared group identity. I will argue that until recently there were mestizos, but no mestizo ethnicity, in the Andes.

The historiography of the Andes, like that for Latin America more broadly, emphasizes the multiplicity and fluidity of racial categories, in contrast to the dominant binary division between black and white in the United States. Increasing miscegenation throughout the centuries complicated the conquest-era dichotomy of two separates "republics"—Spanish and Indian—leading instead to a caste system with multiple categories for various race mixtures.[2] Unlike their colonizing counterparts in North America, Spaniards recognized the potentially infinite shades of the colonial population and in practice regularly referred at least to mulattos, *zambos*, *moriscos*, and *castizos*, as well as mestizos.[3] In their analyses of parish registers, censuses, and lawsuits, historians have emphasized the relative ability of individuals to move across these boundaries.[4] The figure of the Indian who became a mestizo by donning European clothing and moving to the city was a familiar one in colonial chronicles and literature.

Much less is known, however, about what later became of this figure in his new urban life (the example was rarely female). Did he identify himself as a mestizo, and if so what did this identity mean to him and his fellows? Did he share common interests as well as traits with other mestizos?

This essay will question that striking distinction between North American and Andean systems of racial classification, arguing that the original binary definition of race established with conquest continued to shape the caste system even as new categories proliferated and it became possible to move among them. Moreover, the continuing legal separation of Indians during the formative period of nation-state formation militated against the construction of universal notions of citizenship or homogenized national identity. Those identified as Indians, whether by themselves or others, occupied a clear legal and fiscal position in colonial and early republican society: they owed tribute, had access rights to communal land, were under the authority at the local level of ethnic chiefs (caciques or *kurakas*), and held a subordinate but protected legal status similar to minors. In the eighteenth century, the Bourbon royal family reinforced this racial boundary in an attempt to reduce the number of alleged Indians who were evading the head tax. Moreover, one need not ascribe to ideas of cultural authenticity to recognize that Indians could call upon language and custom in asserting a shared identity. The only group attribute uniting mestizos (and others of mixed race), by contrast, was that they were not Indians and were therefore exempt from all these legal rights and obligations.[5] Culturally, they were distinguished from Indians by their adoption of European, not hybrid, attributes. A second, more exclusive, boundary did separate off a colonial elite who could sufficiently demonstrate its purity of blood to attend universities and hold offices. Nevertheless, few of those recognized as white had the resources to claim these privileges, and such restrictions were eliminated with independence.

At either boundary, the definition of a mixed status was in purely negative terms: those so defined were excluded from various rights but held none in common. It is, therefore, difficult to speak of a mestizo *identity* in the colonial or nineteenth-century Andes, and self-conscious movements of mestizos were similarly rare.[6] Indeed, the dominant discourse attributing illegitimacy, moral laxity, and vagrancy to mestizos and other mixed-race peoples made it unlikely that any group would embrace and appropriate the term. Instead, when forced to identify themselves in court, many small farmers and artisans simply called themselves Spanish. Only when such claims were rejected by officials might they content themselves with the label of mestizo to escape the obligations imposed upon Indians.

This analysis is based on the case study of Arequipa, Peru, between 1780 and 1854.[7] The rich agricultural land immediately surrounding this midsized provincial city in the south supported many small and medium-sized landholders who grew food crops. While the city's elites also owned estates near the city, their wealth was based in the colonial period on coastal vineyards and, after independence, on the export of highland wool. The city's position between the coast and highlands thus allowed them to play the role of commercial middlemen. As the region came to play an important role in national political movements of the nineteenth century, the economic and professional elite propagated an image of the local population as similarly in between the colonial aristocrats of the coastal capital of Lima and the backward Indians of the highlands. Some native sons claimed the mantle of authentic *peruanidad*, implying a level of cultural synthesis, but, significantly, they did not use the racialized term "*mestizaje*."[8] On the contrary, Arequipa came to be known as the "White City," a racial double entendre building upon its architecture of white volcanic stone as well as the color of its Hispanic inhabitants. The 1792 census officially classified the urban population of Arequipa as 66.8 percent Spanish, 17.5 percent mestizo, 6.4 percent Indian, and 9.1 percent mulatto and black. Of course, such ethnic identities were not based on precise biological categories, but census takers recognized as white a higher proportion of inhabitants of Arequipa than of any other Peruvian city.[9]

This essay will trace the popular acceptance of an ideology of whitening in the efforts of common folk in Arequipa to gain at least tacit acceptance as Spanish. It begins by examining the important distinction between Indians and others established by colonial law and continued for decades after independence. As long as Indians received land in exchange for paying a head tax, there was an incentive for some villagers of even admittedly mixed race to claim an indigenous identity; as non-Indians increasingly appropriated the farmland around the city, however, the number of self-proclaimed Indians dramatically declined. Those trying to escape the burden of tribute usually asserted that they were Spanish even if they might be identified by officials, and even by their own neighbors, as mixed-race. Given the large proportion of the population of ambiguous genealogy, including members of the local elite, according to travelers, officials often avoided the use of racial labels in the interests of social peace. Arequipa was not unique in its development of a whitened identity, but it was not representative of a region where the majority of the population was identified as indigenous. The final section will discuss racial classification in the Andes more broadly (Ecuador, Peru, and Bolivia), arguing that even in regions with large indigenous populations and where elites were more sparing in whom they would recognize as Spanish, subalterns did not develop a collective identity as mestizos that could be used as a basis for political mobilization.

THE BOUNDARY BETWEEN INDIANS AND OTHERS

The 1792 census identified about 17 percent of the population in the valley of Arequipa as indigenous, the majority in the villages surrounding the city. Although Indians made up a large and distinct minority, various dynamics worked against the formation of cohesive indigenous communities with a politicized ethnic identity, in contrast to other Andean regions or the case of Cauca, Colombia, analyzed by James Sanders in this volume. The royal governor sent to Arequipa in the 1780s, Intendant Antonio Alvarez y Jiménez, noted that Indians in the villages around the city were very acculturated, and that the priests did not need to know Quechua.[10] Within the city, where 6 to 8 percent of the population was identified as indigenous, the cultural difference between Indians and others was even more blurred. As early as 1788, Alvarez y Jiménez noted that it was difficult to distinguish the Indians in their parish of Santa Marta from Spaniards.[11] By 1834 the prefect proposed dividing the parishes by neighborhood rather than race, because the Indians had mixed with Spaniards throughout the city.[12] Nevertheless, Indians were aware of their special status under Spanish law, and they made every effort to use it to their greatest advantage. As those advantages declined from the eighteenth into the nineteenth century, however, so too did the number willing to publicly embrace an indigenous identity.

In a region and period where sustained contact between Indians and Spaniards had resulted in significant acculturation, the strongest common denominator among the former was their right to a plot of land in exchange for paying tribute to the king.[13] Most Indians who lived in the villages earned their livelihood in agriculture, and their most secure access to land was through the periodic distributions of communal holdings. This right to land in exchange for paying tribute was attractive enough during the colonial period that even persons of apparently mixed race might claim an indigenous identity. After the tribute census of 1786, there was not enough community land for each Indian in the village of Tiabaya to get a plot. Agustín Alpaca, the cacique of Cayma who had jurisdiction there, protested that land had been assigned wrongfully to the mestizo sons of Bernardo Pucho. The Puchos initially were expelled from the land in question but subsequently were reinstated by the intendant. According to local interpretations of the law, children acquired their caste from the maternal line; the dispute in this case, therefore, centered on the identity of the Puchos' mother. Alpaca insisted that she was reputed as Spanish or *mestiza*. The Puchos' lawyer admitted that she was mestiza but argued that as the daughter of a Spanish man and an Indian woman she (and her children) were legally Indian.[14] Nine years later the protector of natives still asserted that mestizos should be included as Indians on the tribute rolls so as not to defraud the state of tax revenue.[15]

The rare instances when state officials in Arequipa feared that rebellion was brewing among the native population were during changes in land distribution and tribute collection. Conflict over land brought to the surface the potential tensions between Indians and those they identified as mestizos and, therefore, without legitimate access rights to communal property. Such tensions were exacerbated at the end of the colonial period by the appointment of tribute collectors, often identified as Spanish or mestizo, in place of the ethnic caciques.[16]

In 1811, with the abolition of tribute by the liberal Spanish Parliament, the simmering discontent boiled over in one of the rare instances of indigenous unrest in the valley. The Indian council of Pocsi accused the "cacique" Pedro Rodríguez, the local tribute collector who also happened to be the Spanish mayor, of usurping land, which the council ordered to be distributed among community members. The council argued in court that with the abolition of tribute, Rodríguez lost any authority and land rights he might have had. The subdelegate authorized the council to oversee the distribution of lands but specifically prohibited it from taking land from any individual "on the pretext that he is Spanish."[17] Nevertheless, the fears of non-Indians apparently were not assuaged. In 1812 Rodríguez charged that Pedro Quispe, a member of the Indian council, had tried to foment a riot against the local Spaniards and mestizos.[18] Rodríguez reported that discontent over the land distribution had erupted in a riot, citing rumors that "more blood than water would flow and no mestizo would be left alive in the Village."[19] Because racial category defined access to land in a context of growing scarcity, conflict emerged over who really should be considered "Indian." A potential crisis was averted by higher Spanish offi-

cials through the judicious reaffirmation of the respective rights of both indigenous and Spanish local authorities and a new distribution of lands carried out
in 1813 by the official protector of Indians.[20]

By contrast, because so few of the Indians within the city of Arequipa were
assigned land, there was little incentive for them to pay tribute. Pascual Vargas,
the cacique of *forasteros* (migrants and their descendants) in Santa Marta,
complained in 1803 that not only had many of the Indians in his district died or
moved away, but those who remained were trying to exempt themselves by
shedding their indigenous identity: "All the Indians . . . want to become Spaniards, some because they dress in the Spanish style, others because they learn
Spanish trades such as Barbers, tailors etc., or because their color is somewhat
pale, or because they style their hair, or because their godparents are Spanish
and have them baptized in the Cathedral, and finally because they change their
Indian surnames and take on Spanish ones."[21] The cacique repeatedly pointed
to the transformation of these Indians directly into Spaniards, rather than
mestizos. If measures were not taken immediately to end such abuses, Cacique
Vargas warned, "the day will arrive in which there will be no Indian left, much
less anyone to pay Royal Tribute."[22] Surprisingly, little help was forthcoming
from the state. The intendant was deluged with petitions from persons complaining that Vargas was forcing them to pay tribute even though they were not
Indians; after a presentation of witnesses, most of the petitioners were exempted.[23] In this case, the intendant probably thought it wise to give up some
revenue in order to prevent political unrest.

Indeed, Vargas's dire warning may have sounded ridiculous to the intendant,
because overall tribute revenue had risen during the late eighteenth century.[24]
Nevertheless, a steady decline in indigenous communal landholdings presaged
a later decrease in tribute. As early as 1786, the protector of natives protested
that the Indians were going to be cheated out of their land because the sur-
veyors were using the smaller indigenous *topo* as a measurement instead of the
larger Spanish *topo* (.86 acres), as was customary.[25] By the turn of the century,
the size of the communal share had declined further from the customary four
topos; in the 1801 distribution young men received only two *topos* in Yanahuara
and a mere three-quarters of a *topo* in Tiabaya.[26] After independence, the
Indians' loss of lands accelerated.[27] Landowners in Arequipa seized upon the
change in government and laws as an opportunity to make gains. In early 1826
the new republican state in Lima sent an investigator to Arequipa to hear
denunciations of state property being illegally occupied; those lands would be
auctioned off to raise revenue. There were so many claims filed, most of them

by Spanish landowners against Indians, that by September the prefect ordered that all cases not clearly in the state's favor be discontinued.[28] Two days later, however, several Spaniards who occupied urban lots belonging to the Indian community of Pocsi asked to purchase the property from the state. The community protested that the petitioners had used their connections to the "caciques" (by this period appointed tribute collectors, many of them Spanish) to acquire the best lots, on which they built large homes and shops, while the Indians were forced to live on their agricultural plots or in the hills. The case ended abruptly after the judge gave the Indians nine days to prove their title to the land.[29]

By the last distribution of 1830, each tribute-paying Indian was assigned only one *topo* of land. In compliance with decrees emitted by Simón Bolívar, Indians were granted full ownership of their parcels with the right to pass them on to their heirs. As for their right to sell the land, the laws were confusing: the initial 1824 decree granted them full title, an 1825 decree prohibited the sale of these plots until 1850, and a law passed by the Peruvian congress in 1828 allowed literate Indians to sell their land.[30] It is impossible to know exactly how many Indians sold their land, but there are hints that the Spanish governor of Yanahuara "encouraged" them to do so. Indian Rosa Taco complained that Governor José Butrón had convinced her stepmother to give him power of attorney and then secretly sold a half *topo* that rightfully belonged to Taco.[31] Indian Manuel Mamani testified in his will that following Butrón's advice, "which seemed legal," he had sold his *topo* for 900 pesos. Butrón acted as the intermediary and was paying Mamani in installments; so far Mamani had received only 600 pesos.[32] During the tribute censuses of 1843 and 1852, moreover, several Indians asked to be exempted because they had sold their land shares to support themselves.[33]

Whatever amount was sold or lost, by the mid-nineteenth century it was clear that there was no communal land left in the Arequipa valley to distribute to Indians. When Mariano Quispe, the son of a *forastero* in Yanahuara, asked to be assigned a plot in 1839, the district governor reported that there was not even enough land for *originarios* (the descendants of the original members of the community).[34] In 1846 the Indians of Pocsi argued that because there were no community lands left, the exemption from tithing should extend to private land inherited from their parents.[35] Manuel Quispe of Cayma could not even hold onto the quarter *topo* he had been assigned as a disabled member of the community; because he did not pay tribute the state agreed to sell the land to a retired accountant from the treasury who had denounced the "misappropriation."[36] Indians in many other regions of Peru did not experience as much loss of land, but the market value of agricultural land around Arequipa and the collection of property taxes likely outweighed declines in tribute revenue.[37]

The total number of registered tributaries (males between the ages of eighteen and fifty) in the province of Arequipa varied only slightly from 1789 to 1828, averaging about 1,150.[38] Beginning in the 1790s, however, it became increasingly difficult to collect the full amount of tribute owed in the countryside as well as the city.[39] When the subprefect was sued for debts in 1830, he complained that during the census of 1828, *forasteros* without land had initially been told incorrectly that they only had to pay three pesos, making it impossible to later collect the full rate of over seven pesos.[40] Furthermore, while the first republican tribute census in 1828 showed an increase in the indigenous population, there were already indications of future declines: among the youth, females far outnumbered males, suggesting evasion.[41]

There is evidence that as the land available for this younger generation declined, Indians began trying to escape the racial category to which they had been assigned. Between 1828 and 1836, the number of indigenous taxpayers in Tiabaya dropped by over half.[42] Although the final counts from the tribute census of 1843 are missing, census takers repeatedly questioned community authorities about the high numbers of Indians listed as dead or absent. The answer they received over and over was that the men had gone off in search of work and often died far from home in the coastal valleys.[43] Undoubtedly many Indians did work in the valley plantations, but most were only seasonal migrants. A more intriguing clue to their "disappearance" can be found in the lists of marriages examined by the census takers; suddenly there appeared many villagers listed as "mestizos," which was a term rarely used in Arequipa.

By the time the last tribute census was taken in 1852, the early warning from the cacique of Santa Marta was echoed by the authorities of Yanahuara, who lamented "that they believed with great reason that very soon that caste would disappear." The reason given is revealing: "Since many years ago, the Indians have been disappearing because of the lack of communal land, because since their Fathers obtained private ownership of these plots and sold them, the sons once they reach the age of ten or twelve flee."[44] Once again, however, the officials ignored the increasing proportions of non-Indians, who were now referred to as Spanish or white rather than mestizo, in the parish marriage registers. As there is no evidence to suggest a demographic decline among Indians, they were probably making every effort to avoid being registered on the tax rolls. In Tiabaya the census takers "did not order the censuses required by law to be drawn up because there did not exist any future or present tax-payer."[45] This apparent resignation of even the local officials to the disappearance of the Indians is surprising. They probably knew it would be politically risky to force landless villagers to pay tribute and calculated that the inclusion of valuable property in the local land market would outweigh revenue losses.

The way individual Indians in Arequipa perceived their ethnic identity when they were not dealing with the state may never be known. One case offers a rare glimpse, noting that onlookers unsuccessfully tried to break up a fight between Indians from different villages on the grounds that they were all "people" (likely translated from the Quechua term "*runa*").[46] Nevertheless, it is clear that the incentives for publicly claiming to be Indian or organizing along ethnic lines were declining; the availability of communal lands was steadily decreasing, and neither the ethnic caciques (those who had not been replaced by appointed tribute collectors) nor indigenous councils had much effective power in the province of Arequipa, given the proximity of high officials of the Crown and later the republican state. The advanced degree of acculturation, moreover, made it relatively easy for Indians to blend into the heterogeneous population in both the villages and the city. By the turn of the nineteenth century, urban authorities were complaining of Indians passing into other racial categories. Several decades later, that trend had spread into the countryside. The days had passed when mestizos like the Puchos would claim to be Indians in order to maintain access to communal land. As the Indian share of land around the city decreased, so too did the tribute-paying population. It is unlikely that the "disappearance" of the Indians was due only to migration. Rather, landless Indians probably began to declare they were mestizo, and in many cases even Spanish.[47] Therefore, in Arequipa the decline in the indigenous population did not necessarily translate into an increase in the number of mestizos.

MISSING MESTIZOS

Nowhere in colonial Spanish America did the caste system function according to the ideal, but it is particularly striking that in Arequipa many authorities began to give up even trying to classify people by race. When individuals appeared in court, for example, they were legally obliged to provide pertinent personal data such as occupation, age, civil status, and race. In Arequipa, however, that last item was recorded haphazardly, and the only terms that appeared with any frequency were "Indian" or those indicating African descent such as "black," "mulatto," or "*zambo*." Occasionally witnesses were identi-

fied as Spanish in the smaller villages (where it may have been more important to maintain divisions), or in cases where their testimony was being contrasted with that of Indian witnesses or defendants.[48] Even more surprising—
and revealing—was the absence of racial identifications in the parish registers,
since it was at baptism that a person was theoretically assigned to the proper
caste.[49] A clue to the reason behind such a glaring omission appears in a letter
from Bishop Gonzaga de la Encina to the king in 1815 in which he explained:
"This classification is odious to the parish priests, since having been ordered by
the courts to do it, the priests found themselves obliged either to tell the truth
or to lie. If they did the former, all those who judged themselves to be Spanish
citizens, not being such, believed they had been insulted, and they rose up
against the priests, they insulted, scorned and slandered them. If the latter, it
weighed upon their consciences."[50]

Significantly, the term "mestizo" was rarely used in local documents. Although the 1792 census officially identified 17.5 percent of the population as
mestizo, it was compiled either by authorities from outside Arequipa or at least
under the pressure of Bourbon officials.[51] Similarly, foreign visitors identified
the majority of the population as mestizo or *cholo* (which referred to acculturated Indians), rather than white.[52] On the rare occasions that locals did use
the term "mestizo," it was associated closely with the indigenous population or
its meaning was clarified, as when the priest of Cayma, on the city's outskirts,
advocated settling "Spanish mestizos" in the village who could teach the Indians good habits.[53] In Arequipa, it was customary for one's racial classification
to follow the maternal line. The Puchos of Tiabaya tried to use this law to their
advantage in order to claim a share of communal land; they argued that although their mother was a *mestiza*, her mother was Indian and she and her
children should follow that caste.[54] Francisco Luís de Sosa presumably used the
same principle to justify his petition in 1829 to be assigned a share of land—"as a
mestizo"—and reappointed as a tribute collector.[55] Indian Asencio Huerta, on
the other hand, tried to get his sons exempted from tribute because his wife was
Spanish. He successfully claimed that it was customary "that the mestizos like
my sons, always have been reputed and considered in the class of Spaniards."[56]

When it was used, therefore, "mestizo" had a meaning closer to "*cholo*." One
of the few witnesses identified as "of the mestizo caste," for example, was also
credited with being an "expert in the Spanish Language."[57] Clearly, the assumption was that mestizos were virtually Indians. In 1807 the Spanish mayor of
Yanahuara accused the *cacica* of keeping her Indian lover, Antonio Dias, off the
tribute rolls. The witnesses acknowledged that Dias had a somewhat mixed

heritage, but not enough, apparently, to distance him from the indigenous community. Ignacio Paderes testified that he knew Dias's father by sight as a "mestizo *medio cholo*" and that his mother was an Indian "according to what people said," which made Antonio a "choloized Indian [*indio acholado*]." Simón Corrales described his parents' appearance in a similar fashion, concluding that Antonio "in his judgment is more Indian than *cholo*."[58] Given its association with "Indianness" and the obligation to pay tribute, most people of mixed race probably tried to avoid being labeled mestizos. The sudden appearance of mestizos during the tribute census of 1843 marked a transitional stage that led to the prevalence of Spaniards and whites during the 1852 census. The important legal distinction, therefore, was between Indians and everyone else.

In fact, when claims to Spanish status were investigated for racial purity, few held up under official scrutiny. As in many areas of Latin America, once factors such as dress or customs were considered along with color, categories could become very ambiguous. In the 1770s, for instance, the children of Miguel Gerónimo de Medina petitioned to be declared legally Spanish; even their own witnesses, however, identified their race as mixed. Although they confirmed that Medina was Spanish, one called his wife, Andrea Ati, "*cuarterona*" (one-quarter black), and the other called her "*media Asambada*" (roughly half *zambo*).[59] Clearly, then, people were well aware of the variety of racial categories but often could not agree upon the criteria. Moreover, even if witnesses might apply the terms connoting mixture to others, petitioners often claimed a Spanish identity for themselves.

Pascual Bargas Espinosa y Giles ran into the same problem in 1807 when he tried to exempt himself from paying tribute on the grounds that he was "Spanish." His witnesses described his father variously as *zambo*, half *zambo*, and *cholo*, and his mother as "seeming Spanish," *zamba*, and *mulata*; as for Pascual, one concluded he was Spanish, another *zambo*, and the third mulatto. The cacique seized upon these inconsistencies and pointed out: "If we should judge on appearances, the sentence would come out against Pasqual, because in addition to being an Indian he seems like one, as has been said." Pascual later prevaricated that "it is a question of name that my father seemed *cholo* to him because he was white, and my mother *mulata* because she had somewhat curly hair, but blonde." The judge also investigated whether Pascual's wife was Spanish; witness Bernardo Torres testified that he considered her Spanish, "although she does not appear to be, since her aunts . . . are acknowledged as Spaniards." When the lawsuit entered its third year, a frustrated Pascual accused the cacique and his cohorts of plotting to catch "the persons who are wheat-colored [*del color trigueño*] in order to arrest and oppress them." The emphasis in this case upon skin color and hair over cultural characteristics reflects the increasing shift in the nineteenth century to modern, scientific notions of race. Ultimately, the intendant exempted Pascual from paying tribute on the grounds that he apparently was not Indian, even if not white either.[60]

Even at the highest levels of society, color was in the eyes of the beholder. The eighteenth-century priest and chronicler Travada y Córdova admitted that the Creoles of Arequipa had a few drops of noble Indian blood in their veins but argued that it was more the sun that had darkened their skin.[61] Eighty years later, French traveler Flora Tristan noted with a touch of her characteristic sarcasm: "In aristocratic parlance 'white' means anyone with no negro or Indian ascendants, and I saw several ladies who passed as white, although their skin was the colour of gingerbread, because their fathers were born in Andalusia or Valencia."[62] The elites of Arequipa, therefore, were probably sensitive to suspicions about their racial purity from outsiders, including officials from Spain or Lima. The Bourbon-appointed customs administrator, Juan Bautista Pando, had made precisely that charge when accusing elite Creoles of instigating a tax revolt in 1780.[63] Pando not only asserted that the majority of the common folk were mestizo but implied that many of Arequipa's notable citizens also carried that "stain." The rebellion was organized, he charged, by "those who believed that the fallacies of their nobility would be discovered with the inspection of marriage and baptism books."[64]

Because two-thirds of the population was officially identified as Spanish in the 1792 census, whiteness did not automatically confer elite status in Arequipa. Therefore, there were likely fewer efforts to maintain exclusive standards. In one case, a witness testified that because a woman had claimed that the father of her illegitimate child was Spanish, "therefore her daughter Francisca was Spanish *enough*, and well born."[65] Given that few in Arequipa could claim to be absolutely "pure" Spaniards, Bishop Gonzaga probably reflected a general consensus that in the interests of social peace it was better not to stir up the hornets' nest of racial labels. After all, rumors that tribute would be extended to those of mixed race had helped trigger the 1780 tax revolt. This unspoken agreement could explain the numerous Arequipeños who appeared in official documents without any indication of their caste. Perhaps the scribes could not bring themselves to identify "wheat-colored" witnesses as "white," but leaving their race off the record kept everyone happy and tacitly allowed the majority to consider themselves Spanish.

Such discretion does not mean that Arequipeños were free from racism.

Many expressed prejudices common throughout Peru, but again mestizos were largely absent from local stereotypes. Those of African descent—and particularly the racially mixed mulattos and *zambos*—were widely believed to be devious, crafty, and prone to criminal activities. In 1773, for example, Juan Joseph de Valcarcel sued Bernardo Portugal for slander after the silversmith accused him of theft. Portugal was a mulatto, and therefore it was he, according to Valcarcel, who was "by nature inclined toward the offense of Spaniards, and with a propensity for employment in only the occupation of Thieves."[66] Others accused mulattos of lacking in respect. As Josef Antonio García commented in one case, "Those Zambas have as a custom to stir up quarrels."[67] Indians, on the other hand, were tagged with the vices of laziness, ignorance, and drunkenness. When Vicente Vilca and Isabel Condori, Indians of Santa Marta, complained that their mayor was abusing them, an investigator upheld the mayor's authority and belittled the Indians' complaints: "The leisure and desires of these poor Natives end in drink for which reason one should not pay attention to their outcries."[68] This stereotype was still strong after independence, undermining universal rights of citizenship. Several members of a regional elected council argued that Indians must be forced to work because they were "inclined toward laziness, apathetic, without aspirations to better their sad means of existence, and with the only need to provide themselves a scanty and crude nourishment."[69]

Such stereotypes led Arequipeños to enrich their fighting vocabulary with racial insults. One colorful exchange in 1819 was provoked when Juan de Mata Núñez scolded some boys for throwing garbage from their house into his neighboring lot. Their aunt, Lorenza Escudero, reportedly came out and called him a "black dog." "The Indian calls [me] a Negro?," Núñez retorted. Escudero escalated the exchange by threatening that "the blacks get ridden out of town on the back of a mule." Not to be outdone, Núñez countered with "Indian women get ridden out tied to a llama like a sack of potatoes."[70] Referring to the "pure" racial categories of blacks and Indians, rather than the perhaps more plausible charge of mixed ancestry, may have packed a stronger punch. Even if not meant literally, such insults associated the person's behavior with the stereotypes of the slurred group. Arequipeños were sensitive to that implication, because it could strip away the tacit consent that they were more or less white.

In the colonial and early republican periods, the crucial fiscal and legal boundary for all but the very elite was between those considered to be Indians and all others. Mestizos, rather than developing a unifying identity of their own, tended to be grouped in cultural as well as legal terms with either Spaniards or Indians. The dominant identity of white that emerged in Arequipa, therefore, had both exclusive and inclusive dynamics. Casting the racial "other" as primarily from outside Arequipa—blacks from the coast or Indians from the highlands—denied the cultural contributions of these groups to the local society and justified the assault on communal land. Nevertheless, many of these individuals, who under legal examination might be considered racially mixed, were treated as Spanish in daily life.

AREQUIPA WITHIN THE ANDEAN CONTEXT

Arequipa was not the only place in the Andes where people of apparently mixed race claimed a Spanish' identity. Martin Minchom analyzed petitions for exemption from tribute in Quito, which peaked in the 1770s and 1780s .when colonial administrators, under pressure from the Bourbon regime in Spain, were attempting to catch "tax evaders" and increase revenue. As in Arequipa, the claimants tried to distance themselves as much as possible from the Indian category, claiming to be Spanish or white even when witnesses drew attention to their mixed ancestry.[71] At the official level as well, the emphasis was upon dividing Indians from all others, there being no mestizo category on the censuses. "Thus the official category of Mestizo was very little used in either colonial or Republican Ecuador," concluded Minchom, "and when it was this was in such varied forms that it can be considered a kind of fictitious category to be invented or reinvented by officials, ecclesiastics or outside observers, according to different criteria."[72]

Of course, not all claimants in either Arequipa or Quito were officially recognized as Spanish once their cases were scrutinized. Moreover, there were contexts, especially in more rural areas, in which petitioners to be exempted from tribute did not even try to assert they were white. Most mestizo peasants in Cochabamba (Bolivia), for example, spoke Quechua and differed little from their indigenous neighbors. Bourbon officials there exempted only mestizos with a parent who was recognized as of pure European descent; those who had only a white grandparent were considered *cholos* and were liable for taxation.[73] Nevertheless, accepting the label of mestizo in order to avoid paying tribute did not necessarily mean that peasants embraced it as a collective identity. Indeed, as Brooke Larson asserts, "The relative ease of passing as mestizo cautions against employing this term to define a social group, whether in terms of a common racial identity or a shared function, role, or position in the class structure."[74] In the predominantly indigenous region of Huaylas, Peru, Mark

Thurner found evidence suggesting that peasants who defined themselves for fiscal purposes as mestizo most likely identified with either Spanish or indigenous cultures. For example, a document referred to "mestizos who call themselves whites" who had settled in Indian villages. Conversely, once tribute was abolished, the number of peasants identifying themselves as Indians increased dramatically, implying that many had claimed to be mestizos simply to avoid paying the tax.[75]

Indeed, the rare occasions on which Andeans did collectively assert an identity as mestizos were precisely those moments in which officials tried to lump them with Indians into the tribute-paying population. Bourbon attempts to increase the tax rolls provoked riots among mestizos in Cochabamba in 1730 and Quito in 1762, among other places.[76] Although tax rioters in Arequipa in 1780 had not identified themselves as mestizos, the customs administrator suspected that protesters feared their mixed origins would be discovered by officials drawing up new censuses.

Independence from Spain in the 1820s offered a potential opportunity to disassociate ethnic identity from fiscal status; republican states in the Andes, however, faced financial crises that led them to continue the Indian head-tax. In Peru, the government also created a new tax for people identified as mixed-race (*castas*), but it was very difficult to collect, especially in urban areas. For republican statesmen to promote a collective national identity of mestizo would have clashed with fiscal policies that distinguished between Indians and others, thus denying a universal definition of citizenship. Moreover, incentives to claim a Spanish identity continued or even increased in regions where one might face a *casta* tax, resulting in the rapid increase first in mestizos and then in whites in the villages around Arequipa between the 1843 and 1852 tribute censuses.

In addition to the continuation of a sharp distinction between Indians and others for fiscal purposes, a neocolonial language of civilization and barbarism also flourished in the postindependence Andes.[77] In Peru, the association of the coast with modernity and the highlands with backwardness allowed most Limeños to claim a white identity regardless of skin color. Urban provincial elites, like those of Cuzco or Arequipa, made similar claims based upon their education and "decency," often in opposition to how outsiders perceived them.[78] Nils Jacobsen uncovered a telling drop in the mestizo population and a corresponding increase in whites in Azángaro (Peru) between censuses in 1798 and 1876. He concluded that mestizos had become "a vague, residual ethnic group whose lifestyle, income, and property qualifications could not be easily placed in the emerging polarized ethnic vision of society: on the one hand, the 'civilized' hacendados, civil and ecclesiastical authorities, and better merchants, considered whites, who flouted a 'modern' lifestyle, and on the other, the overwhelming majority of 'barbaric' Indians persisting in their 'anachronistic' habits."[79]

Elite racial ideologies in nineteenth-century Peru, therefore, perpetuated a dichotomy. The few who tried to put a positive face on the racial diversity of the country's population emphasized a whitening version of *mestizaje* with the ultimate goal of Hispanization. In Arequipa, an anonymous article in the official newspaper in 1833 promoted an early assimilationist vision of "diluting and homogenizing" the *castas*. Significantly, the author connected racial policy to liberal politics, asserting that the indigenous population was held back not by inherent defects but by lack of education and true legal equality.[80] Several later proposals to civilize the population through education similarly emphasized a goal of "Hispanism" rather than *mestizaje*. Nevertheless, few intellectuals or politicians at a national level shared this optimism that the entire population could be culturally whitened, and *mestizaje*, therefore, never became official state policy.[81]

An alternative ideology, promoted by the Cuzco elite, rejected the perceived Hispanophilia of the coast and held up the Inca past as the necessary core of Peruvian national identity. But by advocating the maintenance of the racial and cultural purity of the Indian population, as opposed to assimilation, *indigenistas* preserved a similar racial dichotomy. They believed Indians should remain in rural communities and were scornful of mestizos who, they believed, "had 'abandoned' their proper natural/cultural environment and migrated to the cities, where they degenerated morally, as reflected by their deviant sexuality."[82] Between the poles of preserving indigenous "purity" or assimilating to Hispanism, there was little middle ground for the promotion of *mestizaje*.

It was only in the late twentieth century in Peru, according to the analysis of Marisol de la Cadena, that a particular group of Peruvians began publicly to claim a positive identity as mestizos. Ironically, it was precisely the absence of an official state ideology of *mestizaje* that left the term open to appropriation and redefinition.[83] De la Cadena interviewed urban Cuzqueños who rejected binary definitions of race and culture; they claimed to be mestizo by virtue of their education but also to share in "indigenous culture." Therefore, in contrast to colonial and nineteenth-century formulations, they did not see themselves as necessarily in transit from an indigenous to a Hispanic identity. Moreover, the term has provided space for a politicized identity. Whereas oppositional pan-native movements have emerged in countries that officially promote *mestizaje*, de la Cadena found that "not only do indigenous grassroots intellectuals appropriate the label 'mestizo' for self-identification, but crucially, no indigenous social movement exists currently in Peru that rallies around ethnic identities."[84] Although this subaltern identity is counterhegemonic in its redefinition of *mestizaje*, de la Cadena cautions that its acceptance of education as a mark of superiority perpetuates social hierarchies that place illiterate Indians below all others.

De la Cadena was able to interview contemporary Cuzqueños in order to analyze the nuances of their self-definition as "indigenous mestizos." For earlier historical periods, we cannot assert definitively that some Andeans did not construct a mixed identity for themselves away from the eyes of officials who could have described it for the record. Nonetheless, public claims are an important element of ethnic identity, and we can safely conclude that such assertions by mestizos were rare in the eighteenth and nineteenth centuries, the formative period for nation building in the region. As long as the laws continued to distinguish between Indians and all others, those of mixed ancestry had a material incentive either to claim access to land based upon their indigenous roots (perhaps through a maternal line) or deny such ties in order to avoid paying tribute. Because certain categories of mestizos were considered Indians for fiscal purposes, and even the exemption of other mixed castes was precarious, individuals wishing to evade taxation often claimed to be Spanish. The dominant stereotypes against both Indians and mestizos, which continued even after the abolition of tribute, also encouraged individuals to aspire for inclusion in the supposedly civilized Spanish group. Arequipa and Quito may have been unusual in the degree to which such claims were accepted by state officials, but the absence of a collective identity among those who were labeled mestizos was common throughout the Andes. This lack of identification at the popular level, while not the only influence, certainly hindered the emergence of a nationalist discourse of *mestizaje* in the Andes.

NOTES

1. Marisol de la Cadena, *Indigenous Mestizos: The Politics of Race and Culture in Cuzco, Peru, 1919–1991* (Durham: Duke University Press, 2000), 321–23.

2. For an introduction to the caste system, see Magnus Mörner, *Race Mixture in the History of Latin America* (Boston: Little, Brown, 1967). For an excellent recent study, see R. Douglas Cope, *The Limits of Racial Domination: Plebeian Society in Colonial Mexico City, 1660–1720* (Madison: University of Wisconsin Press, 1994).

3. *Zambo* referred to mixed Indian and African ancestry. Mulattos and *moriscos* were mixtures of African with an increasing proportion of European ancestry; mestizos and *castizos* were mixtures of Indian with increasing European ancestry.

4. For a sample, see John K. Chance, *Race and Class in Colonial Oaxaca* (Stanford: Stanford University Press, 1978); Patricia Seed, "Social Dimensions of Race: Mexico City, 1753," *Hispanic American Historical Review* 62, no. 4 (Nov. 1982): 569–606; Rodney D. Anderson, "Race and Social Stratification: A Comparison of Working-Class Spaniards, Indians, and Castas in Guadalajara, Mexico, in 1821," *Hispanic American Historical Review* 68, no. 2 (May 1988): 209–43; and Robert McCaa, "*Calidad, Clase,* and Marriage in Colonial Mexico: The Case of Parral, 1788–90," *Hispanic American Historical Review* 64, no. 3 (Aug. 1984): 477–501.

5. Olivia Harris highlights this paradox of mestizo "identity" in "Ethnic Identity and Market Relations: Indians and Mestizos in the Andes," in *Ethnicity, Markets, and Migration in the Andes: At the Crossroads of History and Anthropology,* ed. Brooke Larson and Olivia Harris with Enrique Tandeter (Durham: Duke University Press, 1995), 362, 373.

6. For a similar conclusion, see David Cahill, "Colour by Numbers: Racial and Ethnic Categories in the Viceroyalty of Peru, 1532–1824," *Journal of Latin American Studies* 26, no. 2 (May 1994): 342–45, and Stuart B. Schwartz and Frank Salomon, "New Peoples and New Kinds of People: Adaptation, Readjustment, and Ethnogenesis in South American Indigenous Societies (Colonial Era)," in *South America,* vol. 3 of *The Cambridge History of Native Peoples of the Americas,* ed. Stuart B. Schwartz and Frank Salomon (Cambridge: Cambridge University Press, 1999), pt. 2, 443–501.

7. For a more thorough context, see Sarah C. Chambers, *From Subjects to Citizens: Honor, Gender, and Politics in Arequipa, Peru, 1780–1854* (University Park: Pennsylvania State University Press, 1999).

8. See, for example, Víctor Andrés Belaúnde, *Meditaciones peruanas* (Lima: Biblioteca Perú Actual, 1933).

9. For census figures, see Günter Vollmer, *Bevölkerungspolitik und Bevölkerungsstruktur im Vizekonigreich Peru zu Ende der Kolonialzeit (1741–1821)* (Bad Homburg: Gehlen, 1967), 253–54. For a warning against the reliability of racial categories in census records, see Robert H. Jackson, "Race/Caste and the Creation and Meaning of Identity in Colonial Spanish America," *Revista de Indias* 55, no. 203 (Jan.–Apr. 1995): 149–73.

10. Víctor M. Barriga, *Memorias para la historia de Arequipa* (Arequipa: Editorial La Colmena, 1941), 1:163, 204, 209, 226, 249, 278.

11. Ibid., 244, 333.

12. Archivo General de la Nación (hereafter AGN), R. J. Ministerio de Justicia: Prefectura de Arequipa: Culto: Legajo 143.

13. This exchange resembles what Tristan Platt has called a colonial "pact" in Bolivia. Tristan Platt, *Estado boliviano y ayllu andino* (Lima: Instituto de Estudios Peruanos, 1982), 40.

14. The case "Don Agustín Alpaca, Cacique de Cayma, contra los hijos de Bernardo

Pucho que como mestizos tratan de usurpar tierras de repartimiento" exists in several pieces in two archives: Biblioteca Nacional del Perú (hereafter BNP), Docs. C2648 (1786), C2629 (1788), C3532 (1793), C3455 (1794), and AGN: Derecho Indígena, Leg. 24, Cuads. 431 and 434 (1788–93).

15. Documents in the archives of Arequipa do not have catalog numbers and will be identified instead by their starting date. Archivo Regional de Arequipa (hereafter ARAR), Intendencia (Int), Administrativo (Adm) (20 Mar. 1795) Sobre que José Condorpusa y Taco debe entrar en el padrón de tributarios.

16. Carlos J. Díaz Rementería, *El cacique en el Virreinato del Perú: Estudio histórico-jurídico* (Sevilla: Universidad de Sevilla, 1977), 235–36.

17. ARAR/Int/Adm (31 Oct. 1811) Sobre si el Cabildo de Naturales de Pocsi puede hacer la repartición de tierras. See also ARAR/Int/Adm (4 May 1803) Sylverio Coaila contra el cacique recaudador Don Pedro Rodríguez, and (12 Mar. 1822) Rosalía y Leonarda Mamani contra Don Bartolomé Málaga. This and all subsequent translations are mine.

18. ARAR/Int/Causas Criminales (Crim) (31 May 1812) Pedro Rodríguez, Alcalde de Quequeña, contra Pedro Quispe y otros por azonada. For a similar case, see ARAR/Int/Adm (5 Aug. 1813) Don Juan de la Cruz Quenaya, indio principal de Pocsi, se queja que el Alcalde de Españoles de Yarabamba Don Bartolomé Málaga quiere despojarle de un solar.

19. ARAR/Int/Crim (31 May 1812) Pedro Rodríguez contra Pedro Quispe y otros por azonada. See also ARAR/Int/Adm (3 Apr. 1813) El Protector de Naturales Dr. Don José Salazar se defiende de un cargo de mala conducta, (5 July 1813) Don Juan de la Cruz Quenaya se queja que el Alcalde de Españoles de Yarabamba quiere despojarle de un solar, and ARAR/Prefectura (Pref) (16 June 1830) Los indígenas de Yanahuara se quejan de los procedimientos del Sub-prefecto y apoderado Fiscal durante la revisita.

20. ARAR/Int/Crim (31 May 1812) Pedro Rodríguez contra Pedro Quispe y otros por azonada, and ARAR/Int/Adm (3 Apr. 1813) El Protector de Naturales Dr. Don José Salazar se defiende de un cargo de mala conducta.

21. ARAR/Int/Adm (20 Jan. 1803) Don Pascual Vargas representa las dificultades. Vargas's predecessors had also encountered such problems; see ARAR/Int/Pedimentos (18 Dec. 1784) Don Carlos Achircana pide que se le mande a Manuel Cavana pagar tributo, and (22 Aug. 1785) Gregorio Flores protesta que el Cacique de Forasteros intenta cobrarle tributo aunque no sea indio.

22. ARAR/Int/Adm (20 Jan. 1803), Don Pascual Vargas representa las dificultades.

23. See petitions in ARAR/Int/Adm (28 May 1802) Melchor Acosta y Pinto, (1 June 1805) Miguel Oblitas y Ramos, (5 Mar. 1806) Gregorio Silva, (24 Apr. 1806) Tomás Cosme, (26 Jan. 1807) Blas Plácido Ortís y Gallegos, (18 Dec. 1807) Pascual Bargas Espinosa y Giles, and (19 Dec. 1808) Bernardo Rocha.

24. See John J. Tepaske and Herbert S. Klein, *Peru*, vol. 1 of *The Royal Treasuries of the Spanish Empire in America* (Durham: Duke University Press, 1982), 39–63; Kendall W. Brown, *Bourbons and Brandy: Imperial Reform in Eighteenth-Century Arequipa* (Albu-

querque: University of New Mexico Press, 1986), 178; Núria Sala i Vila, *Y se armó el Tole Tole: Tributo indígena y movimientos sociales en el Virreinato del Perú, 1790–1814* (Huamanga: Instituto de Estudios Regionales José María Arguedas, 1996), 36–38, 279–87.

25. AGN, Derecho Indígena y Encomiendas, Leg. 24, Cuad. 419 (1786), El Protector de Naturales en Arequipa protesta.

26. ARAR/Int/Adm (30 May 1801) Sobre la mensura, asignación, y reparto de tierras vacantes.

27. Fernando Ponce, "Social Structure of Arequipa, 1840–1879" (Ph.D. diss., University of Texas at Austin, 1980), 128–34, and Betford Betalleluz, "Fiscalidad, tierras y mercado: Las comunidades indígenas de Arequipa, 1825–1850," in *Tradición y modernidad en los Andes*, ed. Henrique Urbano (Cuzco: Centro de Estudios Andinos Bartolomé de las Casas, 1992), 160.

28. AGN, Hacienda, H-1-1, Leg. O.L. 145, Exp. 237 (1826), order dated 21 Sept. 1826 in Informe del Visitador al Sur Don Juan Evangelista de Yrigoyen y Zenteno.

29. ARAR/Pref (28 Sept. 1826) Solicitud de Don Juan Isidro Cárdenas y otros que se les venda unos solares en Quequeña y Yarabamba. Presumably these were the urban lots for which Alvarez y Jiménez had charged a modest rent, payable to the community chest. See Barriga, *Memorias*, 2:124–25.

30. Bolívar's decrees are reprinted in Sociedad Bolivariana de Venezuela, *Decretos del Libertador* (Caracas: Imprenta Nacional, 1961), 1:295–96.

31. ARAR/CS/Crim (17 Oct. 1831) Contra Santos Obando por haber estropeado a María Josefa Coronado.

32. ARAR/Pref (16 Oct. 1835) Juan Manuel Caisa Mendosa protesta que Manuel Mamani murió intestado. The subprefect charged that Indians in Yanahuara had sold or rented out their plots. ARAR/Pref (16 June 1830) Los indígenas de Yanahuara se quejan de los procedimientos del Sub-prefecto y apoderado Fiscal durante la revisita. In 1835 the indigenous community of Pocsi sold eighteen *topos*. ARAR, Notary Francisco de Linares, land sale dated 23 Oct. 1835.

33. Petitions from Mariano Guamani (16 May 1844) and Matías Quispe (26 May 1844) in AGN, Hacienda, H-4-1845, R. 287 (1843), Matrícula de Indígenas de Arequipa, and María Paco (11 Mar. 1852) in AGN, Hacienda, H-4-2191, R. 631 (1852), Matrícula de Indígenas de Arequipa.

34. ARAR/Pref (25 Nov. 1839) Don Mariano Quispe pide probar que es indígena originario contribuyente de Yanahuara.

35. ARAR/Pref (9 July 1846) Unos indígenas de Pocsi protestan que el rematador de diezmos trata de cobrarles indebidamente.

36. ARAR/Pref (25 June 1847) Don Fernando Pacheco hace denuncia de un retazo de tierras en Cayma.

37. Contrast to Nils Jacobsen, *Mirages of Transition: The Peruvian Altiplano, 1780–1930* (Berkeley: University of California Press, 1993), 125–27; Charles F. Walker, *Smoldering Ashes: Cuzco and the Creation of Republican Peru, 1780–1840* (Durham: Duke University

Press, 1999); Paul Gootenberg, "Population and Ethnicity in Early Republican Peru: Some Revisions," *Latin American Research Review* 26, no. 3 (Summer 1991): 109–57; Víctor Peralta Ruíz, *En pos del tributo: Burocracia estatal, elite regional y comunidades indígenas en el Cusco rural, 1826–1854* (Cuzco: Centro de Estudios Andinos Bartolomé de las Casas, 1991); and Erwin P. Grieshaber, "Survival of Indian Communities in Nineteenth-Century Bolivia: A Regional Comparison," *Journal of Latin American Studies* 12, no. 2 (Nov. 1980): 223–69.

38. Vollmer, *Bevölkerungspolitik*, 286; BNP, Doc. D6603 (1813) Matrícula de indios tributarios del Cercado de Arequipa; AGN, Tributos, Leg. 5, Cuad. 160 (1817) Tributo en la Intendencia de Arequipa; AGN, Hacienda, H-4-1623, R. 068 (1828), Matrícula de Indígenas; Betalleluz, "Fiscalidad, tierras y mercado," 152–53; George Kubler, *The Indian Caste of Peru, 1795–1940* (Washington, D.C.: U.S. Government Printing Office, 1952), 11.

39. According to Sala i Vila, between 1795 and 1807 there was consistently a shortfall by about half of the approximately 8,500 pesos owed annually by Indians in the province of Arequipa (*Y se armó el Tole Tole*, 304–8). There are numerous lawsuits in the ARAR against officials for failing to collect all the tribute owed.

40. ARAR/Pref (22 May 1831) Contra el Subprefecto del Cercado Don Manuel Amat y León por deudas.

41. Betalleluz, "Fiscalidad, tierras y mercado," 152–53.

42. ARAR/Pref (15 Apr. 1836) Contribución de Indígenas del Pueblo de Tiabaya.

43. AGN, Hacienda, H-4-1845, R. 287 (1843), Matrícula de Indígenas de Arequipa.

44. Entry dated 14 June 1852 in AGN, Hacienda, H-4-2191, R. 631 (1852), Matrícula de Indígenas de Arequipa.

45. Entry dated 12 June 1852 in ibid.

46. ARAR/CS/Crim (30 Apr. 1834) Contra José Tola y Casimiro Velásquez por la muerte de Gabino Flores.

47. For similar cases, see María Isabel Remy, "La sociedad local al inicio de la República: Cusco, 1824–1850," *Revista Andina* 6, no. 2 (1988): 451–84; Jackson, "Race/Caste," 164–71; and Kubler, *Indian Caste of Peru*, 36–37.

48. See ARAR/Int/Crim (4 Oct. 1800) Contra Matías Alpaca y otros por el robo que hicieron de la caja de Comunidad de Paucarpata, (21 May 1803) Contra Isabel Portugal por maltratos a su esposo Rudecindo Megía, and (2 Feb. 1804) Sebastian Valencia contra María Laguna por injurias. For an example of using the testimony of "Spaniards" against Indians, see ARAR/Int/Crim (7 Oct. 1807) Contra Antonio Dias por concubinato con la Casica de Yanahuara Doña María Tone.

49. One may assume that those baptized in Indian parishes were classified de facto, but the cathedral administered sacraments to all non-Indians and its records list no racial classifications during the period under study.

50. BNP, Doc. D11883, Copiador del Obispo Gonzaga, letter dated 7 July 1815.

51. Vollmer, *Bevölkerungspolitik*, 253.

52. Ernst W. Middendorf, *Perú* (Lima: Universidad Nacional Mayor de San Marcos,

1973–74), 1:164, 2:170, and Heinrich Witt, *Diario y observaciones sobre el Perú* (Lima: COFIDE, 1987), 13.

53. Juan Domingo Zamácola y Jáuregui, *Apuntes para la historia de Arequipa* (1804; reprint, Arequipa: Primer Festival del Libro Arequipeño, 1958), 45.

54. BNP, Doc. C2629 (1788) Apelación de Agustín Alpaca, Cacique de Cayma, contra los hijos de Bernardo Pucho. For similar debates in Colombia, see Frank Safford, "Race, Integration, and Progress: Elite Attitudes and the Indian in Colombia, 1750–1870," *Hispanic American Historical Review* 71, no. 1 (Feb. 1991): 14.

55. *El Republicano*, supplement to 4, no. 40 (3 Oct. 1829): 4. For other references to land being distributed to mestizos, see ARAR/Pref (9 July 1846) Unos indígenas de Pocsi protestan que el rematador de diezmos trata de cobrarles indebidamente, and (25 June 1847) Don Fernando Pacheco hace denuncia de un retazo de tierras en Cayma.

56. ARAR/Int/Adm (5 Mar. 1807) Expediente para que se declare a los hijos de Asencio Huerta, Indio, y Rosa Vílchez, Española, por mestizos. See also ARAR/Int/Adm (26 Jan. 1807) Blas Plácido Ortís y Gallegos pide se le declare exento de tributar. For similar claims in Colombia, see Jaime Jaramillo Uribe, "Mestizaje y diferención social en el Nuevo Reino de Granada en la segunda mitad del siglo XVIII," *Anuario Colombiano de Historia Social y de la Cultura* 2, no. 3 (1965): 36.

57. ARAR/Int/Crim (3 July 1815) Doña María Zenteno y Capas contra Cayetana Riberos y otros por injurias.

58. ARAR/Int/Crim (7 Oct. 1807) Contra Antonio Dias por concubinato con la Casica de Yanahuara Doña María Tone.

59. Archivo Arzobispal de Arequipa/Causas Civiles (1772) María Petrona y María Nieves Medina piden que se les declare españolas.

60. ARAR/Int/Adm (18 Dec. 1807) Pascual Bargas Espinosa y Giles se queja que el Cacique de Forasteros le cobra tributo aunque sea español.

61. Ventura Travada y Córdova, *El suelo de Arequipa convertido en cielo* (1752; reprint, Arequipa: Primer Festival del Libro Arequipeño, 1958), 93.

62. Flora Tristan, *Peregrinations of a Pariah, 1833–1834* (Boston: Beacon Press, 1986), 127.

63. Melchor de Paz y Guiní, *Guerra separatista: Rebeliones de indios en Sur América*, ed. Luis Antonio Eguiguren (Lima: Imprenta Torres Aguirre, 1952), 108.

64. Ibid.

65. BNP, Doc. C3532 (1793), Don Agustín Alpaca, Cacique de Cayma, contra los hijos de Bernardo Pucho. The emphasis is mine.

66. ARAR/Corregimiento/Crim, Leg. 26, Exp. 433 (21 Jan. 1773) Don Juan Joseph de Valcarcel contra Bernardo Portugal. See also Leg. 26, Exp. 434 (18 Mar. 1773) Antonio Zúniga e Ignacio Gordillo contra Diego Navarro, mulato.

67. ARAR/Corregimiento/Crim., Leg. 26, Exp. 445 (19 Dec. 1782) Don Faustino Biamonte y su esposa Petronila de Carpio contra Sebastián Bedoya.

68. ARAR/Int/Crim (13 Nov. 1798) Vicente Vilca y Isabel Condori, indios de Santa Marta, piden su libertad.

69. "Propuesta a la Junta Departamental del Diputado Juan de Dios Ballón para impulsar la minería," in *El Republicano* 4, no. 40 (3 Oct. 1829): 3–4.

70. The original quotes were "que a los negros se sacaba en un aparejo" and "que a las indias se sacaba en una llama con costal y soga." ARAR/Int/Crim (5 Jan. 1819) Juan de Mata Núñez contra Doña Lorenza Escudero por injurias.

71. Martin Minchom, *The People of Quito, 1690–1810: Change and Unrest in the Underclass* (Boulder, Colo.: Westview Press, 1994), 171, 174. See also Martin Minchom, "The Making of a White Province: Demographic Movement and Ethnic Transformation in the South of the Audiencia de Quito (1670–1830)," *Bulletin de l'Institut Français d'Etudes Andines* 12, nos. 3–4 (1983): 23–39.

72. Minchom, *People of Quito*, 199.

73. Brooke Larson, *Cochabamba, 1550–1900: Colonialism and Agrarian Transformation in Bolivia*, exp. ed. (Durham: Duke University Press, 1998), 111, 307.

74. Ibid., 112.

75. Mark Thurner, *From Two Republics to One Divided: Contradictions of Postcolonial Nationmaking in Andean Peru* (Durham: Duke University Press, 1997), 48.

76. Larson, *Cochabamba*, 113, and Minchom, *People of Quito*, 221.

77. Harris, "Ethnic Identity and Market Relations"; Thurner, *From Two Republics to One Divided*; Cecilia Méndez, "Los campesinos, la Independencia y la iniciación de la República," in *Poder y violencia en los Andes*, ed. Henrique Urbano (Cuzco: Centro de Estudios Andinos Bartolomé de las Casas, 1991), 165–88, and "República sin indios: La comunidad imaginada del Perú," in *Tradición y modernidad en los Andes*, ed. Henrique Urbano (Cuzco: Centro de Estudios Andinos Bartolomé de las Casas, 1992), 15–42; Charles F. Walker, "Los indios en la transición de colonia a república," in ibid., 1–14.

78. De la Cadena, *Indigenous Mestizos*, 21–22.

79. Jacobsen, *Mirages of Transition*, 145–46.

80. "Sobre las relaciones del Perú con la Europa, y consigo mismo," *El Republicano* 8, no. 39 (28 Sept. 1833): 7, and no. 40 (5 Oct. 1833): 7–8.

81. De la Cadena, *Indigenous Mestizos*, 17–18, 323–24.

82. Ibid., 24.

83. Ibid., 325–27.

84. Ibid., 323. For discourses of *mestizaje* in Bolivia, see Laura Gotkowitz, "Commemorating the Heroínas: Gender and Civic Ritual in Early-Twentieth-Century Bolivia," in *Hidden Histories of Gender and the State in Latin America*, ed. Elizabeth Dore and Maxine Molyneux (Durham: Duke University Press, 2000), 215–37.

CHAPTER TWO

BELONGING TO THE GREAT GRANADAN FAMILY

Partisan Struggle and
the Construction of
Indigenous Identity and
Politics in Southwestern
Colombia, 1849–1890

James Sanders

In 1991 the Colombian National Constituent Assembly completed a new constitution that granted indigenous communities impressive cultural, economic,
and political rights, including recognition of the territorial integrity and self-
governance of Indian *resguardos* (communal lands).[1] The new political regime
also reserved two Senate seats exclusively to represent indigenous peoples. This
victory capped two intense decades of indigenous organizing, often pioneered
and led by Indians from Colombia's southwest, the Cauca region. While having
formally organized in 1971 as the Consejo Regional Indígena del Cauca (CRIC,
Cauca Regional Indigenous Council), Caucano Indians had been struggling,
often successfully, to protect their lands and lifeways for centuries. During the
nineteenth century, the Cauca's Indians developed both a discourse and strategy for coping with the state and defining themselves that still echoes in contemporary debates. The constitutional guarantees of 1991 emerged out of a long
tradition of Colombia's Indians bargaining with the state over their lands and
the status of indigenous identity within the republican nation.

Ordinary people across the remains of Spain's once-great empire—be they
slaves, freedpeople, Indians, or mestizo peasants—faced the challenge of finding a place for themselves in the new nation-states that emerged after indepen-

dence. Many of the indigenous peoples of southwestern Colombia had supported the dying Spanish monarchy tenaciously, afraid of losing a powerful ally in the Crown to patriot armies led by the very landlords against whom Indians so often found themselves in conflict. After independence, however, Indians attempted to adapt elite republican politics to suit their own needs and social visions. In Colombia, as in many other parts of Latin America, Indians entered a political sphere dominated by Liberal and Conservative Parties vying for control of the state. Social and familial ties often determined the constituencies of these parties, but ideological differences, over the role of the Church or economic policy, also played a role. In Colombia an important division centered over whom the Liberals and Conservatives thought should enjoy the right to be part of the nation and under what conditions. Partisan conflict was fierce; in the Cauca, the parties regularly clashed in elections and, failing that, in civil wars.

The Cauca's Indians faced immense challenges in the republican era. By midcentury, members of the Colombian Conservative Party largely took Indians for granted as potentially dangerous, although usually quiescent, racially inferior peons who at times worked on their haciendas. The newly emerging Liberal Party, at least discursively, promoted the inclusion of popular groups in national politics but regarded indigenous villages as reactionary colonial throwbacks that had to be eliminated in order to transform Indians into productive citizens. Liberals would allow male Indians to be citizens, but only if they abandoned and denied their Indianness. Indians reacted to this quandary by reframing citizenship in a manner compatible with indigenous identity, forging a place for themselves in the new Colombian (or New Granadan) nation.[2]

This essay will explore how Indians reframed citizenship and their own ethnic identities. The first section shows how Indians challenged the elitist and racist definitions of citizenship proposed by the ruling class. In seeking to protect their particular identity, however, indigenous communities participated in maintaining a racialized discourse about other lower-class groups and even perpetuated stereotypes of themselves. The second section examines Indians' actions in the new republican political system and the ways they exploited conflicts between Conservatives and Liberals in the second half of the nineteenth century. The two political parties needed subaltern support at the ballot box and during frequent civil wars. Indians, afraid of Liberal attempts to liquidate their communal landholdings, first turned to Conservatives. Over time, however, Indians forced Liberals to moderate their attacks. During these

MAP 1. *Cauca Region of Nineteenth-Century Colombia*

engagements with the parties, individual indigenous villages initially acted largely independently of each other in pursuit of their political goals, but during the 1860s and 1870s they began to organize beyond the village level. This larger pan-village political collaboration altered the meaning of being Indian, created a potent political discourse, and presaged twentieth-century indigenous politics.

REFRAMING CITIZENSHIP

Indigenous communities formed a small, but politically important part of Caucano society in the nineteenth century. (One observer estimated that Indians constituted approximately 9 percent of the region's population.)[3] The Cauca region centers around the river of the same name, hemmed in by two mountain ranges that parallel the river to the east and west. In addition to the coast and the Amazon rain forest beyond the mountains, the region also includes the southern highlands, where Colombia's three mountain chains join together around the city of Pasto. While some indigenous communities survived in the Cauca River Valley, the majority of Indians lived in the mountains alongside the valley or in the southern highlands. Haciendas controlled the Cauca Valley and other, smaller temperate valleys in the southern highlands.[4] In spite of the haciendas' dominance, most Indians still lived in *resguardos*—communal landholdings they had enjoyed since the colonial era. The *resguardos* were squeezed in between large haciendas and other smallholdings in the mountain valleys or located higher up the slopes, where land was less valuable.[5] Indians were always under threat from the haciendas and neighboring towns, whose owners and residents continually tried to expand their holdings at the *resguardos*' expense.[6] On their *resguardos*, Indians raised some livestock and planted potatoes, wheat, corn, *ocas* (a root crop), barley, and sundry vegetables, while also weaving for local markets.[7] Indians governed their *resguardos* through the *cabildo pequeño* (little council), chosen or elected by the men of each *parcialidad*, a division more or less corresponding to a village within the *resguardo*. An Indian governor led the *cabildo pequeño* and usually conducted the *resguardo*'s business with outsiders.

Since independence, many elites had attacked *resguardos* and Indians' *cabildos pequeños* as colonial institutions unsuitable for a republican nation. Living in these corporate communities most strongly defined the identity of "Indian" as a separate, legal category inherited from colonial caste laws. While most Indians in the settled Cauca (outside the Amazon rain forests) spoke some Spanish, perhaps exclusively, and practiced a culture that was not necessarily so different from that of their poor mestizo and white neighbors, "Indian" also had a cultural connotation, especially for the Indians themselves.[8] They defended their *resguardos* and *cabildos* as not just lands and local governance, but as institutions that helped them maintain "ancient moral and religious traditions" and "our habits and . . . customs."[9] "Indian" also had a racialized significance beyond the legal and cultural lifeways of the *resguardo*, as some "whites" who had married Indians lived in *resguardos* too (but in surveys of the communities were still classified as "white"), and other Indians had lost their *resguardos*.[10] Race was not a sharply defined concept in nineteenth-century Colombia, but, rather, a fluid idea involving notions of phenotype, culture, class, language, legal categories, history, and geography. In spite of its muddled connotations, most elite Caucanos also thought race somehow involved bloodlines or descent from European, African, or American (Indian) ancestors, and they described Indians and Africans as belonging, to a greater or lesser degree, to inferior "*razas*."[11] Many Colombian writers, especially Liberals, thought any racial problem could be overcome by "civilizing," educating, and "whitening" the lower classes. One intellectual noted that a "mixture of the races" would produce "a race of republicans."[12]

In the late 1840s, Colombian Liberals, in a search for popular allies, began to suggest a much broader notion of citizenship than most elites had previously considered. Since independence, most subalterns were legally excluded from official political life; the 1843 constitution, similar to previous constitutions, limited citizenship to adult males with either 300 pesos in property or 150 pesos in annual income (after 1850, literacy was also required), thus eliminating the vast majority of Indians.[13] Many Liberals, inspired by the 1848 revolutions in Europe, began to suggest that citizenship become universal. By universal, Liberals did not mean everyone, but, rather, adult males regardless of class—which they achieved with the 1853 constitution that granted citizenship and suffrage to all adult males. Significantly, however, they also meant that citizenship would replace all other identities—caste, legal, local, or religious—that mediated between the individual and the nation-state. Liberals fulminated against the aristocracy, against slavery, against the Church—all seen as corporate identities limiting liberty—and against Indian villages.

Liberals thought *resguardos* doomed Indians to backwardness and barbarism and prevented them from entering modern society as productive individuals, thus condemning them to poverty.[14] One newspaperman complained that the people around the southern city of Pasto were so filled with "fanaticism" and had so "little civilization" that they could not know their "rights."[15] Liberals warned that until Indians ceased to be governed by special legislation, "they will never become free citizens and active members of the democratic republic."[16] Another Liberal argued that Indians' special legal status was "similar to that of minors, squanderers, the demented, and deaf-mutes."[17] Liberals proposed the division of the *resguardos* so that Indians might lose the last vestiges of their colonial identity as a people separate from the rest of society. Of course, Liberals also coveted the lands Indians held in common, hoping the division of the communal holdings would foster economic development and an active land market. A petition from the village of Silvia in 1852, in which more than forty-five residents sought to have the nearby *resguardos* divided, best reveals the Liberal mindset. The petitioners claimed the new Liberal government had declared "equality of rights for all New Granadans." Equality of law required "that the Indians become citizens and property holders; . . . but to the embarrassment of N.G. [Nueva Granada] within its own territory there today exist, forty-two years after Independence, groups of men with the name communities of Indians." To maintain the *resguardos* and Indian communities meant "maintaining thousands of Granadans tied to the stake of barbarism with the rope of communal goods."[18] Citizenship and civilization, for Liberals, were incompatible with Indians' corporate communities.

The Cauca's Indians were caught in a bind. Either they accepted Liberal citizenship and abandoned their communities, their communal lands, and the very identity of Indian, or they would be cast as colonial throwbacks and excluded from the political life of the republic. Indigenous communities refused the Manichaean choice offered by Liberals, instead laying claim to a citizenship (and republicanism) that did not deny their Indian identity but rather sought to protect it within the new nation. In petitions and letters sent from indigenous communities to regional and national state authorities, Indian leaders insisted they were Granadans (or Colombians) and that they were part of the nation, with all the rights that status entailed. A common opening to petitions included some variation of "using the right to petition that the constitution conceded to every Granadan."[19] Indians from Caldono, involved in a land dispute, wrote to the provincial governor to "implore the protection" they deserved due to "the fact of belonging to the great Granadan family." They also asserted that their rights, guaranteed by "our constitution," had been violated.[20] Indians from Túquerres and Ipiales, claiming to represent all the Indians of their province, argued that maintaining the *resguardos* would hurt neither "national nor provincial interests" and referred to "our legitimate government" and "our *patria.*"[21]

Indians did not just claim to belong to the nation, they also assumed the mantle of citizenship. Indians from Santiago, Sibundoy, and Putumayo criticized local bureaucrats who treated them as "semi-savages . . . instead of giving us the rights that the laws and constitution of the Cauca grant to all citizens."[22] In another petition, Indians from Sibundoy claimed, "We are free citizens, like any other civilized Caucano."[23] Bautista Pechene, governor of a *parcialidad* near Silvia, testified in a court case on election fraud that Indians from his village, in spite of "being citizens, were not able to deposit their votes in the ballot box."[24] Indians from Túquerres demanded that the state respect "our traditions [of] living in community," while asserting that they were "Granadan citizens."[25] The villagers rejected elites' racialized assumptions that "Indian" or indigenous communities were incompatible with republican citizenship.

Indians from Jambaló noted they had the same responsibilities as "other non-Indian citizens" but asserted that they wanted to keep their communal lands.[26] Indians demanded that they be considered part of the nation and be allowed to keep their *resguardos* and *cabildos pequeños*; indeed, the new republic gave Indians "the prerogative to represent ourselves and defend our rights."[27] The most important rights, of course, were possession of their communal lands and local self-governance. Other Indians asserted that it was the duty of "republicans, who proclaim equality" to protect the *resguardos.*[28] Indians seized the idea of citizenship from elite Colombians and insisted not only that Indianness was compatible with citizenship and the republican nation, but that citizenship gave them new rights and standing before the state with which to defend their corporate communities. Indians created a counterdiscourse to elite republicanism, one that did not marginalize Indians or force them to sacrifice their communities and lands in exchange for political status.

Indians couched their republican discourse of citizenship in a colonial language describing their own weakness, coupled with appeals to state authorities for protection: "We, as citizens of the Cauca, are confident that you will hear our pleas."[29] Indians of Túquerres, warning again of the disastrous results of *resguardo* division, noted "that our wretched and unhappy class has not had any help except that which the truly philanthropic government can offer."[30] A village near Barbacoas begged the national president for "your powerful protection" against the "corruption of the municipal officials."[31] Indians from Colimba and Guachucal opened their request: "We implore the conscripted

Fathers of the *Patria* to extend their hand to the thousands of citizens of the Indian class who, here in the South, are the defenseless victims of the whites' abuses and attacks."[32] Indigenous communities called upon the national state to enforce its laws and protect their rights against abuses by local officials or *hacendados* (owners of landed estates). Indians claimed to be citizens and expected the state to fulfill its responsibilities and take their claims and calls for protection seriously.

To justify the need for this protection and the special rights of self-governance and communal landholding, Indians also employed a language of self-denigration, borrowed from the colonial era. The *parcialidad* of Pitayó declared itself "the most wretched and helpless class of society, we are the mine that everyone exploits."[33] Villagers of Toribio, San Francisco, and Tacueyó described themselves as "wretched Indians" who "remain in a state of misery."[34] In one petition from 1877, several communities in the south noted that "the indigenous class is wretched and has very little sense."[35] Harsher still was the judgment made two years earlier from a similar coalition of southern *cabildos* that "civilization and culture are very underdeveloped among all the Indians of the South, without exception" and that "as all the Indians are imbeciles, wretched, and ignorant, it is very easy for the astute to trick them and acquire dominion over their property indirectly."[36] Almost every indigenous petition, with few exceptions, employed some language of humility, ignorance, and wretchedness.

While it may be tempting to dismiss this language as simply the interjections of country lawyers who helped Indians write the petitions, this ignores the strategic employment of the rhetoric to call upon state power. Indians used this language to warn that if they did not enjoy legal protections of the *resguardos*, they could not defend themselves against the whites' power and resources. Indians knew that, isolated as individuals outside the *resguardos*, powerful *hacendados* could wrest away their land (via seizure for debts, threats, sale in times of need, trickery, or outright theft), but that, united in the indivisible *resguardo*, the villagers stood a much better chance.[37] However, by employing such language (or allowing their lawyers to do so), Indians perpetuated stereotypes. While successfully avoiding the Liberals' twin traps of either being equal citizens who lose their special rights or being "Indians" who were not citizens, Indians cast themselves as weak and ignorant, needing protection. They could not completely escape the contradictions and racialized "logic" Liberalism established in defining citizenship. While embracing citizenship, indigenous communities also maintained an older colonial discourse of historical precedent, community, supplication, and appeals to authority in order to legitimate their identity as indigenous citizens.[38] Indians highlighted their supposed weakness, reinforcing elite stereotypes in order to justify their special legal status and maintain their communal landholdings and local self-governance.

In addition to strengthening stereotypes about themselves, Indians' discourse of citizenship also reinforced racialized thinking about other groups in the Cauca. Indians from Pancitará, in a dispute with the town of La Vega, complained that "the white residents of La Vega" did not respect them and that "they do not look upon us as citizens but as slaves."[39] Echoing calls for protection mentioned above, the indigenous governor of Quichaya complained to the provincial governor that "we do not have any authority before whom we can seek redress," as the local officials "treat us as if we were their slaves."[40] I do not want to overly emphasize Indians' use of slavery as an oppositional trope, as many other Caucanos also contrasted slavery and freedom in their discourses. Yet by counterposing their own position with that of slaves, Indians argued for their inclusion in the nation in contrast to excluded African slaves—who were simultaneously engaged in a struggle to redefine both citizenship and the nation. Beyond allusions to slavery, indigenous discourse also contrasted the petitioners and other "Indians."

The petitions cited above originated from Indians who largely spoke some Spanish (if not exclusively), lived in settled villages, practiced the Catholic faith, and in many ways lived lives that were little different from those of their mestizo, mulatto, black, and white peasant neighbors. However, there were other Indians in the Cauca's territory who lived in the Amazon rain forest to the east and the Darien region to the far north along the border with Panama. The Cauca's Indians referred to themselves as civilized "*indíjenas*," in contrast to the uncivilized "*indios*." The Indians of Túquerres and Ipiales who referred to "our *patria*" continually denominated themselves as "*indíjenas*" in their petition but noted that if they lost their *resguardos* they would become "*miserable indios*" and be forced to return to "jungle camps."[41] They counterposed belonging to the nation with the jungle and wild "*indios*." A petition from the governors of Pitayó, Jambaló, and Quichaya complained that "we have been treated like savage *indios* and slaves" by the "whites." They asked for the government of the Cauca state to assume direct control over the area and remove local officials so that "then we will be treated like citizens."[42] Indians of Santiago requested that their village be made part of the municipality of Caldas and not the territory of Caquetá, noting they were "citizens" and not like the residents of the nearby village of Descancé, who have "entirely savage language and customs."[43] Indians promoted their own inclusion in the nation by favorably comparing themselves to "savages" who did not merit such distinction. The Colombian state agreed with such classifications and spent much energy devising schemes by which bureaucrats and missionaries would civilize and control the "*indios*" of the Amazon rain forest.[44]

Citizenship is often defined in contrast to an excluded, noncitizen "other." In the nineteenth century, the "other" most often included women, minors, the lower class, or the "uncivilized."[45] Despite their impressive claims for inclusion on their own terms in the national polity, Indians' arguments supported the exclusion of others: the so-called savage Indians, slaves, and, in a distinct manner discussed below, female members of their own communities. While not possessing the power of intellectuals and politicians to promote their racialized discourses, Indians nonetheless participated in a popular construction of race and citizenship. Indians' petitions reveal the extent to which popular groups were able to challenge the dominant elite political discourse and adapt it to their own needs. However, the petitions also show this indigenous republican discourse's limits, as the hegemonic Liberal discourse forced Indians to perpetuate stereotypes of themselves. While Indians challenged the notions that they were incapable of political action and that they must subsume their racial or ethnic identity to claim citizenship, they nonetheless participated in a racialized discourse, differentiating themselves from slaves and "savage *indios*." The Caucano Indians' experience reflects a central theme of this volume: subalterns' appropriation of race and nation can both undermine and reinforce racism and exclusion.

Yet did this discourse represent Indians' "true" political views, or was it just the invention of country lawyers? The sheer number of petitions, their provenance from different times and places, the ubiquity of such a discourse, and the fact that many indigenous leaders appeared to craft the petitions themselves (literacy may have been more widespread than expected) all suggest that Indians elected to publicly represent themselves this way. Whatever their secret desires, by the 1850s republicanism was hegemonic in the Cauca, and if indigenous communities hoped to have any political influence, they would have to do so within the republican political system.[46] Whether Indians believed such language or not, indigenous republicanism became the way villages talked about and practiced politics.

The above caveat only makes more impressive the significant gains the Cauca's Indians achieved in reframing elite discourse concerning race and national life. Liberal attacks on *resguardos* and the corporate Indian village forced the communities to defend their separate identity as Indians in order to justify their communal landholding and local self-governance. Indians strongly fought to maintain their particular identity, contrasting themselves with whites, mestizos, slaves, and *indios*. While defending their identity as Indians, they also seized upon citizenship as a way to play a role in national life and protect their interests in the new political arena of republicanism that arose after the collapse of colonial rule. Indians amalgamated an older discourse of community and appeals to authority with a new republican discourse of rights and citizenship— which we might call indigenous republicanism.[47] In so doing, they not only strengthened republicanism's hegemony but altered it to better suit their own social visions. Indigenous communities across the Americas faced similar challenges during the nineteenth century, yet the Cauca's communities seemed particularly successful. Charles Walker notes how Indian resistance around Cuzco "ultimately reinforced the division of the nation along the lines of Indians and non-Indians."[48] Cuzco's indigenous communities defended their identity (and lands) but seemed less able to promote their status as citizens. Similarly, as the works of Mark Thurner on Peru and Jeffrey Gould on Nicaragua show, other Indians were less able than the Cauca's indigenous communities to overcome what Thurner calls the "contradictions" of republican nation building, in which elites were able to define citizenship against "Indianness."[49] Aldo Lauria-Santiago argues that while Indian communities in El Salvador conducted fruitful negotiations with the state, they were much less invested in the nation, instead favoring local identities.[50] In general, southwestern Colombia's indigenous communities seemed much more successful in manipulating republicanism, due, in part, to their seizure of the political opportunities opened by Colombia's very contentious partisan politics. The southwest's indigenous villages did not just reframe republican discourse but successfully entered the political sphere to defend their material interests as well.

INDIGENOUS REPUBLICANS IN THE PUBLIC REALM

Indians developed and employed the discourse of indigenous republicanism to support one principal goal—the protection of their *resguardos*. The villagers of Mocondino predicted the consequences of their *resguardo*'s division, claiming that "soon our land would form some rich man's hacienda or the town of people of the white race" and they would have to become "miserable day laborers."[51] Hoping to avoid such a fate, indigenous communities confronted a political scene dominated by the Conservative and Liberal Parties. To prevent their communities' dissolution, they would need to secure the support of one party or the other. Fortuitously, in the Cauca both parties would turn to popular groups for support in the numerous elections and civil wars of the second half of the nineteenth century.

As noted above, when Liberals came to power in 1849—both nationally and in the Cauca—they pushed for the division of *resguardo* land among individual community members as private property. In 1850 the national government ceded the faculty to determine the *resguardos'* future to the provinces, with the expectation that regional legislatures would arrange for division. Many areas quickly moved to do so, with the result that many Indians in central and eastern Colombia lost their land.[52] By the late 1850s, however, Liberals began to realize the political costs of their attitude toward Indians. In reaction to Liberals' attacks on religion and communal lands, the Cauca's indigenous villages, with some exceptions, threw their support to Conservatives in the 1851 and 1854 civil wars.

Conservatives, when they were in power, had at least made some cosmetic efforts at preventing Indians' exploitation by their neighbors.[53] Conservatives accepted that Indians (but not Afro-Colombians) constituted an important part of Colombian society, if not yet always as citizens. Liberals had forged a powerful alliance with Afro-Colombians in the Cauca Valley (around Cali), championing abolition of slavery and the political and social rights of the valley's largely black and mulatto lower class.[54] In a dispute over land around coastal mines, Conservatives chastised Liberals for their obsessive pandering to Afro-Colombians, noting that the Liberals should be more concerned with the welfare of Indians, who "are Granadinos and deserve more than the Africans."[55]

Conservatives reaped the benefits of Liberal attitudes toward Indians during the 1851 civil war. While elite Conservatives rebelled for many reasons in 1851—to regain power, to keep their slaves, to limit the opening of politics, and to protect the Church—in their attempts to mobilize indigenous supporters they mostly focused on the Liberals' godlessness and attacks on property.[56] This had been a traditional method to mobilize popular conservatives, and there seemed to be no reason why it should fail now. Led by the archconservative slaveowner Julio Arboleda, the Conservatives went from village to village throughout the highlands seeking recruits for their planned rebellion. In indigenous villages they spoke out against the godless Liberals, who had expelled the Jesuits, would destroy the Church, and planned to profane the sacrament of marriage.[57] The increasingly hostile debate over religion and the role of the Church alarmed the southwest's Indians. Throughout the colonial epoch, the Church had been an ally—if often unreliable—against the designs of the *hacendados*. President José Hilario López's anticlericalism, especially his expulsion of the Jesuits in 1850, shocked Indians.[58] However, some Liberals' desire to secularize marriage struck even closer to indigenous concerns.[59] One important justification for Indians' local self-government was that it enabled indigenous leaders to exercise patriarchal control over their villages and to maintain order and morality. A coalition of Indians from the south explained the link between patriarchy and the *resguardos* in a metaphor: "Our *parcialidades*, Honorable Deputies, are like a family that lives under one father," and, as such, they follow the rules and customs that they "have received from our ancestors."[60] Nicolas Quilindo, governor of Polindará, noted that "*cabildos* care for the regulation, morality, and good order of their respective indigenous populations."[61] Marriage and the family—sanctified by religion—undergirded the patriarchal structure of indigenous villages, and, therefore, both their culture and communal lands. As with many other forms of popular republicanism, the ability to control dependent women and children legitimized indigenous male citizenship.[62] While elite Conservatives simply hoped Indians would be righteously enraged by Liberals' disrespect of the Church, Indians saw much more than that. Liberals seemed to threaten not only the Church, but also the whole ideological and structural system upon which the indigenous communities rested.

Conservatives also warned that their opponents were communists, and that Liberals' disrespect for property would not just affect the rich but would result in their taking the livestock of even the smallest farmers to distribute to those who had none.[63] Indians' *resguardos*, always legally precarious, now seemed endangered again. As one Liberal succinctly put it, clerics had motivated the masses of the south by "preaching the defense of religion, their women, and their properties."[64]

Generally, Conservatives supported corporate bodies within the state—be they indigenous villages or the Church—and opposed the legal equality that Liberals promoted. While elitist, the Conservatives' conception of citizenship mattered less in their relations with subalterns since Conservatives did not privilege citizenship as the only entrée into political and public life. They accepted that most everyone had some role to play in society—not just citizens—and thus worried much less about the "rationality" of subalterns, especially Indians. Conservatives placed a higher value on received traditions and the importance of local relations for determining political worth as opposed to the new "universal" Liberal citizenship that eclipsed all other identities. For elite Conservatives, Indians might not yet be citizens, but they were Granadans or Colombians with social rights and responsibilities.

When Conservatives revolted in 1851, they enjoyed some indigenous support, but their own arrogance and refusal to treat indigenous leaders as equal allies limited many Indians' enthusiasm. Conservatives relied on dragooning troops, even Indians who might have been more willing supporters if given the opportunity. Nevertheless, some Indians feared Liberal intentions concerning marriage and their *resguardos* enough that they voluntarily enlisted in Conservative ranks.[65] After the Conservatives' initial defeats at Liberal hands, more volunteers began to stream into the Conservative camp, but by then it was too late.[66] Some Liberals with strong patron-client ties to Indians, especially the charismatic José María Obando, convinced many Indians to lay down their arms.[67] Conservatives, hampered by their elitist and racist views, failed to take full advantage of Indians' willingness to fight for their villages.

The Cauca's Conservatives would have another chance in 1854, after a division in the Liberal Party led to one Liberal faction revolting against its own government. Indians fought with Conservatives against the Liberal conspirators, marching into the central valley to stifle any attempted rebellion.[68] A few Indians did support the revolt, due to clientelist ties to Obando (the putative leader of the rebellion), but more sided with Conservatives.[69] After the 1853 constitution gave the vote to all adult males, Indians supported Conservatives at the ballot box as well, guaranteeing them victory throughout the southern Cauca.[70]

The victorious Conservatives did not forget about their subaltern allies. In Túquerres, the legislature and governor passed a law in 1853 allowing *resguardos* to continue indefinitely, unless the Indians themselves decided otherwise.[71] The new governor, Antonio Chaves, moved to strengthen his party's relations with Indians. He astutely demonstrated his understanding of where power lay in the indigenous communities by supporting indigenous governors and *cabildos*. Chaves ordered land that had been sold without the *cabildos'* approval returned to the *resguardos*, and he made it harder for outsiders to claim to be Indians in order to use *resguardo* land; both measures significantly strengthened the *cabildos'* control over their communities' resources.[72] The Conservative legislature of Pasto followed suit in 1855 with a law that assured Indians the *resguardos* would not be divided.[73] Liberal governors had sought to eliminate communal landholding, but Conservatives hoped to paint themselves as the Indians' protectors. While much of the recent literature on state formation has focused on popular liberals, subalterns also sought alliances with conservatives, as noted in the Introduction to this volume. Nineteenth-century politics and nation build-ing cannot fully be understood without considering the motivations and ideol-ogy behind popular liberals' counterparts—popular conservatives.[74]

In the Cauca, however, Conservatives' racism and elitist view of citizenship and politics—and many Conservative *hacendados'* desire for Indian land— prevented them from forging a stronger political bond with Indians. Liberals exploited this in 1859, under the leadership of Tomás Mosquera, a former Conservative turned Liberal who was plotting a revolt against the national Conservative government. Mosquera needed to ensure that the region's Indian communities would not support Conservatives militarily as they had in 1851 and 1854. In an about face, the Liberal state legislature passed Law 90, signed by Mosquera, which ceased attacks on the *resguardos*. The famed legislation ex-plicitly recognized the *cabildos pequeños'* authority to govern Indian life, grant-ing them any customary powers they had traditionally enjoyed, save those that violated state law or their residents' rights as citizens, and giving the *cabildo* officers the duty to correct any "moral" transgressions by their charges. More-over, the law affirmed that Indians would continue to possess their *resguardos*, with no timetable set for division. It also returned illegally sold or rented *resguardo* property back to the control of the community. The law did allow some meddling in Indians' affairs by local and state authorities, but generally it recognized indigenous prerogatives concerning the *resguardos* and community governance. Much like the Indians' own discourse of indigenous republican-ism, which the legislation echoed to a remarkable degree, Law 90 had the unfortunate consequence of reinforcing perceptions of Indians as minors who needed custodianship. This was of less concern, however, than the success of forcing Liberals to abandon at least temporarily their attacks on the *resguardos*, a major triumph for the Cauca's Indians.[75]

The 1860–62 civil war initiated by Mosquera's revolt tested Liberals' rap-prochement with the indigenous villages. Mosquera and his allies had hoped Law 90's concessions would neutralize Indians' support for Conservatives, who would now have trouble saying Liberals wanted to destroy the *resguardos*. They were not mistaken. In contrast to 1851 and 1854, many indigenous communities remained neutral, or at least tried to, resisting efforts by the armies to conscript their menfolk.[76] Law 90 and the Conservatives' brutality during the war toward Indian conscripts soured most indigenous communities on the Conservative Party as a political ally. However, the Liberal Party would prove equally unreli-able. From 1862 until 1879, Liberals dominated the Cauca state. In spite of Law

90, Liberal legislators, time and again, sought to undermine the legislation and renewed their opposition to indigenous corporate life.[77] Neither political party seemed to offer Indians a satisfactory political alliance.

As a result of the continued attacks on their lands, Indians mobilized politically to defend themselves, but in a different manner than before. The continual threats to Indians' property, communities, and lifeways helped to unite many indigenous communities in the south, to create a more forceful indigenous republican discourse, and to redefine what "Indian" would mean in the republic. In 1866 the Cauca state government asked all local officials and indigenous *cabildos* to give their opinion on the compatibility of *resguardos* and the state constitution. Indians resoundingly answered that they wanted to keep their *resguardos*.[78] The village leaders lamented that with individual property holding, "whites" could buy land for ridiculously low prices from "Indians incapable of exactly discerning their true interests," or by corrupting them with liquor or calling in old debts.[79] This constant harassment and persecution by the "whites" or "mestizos" sharply delineated "*blancos*" from "*indíjenas*."[80] Indians also faced the problem of whites claiming that Indians were "more-or-less civilized" and that Indians had fused "the Indian race with the white and mestizo" and therefore did not merit special laws.[81] These accusations forced Indians to defend their "Indianness" and the cohesion of their communities.

The questioning by the state government in the 1860s about the *resguardos'* future helped inspire a greater cohesiveness among the south's indigenous population. Indians had at times acted in pan-village coalitions before the 1860s, but the majority of earlier representations to the Cauca state authorities were conducted by individual or immediately neighboring villages. Indians usually did not unite in petitions and lawsuits beyond the confines of a particular village or *resguardo*. However, under continued pressure from Liberals, in the 1860s large groups of Indians in the south responded together. One petition was sent from many of the *cabildos* of the municipality of Obando—at least fifteen separate *cabildos* were represented under the office of an indigenous community leader known as the *alcalde mayor*. While the language retained much of the humble protestations of other petitions, it emphasized the importance of the local authority of the *cabildo pequeño*. The indigenous leaders stressed how they kept order over their communities and protected them from the invidious schemes of the "whites." They praised Law 90, especially as it allowed the Indians themselves to defend their rights and maintain their communities instead of relying on others.[82] The year 1866 marked a point when the *cabildos* broke from an older language of deference and more forcefully evoked their independence, while acting in supralocal alliances to strengthen their political position.

Indians' new discourse emerged fully in 1873, after the Cauca legislature passed yet another law abrogating Law 90 and ordering the *resguardos*' division. The Indians of Cumbal, engaged in a decades-long land dispute, adopted a stauncher tone. Gone were the protestations of weakness and incompetence, replaced by harsh accusations of the corruption and "clientelism" of the local ruling class.[83] More important, Indians from across the south gathered in Pasto to write to the legislature, chastising it for not consulting them about the law and again exposing the communities to the possibility of losing their lands. They expressed their frustration with the legislature and, noting the continued division of the Cauca into opposing political parties, warned: "If the mentioned law is put into effect or practice, we would find ourselves by necessity standing with the first who gave the shout of rebellion, as long as they assured us the repeal of the aforementioned law."[84]

After threatening to side with any future Conservative rebellion, Indians proposed to Liberals that, unlike in previous civil wars, they would not support the Conservative Party if Liberals acceded to their wishes: "We are convinced that the present legislators would not turn a deaf ear to the voice of more than twenty thousand inhabitants that demand the repeal of a law."[85] The petition did not mark a complete break with the older discourse described above, as the document still contained professions of weakness, calls for justice, appeals to authority to perform its duties, and affirmations of the importance of indigenous families and communities. But this moment did signal an important change in the way the southwest's Indians related to the Cauca's political elites. Before, Indians had reacted favorably to Conservatives' rhetoric and support of their *resguardos*, religion, and families; however, they could only respond to Conservatives, rather than negotiate with them. Conservatives accepted Indian allies, but only on elitist and racist terms. In the 1870s, Indians actively sought to bargain with the powerful, playing one party against the other. They threatened to join the Conservatives in revolt but also held out the promise of supporting the Liberals, if the Liberals gave them what they wanted.

Liberals responded, if somewhat half-heartedly. Cauca state president Julián Trujillo basically gutted the new law, returning Law 90 into effect but also allowing a majority of Indians to ask for division and permitting more outside interference by local authorities in Indian affairs.[86] However, the erosion of Indians' traditional allegiance to Conservatives, begun with Law 90 and the brutality of the 1860–62 war, had now accelerated. The south's indigenous people, acting in a pan-village and regional alliance, had issued a declaration of independence.[87] They would no longer serve as Conservatives' pawns but would make their own independent way between the two parties. Indians mostly remained neutral in the civil wars of 1876–77, 1879, and 1885. Liberals reacted to this new indigenous strategy by attempting in the late 1870s to recruit Indians as more active allies (as they had done with Afro-Colombians since the 1850s). The famed author and Liberal politician Jorge Isaacs urged local Liberal officials to protect indigenous interests against *hacendados'* abuses, so that Indians would see how "the Liberal Party, liberator in all of the nation of slaves of the African race, will also make free, perfectly free, people of the Indian race."[88] Liberals were ousted from power in 1879, however, before the Indians' united front had a chance to respond.

These pan-village actions also redefined what it meant to be Indian. Joanne Rappaport argues that the public identity of Indianness was largely a legal definition.[89] Nancy Appelbaum notes that Indianness was a profoundly local identity in the northern Cauca, connected to immediate landholdings and limiting villages' abilities to unite in regional alliances or acknowledge an extra-local ethnic identity.[90] In the southwest, however, by uniting to confront Liberal attacks, the villagers transformed "Indian" from a local and legal identity to a broader ethnic identity that united disparate villages as political agents under a common appellation. When villagers from across the south came together to act politically, they did not do so as "southerners," as residents of a particular village, or only as Colombians, but as "*indígenas.*" While it is impossible to gauge exactly what subalterns understood their words to mean, the act of coming together with people from other villages and selecting "*indígena*" as their shared designation must have challenged localized forms of imagined identity. Their employment of an "Indian" identity contrasts sharply with the experience of subalterns of African descent in the Cauca, who also banded together politically (in alliance with Liberals), but who never identified themselves as of African descent, as "*negros,*" or as "*mulattos.*"[91] For the indigenous villagers, however, a broader, more politically effective connotation of "Indian" emerged in response to continual Liberal harassment and the constant need to differentiate themselves from "whites" and "mestizos" who coveted their land.

The Cauca's Indians succeeded remarkably at protecting their *resguardos* throughout the nineteenth century. (In central Colombia, meanwhile, Indians lost almost all of their communal land to division by the late 1850s.)[92] In the 1880s a national alliance of Independent Liberals and Conservatives took power and passed Law 89, which bore close resemblance to the Cauca's Law 90.

Law 89 reaffirmed Indians' right to the *resguardos* at the national level, while also classifying indigenous peoples as minors and casting them as dependents of the state.[93] The century's continual partisan conflict opened an opportunity for Indians to exploit both Liberals' and Conservatives' need for popular supporters, an opportunity indigenous villages manipulated with considerable dexterity.[94]

CONCLUSION

Elite intellectuals, caudillos, and bureaucrats did not solely shape racial or national thinking in the nineteenth century. Popular groups also played a significant role. During the colonial period, Indians had turned to Crown and Church, institutions jealous of the power of landlords and provincial officials, for support in their local conflicts. Indians continued this process, often successfully, within the republican state. They challenged the state to act, to perform its duties, to uphold the laws of the nation, and they justified these demands by claiming their due as citizens. This strategy had two principal effects, beyond the immediate goals of retaining land or removing corrupt local officials. First, Indians' constant demands on the state to protect them from local abuses expanded the state's sphere of influence into localities where it had before been nonexistent. Second, Indians made the nation a more powerful— and more democratically and racially inclusive—entity than the imagined community of intellectuals and bureaucrats in Bogotá.[95] Indians had always petitioned higher powers, but as humble subjects; in the nineteenth century, using a republican discourse, they did so as citizens with rights, members in good standing of a national community. However, indigenous reframing of republicanism alone would have mattered little if partisan conflict had not forced elites to bargain with subaltern groups to gain their electoral or military support.

In the southwest, Indians' adoption of republican discourse also altered accepted racial ideas. Indians admitted no contradiction between Indianness and citizenship, contrary to a racialized ideology that sought to either exclude them from national life (much of Colombian Liberalism) or only admit them in peripheral ways (Colombian Conservatism). However, by relying on "just authority" as central to their idea of republicanism, and in asking protection from the state, Indians also reproduced stereotypes about themselves in order to protect their communal landholdings. And by differentiating their legitimate claims to citizenship from those of slaves and "savage Indians," Indians reinforced, at least discursively, the isolation of those two groups from national life and the citizen body.

Indigenous peoples also recast the public meaning of Indianness during the course of the nineteenth century. Under pressure from Liberals to divide their land, and dissatisfied with the opportunities both Liberals and Conservatives offered for political gains, Indians began to unite beyond the village level. During the 1860s and 1870s, villages banded together to present a common front to the state and the two political parties. In addition to this strategy's material success in protecting *resguardos*, the movement helped redefine "Indian" from a legal and local identity to a more regional and broader political identity, foreshadowing the potent indigenous movements of the twentieth century that culminated in the 1991 constitution.

From 1910 to 1918 a number of indigenous communities to the northwest of Popayán united under the leadership of Manuel Quintín Lame to confront powerful *hacendados'* attacks on their lands. The movement would later spread west to Huila and Tolima and is seen as the intellectual and cultural inspiration for Colombia's modern Indian movement. Lame's principal tenets included the defense of the *resguardo*, strengthening the *cabildo* as a political force, reclaiming stolen lands, refusal to pay land rents, and affirmation of indigenous culture.[96] These goals would later influence the founding principles of the CRIC in the 1970s, which spearheaded the national indigenous rights movement.[97]

While Lame's connection to indigenous organizing in the late twentieth century is acknowledged, rarely is any link made back to the nineteenth century, which is often seen as a "long lapse" in indigenous organizing.[98] Yet Lame's goals almost exactly mirrored the discourse of nineteenth-century indigenous republicanism, especially that of the south's communities during the 1860s and 1870s described above. Through the nineteenth-century's long struggles, the Cauca's Indians had maintained sufficient coherence in their communities, which, along with their history of engaging the state and nation, served as the base for future organizing through the CRIC and other organizations before and after the constitutional struggle. The discourse and strategy that Quintín Lame and the founders of Colombia's modern Indian movement employed in the twentieth century emerged out of nineteenth-century politics in the Cauca.[99]

Nineteenth-century indigenous activism bequeathed to future generations of Indians a conception of Colombian citizenship that did not reject, but embraced, indigenous identity. Indians did not accept that they could never be citizens (or could be only second-class citizens) due to elitist notions that they were racially or culturally inferior. Nor did they accept the Liberal idea that they could become citizens only by rejecting their communities and historic lifeways, embracing a universalizing citizenship at the expense of their past, their communal lands, and their communities' coherence. Instead, Indians asserted in their petitions, and reaffirmed in their political actions, that citizenship and Indianness were not incompatible, a claim echoed over a century later by the Zapatistas in the epigraph that opens this volume. The increasing influence of scientific racism in the early twentieth century would erode Indians' gains and lead to further attacks on indigenous communities' existence and rights.[100] The constitution of 1991, however, recognized a notion of indigenous citizenship surprisingly similar to that which Indians had proposed a century earlier: it granted Indians special rights, control over local resources, and representation in the national state.[101] While the constitution was the immediate result of the modern indigenous movement's courageous efforts, the groundwork began in the tumult of nineteenth-century struggles in the Cauca over the meaning of nation, state, and Indian.

NOTES

I would like to thank the staff members of all the Colombian archives cited in this essay for their invaluable help. Michael Jiménez, George Reid Andrews, John Beverly, Aims McGuinness, Brett Troyan, and Jennifer Duncan all provided useful comments and advice, as did the editors of this volume and the anonymous readers for the University of North Carolina Press. All mistakes are solely my responsibility.

1. Throughout the essay, I use the word "Indian" as a translation of the Spanish "*indígena.*" Also, what we now call Colombia possessed several names over the course of the nineteenth century—including Nueva Granada, Confederación Granadina, and Los Estados Unidos de Colombia.

2. The notion of national inclusion lies at the heart of most of the recent literature on the popular role in nation and state formation, which has largely centered on Mexico and Peru. While the literature has grown too large to cite comprehensively, two of the founding texts are Florencia E. Mallon, *Peasant and Nation: The Making of Postcolonial Mexico and Peru* (Berkeley: University of California Press, 1995), and Gilbert M. Joseph and Daniel Nugent, eds., *Everyday Forms of State Formation: Revolution and the Negotiation of Rule in Modern Mexico* (Durham: Duke University Press, 1994).

3. Mosquera's figures from 1852 were an informed guess and should be used with caution. T. C. de Mosquera, *Memoria sobre la geografía, física y política de la Nueva Granada* (New York: Imprenta de S. W. Benedict, 1852), 96.

4. For an overview of Indians' situation during and after the colonial era, see Joanne Rappaport, *The Politics of Memory: Native Historical Interpretation in the Colombian Andes* (Cambridge: Cambridge University Press, 1990), 31–60, and Juan Friede, *El indio en lucha por la tierra* (Bogotá: Editorial Espiral, 1944). For general histories of the Cauca region, see Germán Colmenares, *Historia económica y social de Colombia*, vol. 2, *Popayán: Una sociedad esclavista, 1680–1800* (Bogotá: Tercer Mundo, 1997), and Alonso Valencia Llano, *Estado soberano del Cauca: Federalismo y regeneración* (Bogotá: Banco de la República, 1988).

5. Comisión Corográfica, *Jeografía física i política de las provincias de la Nueva Granada* (Bogotá: Banco de la República, 1959), 2:337; José Francisco Vela to Secretary of Government, Ipiales, 27 June 1866, Archivo Central del Cauca, Popayán (hereafter ACC), Archivo Muerto (hereafter AM), Paquete 94, Legajo 40; Report of Popayán's Jefe Municipal, Popayán, 15 June 1866, ACC, AM, Paq. 94, Leg. 54; Undersigned members of the pequeños cabildos of Túquerres, Obando, and Pasto to Deputies of the State Legislature, Pasto, 29 July 1873, ACC, AM, Paq. 124, Leg. 60 (note that most documents in the Archivo Muerto have no page numbers). See also Friede, *El indio en lucha por la tierra*, and Rappaport, *The Politics of Memory*, 87–116.

6. Communities, like nations and races, are also historical constructions, although internal divisions and hierarchies are not the focus of this essay. See Les W. Field, "State, Anti-State, and Indigenous Entities: Reflections upon a Páez Resguardo and the New Colombian Constitution," *Journal of Latin American Anthropology* 1, no. 2 (1996): 106–7. For community theory, see Mallon, *Peasant and Nation*, 11–12, 63–88, and Gavin Smith, *Livelihood and Resistance: Peasants and the Politics of Land in Peru* (Berkeley: University of California Press, 1989).

For the region's economy, see José Antonio Ocampo, *Colombia y la economía mundial, 1830–1910* (Bogotá: Tercer Mundo, 1998), 255–300, and José Gregorio Fernández to T. C. de Mosquera, Panamá, 28 Sept. 1852, ACC, Sala Mosquera (hereafter SM), Documento 28,406.

7. Pequeño cabildo of Túquerres to District Mayor, Túquerres, 12 Feb. 1866, ACC, AM, Paq. 94, Leg. 54; Comisión Corográfica, *Jeografía física i política*, 161, 225; José María Samper, *Ensayo aproximado sobre la jeografía i estadística de los ocho estados que compondrán el 15 de septiembre de 1857 la Federación Neo-Granadina* (Bogotá: Imprenta de El Neo-Granadino, 1857), 28; Avelino Vela to Secretary of Government, Ipiales, 28 Apr. 1865, ACC, AM, Paq. 92, Leg. 83; Felipe Pérez, *Jeografía física i política de los Estados Unidos de Colombia*, vol. 1, *Comprende la jeografía del distrito federal i las de los estados de Panamá i el Cauca* (Bogotá: Imprenta de la Nación, 1862), 370.

8. Joanne Rappaport, *Cumbe Reborn: An Andean Ethnography of History* (Chicago: University of Chicago Press, 1994), 26–28.

9. First quotation from Indian Alcalde Mayor of Obando Municipality (with signers from the parcialidades of Potosí, Mayasquer, Yaramal, Cumbal, Guachucal, Muellamuez, Colimba, Carlosama, Caserío de Pastas, Pupiales, Anfelima, Girón, Iles, Ospina, and

Puerres) to Secretary of State Government, Ipiales, 4 Mar. 1866, ACC, AM, Paq. 94, Leg. 54; second from the Alcaldes Mayores of Túquerres and Ipiales Cantones, with all the pequeños cabildos de indígenas of the Provinces, to President of the Provincial Legislature, Túquerres, 17 Sept. 1848, ACC, AM, Paq. 44, Leg. 39. This and all subsequent translations are mine.

10. Pequeño cabildo of Túquerres to District Mayor, Túquerres, 12 Feb. 1866, ACC, AM, Paq. 94, Leg. 54; Pequeño cabildo of Piedra-ancha to District Mayor, Piedra-ancha, 21 Feb. 1866, ACC, AM, Paq. 94, Leg. 54.

11. The Caucano politician Tomás Mosquera divided society into three "*razas*"— "Caucasian whites," "Civilized Americans," and "Ethiopian blacks"—and four "*castas*"— "quadroons," "mestizos," "mulattos," and "*zambos.*" Mosquera, *Memoria sobre la geografía*, 96; Sergio Arboleda, *Rudimentos de geografía, cronología e historia: Lecciones dispuestas para la enseñanza elemental de dichos ramos en el seminario conciliar de Popayán* (Bogotá: Imprenta de El Tradicionalista, 1872), 18. On the "inferior races," see Sergio Arboleda, *El clero puede salvarnos i nadie puede salvarnos sino el clero* (Popayán: Imprenta del Colejio Mayor, 1858), 16. See also *Ariete* (Cali), 20 Oct. 1849.

For nineteenth-century Colombian thinking on race, see Frank Safford, "Race, Integration, and Progress: Elite Attitudes and the Indian in Colombia, 1750–1870," *Hispanic American Historical Review* 71, no. 1 (Feb. 1991): 1–33; Nancy P. Appelbaum, "Remembering Riosucio: Race, Region, and Community in Colombia, 1850–1950" (Ph.D. diss., University of Wisconsin–Madison, 1997), 2–8; Peter Wade, *Blackness and Race Mixture: The Dynamics of Racial Identity in Colombia* (Baltimore: Johns Hopkins University Press, 1993), 29–37, 54–59; J. León Helguera, *Indigenismo in Colombia: A Facet of the National Identity Search, 1821–1973* (Buffalo: Council on International Studies, 1974), 7–9.

12. José María Samper, *Ensayo sobre las revoluciones políticas y la condición social de las repúblicas colombianas (Hispano-Americanas), con un apéndice sobre la orografía y la población de la Confederación Granadina* (1861; reprint, Bogotá: Universidad Nacional de Colombia, 1969), 266–67, 292, 299, quotation on 300. Some Caucano Liberals claimed race did not exist. *El Montañés* (Barbacoas), 15 Feb. 1876.

13. William Marion Gibson, *The Constitutions of Colombia* (Durham: Duke University Press, 1948), 160–62.

14. Joaquín Garcés, "Mensaje del Gobernador de la provincia de Túquerres á la Cámara en 1850," Túquerres, 15 Sept. 1850, ACC, AM, Paq. 48, Leg. 25; Safford, "Race, Integration, and Progress," 1–11.

15. *Las Máscaras* (Pasto), 26 Sept. 1850. See also Report of Juan Antonio Arturo, Governor of Pasto, to the Provincial Legislature, Pasto, 20 Oct. 1853, ACC, AM, Paq. 54, Leg. 26.

16. Anselmo Soto Arana and E. León to Deputies, Popayán, 9 Sept. 1871, ACC, AM, Paq. 112, Leg. 2.

17. Eliseo Payán, "Mensaje que el Presidente del Estado Soberano del Cauca dirije a la Lejislatura en sus sesiones ordinarias de 1865," Popayán, 1 July 1865, ACC, AM, Paq. 90, Leg. 49.

18. Citizens and residents of Silvia parish [over forty-five names] to Senators and Representatives, Silvia, 19 Mar. 1852, Archivo del Congreso—Bogotá (hereafter AC), 1852, Senado, Informes de Comisión IV, 137. Ellipses in original.

19. Cabildo pequeño de indígenas of Yascual to President of the Provincial Legislature, Túquerres, 8 Oct. 1852, ACC, AM, Paq. 48, Leg. 4. Others referred to "our Republic"; see Parcialidad de indígenas of Fúnes to President, Pasto, 27 July 1882, Archivo General de la Nación—Bogotá (hereafter AGN), Sección República (hereafter SR), Fondo Ministerio de Industrias—Correspondencia de Baldíos, Tomo 4, 136.

20. Cabildo de indígenas of the village of Caldono to Provincial Governor, Caldono, 19 Nov. 1853, ACC, AM, Paq. 55, Leg. 85.

21. Alcaldes Mayores of Túquerres and Ipiales Cantones, with all the pequeños cabildos de indígenas of the Provinces to President of the Provincial Legislature, Túquerres, 17 Sept. 1848, ACC, AM, Paq. 44, Leg. 39.

22. The three pequeños cabildos of Santiago, Sibundoy, and Putumayo to State Legislators, Santiago, 20 Jan. 1870, ACC, AM, Paq. 112, Leg. 8.

23. Cabildo pequeño de indígenas and adults of the village to State President, Sibundoy, 8 Nov. 1874, ACC, AM, Paq. 129, Leg. 45.

24. Testimony of Governor Bautista Pechene, Popayán, 18 Aug. 1856, ACC, AM, Paq. 62, Leg. 45.

25. Indigenous Alcalde Mayor and cabildos pequeños of Túquerres Province to President of the House of Representatives, Túquerres, 30 Dec. 1848, AC, 1849, Cámara, Informes de Comisiones IX, 184. See also Governor and Regidor of the pequeño cabildo de indígenas of Rioblanco to Jefe Municipal, Popayán, 4 Oct. 1878, ACC, AM, Paq. 140, Leg. 62.

26. Report of pequeño cabildo de indíjenas of Jambaló, Jambaló, 6 Mar. 1866, ACC, AM, Paq. 94, Leg. 54.

27. Indian Alcalde Mayor of Obando Municipality (with signers from the parcialidades of Potosí, Mayasquer, Yaramal, Cumbal, Guachucal, Muellamuez, Colimba, Carlosama, Caserío de Pastas, Pupiales, Anfelima, Girón, Iles, Ospina, and Puerres) to Secretary of State Government, Ipiales, 4 Mar. 1866, ACC, AM, Paq. 94, Leg. 54.

28. Indigenous residents of Cajamarca to State President, Cajamarca, 30 July 1871, ACC, AM, Paq. 112, Leg. 29; Cabildo de indígenas of Guachucal and Colimba to Legislators, Guachucal, 12 Aug. 1873, ACC, AM, Paq. 124, Leg. 60.

29. Cabildo pequeño de indígenas of Santiago de Pongo to Deputies, Santiago de Pongo, 8 Aug. 1869, ACC, AM, Paq. 103, Leg. 3. For an analysis of indigenous petitions from the colonial era, see Margarita Garrido, *Reclamos y representaciones: Variaciones sobre la política en el Nuevo Reino de Granada, 1770–1815* (Bogotá: Banco de la República, 1993), 229–66.

30. Cabildo de indígenas of Túquerres to President of the Legislature, Túquerres, 26 July 1871, ACC, AM, Paq. 112, Leg. 15.

31. Indians from the Felpí River to President, Barbacoas, 20 June 1866, Archivo del

Instituto Colombiano de la Reforma Agraria—Bogotá, Bienes Nacionales, Tomo 21, 482. See also Pequeño cabildo de indígenas of Cumbal to State President, Cumbal, 29 July 1871, AGN, SR, Fondo Ministerio de lo Interior y Relaciones Exteriores, Tomo 82, 986.

32. Cabildo de indígenas of Guachucal and Colimba to Legislators, Guachucal, 12 Aug. 1873, ACC, AM, Paq. 124, Leg. 60. See also Alcalde indígena of Paniquitá to Provincial Governor, Popayán, 15 Mar. 1850, ACC, AM, Paq. 48, Leg. 57.

33. Governor and Alcaldes of the parcialidad of Pitayó to State Governor, Popayán, 24 Nov. 1858, ACC, AM, Paq. 67, Leg. 19.

34. Indians of Toribio, San Francisco, and Tacueyó to Governor of the State, Toribio, 25 May 1868, ACC, AM, Paq. 101, Leg. 60.

35. Cabildos pequeños de indígenas of Túquerres, Cumbal, Guachucal, Muellamuez, Sapuyes, Guaitarilla, Ospina, Yascual, Mallama, and Imués to Deputies of the State Legislature, Túquerres, 14 Aug. 1877, ACC, AM, Paq. 137, Leg. 18.

36. Cabildos pequeños de indígenas of Túquerres, Sapuyes, Imués, Ospina, Cumbal, Guachucal, Muellamuez, Yascual, and Puerres to Honorable Deputies of the Legislature, Pasto, 19 July 1875, ACC, AM, Paq. 133, Leg. 75.

37. Cabildos pequeños of Guachucal and Muellamuez to Provincial Governor, Guachucal, 4 Oct. 1852, ACC, AM, Paq. 53, Leg. 56; Indian Alcalde Mayor, Governor, and Regidores of Túquerres to Deputies of the Legislature, Túquerres, 20 Sept. 1852, ACC, AM, Paq. 48, Leg. 4.

38. See especially Pequeño cabildo de indígenas of Genoy to President of the Legislature, Pasto, 15 Aug. 1877, ACC, AM, Paq. 137, Leg. 18, and Indians and Members of the pequeño cabildo of Túquerres to President of the Legislature, Túquerres, June 1869 [no day listed], ACC, AM, Paq. 103, Leg. 3.

39. This language is particularly interesting as at least technically the Indians were not citizens under the law at this time, given that most would not have owned enough property to qualify under the constitution of 1843. Governor and cabildo pequeño de indígenas of Pancitará to Provincial Governor, Pancitará, 24 Aug. 1850, ACC, AM, Paq. 48, Leg. 57.

40. Governor de indígenas of Quichaya to Provincial Governor, Popayán, 1 Apr. 1853, ACC, AM, Paq. 55, Leg. 85. See also Indian Alcalde Mayor of Obando Municipality (with signers from the parcialidades of Potosí, Mayasquer, Yaramal, Cumbal, Guachucal, Muellamuez, Colimba, Carlosama, Caserío de Pastas, Pupiales, Anfelima, Girón, Iles, Ospina, and Puerres) to Secretary of State Government, Ipiales, 4 Mar. 1866, ACC, AM, Paq. 94, Leg. 54.

41. Alcaldes Mayores of Túquerres and Ipiales Cantones, with all the pequeños cabildos de indígenas of the Provinces, to President of the Provincial Legislature, Túquerres, 17 Sept. 1848, ACC, AM, Paq. 44, Leg. 39.

42. The signatories referred to themselves as "indíjenas." Governors of Pitayó, Jambaló, and Quichaya to Governor of the State, Jambaló, 1 Aug. 1859, ACC, AM, Paq. 74, Leg. 51.

43. Caquetá was a territory, so the people living there did not have the same rights as those living in the states. Cabildo pequeño de indígenas of Santiago de Pongo to Deputies, Santiago de Pongo, 8 Aug. 1869, ACC, AM, Paq. 103, Leg. 3.

44. The undersigned members of the Second Provincial Ecclesiastical Council (including the Bishop of Popayán) to Senators and Representatives, Bogotá, 12 Feb. 1874, AC, 1874, Senado, Proyectos de Ley IV, 184; *El Seminario* (Popayán), 24 Nov. 1857; *Rejistro Oficial (Organo del Gobierno del Estado)* (Popayán), 31 Mar. 1880; *El Ferrocarril* (Cali), 16 Mar. 1883. Ecuadorian elites made similar distinctions between the "civilized" Otavaleño Indians and other indigenous peoples. Derek Williams, "Indians on the Verge: The 'Otavalo Indian' and the Regional Dynamics of the Ecuadorian 'Indian Problem,' 1830–1940" (paper presented at the Conference on Latin American History, Boston, 4–7 Jan. 2001).

45. Uday Singh Mehta, *Liberalism and Empire: A Study in Nineteenth-Century British Liberal Thought* (Chicago: University of Chicago Press, 1999), 1–114; Elizabeth Dore, "One Step Forward, Two Steps Back: Gender and the State in the Long Nineteenth Century," in *Hidden Histories of Gender and the State in Latin America*, ed. Elizabeth Dore and Maxine Molyneux (Durham: Duke University Press, 2000), 14–21.

46. Afro-Colombians and Antioqueño migrants did not represent themselves in the same manner as did Indians. While the role of scribes and country lawyers was important in introducing republican ideas to communities, ultimately the communities themselves usually decided how to adapt such language to suit their interests. For opposing views see Gayatri Chakravorty Spivak, "Can the Subaltern Speak?," in *Marxism and the Interpretation of Culture*, ed. Cary Nelson and Lawrence Grossberg (Urbana: University of Illinois Press, 1988), 271–313, and James C. Scott, *Domination and the Arts of Resistance: Hidden Transcripts* (New Haven: Yale University Press, 1990).

47. María Teresa Findji notes that many republican policies sought to eliminate Indians from national life, yet she underestimates Indians' abilities to reframe the language of republicanism to defend their communities within the new nation. María Teresa Findji, "From Resistance to Social Movement: The Indigenous Authorities Movement in Colombia," in *The Making of Social Movements in Latin America: Identity, Strategy, and Democracy*, ed. Arturo Escobar and Sonia E. Alvarez (Boulder, Colo.: Westview Press, 1992), 112–13.

48. Charles F. Walker, *Smoldering Ashes: Cuzco and the Creation of Republican Peru, 1780–1840* (Durham: Duke University Press, 1999), 186.

49. Mark Thurner, *From Two Republics to One Divided: Contradictions of Postcolonial Nationmaking in Andean Peru* (Durham: Duke University Press, 1997), 146–52; Jeffrey L. Gould, *To Die in This Way: Nicaraguan Indians and the Myth of Mestizaje, 1880–1965* (Durham: Duke University Press, 1998), 11–15, 285. Indian elites in Quetzaltenango had some success in promoting indigenous citizenship, but at a somewhat later historical moment and with a less popular cast. See Greg Grandin, *The Blood of Guatemala: A History of Race and Nation* (Durham: Duke University Press, 2000), 125–46.

50. Aldo A. Lauria-Santiago, *An Agrarian Republic: Commercial Agriculture and the Politics of Peasant Communities in El Salvador, 1823–1914* (Pittsburgh: University of Pittsburgh Press, 1999), 112–31, 218–21.

51. Pequeño cabildo de indígenas of Mocondino to President of the Sovereign State of Cauca, Pasto, 18 Feb. 1866, ACC, AM, Paq. 94, Leg. 54.

52. The national government had made tentative efforts to divide the *resguardos* since independence, but such efforts had generally failed. Jorge Villegas and Antonio Restrepo, *Resguardos de indígenas, 1820–1890* (Medellín: Universidad de Antioquia, 1977), 6–37; Glenn Thomas Curry, "The Disappearance of the Resguardos Indígenas of Cundinamarca, Colombia, 1800–1863" (Ph.D. diss., Vanderbilt University, 1981).

53. Governor Vicente Cárdenas to Jefe Político of Almaguer Cantón, [no place or day listed, but Popayán], June 1848, ACC, AM, Paq. 44, Leg. 16; Francisco Lémos to Treasury Court, Popayán, 13 Mar. 1848, ACC, Sala República, Archivo de "El Carnero," Signatura 2,708, unpaginated.

54. James Sanders, "Contentious Republicans: Popular Politics, Race, and Class in Nineteenth-Century Southwestern Colombia" (Ph.D. diss., University of Pittsburgh, 2000). See also Aims McGuinness, "In the Path of Empire: Land, Labor, and Liberty in Panamá during the California Gold Rush, 1848–1860" (Ph.D. diss., University of Michigan, 2001).

55. The landowners of Barbacoas Cantón [over thirty names] to Secretary of Foreign Relations, Barbacoas, 16 Aug. 1852, AGN, SR, Fondo Gobernaciones Varias, Tomo 179, 147.

56. Manuel Bueno to José Hilario López, Popayán, 25 June 1850, AGN, Sección Academia Colombiana de Historia (hereafter SACH), Fondo José Hilario López (hereafter FJHL), Caja 3, Carpeta 8, 630; R. Diago to José Hilario López, Popayán, 28 Dec. 1853, AGN, SACH, FJHL, Caja 9, Carpeta 1, 64.

57. Manuel Bueno to Provincial Governor, Popayán, 11 Jan. 1851, ACC, AM, Paq. 51, Leg. 65; Julio Arboleda, "El Misóforo: Número noveno—Popayán, 27 de noviembre 1850," in *Prosa de Julio Arboleda: Jurídica, política, heterodoxa y literaria*, ed. Gerardo Andrade González (Bogotá: Banco de la República, 1984), 336; Manuel M. Alaix to José H. López, Popayán, 18 Oct. 1850, AGN, SACH, FJHL, Caja 4, Carpeta 15, 1,337; *Las Máscaras* (Pasto), 21 Nov. 1850.

58. *Las Máscaras* (Pasto), 7 Nov. 1850.

59. *El Clamor Nacional* (Popayán), 8 Feb. 1851.

60. Undersigned members of the pequeños cabildos of Túquerres, Obando, and Pasto to Deputies of the State Legislature, Pasto, 29 July 1873, ACC, AM, Paq. 124, Leg. 60.

61. Indian officials' claims to power and citizenship rested, in part, on their ability to control the members of their communities, especially women. Governor of indígenas of Polindará to Mister Governor, Popayán, 1855 [page torn, so full date illegible], ACC, AM, Paq. 60, Leg. 56.

62. See especially Cabildo pequeño de indígenas of Guachavéz to Honorable Deputies,

Pasto, 6 Oct. 1856, ACC, AM, Paq. 61, Leg. 6; Indigenous Alcalde Mayor and cabildos pequeños of Túquerres Province to President of the House of Representatives, Túquerres, 30 Dec. 1848, AC, 1849, Cámara, Informes de Comisiones IX, 184; Sarah C. Chambers, *From Subjects to Citizens: Honor, Gender, and Politics in Arequipa, Peru, 1780–1854* (University Park: Pennsylvania State University Press, 1999), 189–215.

63. *El Cernícalo* (Popayán), 22 Sept. 1850.

64. J. N. Montero to Secretary of Government, Barbacoas, 26 June 1851, AGN, SR, Fondo Gobernaciones Varias, Tomo 165, 706.

65. Undersigned landowners to the President of the Provincial Legislature, Pasto, 20 Sept. 1852, ACC, AM, Paq. 53, Leg. 70. See also *Boletín Político i Militar* (Pasto), 20 July 1851.

66. Anonymous, "Diario de la guerra de 1851," ACC, Fondo Arboleda, Signatura 988, unpaginated.

67. Obando had led many Indian and Afro-Colombian rebels in the civil war of 1839–42, called the War of the Supremes. Anonymous, *Contestación al folleto del Jeneral Franco titulado "A la nación i al gobierno"* (Popayán: Imprenta de Hurtado, 1852).

68. M. D. Quijano to Governor of Túquerres, [n.p.], 24 Aug. 1854, ACC, AM, Paq. 56, Leg. 1, 124; Vicente Cárdenas to Governor of Popayán, Pasto, 12 Aug. 1854, ACC, AM, Paq. 58, Leg. 75; Enrique Diago, "Mensaje del Gobernador de Barbacoas á la Lejislatura provincial en sus sesiones de 1854," Barbacoas, 15 Sept. 1854, ACC, AM, Paq. 57, Leg. 39; Ramón M. Orejuela to Tomás C. de Mosquera, Barbacoas, 30 May 1854, ACC, SM, Doc. 31,796.

69. Manuel [Luna] to Sergio Arboleda, Popayán, 25 Oct. 1854, ACC, Fondo Arboleda, Signatura 1,518, unpaginated; José Tomás Diago to Tomás C. de Mosquera, Popayán, 8 Nov. 1854, ACC, SM, Doc. 29,852. For Obando, see J. M. Mosquera to Secretary of Government, Popayán, 28 Oct. 1854, AGN, SR, Fondo Gobernaciones Varias, Tomo 201, 116.

70. Gustavo Arboleda, *Historia contemporánea de Colombia*, vol. 4, *1851–1853* (Bogotá: Banco Central Hipotecario, 1990), 269–70.

71. "Ordenanza 6ª sobre resguardos de indíjenas," Túquerres, 16 Nov. 1853, ACC, AM, Paq. 54, Leg. 36.

72. Antonio J. Chaves to President of the Legislature, Túquerres, 7 Oct. 1854, ACC, AM, Paq. 57, Leg. 45.

73. "Ordenanza 7ª sobre resguardos de Indíjenas," Pasto, 18 Oct. 1855, ACC, AM, Paq. 59, Leg. 40.

74. For example, Peter Guardino details the ideology of popular federalism in his engaging study of peasants and Mexican state formation, yet popular centralists/conservatives remain largely absent. Peter F. Guardino, *Peasants, Politics, and the Formation of Mexico's National State: Guerrero, 1800–1857* (Stanford: Stanford University Press, 1996). Florencia Mallon notes the existence of popular conservatives and the role of religion in her pioneering study of popular liberals. Mallon, *Peasant and Nation*, 94–95. Charles Walker notes how the Conservatives largely failed to gain any voluntary indigenous support around Cuzco. Walker, *Smoldering Ashes*, 212–21. See also Lauria-Santiago,

An Agrarian Republic; Grandin, *The Blood of Guatemala*, 5–6, 16, 101–9; Jennie Purnell, *Popular Movements and State Formation in Revolutionary Mexico: The* Agraristas *and* Cristeros *of Michoacán* (Durham: Duke University Press, 1999).

75. *Gaceta del Cauca* (Popayán), 29 Oct. 1859. See also M. M. Castro, *Informe que el Secretario de Gobierno en el Estado del Cauca presenta al Gobernador* (Popayán: Imprenta del Colejio Mayor, 1859), 47–48. For a different interpretation of the law, see María Teresa Findji and José María Rojas, *Territorio, economía y sociedad Páez* (Cali, Colombia: Universidad del Valle, 1985), 68–69.

76. Governor of the Indians of Quichaya to Commander in Chief of the state militias, Popayán, 5 Oct. 1860, ACC, AM, Paq. 78, Leg. 44; Indian bosses of the Aldea de Coconuco to Alcalde of Popayán district, Coconuco, 1 Aug. 1860, ACC, AM, Paq. 129, Leg. 45; District Alcalde to Provincial Governor, Cajibío, 5 Oct. 1861, ACC, AM, Paq. 82, Leg. 26; Marcelino Rodríguez to Provincial Governor, Silvia, 1 Oct. 1861, ACC, AM, Paq. 82, Leg. 26; *Boletín Oficial* (Bogotá), 20 Jan. 1862, 24 July 1862.

77. These attacks were led by Liberals with interests in the north around Riosucio, where indigenous villages were smaller and more vulnerable than those in the south. Nancy Appelbaum, "Whitening the Region: Caucano Mediation and 'Antioqueño Colonization' in Nineteenth-Century Colombia," *Hispanic American Historical Review* 79, no. 4 (Nov. 1999): 652–63; Manuel de J. Quijano, *Informe del Secretario de Gobierno del Estado Soberano de Cauca, a la Convención de 1872* (Popayán: Imprenta del Estado, 1872), 34.

78. See multiple petitions and reports found in ACC, AM, Paq. 94, Leg. 54.

79. Quotation from Indian Alcalde Mayor of Obando Municipality (with signers from the parcialidades of Potosí, Mayasquer, Yaramal, Cumbal, Guachucal, Muellamuez, Colimba, Carlosama, Caserío de Pastas, Pupiales, Anfelima, Girón, Iles, Ospina, and Puerres) to Secretary of State Government, Ipiales, 4 Mar. 1866, ACC, AM, Paq. 94, Leg. 54. See also Members of the indigenous cabildos of Cumbal, Muellamuez, Imués, and Túquerres to Legislature, Túquerres, 31 July 1871, ACC, AM, Paq. 112, Leg. 14.

80. In indigenous discourse, "*blanco*" could signify any non-Indian, regardless of race. Pequeño cabildo de indígenas of Mocondino to State President, Pasto, 18 Feb. 1866, ACC, AM, Paq. 94, Leg. 54; Javier Muñoz to Jefe Municipal, Timbío, 1 Nov. 1864, ACC, AM, Paq. 84, Leg. 46; Indians and Members of the pequeño cabildo of Túquerres to President of the Legislature, Túquerres, June 1869 [no day listed], ACC, AM, Paq. 103, Leg. 3.

81. First quotation from Undersigned members of the Cumbal town council to President of the Legislature, Cumbal, 24 July 1871, ACC, AM, Paq. 112, Leg. 15; second from Undersigned residents of Riosucio district to Deputies of the Legislature, Riosucio, 27 June 1875, ACC, AM, Paq. 130, Leg. 17. Appelbaum, "Whitening the Region," 645–62; Rappaport, *Cumbe Reborn*, 30–36.

82. Indian Alcalde Mayor of Obando Municipality (with signers from the parcialidades of Potosí, Mayasquer, Yaramal, Cumbal, Guachucal, Muellamuez, Colimba, Carlosama, Caserío de Pastas, Pupiales, Anfelima, Girón, Iles, Ospina, and Puerres) to Secretary of State Government, Ipiales, 4 Mar. 1866, ACC, AM, Paq. 94, Leg. 54.

83. Pequeño cabildo of Cumbal to Citizen Deputies, Cumbal, 22 July 1873, ACC, AM, Paq. 124, Leg. 56.

84. The petition was signed by members of the pequeños cabildos of Túquerres, Guaitarilla, Ospina, Mallama, Imués, Pasto, and Yascual as well as over 525 other Indians, all names marked with a cross or a sign. Undersigned members of the pequeños cabildos of Túquerres, Obando, and Pasto to Deputies of the State Legislature, Pasto, 29 July 1873, ACC, AM, Paq. 124, Leg. 60.

85. Ibid.

86. *Registro Oficial (Organo del Gobierno del Cauca)* (Popayán), 25 Oct. 1873, 1 Nov. 1873, 6 Dec. 1873.

87. Indians from the south would continue to act in unison to lobby the state government. Cabildos pequeños de indígenas of Túquerres, Sapuyes, Imués, Ospina, Cumbal, Guachucal, Muellamuez, Yascual, and Puerres to Honorable Deputies of the Legislature, Pasto, 19 July 1875, ACC, AM, Paq. 133, Leg. 75; Members of the indigenous cabildos pequeños of Cumbal, Muellamuez, Imués, and Túquerres to Legislature, Túquerres, 31 July 1871, ACC, AM, Paq. 112, Leg. 14.

88. *Registro Oficial (Organo del Gobierno del Cauca)* (Popayán), 8 Dec. 1877.

89. Rappaport also notes how Indians coupled this political identity with a cultural identity based on certain traits (even though they may have shared these traits with their mestizo neighbors) and a storytelling tradition. Rappaport, *Cumbe Reborn*, 25–37.

90. Appelbaum, "Remembering Riosucio," 270–73, 532–33. In the nineteenth century, the southwest's Indians did not publicly refer to themselves by any tribal or national affiliations. They simply identified themselves as Indians from a particular village.

91. See Sanders, "Contentious Republicans," and petitions found in the AC, ACC, AGN, and Archivo Histórico Municipal de Cali (Cali). Some petitioners did refer to themselves as slaves or ex-slaves, but never as "blacks" or "mulattos."

92. Villegas and Restrepo argue that the economic symbiosis of *resguardos* and haciendas was the key to allowing *resguardos* to survive, but I think Indians' political action was most important. Villegas and Restrepo, *Resguardos de indígenas*, 37, 45–49.

93. Joanne Rappaport argues that the law also politically weakened communities by dividing larger cultural groups into individual *resguardos*, which then had less ability to resist the state and large landowners. Rappaport, *The Politics of Memory*, 93, 143.

94. Alejandro de la Fuente notes the importance of party competition in increasing subalterns' political influence in Cuba. Alejandro de la Fuente, "Myths of Racial Democracy: Cuba, 1900–1912," *Latin American Research Review* 34, no. 3 (1999): 53–68. Similarly, much of the recent literature on the popular contribution to nation building suggests the importance of partisan or international conflict in opening political space to subalterns. See especially Mallon, *Peasant and Nation*, and Ada Ferrer, *Insurgent Cuba: Race, Nation, and Revolution, 1868–1898* (Chapel Hill: University of North Carolina Press, 1999).

95. Benedict Anderson, *Imagined Communities: Reflections on the Origin and Spread of Nationalism*, rev. ed. (London: Verso, 1991).

96. Rappaport, *The Politics of Memory*, 112–16; Gonzalo Castillo Cárdenas, *Liberation Theology from Below: The Life and Thought of Manuel Quintín Lame* (Maryknoll, N.Y.: Orbis Books, 1987); Manuel Quintín Lame, *En defensa de mi raza*, ed. Gonzalo Castillo Cárdenas (Bogotá: Comité de Defensa del Indio, 1971).

97. The CRIC helped found the Organización Nacional Indígena de Colombia (ONIC, National Indigenous Organization of Colombia) in 1982. Donna Lee Van Cott, *The Friendly Liquidation of the Past: The Politics of Diversity in Latin America* (Pittsburgh: University of Pittsburgh Press, 2000), 46; Nina S. de Friedemann, "Niveles contemporáneos de indigenismo en Colombia," in *Indigenismo y aniquilamiento de indígenas en Colombia*, ed. Juan Friede, Nina S. de Friedemann, and Darío Fajardo (Bogotá: Universidad Nacional de Colombia, 1975), 35–37; Findji, "From Resistance to Social Movement," 112–33.

98. Quotation from Myriam Jimeno Santoyo, "Pueblos indios, democracia y políticas estatales en Colombia," in *Democracia y estado multiétnico en América Latina*, ed. Pablo González Casanova and Marcos Roitman Rosenmann (Mexico City: La Jornada Ediciones, 1996), 226. Rappaport describes the Lamista movement: "For the first time, communities pressed indigenous demands within the national arena, using Colombian political language." Rappaport, *The Politics of Memory*, 114. See also Findji, "From Resistance to Social Movement"; Field, "State, Anti-State, and Indigenous Entities," 105–10; Van Cott, *The Friendly Liquidation of the Past*.

99. Two indigenous deputies to the 1991 National Constituent Assembly came from the Cauca and another from the Chocó (which had been part of the nineteenth-century Cauca). Van Cott, *The Friendly Liquidation of the Past*, 67–68. For twentieth-century social movements, see Peter Wade, "Negros, indígenas e identidad nacional en Colombia," in *Imaginar la nación*, ed. François-Xavier Guerra and Mónica Quijada (Münster: Lit, 1994), 257–88; Findji, "From Resistance to Social Movement"; Myriam Jimeno and Adolfo Triana, "El estado y la política indigenista," in *Estado y minorías étnicas en Colombia*, ed. Myriam Jimeno and Adolfo Triana (Bogotá: Cuadernos del Jaguar, 1985), 65–147; Jesús Avirama and Rayda Márquez, "The Indigenous Movement in Colombia," in *Indigenous Peoples and Democracy in Latin America*, ed. Donna Lee Van Cott (New York: St. Martin's Press, 1994), 83–105; Brett Troyan, "The Indigenous Rural Folk's Discourses and Identities in the '30s and '40s of the Twentieth Century in Cauca, Colombia" (paper presented at the Conference on Latin American History, Boston, 4–7 Jan. 2001).

100. Roberto Pineda Camacho, "La reivindicación del indio en el pensamiento social colombiano (1850–1950)," in *Un siglo de investigación social: Antropología en Colombia*, ed. Jaime Arocha and Nina S. de Friedemann (Bogotá: ETNO, 1984), 206–11.

101. Of course, the implementation of these provisions is an ongoing struggle. See Joanne Rappaport and Robert V. H. Dover, "The Construction of Difference by Native Legislators: Assessing the Impact of the Colombian Constitution of 1991," *Journal of Latin American Anthropology* 1, no. 2 (1996): 22–45; Van Cott, *The Friendly Liquidation of the Past*; Wade, "Negros, indígenas e identidad nacional," 257–88.

CHAPTER THREE

SEARCHING FOR "LATIN AMERICA"

Race and Sovereignty
in the Americas
in the 1850s

Aims McGuinness

During the twentieth century, the comparative study of race in the United States and Latin America emerged as an important field of academic inquiry. Beginning with the publication of Frank Tannenbaum's *Slave and Citizen* in 1946, scholars working in a comparative mode challenged many received ideas about race, including the ideology of racial democracy in Brazil and the perception that racial segregation in the U.S. South was somehow an inevitable outgrowth of the institution of slavery. Yet the scholarship on comparative race relations also suffered from its own blind spots. As Rebecca Scott, Frederick Cooper, and Thomas Holt have pointed out in a recent collection of essays, the nearly exclusive emphasis on the importance of slavery for the rise of contemporary racial regimes led Tannenbaum and many of those who followed him to overlook the importance of events that followed abolition.[1] Even as race-relations scholars scrutinized the workings of race in Latin American societies, they tended to think less critically about the geographical category of "Latin America," often writing as if that category existed outside the processes of racial formation that they sought to elucidate.

According to Martin Lewis and Kären Wigen, "Latin America" is one of the oldest world regional designations, dating back at least to the mid-nineteenth century.[2] Nevertheless, the precise origins of the term remain controversial. In an essay published in 1968, the U.S. historian John L. Phelan credited the concept to pan-Latinist intellectuals close to Napoleon III, including Michel Chevalier, who sought to justify French intervention in Mexico in the 1860s by asserting solidarity between France and Mexico based on shared belonging to the "Latin race." According to Phelan, it was only after the French coined the term that Spanish-speaking intellectuals in the Americas adopted the geopolitical category for themselves.[3] A very different account of the origins of "América Latina" has been written by Arturo Ardao, the Uruguayan philosopher and historian of ideas. Ardao and more recently Miguel Rojas Mix have found numerous instances of the geopolitical designations "América Latina" and "*latinoamericano*" in the writings of important intellectuals from the Americas writing in Spanish in the decade before the French intervened in Mexico, including José María Torres Caicedo and Justo Arosemena of New Granada (predecessor of contemporary Colombia), Santiago Arcos and Francisco Bilbao, both of whom were Chileans, and Francisco Muñoz del Monte of the Dominican Republic. In his first major work on the subject, *Génesis de la idea y el nombre de América Latina*, Ardao hypothesized that the concept of "América Latina" as a distinct geopolitical entity, as opposed to an extension of the Latin nations of Europe, first appeared in print in a poem entitled "Las dos Américas." Apparently written in September 1856 by Torres Caicedo, an expatriate based primarily in Paris, the poem was published in February 1857 in *El Correo de Ultramar*, a Spanish-language newspaper published in Paris.[4]

The matter of who first conceived the term "América Latina" and when is unlikely to be resolved definitively any time soon, if ever. Rojas Mix, for example, has located a use of "América Latina" prior to the writing of Torres Caicedo's poem in a speech delivered in Paris by Francisco Bilbao in June 1856.[5] But while Phelan's account retains significant influence in the world of English-language scholarship and in France, the works of Ardao and Rojas Mix and more recent essays by Paul Estrade and Mónica Quijada have clarified that the concept of Latin America as a geographical and political entity predates French intervention in Mexico in the 1860s.[6]

THE PANAMA ROUTE IN THE MID-NINETEENTH CENTURY

Why and how did the concepts of "América Latina" and a "Latin race" take on importance among a number of important Spanish-speaking intellectuals from the Americas in the mid-1850s? Part of the answer to this puzzle lies in the intensely violent struggles over the forging of international trade routes, the expansion of U.S. capital, and conflicting racial practices on the Isthmus of Panama in the late 1840s and 1850s. In the mid-nineteenth century, Panama formed the westernmost part of New Granada, and it would remain part of Colombia (as New Granada was known after 1863) until its separation and independence in 1903.

During the late 1840s and early 1850s, Panama was remade into one of the principal points of transit for commodities and people along trade routes linking the eastern United States to California, which the United States conquered during the 1846–48 war against Mexico. The news of gold in California, discovered at Sutter's Mill in January 1848, prompted a massive migration from the eastern United States along a number of trajectories, including overland routes across the Great Plains, the sea route around the horn of South America, and a combination of sea routes and overland crossings at points such as the Isthmus of Tehuantepec, Nicaragua, and the Isthmus of Panama.

Gold seekers bound for California began to arrive in Panama at the end of 1848. These early emigrants landed at the Atlantic port of Chagres. From there, boatmen provided transport up the Chagres River in canoes known as *bongos* to the town of Gorgona or, if water levels permitted, to the town of Cruces. After arriving at one of these river ports, emigrants typically hired mules or porters (*cargadores*) to carry them the rest of the way to Panama City, on the Pacific coast. Once in Panama City, boatmen again provided transport from the shore to California-bound ships anchored off the coast.

In the late 1840s, river and overland transport across Panama was controlled mainly by small operators—Panamanians as well as more recent arrivals from the British West Indies and South America, including other regions of New Granada and Peru. Almost immediately after the beginning of the gold rush, capitalists from the United States and Great Britain began to make inroads into this system, often through alliances with members of elite mercantile families based in Panama City or other regions of New Granada. Their strategies included the formation of freight companies with large fleets of mules imported from abroad and the introduction of steamboats into the Bay of Panama and the Chagres River. The most wrenching changes in the Panamanian transit economy came when the Panama Railroad Company of New York City constructed a railroad across Panama between 1850 and 1855. Built largely with the labor of workers from Cartagena, Jamaica, and South China, the railroad was inaugurated in January 1855. The outbreak of war in Nicaragua in the same year posed a major impediment to travel on the Nicaragua Route, Panama's chief

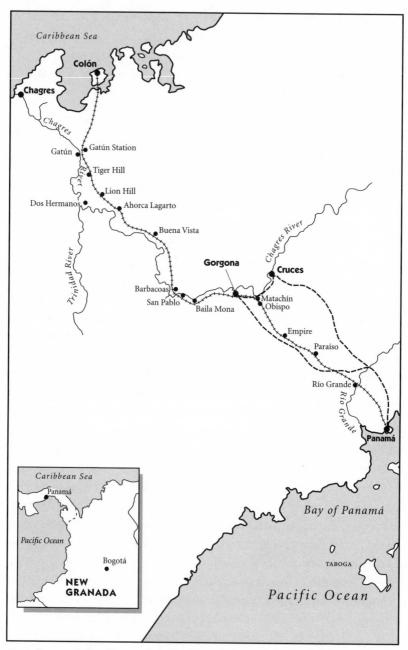

MAP 2. *Panama Railroad Route, 1855. Adapted from a 1940 map in John Haskell Kemble,* The Panama Route, 1848–1869 *(1943; reprint, Columbia: University of South Carolina Press, 1990), 168; used with permission of University of South Carolina Press.*

competitor. Thus by 1856 the Panama Route had emerged as the fastest path between the Atlantic and Pacific coasts of the United States and would remain so until the completion of the second transcontinental railroad in 1869.[7]

THE WATERMELON SLICE INCIDENT

Members of Panama's merchant elite heralded the inauguration of the railroad as a sign that Panama was poised to realize what they viewed as its destiny to become an emporium to the world—a nexus of intercontinental routes and a marketplace for all nations.[8] This rosy vision of Panama as a mercantile paradise would be thrown into question a little more than a year after the inauguration of the railroad, as violence in the streets of Panama City exposed the underside of Panama's transformation into a nexus of the world economy. The conflict that took place in Panama City on the evening of 15 April 1856 has been dubbed the "*Incidente de la tajada de sandía* [Watermelon Slice Incident]" by Panamanian historians, after an altercation over a slice of watermelon that allegedly initiated the violence.

An account of this altercation was given to Panamanian police by a fruit vendor named José Manuel Luna. Luna testified that he was working at his stand when a small group of inebriated travelers from the United States approached him. One of the travelers seized a slice of watermelon, tasted it, and threw it to the ground. Luna, who spoke English, asked the traveler for payment. When the traveler responded with a vulgarity, Luna asked him again for payment, reminding the traveler, "Take care, we are not in the United States here." Instead, the drunken traveler removed a pistol from his belt, and a scuffle began that resulted in the disarming of the traveler by a bystander.[9]

Soon afterward, many other people began to gather in La Ciénaga, the neighborhood where the altercation occurred. As darkness fell, fighting began between groups of people from outside the city walls of Panama City (an area of relatively poor neighborhoods known collectively as "*el arrabal*") and travelers bound for California, more than 800 of whom had arrived in Panama City earlier the same day by railway from the Atlantic coast. By the dawn of the next day, according to the official death toll released by the Panamanian state government, seventeen people had been killed, including two Panamanians and fifteen foreigners. Significant damage was also done to property, particularly buildings belonging to the Panama Railroad Company.[10]

José Manuel Luna was one among many residents of Panama City in the mid-1850s who had come to the city from elsewhere. Recent arrivals included hundreds of immigrants drawn by the booming transit economy from places such as Cartagena, other regions of Central and South America, the Caribbean, the United States, Europe, and China. Panamanian judicial records identify Luna himself as a native of Parita, a small town located to the west of Panama City. In contrast to judicial records in Panama, which conventionally made no mention of the race or color of parties to judicial cases in the mid-1850s, U.S. officials described Luna flatly as a "negro."[11]

How Luna perceived himself in terms of color or race, or whether such markers were even important to him, cannot be discerned from these records. But Luna was required by legal conventions in Panama to state his occupation, which he identified as "*platero*," or silversmith. Why would an artisan be selling fruit in the streets of Panama City in 1856? The dramatic rise in demand for food, shelter, and transport led to high prices in the late 1840s and early 1850s that may have made fruitselling appealing to Luna as a way to earn cash from emigrants. By the mid-1850s, however, this boom had largely dissipated, as the completion of the railroad and increased coordination of shipping lines to and from the isthmus reduced the amount of time that emigrants spent in Panama from a matter of days to hours. The increase in the importation of manufactures from the United States and Europe into Panama during the gold rush also had negative effects on artisans in Panama City, some of whom found it difficult to compete against cheaper imports.[12]

The fact that the work of a fruitseller was strongly identified with women in Panama in the mid-nineteenth century also suggests that it was likely Luna the *platero* turned to selling watermelon from a stand because of economic hardship. If so, he would have been one of many in Panama City, particularly in the *arrabal*, who had suffered due to the completion of the railroad. Witnesses deposed by U.S. officials interpreted the damage done to the property of the Panama Railroad Company and other U.S. firms in Panama City in part as a response by *arrabaleños* to the damage done to the local mule and carrying trades and to the introduction of the *Taboga*, a small steamboat that had a devastating effect on boatmen in the Bay of Panama.[13] The report produced by the national government of New Granada also explained the violence as a response to the completion of the railroad, particularly by black workers from the British West Indies whom the railroad company had employed as laborers and then discharged without regard for their future subsistence.[14] One witness for the United States indicated that the company had inspired further enmity from the "negroes" living in the *arrabal* by claiming ownership over the neighborhood of La Ciénaga, which raised fears among people living there that they would soon be driven from their homes without compensation for their lost property.[15]

ELECTORAL POLITICS, COMMERCE, AND RACE IN PANAMA IN THE 1850S

José Manuel Luna also took part in the political revolution that swept the Isthmus of Panama and other areas of New Granada in the early 1850s. Following the ascension of the Liberal José Hilario López to the presidency of New Granada in 1849, a number of reforms opened up the realm of electoral politics to previously excluded groups.[16] While slavery was nearly moribund on the Isthmus of Panama by the early 1850s, its official demise on 1 January 1852 was greeted with great fanfare in a city with a large population of people of African descent, particularly in the *arrabal*, which was known by Panamanians and foreigners alike as the part of the city where people of color predominated.[17] In 1853 a new national constitution established universal manhood suffrage and the provincial governorship of Panama became an elective office. Two years later, in 1855, the congress of New Granada established Panama as the nation's first semiautonomous federal state.

Poll records for Panama City indicate that José Manuel Luna voted in the 1851 elections for the *cabildo*, or city council, of Panama City as a resident of the parish of Santa Ana.[18] In 1853 his name appeared again in the electoral list for the parish of Santa Ana, which also noted that Luna could both read and write.[19] By the mid-1850s, the *arrabal* and, more generally, people of color in Panama City had become strongly identified with the Liberal Party. *Arrabaleños* played a critical role in gubernatorial elections in 1856 and again in 1858, both as voters and as defenders of the party in street battles fought with adherents to Panama's Conservative Party, whose base of power lay within the city walls, in the more elite parish of San Felipe.[20]

The intensified U.S. presence posed a number of threats to these newly won gains in the realm of politics and the public sphere. The early years of the gold rush saw a convergence in Panama not only of people from many different places but also of different racial practices, which frequently proved to be incompatible in the streets of Panama City and along the transit route. White people from the United States, from the North and South alike, commented on what they perceived as a troubling ambiguity in the relationship between color and status in Panama. Theodore Johnson noted what he regarded as a general tendency for "Creoles," or people with some "white blood," to dominate "Negroes" and "Indians."[21] Yet even the whiteness of many members of the Panamanian elite seemed suspect to some U.S. observers. Writing in 1855, Robert Tomes acknowledged that in Panama City there were "a few families which boast themselves of pure Castilian blood; but I hardly think they could pass muster before the discerning eye of a shrewd Mississippi dealer in the Negro variety of mankind."[22]

As Brian Roberts has discussed, white travelers from the United States often perceived Panamanian society in terms of "minstrelsy"—a form of theater popular in much of the United States in the antebellum period in which white actors blackened their faces with charcoal and acted out comic scenes from what they imagined to be the lives of African Americans.[23] Indeed, many travelers from the United States treated their entire journey across the isthmus as if it were a prolonged minstrel show. For instance, Theodore Johnson, who crossed Panama in 1849, described a cockfight he witnessed in Panama City as if it were a minstrel performance, with "*fancy* darkies and Creoles shuffling and pushing about the ring, chattering like monkeys and gesticulating like ourangoutangs." He recounted how he and his traveling companions had made fun of the *patrón* (owner and boss) of their canoe, a man Johnson described as a racially mixed Creole. After the *patrón* entered the water to move the *bongo* beyond a low point in the river, Johnson and his friends prevented him from boarding the *bongo* and then joked that the scare had whitened the *patrón*'s skin.[24] Bayard Taylor, in his account of his passage up the Chagres River in 1849, discussed the popularity of minstrel songs from the United States in Panama and described how one of the Panamanian boatmen he hired had sung "Oh Susanna!" and other "Ethiopian melodies" that he had learned from emigrants from the United States.[25]

Moments of racialized "fun" such as that described by Johnson could easily turn into expressions of terror and rage when whites from the United States found themselves in circumstances that in their view placed them on an equal or lower plane in relation to individuals whom they regarded as inferior to themselves. As Albert Hurtado has noted, this was especially true when white women from the United States were present. Sarah Brooks, who traveled up the Chagres River in 1852, described the tumult that resulted when the boatmen who transported her party discarded clothing to perform their work. While she and her female traveling companions retreated beneath their umbrellas, their male companions demanded that the boatmen replace their garments, whereupon a "stormy scene ensued."[26] As Brooks's account suggests, attempts by white people from the United States to impose their own notions of racial order on others in Panama could easily lead to tension and violence.

Commercial exchange—the sale of labor or goods—was another situation in which conflicting notions of racial propriety and fairness could produce conflict. Johnson described how his party was declined service by the boatmen whom they thought they had contracted to take them up the Chagres River after the boatmen found a better price from other customers. In response, Johnson's compatriots drew bowie knives and revolvers and waved them about, threatening to whip the boatmen and calling for the annexation of the Isthmus of Panama by the United States. Johnson offered this and other stories as proof of the incapacity of Panamanians to engage in fair dealing.[27] The same argument was made by James Tyson, who traveled across Panama twice in 1849 and asked rhetorically, "Who that has bargained with these slothful and dilatory people, ever knew them to adhere to a contract?"[28] But in their efforts to enforce what they thought were fair deals, white North Americans often ran afoul of other conceptions of what constituted a just contract. In another instance related by Johnson, a white man from the United States claimed to have been double-crossed in the purchase of a deer that a Panamanian man had shot. When Johnson's "Yankee friend" attempted to enforce his notion of the contract by drawing a knife, the Panamanian man drew his own blade.[29]

Taylor reported his conversation with a "negro boatman" named Ambrosio Mendez on the subject of fair dealing and race during his crossing of Panama in early 1849. According to Taylor, Mendez told him, "If the Americans are good, we are good; if they abuse us, we are bad. We are black, but *muchos caballeros*."[30] The boatman's words, when combined with many other accounts of tense negotiations between U.S. travelers and workers in the transit zone, suggest a more general insistence among working people in Panama on equality in commercial transactions in this period.

Informal acts of racist abuse by white forty-niners were a small step away from more organized threats to black political power on the Isthmus of Panama. Mary Seacole—a woman of mixed race who migrated from Jamaica to Panama in the early 1850s—described in her autobiography how white travelers from the United States reacted when the alcalde of Gorgona ordered soldiers under his command to arrest one of the travelers' compatriots for stealing from a party of Chileans. The arrested man's "brother Americans" resisted the soldiers and alcalde, "abusing and threatening the authorities in no measured terms, all of them indignant that a nigger should presume to judge one of their countrymen."[31] According to Seacole, the alcalde held his ground, delivering a searing denunciation of U.S. emigrants to California and declaring his "determination to make strangers respect the laws of the Republic."[32]

As Seacole's story indicates, white travelers from the United States often questioned and sometimes challenged outright the political power of Panamanians whom they perceived as racially inferior to themselves. John Forster, a native Pennsylvanian, expressed astonishment when he encountered the alcalde of Gorgona. (The alcalde goes unnamed in both Seacole's and Forster's accounts, although the fact that both incidents occurred within four or five years of one another makes it possible that it was the same man whom they encountered.) Coming from a country where the voting rights of men of African descent had been virtually extinguished, Forster was both impressed by and suspicious of the power exercised by the alcalde, whom he described as a "half-breed-Spanish-negro" and a "generalissimo in civil affairs—executive, judge and jury." Taking careful note of what he alleged was the alcalde's "harem," which according to Forster included "five wives," he described the alcalde as if he were an exotic king rather than an official of a republic that many Liberals in New Granada regarded as the vanguard of democracy in the Americas, if not the world.[33]

A petition signed in Panama City in March 1850 by white citizens from the United States further illustrates how everyday acts of racialized violence could be translated into attempts to infringe on New Granadan sovereignty in Panama. The petitioners acknowledged that many of the conflicts between U.S. travelers and Panamanian officials had their roots in "the prejudice arising from color" shared by many of their countrymen. Among the solutions they proposed for reducing these conflicts was to avoid imprisoning white U.S. citizens alongside "colored" men. If the government of New Granada could not stop officials who were not white from attempting to enforce local laws against U.S. travelers, then the petitioners proposed that U.S. citizens be permitted to establish a judicial system for themselves in Panama, parallel to that of New Granada.[34]

In many ways the most dramatic threat to local sovereignty posed by the influx of U.S. whites into Panama during the gold rush was that of the filibusters, or *filibusteros*—adventurers who radiated outward from the United States in the early 1850s with aspirations that ranged from prying Cuba away from Spain to overthrowing independent governments elsewhere in the Spanish-speaking Americas. The most famous of the filibusters was William Walker, a native of Tennessee, who arrived in Nicaragua in early 1855 as a mercenary fighting for the Liberal Party against the Conservatives. Walker and his allies (including Nicaraguans and recruits from the United States) managed to establish control over much of Nicaragua by October of the same year, and

Walker would proclaim himself president in July of 1856. Spanish- and English-language newspapers kept the populace of Panama City well informed of fili-bustering and annexationism in the United States and their likely effects on people of color in Panama. In response to an article advocating annexation in an English-language newspaper called the *Panama Echo*, an anonymous writer commented sardonically in the *Revisor de la Política y Literatura Americana* that while he did not doubt that annexation would lead to prosperity in Panama, he was also sure that the fruits of that prosperity would be restricted to "the hyperactive descendants of the Anglo-Saxon race," while the current property-owning class of Panama would be left in poverty and "*gente de color* [people of color]" would be subjected to the "ultimate degradation," meaning their reenslavement.[35]

Granadinos in both Panama City and Bogotá attributed the events of 15 April in part to beliefs among *arrabaleños* and other residents of Panama City that they were under attack by filibusters. Fears of filibuster attack had intensified in early April 1856 after the arrival in Panama City of the *Cortes*, a ship bearing recruits from California for William Walker's army in Nicaragua, one of whom would be listed among the dead following the violence of 15 April.[36] Antonio Abad Monteser, an artisan from the parish of Santa Ana, testified how another man, Pedro Jiménes, had reproached him the day after the violence for not joining other men from the *arrabal* in defending the city from what Jiménes believed was an imminent attack by "*filibusteros.*"[37]

Investigators from both New Granada and the United States attributed other aspects of the violence of 15 April to the longer history of tension and outright conflict between people of African descent in Panama and white travelers from the United States. New Granadan officials observed that opposition to "*fili-busteros*" was particularly strong among the "poorer classes" of Panama City, who were "frequently the victims of the outrages committed by the passing emigrants."[38] Arthur MacKenzie testified to U.S. officials after 15 April that he had frequently witnessed fights on the beach in front of La Ciénaga between boatmen and travelers from the United States, which he blamed both on the boatmen, for charging what he regarded as exorbitant prices, and on pas-sengers, who when drunk were often "insulting to the negroes."[39]

RACE AND SOVEREIGNTY

It is noteworthy that when faced with attempts by white men from the United States to impose their wills upon them, both José Manuel Luna and the alcalde of Gorgona framed their retorts by reminding the travelers that they were in a different country. Mediated as such utterances were by the Panamanian judicial process and the prose of Mary Seacole, the words nevertheless suggest how intimately the defense of local sovereignty came to be intertwined with the defense of equality and the rights of citizenship, particularly for people of color in Panama, who had the most to lose in the event of annexation to the United States or conquest by filibusters. The drunken man who seized the slice of watermelon from José Manuel Luna might well have found more support for his actions had the two men been standing on a street in the United States.[40] But Panama in 1856 was a place where the white traveler and his companions found themselves not only vastly outnumbered but also in a very different relationship to the state, whose laws proclaimed the equality of all its male citizens.

The issues of race and sovereignty also came to be intertwined in many of the reactions by officials and elite commentators in New Granada to the conflict of 15 April. As Frank Safford has discussed, the events of 15 April and the subsequent diplomatic controversy between the United States and New Granada over claims for lost property and lives led to a conflicted response from both Liberals and Conservatives in Bogotá. Some Liberals advocated resistance to U.S. demands against New Granada and interpreted events in Panama as a justification for a deeper commitment to federalism and even for the reestablishment of Colombia, which in its newly federated form might include not only New Granada, Venezuela, and Ecuador but also Central America and other places in the Spanish-speaking Americas such as the Dominican Republic. Other commentators, particularly Conservatives, interpreted the violence and its diplomatic denouement as a sign that New Granada would soon lose Panama to the United States through what they perceived to be a combination of U.S. acquisitiveness and the fecklessness of Panamanian officials. After losing hope that Great Britain or France would come to New Granada's aid, the Conservative president Mariano Ospina even proposed the annexation of the entirety of New Granada to the United States, reasoning that the northern power was in any event likely to conquer most of the continent in the near future.[41]

The conflict in Panama also led to consternation among *granadinos* abroad, including the young poet Rafael Pombo, a diplomat based in the United States who took part in the negotiations with the U.S. government over claims related to 15 April and who authored a number of poetical works denouncing annexationism and filibustering in the late 1850s.[42] In France, José María Torres Caicedo—the *granadino* to whom Ardao attributed the authorship of the concept of "América Latina"—denounced U.S. actions in Panama and offered a defense of Panamanians in an article that appeared in Paris in June 1856 entitled "Confederación de las naciones de la América española." As early as 1850, while editor of *El Día*, a newspaper in Bogotá, Torres Caicedo had warned of the United States's designs on the Isthmus of Panama. He returned to this same theme in "Confederación de las naciones," in which he praised the "sons of Panama" for their actions on 15 April and then compared U.S. claims for damages from the government of New Granada to William Walker's aggression against Nicaragua. Torres Caicedo's call for a "confederation" echoed earlier notions of political unity advanced by Simón Bolívar in the context of the Congreso de Panamá of 1826.[43] But while Bolívar was chiefly concerned with threats to American sovereignty emanating from Europe, Torres Caicedo, like Francisco Bilbao and other advocates of Hispanic American unity in the mid-1850s, identified the greatest danger to Latin sovereignty in the Americas as the United States. Torres Caicedo's articulation of the antagonism between "América del Norte" and "América del Sud" also relied on an opposition between the "Saxon race" and a "Latin race" that owed more to theories of race circulating in the 1850s than to Bolívar and included notions of pan-Latin racial unity similar to those advanced in France by Saint-Simonians such as Michel Chevalier. By the mid-1850s, as Phelan discussed in his study of pan-Latinism and French expansionism, Chevalier had developed a vision of pan-Latin diplomacy that pitted the Latin nations of Europe (including Belgium, Spain, and Portugal, and led, of course, by France) against the Germanic or Anglo-Saxon peoples of northern Europe and the Slavic nations of eastern Europe.[44] A similar opposition between the Latin and Anglo-Saxon "races" found its expression in Torres Caicedo's 1856 poem "Las dos Américas," which was concerned principally with Walker's filibustering in Nicaragua:

> The race of Latin America [*América latina*]
> Finds itself confronted by the Saxon Race,
> Mortal enemy who now threatens
> To destroy its liberty and its banner.[45]

But in contrast to the expansionist thought of Chevalier, for whom the Latin peoples of the Americas were essentially an extension of the Latin powers of Europe, "Latin America" in Torres Caicedo's poem stood alone in its confrontation against the United States.

In July 1856, on the other side of the Atlantic, Justo Arosemena employed similar language in his own account of the violence of 15 April and its diplomatic repercussions, entitled "La cuestión americana i su importancia," which appeared in *El Neogranadino*, a newspaper in Bogotá.[46] A scion of one of Panama City's elite families, Arosemena was a prominent figure in Liberal Party politics on a national level and a key figure in the establishment of Panama as a federal state in 1855, briefly serving as the state's first executive. Following the onset of the California gold rush, Arosemena emerged as one of the most visible critics of what he perceived as the arrogance of U.S. citizens and the U.S. government on the isthmus. Writing in November 1850, he warned that if Panamanians did not find an effective form of self-defense, they would soon find themselves reduced to the status of servants or slaves of other "*razas*," who would never regard "*istmeños*," or inhabitants of the isthmus, as members of the "*pueblos civilizados*."[47]

In his response to the violence of 15 April 1856, Arosemena reiterated the same opposition between the Latin race ("*raza latina*") and the United States that had appeared in Torres Caicedo's writings on the other side of the Atlantic, but he referred primarily to the "*raza yankee* [Yankee race]" rather than the "*raza sajona* [Saxon race]." Arosemena's characterization of the "*raza yankee*" was in many ways similar to depictions of the Anglo-Saxon race by U.S. expansionists in the same period and suggests that he was familiar with the writings of ideologues of U.S. empire such as James Buchanan and John L. O'Sullivan. Like these advocates of Manifest Destiny, he regarded Anglo-Saxons as inherently a conquering people, predisposed toward the domination of other races. But while expansionists in the United States celebrated this characteristic, Arosemena condemned it, denouncing Yankees as "highwaymen of nations" who had become excessively materialistic and corrupted by the "invasive spirit of conquest."[48] Already distended after devouring Mexican territory, the United States's integrity as a nation was further imperiled in Arosemena's view by slavery, which he saw as a contradiction of republican ideals and predicted would cause an unbridgeable rift between the northern and southern states.[49]

In contrast to Yankees, *latinos* were, according to Arosemena, less materialistic, more chivalrous, and more spiritually inclined. But while spokesmen of U.S. expansion in this period tended to view such qualities as evidence of the decadence and even the femininity of the peoples living to the south, Arosemena reclaimed these characteristics as masculine virtues, declaring the "*raza latina*" to be "the most noble and sentimental race." And while he acknowledged that the Latin peoples of the Americas were weak in the present, he argued that as opposed to the hypocritical United States, they could only grow in strength because they had "Democracy" on their side, which in Arosemena's usage entailed commitments to federalism, free trade, and free labor.[50] While inherited from the past, the defining characteristics of *latinos* were not fixed in a biological or any other sense. The key distinguishing characteristics were reflected in the realm of temperament and governing institutions rather than skin color or other putatively physical characteristics.[51]

Arosemena argued that recent acts of U.S. aggression in Central America and New Granada had upset the "equilibrium of nations and races" in the Americas. The plight of Panama was thus a question of "Latin American interest [*interés latinoamericano*]." By appealing to "Latin American interest," Arosemena meant that the plight of Panama was vital for the future of all the peoples of the "Spanish race [*raza española*]" in the Americas, from the northern border of Mexico to Argentina. The ultimate salvation for the "peoples of the Latin race existing in America," according to Arosemena, lay in the creation of what he called a "Hispanic American Confederation." The basis of this confederation would be a re-united "Colombia," including but not necessarily limited to the constituent parts of what historians now refer to as Gran Colombia (including present-day Panama, Venezuela, Colombia, and Ecuador). As Arosemena expressed in a speech that he delivered in Bogotá on July 20, 1856, this re-united Colombia could conceivably stretch from Panama to Cape Horn.[52]

While the characteristics that Arosemena attributed to the Latin race in some ways resembled those celebrated by pan-Latinists in France such as Chevalier, the possibility of an alliance with France had no role in Arosemena's vision of Latin unity. As in the writings of Torres Caicedo, the Latin race of the Americas in Arosemena's vision had no choice but to stand alone. A Liberal with anticlerical tendencies, Arosemena had a dim view of the Catholic Church and the institution of monarchy, and thus he regarded the Latin race of the Americas to be superior to its brethren in Spain, who in his view had entered into decline due to religious and political despotism. Both France and Spain were too weak, in Arosemena's view, to offer any real assistance, while Great Britain seemed to him too self-interested to offer any succor, at least in the short term.[53]

Those who fell outside the bounds of Arosemena's vision of a Latin race included not only Yankees but also people in Panama whom he characterized as "upstart blacks," and whom he blamed no less than people from the United States for the violence of 15 April. While Torres Caicedo had portrayed Panamanians as active combatants in the riot, Arosemena wrote as if the "*hijos del país* [children of the country]" on 15 April were mere bystanders caught between two warring parties: travelers from the United States and "a few of those upstart blacks [*unos pocos de esos negros advenidizos*], with origins in many countries, particularly the Antilles," who constituted "the corrupted scum that always accumulates in large cities or along the great commercial routes."[54]

If West Indians of African descent were clearly excluded from Arosemena's dreams of Latin unity, the role of indigenous peoples and native people of color in his vision of the future was less clear. He made no explicit reference to either group in "La cuestión americana." One year before, in a book entitled *El Estado Federal de Panamá*, Arosemena had written of indigenous peoples in Panama as if they had ceased to exist after the Spanish conquest—a destruction he regarded as a lost opportunity to educate and civilize native peoples. In the same book, Arosemena had criticized the United States for its discrimination against people of color. By implication, then, people of indigenous and African descent might form part of Arosemena's Latin American polity, provided they were properly civilized. But neither they nor projects for their uplift played significant roles either in Arosemena's argument for Panamanian statehood in 1855 or in his call for Latin unity in the Americas in 1856.[55]

CONCLUSION

In our explorations of race and nation within the region that we now call Latin America, latter-day scholars would do well to recall how "América Latina" as a geopolitical category has itself been racialized in different ways over time. The events of 15 April 1856 and the debate they helped to provoke over the political future of the "Latin race" indicate how early formulations of "América Latina" were intimately related to struggles over race and sovereignty not only on the level of elite political discourse but also in the context of everyday struggles over the terms of U.S. expansion.[56] Rather than being viewed as the invention of any single individual or the product of any single place, calls for a specifically "Latin American" unity in the mid-1850s are perhaps better understood as critical engagements with a larger, transatlantic debate over the relationship between race and political destiny that encompassed not only individuals such as Torres Caicedo and Arosemena but also French pan-Latinists and advocates of Manifest Destiny in the United States, among others. Yet participation in transnational intellectual circuits did not insulate Arosemena from developments within Panama itself. The conflict that began with an argument over a piece of fruit in Panama City and the calls for Latin unity made in Bogotá and Paris by elite intellectuals thus formed part of a continuum, even as the uneasy place of people of African and indigenous descent in Arosemena's writings suggests the racial limits of Latin America in the mid-nineteenth century.

NOTES

I would like to thank the editors of this volume as well as Jasmine Alinder, Alfredo Castillero Calvo, Sueann Caulfield, Fernando Coronil, Paul Eiss, Alfredo Figueroa Navarro, David Pedersen, Angeles Ramos Baquero, James Sanders, Rebecca J. Scott, Julie Skurski, Argelia Tello Burgos, J. Mills Thornton, and Michael Zeuske.

1. Frank Tannenbaum, *Slave and Citizen: The Negro in the Americas* (New York: Random House, 1946); Frederick Cooper, Thomas C. Holt, and Rebecca J. Scott, *Beyond Slavery: Explorations of Race, Labor, and Citizenship in Postemancipation Societies* (Chapel Hill: University of North Carolina Press, 2000), 1–2.

2. Martin W. Lewis and Kären Wigen, *The Myth of Continents: A Critique of Metageography* (Berkeley: University of California Press, 1997), 181.

3. John L. Phelan, "Pan-Latinism, French Intervention in Mexico (1861–1867), and the Genesis of the Idea of Latin America," in *Conciencia y autenticidad históricas*, ed. Juan A. Ortega y Medina (Mexico City: Universidad Nacional Autónoma de México, 1968), 279–98.

4. Arturo Ardao, *Génesis de la idea y el nombre de América Latina* (Caracas: Centro de Estudios Latinoamericanos Rómulo Gallegos, 1980), 82–86. See also Ardao, *América Latina y la latinidad* (Mexico City: Universidad Nacional Autónoma de México, 1993).

5. Miguel Rojas Mix, "Bilbao y el hallazgo de América latina: Unión continental, socialista y libertaria," *Cahiers du Monde Hispanique et Luso-Brasilien—Caravelle* 46 (1986), 35–47.

6. Paul Estrade, "Del invento de 'América Latina' en París por latinoamericanos (1856–1889)," in *París y el mundo ibérico e iberoamericano*, comp. Jacques Maurice y Marie-Claire Zimmerman (Paris: Université Paris X-Nanterre, 1998), 179–88; Mónica Quijada, "Sobre el origen y difusión del nombre 'América Latina': O una variación heterodoxa en torno al tema de la construcción social de la verdad," *Revista de Indias* 58, no. 214 (Sept.–Dec. 1998), 595–616.

7. On changes in the Panamanian transit economy in the late 1840s and 1850s, see Aims McGuinness, "In the Path of Empire: Labor, Land, and Liberty in Panamá during the California Gold Rush, 1848–1860" (Ph.D. diss., University of Michigan, 2001), and John Haskell Kemble, *The Panama Route, 1848–1869* (1943; reprint, Columbia: University of South Carolina Press, 1990). Kemble estimated that between 1848 and 1854 an "assured minimum" of 144,847 people traveled between New York City and San Francisco by way of Panama. From 1855 through 1859, the total reached an assured minimum of 150,989. See Kemble, *The Panama Route*, 253–54.

8. On the commercial aspirations of Panama City's merchant elite during the California gold rush, see Alfredo Figueroa Navarro's classic study of society and politics in nineteenth-century Panama, *Dominio y sociedad en el Panamá colombiano (1821–1903)* (Panama City: Editorial Universitaria, 1982), 259–61.

9. Declaration of José Manuel Luna reprinted in *Gaceta del Estado*, 26 Apr. 1856. This and all subsequent translations are mine. I have translated Luna's words, which according to Luna were spoken originally in English, from the Spanish in which they were rendered in the published version of his testimony.

10. For the official report of the U.S. government regarding the events of 15 April 1856, see Amos B. Corwine, "Report of Amos B. Corwine, United States Commissioner, respecting the Occurrences at Panama on the 15 April 1856," U.S. National Archives, Department of State, Record Group 59, Microfilm Series 139 (hereafter USNA, DS, RG 59, M-139), roll 5. The official report of the government of New Granada came in the form of a compilation of diplomatic correspondence and other documents related to the violence; see New Granada, *Final controversia diplomática con relación a los sucesos de Panamá del día 15 de abril de 1856* (Bogotá: Imprenta del Estado, 1857). See also Mercedes Chen Daley, "The Watermelon Riot: Cultural Encounters in Panama City, 15 April 1856," *Hispanic American Historical Review* 70, no. 1 (Feb. 1990), 85–108.

11. *Gaceta del Estado*, 26 Apr. 1856; Corwine, "Report."

12. On the effects of imported goods on local production and other economic effects of the gold rush in Panama, see Justo Arosemena, *El Estado Federal de Panamá* (1855; reprint, Panama City: Editorial Universitaria de Panamá, 1982), 76.

13. See, for example, the affidavit of Moses Brinkerhoff, June 25, 1856, USNA, DS, RG 59, M-139, roll 5.

14. "Fragmento de la 'Esposición' del Secretario de Relaciones Esteriores al Congreso, de fecha 2 de febrero de 1857," in New Granada, *Final controversia diplomática*, 68–80.

15. Affidavit of Arthur MacKenzie, 10 July 1856, USNA, DS, RG 59, M-139, roll 5.

16. For an overview of these reforms, see David Bushnell, *The Making of Modern Colombia: A Nation in Spite of Itself* (Berkeley: University of California Press, 1993), 104–13.

17. Alfredo Castillero Calvo, *Los negros y mulatos libres en la historia social panameña* (Panama City: n.p., 1969), 26–27. For a description of the liberation of the last slaves in Panama City at the city's cathedral, see *El Panameño*, 4 Jan. 1852. On the spatial organization of race in Panama City, see Alfredo Castillero Calvo, *La vivienda colonial en Panamá: Arquitectura, urbanismo y sociedad: Historia de un sueño* (Panama City: Biblioteca Cultural Shell, 1994), 198–204, and Figueroa Navarro, *Dominio y sociedad*, 79–100.

18. Election Results for Cabildo of Panama City in 1851, Archivo del Consejo Municipal de Panamá, Tomo 5 (1851).

19. Padrón Electoral de la parroquia de Santa Ana, 21 Aug. 1853, Archivo del Consejo Municipal de Panamá, Tomo 11 (1853).

20. Figueroa Navarro, *Dominio y sociedad*, 342–44, and Helen Delpar, *Red against*

Blue: The Liberal Party in Colombian Politics, 1863–1899 (University: University of Alabama Press, 1981), 16–21. On the relationship between categories of race and region in nineteenth-century Colombia, see Nancy Appelbaum, "Whitening the Region: Caucano Mediation and 'Antioqueño Colonization' in Nineteenth-Century Colombia," *Hispanic American Historical Review* 79, no. 4 (Nov. 1999): 631–67, and "Remembering Riosucio: Race, Region, and Community in Colombia, 1850–1950" (Ph.D. diss., University of Wisconsin–Madison, 1997). For a discussion of the formation of race and space with a focus on contemporary Colombia, see Peter Wade, *Blackness and Race Mixture: The Dynamics of Racial Identity in Colombia* (Baltimore: Johns Hopkins University Press, 1993). On the participation of former slaves and blacks in the Liberal Party in Cauca and its environs, see the above-cited works by Nancy Appelbaum and also James Sanders, "Contentious Republicans: Popular Politics, Race, and Class in Nineteenth-Century Southwestern Colombia" (Ph.D. diss., University of Pittsburgh, 2000).

21. Theodore T. Johnson, *Sights in the Gold Region, and Scenes by the Way* (New York: Baker and Scribner, 1849), 12.

22. Robert Tomes, *Panama in 1855* (New York: Harper and Brothers, 1855), 215. On U.S. views of Mexicans during the U.S.-Mexican War of 1848, see Reginald Horsman, *Race and Manifest Destiny: The Origins of American Racial Anglo-Saxonism* (Cambridge, Mass.: Harvard University Press, 1981), 229–48.

23. Brian Roberts, *American Alchemy: The California Gold Rush and Middle-Class Culture* (Chapel Hill: University of North Carolina Press, 2000), 140. On minstrelsy, see also Eric Lott, *Love and Theft: Blackface Minstrelsy and the American Working Class* (Oxford: Oxford University Press, 1993); David R. Roediger, *The Wages of Whiteness: Race and the Making of the American Working Class* (London: Verso, 1991); and Alexander Saxton, *The Rise and Fall of the White Republic: Class Politics and Mass Culture in Nineteenth-Century America* (London: Verso, 1990), 141–42, as well as Thomas C. Holt's discussion of these issues in "Marking: Race, Race-making, and the Writing of History," *American Historical Review* 100, no. 1 (Feb. 1995): 1–20.

24. Theodore T. Johnson, *Sights in the Gold Region*, 64, 28.

25. Bayard Taylor, *Eldorado* (1850; reprint, New York: Alfred A. Knopf, 1949), 12–15.

26. Sarah Merriam Brooks, *Across the Isthmus to California in '52* (San Francisco, 1894), as quoted in Jo Ann Levy, *They Saw the Elephant: Women in the California Gold Rush* (Hamden, Conn.: Archon Books, 1990), 46–47. Albert L. Hurtado discusses Brooks's account in "Crossing the Borders: Sex, Gender, and the Journey to California," in *Intimate Frontiers: Sex, Gender, and Culture in Old California* (Albuquerque: University of New Mexico Press, 1999), 45–73. On the role of race and gender in conflicts in the California goldfields, see Susan Lee Johnson, *Roaring Camp: The Social World of the California Gold Rush* (New York: Norton, 2000).

27. Theodore T. Johnson, *Sights in the Gold Region*, 17.

28. James L. Tyson, *Diary of a Physician in California* (New York: D. Appleton and Company, 1850), 19.

29. Theodore T. Johnson, *Sights in the Gold Region*, 74–75.

30. Taylor, *Eldorado*, 16.

31. Mary Seacole, *Wonderful Adventures of Mrs. Seacole in Many Lands*, ed. Ziggi Alexander and Audrey Dewjee (1857; reprint, Bristol: Falling Wall Press, 1984), 44–45.

32. Ibid., 45.

33. John Harris Forster, "Field Notes of a Surveyor in Panama and California" (1849), unpublished manuscript, Michigan Historical Collections, Bentley Library, University of Michigan, 25.

34. John L. Brown, William S. Safford, A. B. Miller, William Miller, and I. D. Farwell to President José Hilario López, 20 Mar. 1850, Archivo del Ministerio de Relaciones Exteriores (Colombia) (hereafter AMRE), Correspondence from the U.S. Legation in New Granada.

35. *Revisor de la Política y Literatura Americana* (New York City), 16 Mar. 1850. On William Walker, see E. Bradford Burns, *Patriarch and Folk: The Emergence of Nicaragua, 1798–1858* (Cambridge, Mass.: Harvard University Press, 1991), 194–203.

36. *Panama Star and Herald*, 19 Apr. 1856.

37. Testimony of Antonio Abad Monteser, 4 Aug. 1856, Archivo Nacional de Panamá, Período Colombiano (hereafter ANP, PC), Cajón 850, Tomo 2166 [originally located in Tomo 2160], 252–53.

38. New Granada, *Final controversia diplomática*, 42.

39. Affidavit of Arthur MacKenzie, 10 July 1856, USNA, DS, RG 59, M-139, roll 4.

40. Peter Wood and Karen C. C. Dalton write that while visual images of African Americans with watermelon predate Reconstruction, the racist association of watermelon with grotesque portrayals of African Americans did not become a commonplace in U.S. racism until after Reconstruction's end, in the 1880s. See Peter Wood and Karen C. C. Dalton, *Winslow Homer's Images of Blacks: The Civil War and Reconstruction Years* (Austin: University of Texas Press, 1988), 122 n. 192.

41. See Frank Safford and Marco Palacios, *Colombia: Fragmented Land, Divided Society* (Oxford: Oxford University Press, 2002), 217–21.

42. On Rafael Pombo's critiques of U.S. expansionist activity in the late 1850s, see Kirsten Silva Gruesz, *Ambassadors of Culture: The Transamerican Origins of Latino Writing* (Princeton: Princeton University Press, 2001).

43. José María Torres Caicedo, "Venta del Istmo de Panamá," *El Día*, 10 Aug. 1850, reprinted in Ardao, *Génesis de la idea*, 171–72, and "Confederación de las naciones de la América española," dated June 1856, reprinted in the same volume on 172–74.

44. Phelan, "Pan-Latinism," 281–82. On Saint-Simonianism and Torres Caicedo's career in Europe, see Paul N. Edison, "Latinizing America: The French Scientific Study of México, 1830–1930" (Ph.D. diss., Columbia University, 1999).

45. José María Torres Caicedo, "Las dos Américas," *El Correo de Ultramar* (Paris), 15 Feb. 1857, reprinted in Ardao, *Génesis de la idea*, 175–85.

46. Justo Arosemena, "La cuestión americana i su importancia," *El Neogranadino*, 15

and 29 July 1856, reprinted in *Escritos de Justo Arosemena: Estudio introductorio y antología*, ed. Argelia Tello Burgos (Panama City: Universidad de Panamá, 1985), 247–63. For a sampling of some of the most important scholarship on Justo Arosemena, including selections by José Dolores Moscote, Octavio Méndez Pereira, Ricaurte Soler, Argelia Tello Burgos, Nils Castro, Humberto Ricord, and Miguel Candanedo, see the special issue of *Tareas* 92 (Jan.–Apr. 1996).

47. Justo Arosemena, "¡¡¡Alerta Istmeños!!!," *El Panameño*, 17 Nov. 1850, reprinted in Tello Burgos, *Escritos*, 78.

48. Arosemena, "La cuestión americana," 250–51.

49. Ibid., 259–61. On Anglo-Saxonism and U.S. expansion in Mexico and elsewhere in Latin America in the late 1840s and 1850s, see Horsman, *Race and Manifest Destiny*, 229–48, and Matthew Frye Jacobson, *Whiteness of a Different Color: European Immigrants and the Alchemy of Race* (Cambridge, Mass.: Harvard University Press, 1998), 205–13.

50. Arosemena, "La cuestión americana," 250.

51. Ibid., 249–50.

52. Ibid., 258–63. Arosemena's speech is reprinted in Octavio Méndez Pereira, *Justo Arosemena*, 2nd ed. (Panama City: Imprenta Nacional, 1970), 208–10.

53. Ibid., 262–63. Also see Arosemena's speech in Bogotá in July 1856 calling for a united "Colombia," reprinted in *Panamá y nuestra América*, ed. Ricaurte Soler (Mexico City: Universidad Nacional Autónoma de México/Biblioteca del Estudiante Universitario, 1981), 157–60.

54. Arosemena, "La cuestión americana," 257. On the role of indigenous peoples in Pan-Latin and Americanist discourse in France in the 1850s and 1860s, see Edison, "Latinizing America," particularly 192–96. On indigenous peoples in the pan-Latin writings of Torres Caicedo and Francisco Bilbao, see Quijada, "Sobre el orígen," 612–15.

55. Arosemena, *El Estado Federal*, 23–24, 74–75.

56. On the "geographical distribution of cultural difference," see Peter Wade, *Race and Ethnicity in Latin America* (London: Pluto Press, 1997), 18–19.

CHAPTER FOUR

IMAGINING THE COLONIAL NATION

Race, Gender,
and Middle-Class
Politics in Belize,
1888–1898

Anne S. Macpherson

ERASING THE BLACK MOTHER

On 10 September 1798 a Spanish fleet engaged off the coast of Belize with a smaller force of British sailors, slaveowning settlers and male slaves, and poor white and free colored men.[1] The Spaniards intended to seize the rich mahogany lands of the interior by driving the British of the Bay Settlement out of Bourbon territory. But the fleet retreated after a two-hour exchange of fire, and the settlement survived, evolving in the nineteenth century into the colony of British Honduras.[2] By the 1890s that naval engagement, known as the Battle of St. George's Caye, was being sanctified in a political origin myth that imagined the Creole proto-nation as an unequal cross-race fraternity. Created by the pivotal Creole middle class—a small strata of mixed-ancestry urban artisans, shopkeepers, and government officers[3]—the battle myth commemorated their white settler forefathers as patriots and male slaves as loyal dependents, while erasing the presence of the black, colored, and sometimes enslaved foremothers of the leading Creole families. Thus it coded the battle's male "nation"-founding protagonists as white or black, but never both.

This essay traces the emergence of the myth during the politically contentious decade of 1888–98; the introductory section situates its enduring 1898 form in the context of dominant late-nineteenth-century racial ideology. The nation imagined by middle-class Creoles in the 1890s matched their goal of regaining legislative representation within an imperial power structure profoundly hostile to racial hybrids and black self-government. Thus, leading Belizean Creoles posited a definitively colonial nation, disavowing a Cuban-style struggle for independence, with its popular political participation and racially egalitarian potential.

The myth of the colonial nation's origins excluded women on gendered grounds, but also because Creoles sought to make taboo the history and reality of interracial sex. In the late nineteenth century an elite North Atlantic consensus coalesced about the biologically fixed inferiority of Africans, New World blacks, and hybrid mulattos.[4] Integral to this consensus was an obsession with degeneracy, which was "incarnated in the black mother," in white colonizing men's ambivalent and supposedly disastrous desire for non-European women, and in the hybrid results of sexual unions between white men and black women.[5] Concretely, Britain's Colonial Office acted on the assumption "that democratic government could not function in a racially mixed society."[6] In claiming rights to legislative representation, middle-class Belizean Creoles thus suppressed their own mixed-race lineages by removing the black mother and her mixed-race offspring from the founding moment of the Creole nation.[7]

The imagined nation was therefore born "in war—and not in sex," as Ada Ferrer has argued of Cuba, and specifically in the "physical and spiritual embrace between black and white men in battle."[8] Male slaves' loyalty to their white masters in jointly repudiating the Spaniard in 1798, according to the myth, symbolized the absence of racial hatred that had plagued other British possessions. This was a thinly veiled reference to the 1865 Morant Bay Rebellion in Jamaica, which had ended midcentury optimism that former slaves would learn to behave according to emerging white bourgeois norms and consolidated the view that blacks lacked any capacity for self-government.[9] In denying that a Morant—or, implicitly, a Cuban Ten Years' War or a Haitian Revolution— could occur on British Honduran soil, the myth's authors did not contest the linkages between whiteness and civilization or among blackness, hybridity, and degeneracy. Instead they asserted their white male ancestors' command of loyal male slaves as a metaphor of their own ability to lead and control the Creole working class, and thus of their fitness to legislate. By associating themselves with whiteness without explicitly claiming to be white, middle-class Creoles presented themselves as authentic natives who, as Britain's junior partners in governance, could secure a racially harmonious and loyal colonial nation.

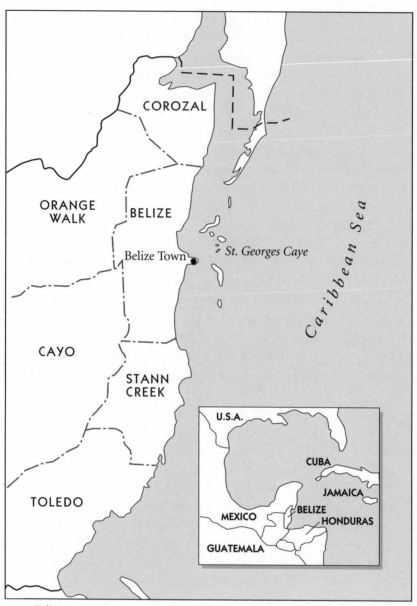

MAP 3. *Belize*

The mythmakers sought to suppress the source of supposed racial democracy and harmony celebrated four decades later in Brazil by Gilberto Freyre: racial mixing originating in sexual relationships between white masters and black female slaves or free colored women.[10] Freyre's enthusiasm for miscegenation did not displace a commitment to whitening his nation, and in this he was typical of Latin American reformers who sought to rework the racist North Atlantic consensus that relegated their nations to permanent "uncivilized" status. Where white immigration failed, the neo-Lamarckian emphasis on environmental racial improvement allowed the mulatto and mestizo to be construed not as degenerates, but as hybrid agents of a long-term project of national whitening.[11] The Latin American idea of whitening miscegenation seems to have had less currency in the British Caribbean both pre- and post-abolition, where mixed-race middle groups sought clear separation between themselves and the black masses, and where a post-Morant imperial policy prevailed of limiting social mixing between British administrators and locals.[12] Similar but perhaps less intense anxieties about racial hybridity among Cuban nationalists and Puerto Rican autonomists in the 1890s yielded constructions of race and nation that marginalized and discursively whitened women and led to policies of progress that focused on social reform rather than miscegenation.[13] The more absolute exclusion of women in the battle myth is suggestive of middle-class Creoles' acute concern with their own, not just the nation's, racial hybridity. The fraternal embrace, defined by male slaves' platonic loyalty to their "native" masters, was the only workable metaphor for middle-class Creoles' colonial *patria*.

In reconsidering the creation of the battle myth, this essay complicates a twentieth-century critique by Belizean nationalists who condemned it as an Anglophile impediment to independence, a "glorying in our subservience and colonial status."[14] Indeed, the myth did deny prior Mayan claims to indigenous status, allege that British Honduran slavery was benign, demonize all things Spanish, legitimize imperial authority, and draw a racialized distinction between the respectable middle class and the unruly masses. And in erasing the historic roles of black and mixed-race women in building the Creole nation, the myth offered no means for women to claim political rights. These criticisms notwithstanding, the myth was not a celebration of slavery or of absolute British dominance. As anthropologist Karen Judd has argued, the leading Creole men who launched the battle myth in 1898 prided themselves on being "true patriots," cast the battle as a distinctly "creole heritage," and sought "native" legislative rights.[15] Such terms are ambiguous, though, for the lines between local patriotism and empire loyalty, between Creole and British identities, were always blurred for the Creole middle class. The myth did posit a nation, but not one that was independent, democratic, or inclusive of anyone but middle-class Creole men as rights-bearing citizens.

A CENTURY OF DECLINE AND THE EMERGENCE OF THE BATTLE MYTH

The centennial of the battle in 1898 was an opportune moment to justify the middle-class project of reclaiming power lost over the preceding century. In the late 1700s free colored men held militia commissions, and some of them were counted among the wealthiest slaveowners in the settlement. But they were excluded from the Public Meeting, a homegrown legislature that institution-alized white slaveowning power and contested that of British superintendents.[16] As local mahogany contractors became subordinate agents to metropolitan capitalists in the 1850s, the Public Meeting was replaced by a Legislative Assembly elected on a narrow male franchise and generally representative of British interests.[17] In 1870 its members extinguished all voting rights by dissolving the assembly in favor of Crown Colony rule. This "imperial paternalism" concentrated political power in the hands of the appointed governor, Executive Council, and Legislative Council.[18] The English and Scots merchant-landowner elite quickly entrenched its power on these councils and in 1892 won from the Colonial Office a voting majority over government officials on the Legislative Council, which it used to minimize spending on agriculture, infrastructure, education, and health. This "Unofficial Majority" of powerful legislators was a primary target of the 1898 battle mythmakers.

The white elite, however, was attacked first by the black working class. Legally freed in 1838, this group experienced the postemancipation period as a crisis of poverty and political exclusion barely relieved by church education. In December 1894 Creole mahogany laborers and their female kin petitioned and rioted in Belize Town against a currency devaluation that cut their purchasing power. They looted merchant stores, declared themselves to be the colony's true natives, and condemned the Unofficial Majority without evincing any loyalty to the Creole middle class. Thus, by the mid-1890s a potential black threat from below combined with white political and economic dominance to uncomfortably pressure middle-class Creoles from both directions.

Declining economic power yielded an emphasis in middle-class culture on social status and political rights, specifically in a revived legislature. In the 1870s–90s very few men from what Judd defines as "middle-class" Creole families were landowning mahogany contractors or planters. Fully one in three was a laborer, while the balance were fishermen, mercantile clerks, shopkeepers, civil servants, and skilled tradesmen.[19] Only a fraction of these families could be defined as "leading" or "elite," among them the four that Judd examines in depth. Key men in these four families, most of whom participated in the making of the battle myth, were Henry Charles Usher, a senior civil servant; Wilfred A. Haylock, a grocer, civic activist, and sometime timber contractor; Benjamin Fairweather, a master carpenter and the only Creole Unofficial in the 1890s; and Absalom Hyde, a blacksmith. Usher's and Haylock's fathers had been among the few free colored men to enter the Public Meeting, while Haylock and Hyde sent their sons to high school. All but Fairweather descended from unions between free colored women and white men, both partners having been wealthy slaveowners in the cases of Usher and Hyde. Typical of the Creole elite, three of the four were Anglicans, while Haylock was Catholic; none attended the Wesleyan and Baptist churches patronized by lower-class Creoles. The man who gave this Creole elite voice was Dr. Frederick Gahne, a physician employed by one of the largest mahogany firms and founder-editor of the *Colonial Guardian* newspaper from 1882 to 1913. Gahne, a Creole from Honduras's Bay Islands, made his paper the primary vehicle for the articulation of the battle myth. For Gahne, his leading Creole associates, and his largely middle-class audience, the rights to legislative representation justified by the myth would help to compensate for their families' loss of economic power since the late 1700s.

The 1898 battle myth took shape through the previous decade of political conflict, during which three competing political projects were launched by distinct groups in colonial society. First was the 1888–93 Emancipation Jubilee and People's Hall project, carried out by black-identified workers to commemorate slave abolition, which earned middle-class disapproval as racially divisive and contrary to the spirit of 1798. Second was the British merchant-landowner elite's 1888–92 flirtation with ritualizing the battle anniversary and its campaign for absolute legislative power. Middle-class Creole men collaborated in this campaign, briefly deploying a construction of the battle that was surprisingly anti-British and that sustained meanings of racial equality as well as racial loyalty. Third was the black working class's 1894 protest and riot, which expressed popular anger at the merchants' political as well as economic power. Only after the riot did the Creole middle class break with the white expatriates to construct the battle as a clearly Creole heritage and themselves as Britain's rightful allies in containing both mercantile and proletarian extremes. This was the decade in which the Creole middle class clarified its political identity and interests and ultimately articulated an enduring political and cultural strategy.

Key elements of the battle myth originated in two early-nineteenth-century references. In 1823 local slaveowners cited slaves' loyalty in 1798 as evidence that their slaves were well treated and argued that the slaves had preferred British bondage over Spanish freedom.[20] In 1827 free colored slaveowner George Hyde, son of Scottish-born James Hyde and ancestor of Absalom, traveled to London to argue for free colored civil rights. Insisting that he should not "remain in a condition of comparative degradation, on the sole ground of his mother being a woman of colour," Hyde did not exactly repudiate racial hierarchy. He identified himself with his "brethren of the mix'd race" and never supported civil rights for free blacks, making his white male ancestry the basis for his claims.[21] This argument, and the slaveowners' emphasis on slave loyalty, survived in the official 1898 myth, although Hyde's frank admission of having a nonwhite mother did not.

THE EMANCIPATION JUBILEE AND PEOPLE'S HALL PROJECT, 1888–1893

On 1 August 1888 those Belizeans who identified themselves as descendants of slaves celebrated the fiftieth anniversary of emancipation, presenting themselves to the governor as representative of "the coloured population of this Colony."[22] Organized by an all-male committee headed by laborer Simon Lamb, along with "a considerable number of women" and several schoolteachers, the Emancipation Jubilee indicated the capacity for black-identified self-organization involving black and mixed-race women and made no mention of 1798 as a date of any significance for black Belizeans. Organizers asked for an educational institution rather than political rights, but they did not look to middle-class Creoles as their spokesmen.

Three notable features of the jubilee parade were the pairing of "woodcutters" and "Baymen," the inclusion of women, and the presence of blackface minstrels. The band of "woodcutters" led off, carrying axes and paddles as "the emblems of their occupation," while the "Baymen" carried a banner with the old coat of arms reading "Sub umbra floreo [In the shade we flourish]."[23] In the 1898 myth the "Baymen" would be coded as white slaveowners, but here their identity was less clear and potentially subversive, as they were played by "coloured people" and could perhaps be seen as sharing a common black ancestry with the woodcutters. The first of three groups of women was a "large army of females" in red dresses, "snowy white muslin pinafores," and straw hats trimmed with red; the others were in white with blue and white with pink respectively. Although distinct from male "citizens," women were at least present, unlike in the battle centennial parade a decade later. Two carts of "amateur Christy's Minstrels dressed in appropriate costume with countenances as hideous as could be desired by their greatest admirers" brought up the rear. Whether the parade organizers had sanctioned the blackface players' presence is as difficult to know as their reactions to the minstrels: indifference, suppressed outrage, or hilarity at whites' attempt at mimicry seem equally plausible.[24] One could even speculate that black Belizeans played Baymen in a reverse minstrelsy.

Although there were gestures of racial humility and even empire loyalty in the speeches presented to the governor, they also defied dominant biologized racism by linking improvement through education to ancestral values and Creole pride. Lamb's committee praised William IV and Queen Victoria, who "set our ancestors at liberty," and gave thanks that since emancipation "our rights as a freed people have been maintained and honoured." Grateful that fifty years of enlightenment had enabled "the majority of Creoles of this town, though not highly educated," to read the Bible, the committee thanked the governor for his aid in starting an emancipation institute. The "schoolchildren's" speech, undoubtedly written by the teachers who signed it, differed in describing slavery as "misery . . . cruelty . . . [a] galling yoke . . . humiliation . . . degradation," a memory that the middle class would consistently deny. Yet it too attributed emancipation to Queen Victoria and expressed gratitude for "education, liberty, all supported by Britain." The speech concluded, "As the children of a people remarkable for loyalty we desire to grow up more intelligent than our ancestors, and to inherit their magnanimity," and thanked the governor for his commitment to help with the emancipation institute.

Gahne's coverage of the jubilee in the *Colonial Guardian* emphasized its orderliness. This was clearly an expression of relief, for a few days earlier he had warned the organizers not to allow memories of slavery to provoke unrest. A feature in the newspaper argued that "the slavery of British Honduras . . . was unlike that of the other British colonies in the New World, as slavery but in name."[25] The "evidence" presented to support this view is familiar to most adult Belizeans today as part of the battle myth. Although armed and isolated in the woods with their masters, male slaves did not attack whites. Indeed, according to this view, the slave gang was in fact more like a colonial militia, ready to protect its officer's "life and property against marauders from Yucatan," or like the clansmen of a Scottish chief.[26] Thus, "the hatred of race and of class which arose in other portions of the British Empire where slavery existed" never developed in British Honduras, and "the Creole labouring class" had neither the desire nor capacity to engage in "crimes of violence."

On 1 August 1889 Lamb's committee and a group of women wearing the red and white costumes of 1888 marched to an empty lot in the center of Belize Town where the governor granted ownership to the group. Here the promised emancipation institute, now dubbed the People's Hall, was to be built by private donations. Little progress had been made by early 1892, when Gahne called for the return of the lot to the government for a general colonial museum. In August 1892 the People's Hall Committee met with Governor Moloney to discuss its financial insolvency. A veteran of the colonial service in West Africa, Moloney demonstrated a sympathetic understanding of the causes of slavery and the meaning of emancipation and committed the administration to aiding the project. The People's Hall was partially complete by March 1893, when Moloney withdrew support, now advocating Gahne's idea of a general museum that would "recognize no distinctions of class or colour" and would not "keep alive the memory of those atrocities." The governor implied at an open meeting that suspicions of racial motives, and of the project being by and for members of the Wesleyan Church, had hampered its success.[27] The committee members voted to turn over the project to the administration but then withdrew their resignations. The passions and goals motivating this reversal are undocumented, but we do know that Gahne roundly disapproved of the committee's persistence. By July 1893 the People's Hall was almost complete when a severe tropical storm razed it. The committee held a final fund-raiser at Christmastime in 1893 and then vanished. Middle-class Creoles, lacking any desire to commemorate slavery and emancipation, or to identify with their black ancestry, made no effort to revive the project. Gahne's criticisms of it as sectarian and racially divisive heralded middle-class claims to be generally representative and racially neutral.

THE EXPATRIATES' BATTLE AND THE UNOFFICIAL MAJORITY, 1888–1892

By the time the People's Hall was destroyed, the white mercantile elite had gained unprecedented power through the Unofficial Majority. In 1888, however, expatriates reacted to the August Emancipation Jubilee by marking the battle anniversary a month later with a private evening entertainment, possibly portraying it as a British victory.[28] A year later, members of the whites-only Colonial Club worked up an entertainment depicting the 1798 battle, which they performed for club members and as a free entertainment for the public. "Several gentlemen dressed as cutters" sang and told humorous stories in Creole, a clear example of minstrelsy.[29] The "Tenth," as the battle anniversary came to be known, was not marked again in the 1890–96 period, with the exception of an editorial by Gahne in 1893. Here he praised the "nominal" slaves' "self-abnegation" as the most heroic aspect of the battle and suggested that the approaching centennial should be a public holiday. What began as a reassuring entertainment for affluent British expatriates in 1888 would become a deeply serious ritual for middle-class Creoles a decade later.

The battle myth was invoked repeatedly during the elite's and middle class's campaign for the Unofficial Majority from 1890 to 1892, but in a rather different form from that of 1898 and beyond. The campaign began in March 1890 when a British court held the colony responsible for paying the canceled contract of an English engineer. Immediately, "the vast majority of the mercantile community" and "a considerable number of the better class of artisans" held a "Public Meeting" (the capitals deliberately meant to invoke the early-nineteenth-century institution), which forwarded a protest memorial to the Colonial Office.[30] In April, when the officials on the Legislative Council approved payment by the colony's taxpayers, the Unofficials (four white merchants and Benjamin Fairweather) walked out, and the governor formed an unconstitutional all-official council.[31] A second public meeting denounced the payment and Crown Colony rule and proposed a Legislative Council with a partly elected Unofficial Majority. The nine-member committee formed to consider this proposal included just one Creole, publican C. M. Vernon. Gahne applauded the proposal and attacked the Colonial Office and governor as despotic.[32] By October, Gahne was claiming that "the people" had enjoyed the franchise for over a century before Crown Colony rule, a gross misrepresentation of the white oligarchic Public Meeting.[33] In December, while the mahogany laborers were returning to town for Christmas, the Colonial Office refused to empower the colony's small white population with an Unofficial Majority, for it would not contemplate a broader franchise that might make voters of nonwhites.

In reaction, Gahne penned an outraged critique of Crown Colony rule that directly invoked the 1798 battle.[34] Denouncing the Colonial Office view that "we are unfit to have even a majority of one in the Legislative Council" because "there are only 400 inhabitants of European descent in the colony," Gahne argued that race should not be paramount in determining political rights. "Even in the days of slavery," he claimed, "the men of European descent, those of mixed European blood and those of purely African descent, stood shoulder to shoulder to resist the Spaniard." This reference to people of mixed race was unique in the 1888–98 decade, and although it was softened with the "European" adjective, it stands in contrast to the myth of 1898, which retained only the "shoulder to shoulder" rhetoric. It seems probable that the very anti-Britishness of the moment opened a small space to assert an identity at odds with British racial ideology, and to speak to a local rather than an imperial audience. Gahne, however, began to negotiate in the same breath, demonstrating the fragility of his commitment to an *equal* fraternity. Given the high proportion of people of "mixed European descent," he argued, British Honduras should qualify for some electoral representation. Notable in his discourse were a strong emphasis on nonwhite loyalty to constituted authority and an emphasis on white European rather than black African ancestry. His populist appeal against official British racism had clear limits.

Those limits were already plain in the *Guardian*'s coverage during 1890 of popular morality and women's behavior within the urban black working class. First Gahne called for a diminution of the 50 percent illegitimacy rate. Next the paper denounced the "filthy streams of obscenity" uttered by "the fallen sisterhood," demanding that such "viragoes . . . the foul-tongued women who disgrace the community" be silenced and shunned.[35] Finally, in highly unusual coverage of a popular gathering, the paper condemned the *sambye* dance, "a dance of African origin, patronised by the lower orders of the community." Of particular concern were the "chorus of shrill-voiced females, with arms akimbo" and the lead female screaming a song "pregnant with indecency," who together danced to the drums, rendering the night "hideous." Labeling the *sambye* dances "obscene orgies," the *Guardian* urged that they be banned for the sake of "morality, law and order."[36] These criticisms of popular black culture and poor women marked a gendered and racialized boundary around the respectable, deserving proto-nation that Gahne was asserting against overt British racism.[37]

In January 1891 the merchant-landowner elite, Gahne, two British doctors, and two Creoles, Benjamin Fairweather and C. M. Vernon, formed the People's Committee to defy British "despotism" through pursuit of the Unofficial Majority.[38] Notably, the committee formed not when the Unofficials walked out of the Legislative Council, or even when the Colonial Office rejected proposals for a partly elected Unofficial Majority, but when the Emancipation Jubilee Committee was laying the cornerstone of its People's Hall. Only then did the leading British and Creole men of the community label themselves the "people's" committee and claim to rely on "the sovereignty of the people," as if they had been popularly elected. The People's Committee met almost monthly through 1891 and hired a London lawyer to lobby the Colonial Office for either representative government or an appointed Unofficial Majority. Gahne defended the committee as representative and patriotic, portraying it as a racially inclusive popular assembly, foreshadowing his 1892–93 critique of the People's Hall project as irresponsibly divisive. Again invoking 1798, he cast the Colonial Office in the role of the Spanish tyrant to be resisted by the colonists, "irrespective of colour, race, or creed, standing shoulder to shoulder."[39] Ultimately an English court found the all-official Legislative Council to be unconstitutional, forcing the Colonial Office to grant an appointed Unofficial Majority in January 1892.[40] After rejoicing in the achievement of "liberty," Gahne quickly turned to attack the People's Hall Committee for the slow pace of construction, and for pursuing a sectarian project. With power achieved, the precarious language of inclusivity and equality could be dispensed with. Soon, though, middle-class Creoles would question how much power they had gained through the Unofficial Majority and would begin their own campaign for a partially elected legislature, a campaign in which the rearticulation of the battle myth as fundamentally Creole was central.

THE 1894 LABORERS' RIOT

Creole disenchantment with the Unofficial Majority solidified in reaction to the black working-class riot of 11 December 1894. When currency devaluation was discussed at a People's Committee public meeting in late 1892, laborers shouted down a wealthy Scottish merchant who claimed that it would hurt the "well-to-do" most.[41] They were delighted, however, by lawyer F. E. Maxwell's argument that devaluation would benefit exporter-employers. Maxwell's view that a different kind of government was needed was one of the earliest criticisms of the Unofficial Majority. After the riot against devaluation in 1894, the middle class as a whole began to shift toward Maxwell's position.

As the colonial authorities moved toward currency devaluation after September 1894, public anger rose, erupting first in a police force mutiny over pay, and then in the riot carried out by women, children, and woodcutters home for Christmas. The riot was preceded by a delegation of workers calling on the governor with a petition for increased wages and carrying a banner reading "Justice we Desire." Led by Jon Alexander Tom, the petitioners identified themselves as "the real inhabitants of this Colony," those who toiled in the forests to produce its wealth but were "without anyone to protect their interests while both Councils are filled with merchants and other employers of labourers."[42] Labor's definition of colonial citizenship was based not on slaves' battle service in 1798 but on the working class's contemporary importance; it made the governor less a benevolent patriarch than an arbiter of just principle. When the governor rejected the petition, the riot ensued. According to testimony during rioters' trials, on 11 December crowds of 200–600 people controlled the central business district, looting stores and surrounding the police station to force one leader's release. Poor women participated actively in the riot, displaying the "unladylike" behavior deemed degenerate by the imperial authorities and from which respectable Creoles sought to distance themselves.[43] But the Creole middle class now had to reckon with the black laborers' extreme hostility to the white merchant elite, as well as the British authorities' importance in restoring order. The black working class had become a political factor that middle-class Creoles could neither ignore nor ally with.

Gahne characterized the riot as "alien to the character of the people" and demanded permanent troops to protect "law-abiding inhabitants against future outbreaks of proletarian fury." He called for a new Legislative Assembly, more representative than the assembly of 1853–70 and with less security of tenure for Unofficials.[44] The *Guardian* soon berated the Unofficials for lowering tariffs on luxury goods and refusing to increase education spending.[45] Most significantly, Gahne published F. M. Maxwell's radical critique, which decried the Colonial Office for granting "irresponsible power to . . . legislative councillors" with narrow self-interests.[46] Neither officials nor Unofficials were "in touch with the main body of the people," Maxwell claimed, and thus required "brute force to sustain their authority."[47] Arguing that British Hondurans were not citizens but only subjects, Maxwell concluded that "the unofficial element in the Council [Fairweather excepted] has not proved of the slightest benefit to the community." In sum, he wrote, "The government of this colony is absolute; we the people . . . have no more voice in the management of our public affairs . . . than serfs or slaves have."[48] Crucially, Maxwell reminded his readers that in 1891 the People's Committee had floated the idea of elected representation. Gahne agreed but—moving sharply away from his egalitarian and inclusive "shoulder to shoulder" rhetoric of 1890 and 1891—claimed that manhood suffrage was unthinkable "for obvious reasons."[49] He suggested a legislature of three officials and eleven Unofficials, seven of them elected. Candidates and voters would have to meet steep property qualifications. Gahne had clearly articulated what would become the middle-class political platform for the next half-century, a platform that the merchant elite would successfully resist until the 1930s and the popular classes would dismiss as wholly inadequate.

In late 1895 the Creole middle class formed the Committee for the Advancement of the Colony, which began to openly criticize the Unofficial Majority for lack of progress in education, agricultural development, transportation, and communications.[50] By April 1896 Gahne editorialized that "the people"—a category now excluding the merchant-landowner elite—were tired of "hope deferred and of neglect of their welfare."[51] That summer Gahne made two key moves: he argued that the mahogany economy had arrested colonial development, and he suggested that the people should be prepared to properly celebrate the centennial of the battle in September 1898. The Unofficial Majority, rejected by the laborers themselves in late 1894, was now acknowledged by its original middle-class proponents as the opposite rather than the epitome of representative government. In constructing their own version, however, middle-class men would reject both the respectful black identity of 1888 and the combative one of 1894, instead courting alliance with the British authorities.

THE BATTLE MYTH, 1897–1898

In the aftermath of the riot, leading Creole men seized on the history of the battle as a vehicle for their demands for a restored representative legislature, in which they would sit as elected members, chosen by their peers. Middle-class Creoles used the occasion of Queen Victoria's Diamond Jubilee in 1897 to elaborate their Creole heritage within the context of the British Empire. At the public meeting held to plan local celebrations, Wilfred Haylock told the story of his great-granduncle's participation in the 1798 battle, and Benjamin Fairweather too said that he "felt proud to be the descendant of a Bayman." The meeting agreed to mark the royal occasion by building a jubilee library, which Gahne suggested be opened on the centenary of the battle.[52] Also connecting the two anniversaries was a proposal for a jubilee stamp commemorating the battle. Jubilee celebrations included parades, sports, speeches, and fireworks but were not followed up by any collective marking of the Tenth.[53] Gahne, however, editorialized that without the battle, British Honduras would be like Cuba and the Philippines, forced to rebel against Spain.[54] In early 1898 Haylock renewed the request for a stamp, submitting a sketch of a black soldier and a white one clasping hands over a banner proclaiming "Shoulder to shoulder." Again London turned down the request, causing Gahne to regret that the British did not properly appreciate British Hondurans' loyalty.[55] This rhetoric was far milder than his condemnation of Britain as a despot in the early 1890s and is indicative of the new Creole strategy of alliance with British officials. In April 1898, as U.S. troops were landing in eastern Cuba, Gahne criticized Irish nationalists as unfit for self-government because of their disloyalty. In this moment Gahne cemented his post-riot dismissal of manhood suffrage and drained the battle myth of its precarious 1890 meaning as a site of black and mixed-race equality with whites, for now "shoulder to shoulder" unequivocally meant slaves' loyalty to their masters, and colonial loyalty to the metropole. As in Cuban nationalist rhetoric, the battle myth constructed an idealized black insurgent: loyal to whites, lacking any sexual desire for white women, and "incapable of imagining a black republic."[56]

The Centenary Committee was formed at an April 1898 meeting chaired by Henry Charles Usher, a career civil servant. Both Wilfred Haylock and Benjamin Fairweather spoke.[57] After painting the naval engagement of 1798 as a thrilling David and Goliath adventure story, Usher zeroed in on the central theme:

> The most distinguishing feature of that remarkable event was the gallantry and true nobleness of nature displayed by the slaves, who, regardless of the bondage in which they were held and remembering only the kindness they had received from their masters, when they heard that danger threatened their masters' works and homesteads . . . abandoned their peaceful homes and safe retreats in the bush where they were working and rushed to the assistance of their masters, and there assembled around their masters in force and numbers, armed with machetes, axes and muskets; some in the absence of a better weapon of defence armed themselves with "poke-and-do boy" sticks, sharpened to a needle like point, and all right loyally and devotedly declared their intention, to aid in beating off the Spaniards or dying with their masters in the conflict then evidently at hand.

Usher concluded by recalling that his father was only three in 1798, but that his grandfather, James Usher, "together with his slaves took a very active part and fought on that occasion." He remained silent about his free colored grandmother, Jane Trapp, who owned slaves in her own right. Fairweather, who may have known that his family could not trace its roots to the battle, was vaguer, recalling that his father was also three years old at the time and had later instructed his son that "the loyalty of the slaves caused [the Spaniards'] defeat." He did not air the family story that his own mother was a Miskito Indian or mention that his wife's parents were both free colored. Haylock was able to

Belize coat of arms. Located at the center of the modern Belizean flag, this coat of arms incorporates both the motto mentioned in the 1888 Emancipation Jubilee and the white and black male figures added in the formation of the 1898 battle myth. Note that these figures have been changed since 1898 from soldiers to woodcutters and their racialized differences have been minimized.

recount that his great-grandmother had told him about his great-granduncle's participation in the battle. This was probably his grandfather Jonas's older brother Francis Haylock Jr., a free colored turtler; both were sons of Francis, a white turtler, and Rebecca Fitzgibbon Haylock, a free colored woman. In 1898 Rebecca's great-grandson did not mention the family's racial hybridity.[58]

By reproducing the boundaries of memory that Usher had just established, Haylock and Fairweather implied that they too had white slaveowning forefathers who had fought in the battle and made taboo their nonwhite foremothers and their own mixed-race status. The audience quite likely knew that these speakers' backgrounds included free colored slaveowners and women, nonslaveowning whites, and possibly Indians, but such complexities were smoothed out into a discourse of masters and loyal slaves, each tacitly racialized as white or black, but not both, and each male. Cementing this discourse by separating "the descendants of the masters" from "the descendants of the slaves," Haylock concluded that "the subject before them ought to interest all. . . . The heroism of the slaves was very great, because had they joined the Spaniards they would have been free. . . . If the Baymen had not secured to them liberty under the British flag they would be now suffering like Cuba." It is not clear whether Cuba's suffering consisted of Spanish colonial rule, U.S. intervention, or both, but the way to avoid it was through a generic British "liberty," not national independence.

The final speaker of the evening, a British medical officer in the colonial service, further racialized the division between masters and slaves in presenting the resolution to celebrate the battle centenary. His role is indicative of the middle class's desire to ally with colonial officials. Distinguishing "the race of the Baymen" and "the race of the slaves," and again referring to "the two races of Baymen and their slaves," he also identified the slaves' loyalty as "the central fact of this battle" and mentioned that those slaves' "descendants . . . are in our midst." He called on people to put aside distinctions of creed, caste, and color to celebrate the empire as a common country, concluding, "Let us cheerfully and joyfully yield to our Creole brethren the first place" and do honor to their ancestors on the Tenth. Clearly "the race of Baymen" meant white slaveowners and was thus distinct from the slaves' descendants in this discourse, but the phrase "our Creole brethren" was more ambiguous. Usher, Fairweather, Haylock, and Gahne might have been willing to include "the descendants of the masters" and "the descendants of the slaves" in this category, but only because they had firmly linked themselves to the white Baymen masters. In short, they knew they were not white and feared to have their black maternal origins exposed.

The all-male committee put on a splendid show to celebrate the battle centenary. On the morning of 9 September 1898 the grand procession was led by "Minstrels with the usual blackened faces," followed by "men dressed as cutters with axes and paddles on shoulders," musicians, and a group of friendly society members, some of whom may have been women.[59] Absent were the "citizens" and women's bands of the Emancipation Jubilee; presumably those people were relegated to the "great crowds" watching from the sidelines. The acting governor made a politic speech about the importance of natives as well as British sailors in 1798. He regretted the slowness of the Colonial Office in appreciating the victory and including British Honduras properly in the empire. Had the loyalty of the inhabitants not enabled London to finally see the light, he feared that the colony would be suffering the fate of Cuba and the Philippines. This further reference to the U.S. interventions in the Caribbean and Pacific presumably resonated with leading Creoles eager to confirm their loyalty. To the assembled schoolchildren the governor emphasized their ancestors' courage and the "privileges and advantages of living as British subjects and citizens of the British Empire." Each child then received a bag of sweets. The Tenth itself was marked by a military parade and sports competition, and the next day by special church services.

Missing from these events was the address of loyalty to the governor, monarch, and empire, which became a central tradition of the twentieth-century ritual; thus there was no opportunity for leading Creoles to articulate their demands for legislative autonomy. Those demands were drowned out by displays of empire loyalty and children's voices singing "Rule Britannia." It was almost as if the fear that removed free colored foremothers from the middle class's political origin myth, and placed working-class men in a firmly junior position, had become a fear of expressing anything but empire loyalty. Middle-class legislative rights would not be restored for another thirty-seven years.

"PREGNANT WITH INDECENCY"

Gahne's risky articulation of the battle myth in the early 1890s was both anti-British and assertive of racial equality and native unity. But these attributes were superficial and dependent on the white merchant-landowner elite's leadership of the campaign against Crown Colony rule. The Creole middle class was incapable of independently standing against the colonial authorities and genuinely allying with their "Creole brethren" in the working class. Such an alliance risked a loss of control and status to an "uncivilized" majority that the middle class and its free colored ancestors had always disdained and feared. Fear rose slightly in 1888 and sharply in 1894, assuring that middle-class Creoles, in breaking with the economic elite, would seek out colonial officials as their new allies, while making only rhetorical gestures toward the working class. Bound up with these political choices was the middle class's construction of race through the battle myth. Claiming to be Creole in terms of culture and native belonging, the middle class nonetheless "decreolized" itself racially, at least on the terrain of politics. This strategy entailed a construction of the Baymen as white, the slaves as black, and both as male. It also meant that free colored men and women could not be mentioned in connection with 1798, particularly the women, whose "indecent" pregnancies had produced the mythmakers themselves. By associating themselves only with their white Baymen ancestors, and by twisting "shoulder to shoulder" into a metaphor for black loyalty, middle-class Creoles hoped to convince the Colonial Office of their fitness as colonial voters and legislators. The battle myth's content illustrates how such tensions were partly overcome—but also extended—through masculinizing cross-class and cross-race relations. The rhetoric of equal fraternity remained as a weak gesture toward the politically restless Creole working class, which gave the traditional myth no support until the late 1950s.[60]

A different kind of interpretation emerged at the height of anticolonial labor rebellion in 1934, when labor leader Antonio Soberanis Gómez led the first mass Tenth celebration.[61] Linking the battle to national rebellion, Soberanis made it palatable to a popular multiracial coalition that did not base its political claims on white ancestry. He did not carve out a place for women in the myth, but they were central in articulating and pursuing labor's anticolonial agenda.[62] In 1949, after a stint in the Panama Canal Zone that apparently radicalized him, Soberanis penned a lucid deconstruction of the battle myth in arguing for Belize's national self-determination as a black and Indian nation with deep historical roots.[63] Questioning the myth's historical sources, he noted that no records of "Negro" voices or opinions in 1798 existed, and that the mythmakers had ignored an oral "native tradition." This tradition maintained that the Spaniards retreated when Africans on their ships mutinied after communicating by drum to Africans in the Bay Settlement their desire to escape. The mythmakers ignored this memory in order to swallow up "all rights to self-determination of the descendants of the Negroes" and to "foster loyalty and devotion to His Majesty the King and the British Empire rather than unite in a native claim to self-determination." Soberanis explained their choice: "A few wicked half-breeds and white officials seeing an opening because the mass of Negroes had no education or written records decided to give such interpretations to what documents existed as would deprive oppressed natives of their right to self-determination, with the hope that they, having found favour with the British Crown, would be set up as aristocrats and descendants of the 'Baymen' who could then be proven to be *white*."[64] Soberanis downplayed the fact that some Baymen *were* white but accurately identified middle-class Creoles' attachment to the white portion of their ancestry.

The myth perpetuated the political exclusion not only of blacks, Mayans, and mestizos, but also of Belizean women. The contradictions of including women in the myth of 1798 were exposed in 1952, when the leading female middle-class reformer of the 1920s–50s period, Vivian Seay, attempted to do so.[65] Her story was that during the Public Meeting held in 1798 to debate the approaching Spanish attack, "a few" men argued for evacuation in order to prevent women being "subjected to the most galling of insults and humiliation by the Spaniard." Seay applauded the women who "jeered and derided" those men who thought to abandon the settlement for the sake of female virtue, insisting that loyalty to home and empire must come first. Only then did the men resolve to go out with their male slaves to fight and defeat the Spaniards. "These are the women from whom we are descended," claimed Seay. But she could not acknowledge that most women present in the settlement in 1798, even among the free, and likely including these heroic foremothers, were not white.[66] The male mythmakers could invoke race in connecting to their white forefathers, but Seay and other respectable women reformers had to maintain an absolutely raceless imagining of these female instigators to the fraternal embrace. This silence compounded middle-class women's inability to connect with poor black women, who in 1952 were flocking to the nationalist movement and bringing to a close the era of colonial patriotism.

For Seay, as for the myth's creators in the 1890s, interracial sex was publicly taboo, and black women's historical roles could never be safely contained. Boxed in by transatlantic ideologies of race and hybridity, pincered by the white merchant elite and the black working class, and, not least, constrained by its own acceptance of imperial norms, the Creole middle class had few options in constructing an origin myth for the colonial nation. In attempting to articulate a justification for representative government, it faced its own ambivalence about its racial identity, an ambivalence that centered on its black and colored foremothers. When leading Creoles did mention black women in the 1890s, they were the *sambye* singers and dancers denounced by Gahne as hideous, obscene, orgiastic, immoral, disorderly, and African. How distressed the mythmakers would be to witness the centerpiece of contemporary Tenth celebrations in Belize: an off-season carnival in which black women, many of them poor, dance down the streets to the drum beats of the latest Afro-Caribbean music. Blackness and national identity have become more compatible in much of the contemporary British Caribbean than anywhere in Latin America, but only to the degree that the region's popular classes have broken free of the imperial and middle-class racial thinking that defined the late nineteenth century.[67]

NOTES

My thanks to the audience and my copanelist Patrick McNamara at the 2000 American Society for Ethnohistory meeting, where I presented an early version of this essay. Thanks also to my coeditors for fine-tuning the final essay. Richard Black and Kim Scott of SUNY College at Brockport's Office of Design and Production prepared the figure and map.

1. Throughout the British Caribbean the "free colored" were people of mixed European and African ancestry who were born free or gained their freedom prior to the abolition of slavery in the 1830s. They tended to distance themselves from the black majority that was freed at that time.

2. O. Nigel Bolland, *The Formation of a Colonial Society: Belize, from Conquest to Crown Colony* (Baltimore: Johns Hopkins University Press, 1977), chaps. 3, 10, 11.

3. The term "Creole" in Belize refers to the ethnic group descended from non-Iberian Europeans and/or Africans and to the language they have developed since the seventeenth and eighteenth centuries. Most middle-class Creoles had both African and European ancestry.

4. Michael Banton, *Racial Theories* (Cambridge: Cambridge University Press, 1987), 52–60; Ada Ferrer, *Insurgent Cuba: Race, Nation, and Revolution, 1868–1898* (Chapel Hill: University of North Carolina Press, 1999), 4; Anne McClintock, *Imperial Leather: Race, Gender, and Sexuality in the Colonial Contest* (New York: Routledge, 1995), 43–54; George L. Mosse, *Toward the Final Solution: A History of European Racism* (New York: Howard Fertig, 1978), 70; Nancy Leys Stepan, *"The Hour of Eugenics": Race, Gender, and Nation in Latin America* (Ithaca: Cornell University Press, 1991), 45; George W. Stocking Jr., *Race, Culture, and Evolution: Essays in the History of Anthropology* (New York: Free Press, 1968), 48–49; Robert J. C. Young, *Colonial Desire: Hybridity in Theory, Culture, and Race* (London: Routledge, 1995), introduction and chaps. 4–6.

5. The quote comes from McClintock, *Imperial Leather*, 49. See also Young, *Colonial Desire*, 5–16, 150–58; Stepan, *"The Hour of Eugenics,"* 24, 44–46; Ann Laura Stoler, *Race and the Education of Desire: Foucault's* History of Sexuality *and the Colonial Order of Things* (Durham: Duke University Press, 1995), 8.

6. Thomas C. Holt, *The Problem of Freedom: Race, Labor, and Politics in Jamaica and Britain, 1832–1938* (Baltimore: Johns Hopkins University Press, 1992), 340.

7. Blanca Muratorio, "Images of Indians in the Construction of Ecuadorian Identity at the End of the Nineteenth Century," in *Latin American Popular Culture: An Introduction*, ed. William H. Beezley and Linda A. Curcio-Nagy (Wilmington, Del.: Scholarly Resources, 2000), 105–21, shows that the Ecuadorian Liberal elite "desexed" its aristocratic Incan heritage by emphasizing images of noble male warriors.

8. Ferrer, *Insurgent Cuba*, 4, 9.

9. Catherine Hall, "Gender Politics and Imperial Politics: Rethinking the Histories of Empire," in *Engendering History: Caribbean Women in Historical Perspective*, ed. Verene Shepherd, Bridget Brereton, and Barbara Bailey (New York: St. Martin's Press, 1995), 48–

59; Holt, *The Problem of Freedom*, chap. 8; Gad J. Heuman, *The Killing Time: The Morant Bay Rebellion in Jamaica* (Knoxville: University of Tennessee Press, 1994).

10. See Sueann Caulfield's chapter in this volume.

11. Stepan, *"The Hour of Eugenics,"* chap. 3; Lourdes Martínez-Echazábal, *"Mestizaje and the Discourse of National/Cultural Identity in Latin America, 1845–1959,"* *Latin American Perspectives* 25, no. 3 (May 1998): 27–30.

12. Patrick E. Bryan, *The Jamaican People, 1880–1902: Race, Class, and Social Control* (London: Macmillan, 1991), 254, captures this West Indian middle-class attitude in arguing that Jamaica's "black intellectuals were alienated from the Creole society which gave them birth." On British policy, see Young, *Colonial Desire*, 144.

13. On the gendered constructions of the Cuban nation, see Ferrer, *Insurgent Cuba*, 126–27, and Jean Stubbs, "Social and Political Motherhood of Cuba: Mariana Grajales Cuello," in Shepherd, Brereton, and Bailey, *Engendering History*, 296–315. On the inclusion of "white wives and mothers" as instigators of the Puerto Rican autonomists' *gran familia*, see Eileen Suárez Findlay, *Imposing Decency: Race and Sexuality in Puerto Rico, 1870–1920* (Durham: Duke University Press, 1999), 54–59, 85–87.

14. Lloyd Griffiths, a schoolmaster's son, rejected the myth in a letter to the *Daily Clarion* newspaper, 20 July 1948, quoted in Assad Shoman, *13 Chapters of a History of Belize*, ed. Anne S. Macpherson (Belize: Angelus Press, 1995), 155.

15. Karen H. Judd, "Elite Reproduction and Ethnic Identity in Belize" (Ph.D. diss., City University of New York, 1992), 202, 222.

16. Bolland, *Formation of a Colonial Society*, 45–46, 90–93, 180–82. London forced the Public Meeting to admit free colored men on equal property qualifications in 1831, but little changed.

17. O. Nigel Bolland and Assad Shoman, *Land in Belize, 1765–1871* (Mona, Jamaica: Institute for Social and Economic Research, University of the West Indies, 1977), chap. 3; Bolland, *Formation of a Colonial Society*, 189, 191.

18. Bryan, *The Jamaican People*, 11, 17, uses the phrase "imperial paternalism."

19. Judd, "Elite Reproduction," 183–88, 214. These statistics are based on Judd's research on men with twenty-two "creole surnames associated with the creole elite."

20. *Defence of the Settlers of Honduras Against the Unjust and Unfounded Representations of Col. George Arthur, Late Superintendent of the Settlement* (London: A. J. Valpy, 1823).

21. CO 123/38, George Hyde to Earl of Bathurst, 3 Feb. 1827.

22. *Colonial Guardian* (hereafter *CG*), 21 July and 4 Aug. 1888.

23. See the figure later in this chapter for the version of this coat of arms incorporated into Belize's national flag.

24. The presence of blackface minstrels in the 1888 jubilee and the 1898 and 1899 battle anniversary parades is fascinating but uninterpretable because the identities of the minstrels are unknown. As recent minstrelsy scholarship shows, the meaning of blackface is highly dependent on players, audience, and local context. See, for example, Leslie S. Katz, " 'Julius the Snoozer': Independence Day in Blackface," *Theatre History Studies* 13 (1993):

17–32, and Annemarie Bean, James V. Hatch, and Brooks McNamara, eds., *Inside the Minstrel Mask: Readings in Nineteenth-Century Blackface Minstrelsy* (Hanover, N.H.: Wesleyan University Press, 1996).

25. *CG*, 28 July 1888.

26. These claims have been debunked in O. Nigel Bolland, "Slavery in Belize," in *Colonialism and Resistance in Belize: Essays in Historical Sociology* (Belize: Cubola/ISER/SPEAR, 1988), 61–65, and Anne S. Macpherson, "Viragoes, Victims, and Volunteers: Female Political Cultures in Nineteenth-Century Belize," in *Belize: Selected Proceedings from the Second Interdisciplinary Conference*, ed. Michael Phillips (Lanham, Md.: University Press of America, 1996), 23–44.

27. *CG*, 25 Mar. and 1 Apr. 1893. For further details on the People's Hall, see *CG*, 24 Jan. and 14 Feb. 1891, 19 Mar. and 13 Aug. 1892, 11 and 18 Mar., 8 July, and 23 and 30 Dec. 1893.

28. *CG*, 14 Sept. 1888, cited in Judd, "Elite Reproduction," 225.

29. *CG*, 5 Oct. 1889.

30. *CG*, 8 Mar. 1890.

31. *CG*, 19 Apr. 1890.

32. *CG*, 31 May 1890.

33. *CG*, 25 Oct. 1890.

34. *CG*, 27 Dec. 1890.

35. *CG*, 24 May and 6 Dec. 1890.

36. *CG*, 6 Dec. 1890.

37. Findlay, *Imposing Decency*, chap. 3, finds that Puerto Rican artisans drew similar boundaries in Ponce in the 1890s, culminating in an antiprostitution campaign.

38. *CG*, 24 Jan. 1891.

39. *CG*, 15 Aug. and 5 Dec. 1891.

40. *CG*, 23 Jan. 1892.

41. *CG*, 3 Dec. 1892.

42. Shoman, *13 Chapters*, 176–77.

43. Every issue of the *Colonial Guardian* from 22 Dec. 1894 to 2 Feb. 1895 mentions women in coverage of testimony from rioters' trials.

44. *CG*, 20 Apr. 1895.

45. *CG*, 16 Mar. 1895.

46. *CG*, 19 Jan. 1895.

47. *CG*, 6 Apr. 1895.

48. *CG*, 9 Feb. 1895.

49. *CG*, 4 May 1895.

50. *CG*, 7 and 14 Dec. 1895, 8 and 15 Feb. 1896.

51. *CG*, 18 Apr. 1896.

52. *CG*, 8 May 1897.

53. *CG*, 26 June 1897.

54. *CG*, 11 Sept. 1897.

55. Judd, "Elite Reproduction," 227–28, citing *CG*, 2 Sept. 1898.

56. Ferrer, *Insurgent Cuba*, 117–22.

57. *CG*, 9 Apr. 1898.

58. On the Usher, Fairweather, and Haylock family histories, see Judd, "Elite Reproduction," 240, 257, 249.

59. *CG*, 17 Sept. 1898.

60. On early battle celebrations, see *CG*, 16 Sept. 1899, 15 Sept. 1900, 14 Sept. 1901, 13 Sept. 1902, 12 Sept. 1903, 10 Sept. 1904, 16 Sept. 1905, 15 Sept. 1905, 22 Sept. 1906.

61. Anne S. Macpherson, " 'Those Men Were So Coward': The Gender Politics of Social Movements and State Formation in Belize, 1912–1982" (Ph.D. diss., University of Wisconsin–Madison, 1998), chap. 3.

62. Ibid.

63. Antonio Soberanis Gómez and Luke D. Kemp, *The Third Side of the Anglo-Guatemalan Dispute over Belize or British Honduras* (Belize: Open Forum, 1949). Kemp wrote the introduction, but the body of the pamphlet seems to be Soberanis's independent work.

64. Ibid., 7–8, emphasis in original. Peter Linebaugh and Marcus Buford Rediker, in *The Many-Headed Hydra: Sailors, Slaves, Commoners, and the Hidden History of the Revolutionary Atlantic* (Boston: Beacon Press, 2000), 268–72, portray the slaveowning Baymen as white. The mythmakers of the 1890s made the same implication for different reasons.

65. *Daily Clarion*, 3 Sept. 1952.

66. Bolland, *Formation of a Colonial Society*, 42, indicates that of 693 women in the Bay Settlement in 1790, 46 were white, 132 were free colored, and 515 were slaves. The corresponding numbers for 1803 are 50, 275, and 675.

67. A black national identity has never become normative in Belize, given its multiracial character and the nationalist movement's promotion of a Central American/Mayan national identity in the 1960s. In Trinidad and Guyana, with their large East Indian populations, assertions of a normative black national identity have proved tragically divisive.

CHAPTER FIVE

FROM REVOLUTION TO INVOLUTION IN THE EARLY CUBAN REPUBLIC

Conflicts over Race,
Class, and Nation,
1902–1906

Lillian Guerra

Late in the afternoon of 21 May 1902, a day after U.S. military forces had formally ceded control of the island of Cuba to elected Cuban officials, festivities in the downtown districts of Havana had long since died down. Yet in the black working-class neighborhood of Jesús, María y José on the outskirts of the city, national celebrations inaugurating the republic had given way to gatherings of a different kind. At a rented house on Jesús Peregrino Street, eighty to ninety men added the sonic tones of *claves*, hand-held wooden sticks, to the rhythm of African drums as three elaborately costumed *diablitos*, or tricksters, danced what a participant later called "*el ñáñigo*." Suddenly, a shout rang out from the doorway. Those who heard it jumped through windows or climbed over patio walls to escape. The *diablitos*, a mulatto and two whites, ran for an inner room where they struggled (with little success) to free themselves of their attire. Police identified and captured all three, together with their costumes.[1] Within minutes, the raid netted a total of fifty-nine prisoners, among them twenty-five mulattos, thirty-two blacks, and two whites. All were gainfully employed, fifty-one of them skilled artisans.[2]

After looting the house on Jesús Peregrino and confiscating hundreds of objects including sacrificial roosters and carved wooden staffs (*palos mecongos*), police took the men to headquarters.[3] Despite most prisoners' summary denials, police charged them with being *ñáñigos*, members of a secret society known as the Abakuá that practiced African-derived rituals and beliefs.[4] At least one prisoner, who had crossed the bay from his home in Regla (the historical focal point of Abakuá activity) to attend the event, protested. The purpose of the gathering, he said, was to celebrate the new republic.[5] Regardless, police officers justified the arrest on the grounds that the Abakuá society "had been recognized as criminal" through public consensus and had been "persecuted and punished from time immemorial." In setting bond at the exorbitant level of $1,000 per defendant, the district court judge apparently concurred. Authorities charged the men with violating Article 186 of the Spanish Penal Code and Order 109, issued by the U.S. Military Government in 1899. Eventually, the judge found them guilty of "illicit association."[6]

Defense attorneys did not contest the "savage" origins or "barbaric" practices of the society. Rather, they argued that the arrest itself was legally invalid. Throughout the proceedings, the defense accused the court of deliberately ignoring key articles of the 1901 Cuban constitution whose sanctity its officers had sworn to protect. These articles annulled preexisting legal codes, especially laws restricting or violating the civil rights that the constitution granted all citizens, including the right of assembly and of association.[7] In December 1902, Cuba's Supreme Court upheld the lower court's conviction and sentence.[8] Ironically, neither the district court judge nor the judges of the Supreme Court had relied on Spanish legal precedents to render their verdicts. If they had, most of the men arrested would have been freed without charge. Only those shown to be leaders of the Abakuá would have served any jail time.[9] In other words, Cuba's republican judiciary defied the new constitution to interpret Spanish law even more rigidly than the Spanish had. The men's "crime" was their membership in a fraternal organization whose character transgressed the boundaries of what officials of the new republic considered ideologically acceptable expressions of identity and affinity with the nation.

As one of the first criminal trials of the new republic, this case illustrates the debate on the meaning of freedom that lay at the core of Cuba's political struggle to form a viable nation-state in the early twentieth century. Embedded in this debate were three distinct approaches to citizenship, race, and nation that key political actors in the early republic adopted and fought over for years to come. Class and race became salient features of political conflict precisely because they formed the referential axes that distinguished each sector's vision of nation from that of the others.

Like the judge and prosecution in the *ñáñigos'* trial, social conservatives at the helm of Cuba's first republican administration confined their interpretation of the nation and its citizenry to those Cubans who adhered to cultural values typified by the colonial elite. Most state officials appointed by President Tomás Estrada Palma had served as civilian leaders of Cuba's last independence war of 1895–98. Yet once in power, these officials actively supported Estrada Palma's goals of fusing a modernizing republic onto the social order of a Spanish colonial past. During the first several months of the republic, conservatives' disdain for social elements they considered inimical to Cuba's embrace of modernity extended toward white Cubans. These included working-class whites who expressed solidarity with blacks as well as liberal politicians whose presumed ideological kinship with black veterans of the 1895 war threatened the state's moral, cultural, and political authority. Popular resistance to state efforts to enforce a Hispanophilic vision of nation led Estrada Palma and his supporters to racialize their policies of social control and ideological exclusion. Ultimately, they promoted European immigration in order to jump-start the cultural process of homogenization through biological engineering. Their goal was to construct a wholly Europeanized society that matched their vision of a Cuban nation stocked with ideal, white citizens.

In contrast, liberal leaders of the political opposition acted much as the defense lawyers in the 1902 trial of the *ñáñigos* had. On the one hand, liberals refused to concede the cultural legitimacy of popular-class clients' efforts to express an identity or affinity for the nation in non-European or creolized, African-derived terms. On the other hand, liberals did not condemn the continued coexistence of difference among citizens as long as citizens subsumed expressions of difference into political channels that liberals controlled. From 1902 to 1906, liberal leaders understood the relationship of race to nation in meritocratic terms: they wanted to re-orient society away from colonial norms by developing lines of political patronage and a gradual, top-down process of social change. This liberal national vision incorporated key lessons not only from the military experience of commanding and controlling an impoverished guerrilla army but also from a U.S. occupation that had made a mockery of the Cuban revolutionaries' claim to national sovereignty. Thus, liberal promises to include the popular classes as state constituents rested on two conditions. First, the popular classes could only articulate grievances against the state through the historic, war-tested discourse of raceless social unity that liberals, as the most progressive of Cuba's pro-independence leaders, had officially championed. Second, any autonomous political action by popular-class activists constituted a betrayal of liberal authority and an invitation for the United States to intervene.

In this sense, "racelessness" as the foundation of the liberals' nation implied a toleration of racial and cultural differences among citizens only to the extent that they recognized liberals' authority as a political elite. Thus, even as they lambasted the pro-Spanish posture of the Estrada Palma administration, liberal leaders, both white and black, failed to condemn de facto discrimination against blacks and the racial preferencing of Spaniards in government policy. For most liberal leaders, Cuban identity remained "raceless" so long as the cultural standards of the educated middle and upper classes reigned supreme. If, in asserting equality, blacks who could not measure up to such standards promoted an alternative, African-derived or autonomous, mixed Creole identity instead, liberals were not above changing their tune. At key moments between 1902 and 1906, liberals withdrew their support from striking workers and black veteran activists as testament to the political conditions they imposed on citizens for inclusion in the nation. Workers whose activism not only crossed racial lines but also derived its cultural or ideological authority from outside the ranks of the liberal political elite threatened the liberal nation. Such activists violated the means by which this nation had been made possible in the 1895 war: adherence to a political order based on a meritocratic social hierarchy.

The inclusion of white, black, and mulatto Cubans at the Abakuá celebration of the new republic in 1902 reveals how differently popular-class Cubans and political elites interpreted the nation and its foundational principles of citizenship. Rather than seeing the nation as the projection of the state, like conservative supporters of Estrada Palma, or as the projection of a patron-client power structure, like the liberals, popular-class activists interpreted the nation on their own terms. Although the working-class and African-descended rank-and-file of the 1895 war perceived and defined race in a variety of ways, they saw the past as more intrinsic to contemporary discussions of race in relationship to nation and state policy than either liberal or conservative leaders did. If the colony had entailed state repression of individual rights through enslavement and persecution, then the republic required subversion of those legacies in all forms. Those whom the colony had marginalized or oppressed were, by default, the nation's originators and the republic's citizens. Like the *ñáñigos* who included whites in an African-derived cultural practice, popular-class Cubans espoused a form of *mestizaje* as the foundation of the nation. Closer to common meanings of "*mestizaje*" as a racial and cultural mixture, the *mestizaje* at the core of the popular-classes' nation was more egalitarian than the racial and cultural homogeneity conservatives preferred or the meritocratic heterogeneity that liberals offered. Like the multiracial, culturally mixed *juego de ñáñigos* in Havana's working-class barrio, the fraternal nation projected through the actions of organized workers and black veteran activists in the first years of the republic admitted all males to citizenship. It also implicated the state as the primary defender of their right to promote social change.

This essay argues that, as illustrated in the judicial system's 1902 trial of the *ñáñigos*, political elites within and outside the state offered black and working-class activists little chance for engagement in the early years of the republic. Through an analysis of the black veterans' movement, the general strike of 1902, and the culmination of the state's Hispanophilia in the call for white immigration, this work tracks disagreements over the meaning of nation in terms of state policies. In particular, it analyzes the degree to which debates over these policies included or excluded discussions of race as a cultural, historical, or biological marker. In short, this essay seeks to explain the process by which political elites moved away from revolution, defined here as the inversion of the colonial order, as a mandate for guiding and justifying their actions in the republic. As a result of their encounters with the popular classes, political elites turned increasingly toward political involution, the selective retrieval and incorporation of the colonial order as the basis for political power. Both conservative and liberal ex-revolutionaries participated equally, if differently, in this process. Ultimately, conservative culpability and liberal complicity in the republic's political involution led to declining possibilities for popular-class activists to foreground class-specific demands or race-conscious critiques of continuing inequalities in their calls for social change.

The first four years of the republic demonstrate how advocates of at least three different visions of nation fought to see the state fulfill three very different agendas. To the extent that both conditional toleration through acculturation and exclusionary racialization characterized the ideologies and actions of Cuba's political elites, the early years of the Cuban republic represent a transition between the second and third moments of the historical process of nation building in Latin America. Although forged in a hemispheric context defined by the "civilizing" impulse to modernize and by scientific racism, Cuban independence was both ideologically and practically the product of mass mobilizations. As a result, Cuba's conservatives experimented with positivism while liberals weighed the potential for corporatism as guiding political ideologies. Like most elites of early-twentieth-century Latin America, neither Cuba's liberals nor its conservatives could escape demands articulated from below. Cuban conservatives responded to such demands with policies of social control. Cuban liberals turned to softer methods of conditional engagement for the purpose of social containment.

TRACING THE ORIGINS OF DIVERGENT INTERPRETATIONS OF RACE AND NATION IN CUBA

Recently historians have struggled to untangle the paradox of Cuba's official commitment to a "raceless" national identity during the 1895 war and the contradictory interpretations Cubans subsequently derived from that commitment in the early years of the republic. The relationship between race and nation building in the early republic hinged on the contradiction between Cuba's revolutionary discourse of liberation and the political practice to which this discourse gave rise before and after 1902.

In the first in-depth study of the dynamic between race and nation in Cuba, Aline Helg posits that the revolution produced a "myth of racial equality" rather than racial equality itself. Helg argues that by militarily and discursively including blacks in the 1895 revolution, white leaders exempted the state and wealthy elites from having to pay restitution for slavery or promoting state policies in favor of the former slaves. Consequently, Helg contends, the myth of racial equality trapped Cubans of color in an impossible position in the republic. If they protested continuing discrimination on the basis of race, whites accused them of betrayal. Conversely, if Cubans of color conformed to the myth, they became participants in their own sector's political demise.[10] Helg's work thus set the stage for historians to question why the promise of racelessness promoted during the 1895 war contrasted so sharply with the continuing reality of discrimination in the republic.

Ada Ferrer's work on Cuba's thirty-year independence struggle (1868–98) contends that the effacing of racial identities and race-based rights within the revolution, rather than asserting racial equality, came to form the bedrock of political discourse and ideology on nation. Ferrer finds that the revolutionary leadership's official commitment to anti-racism—not necessarily the conceptual equivalent of racial equality—constituted both a point of attraction for Cubans of all social classes and a central tension in the independence process. This "rhetoric of anti-racism" not only facilitated the recruitment and inclusion of a majority of poor black and mixed-race soldiers in the Liberating Army, it also facilitated the advancement of black Cubans through the ranks of the army. Ultimately, the language of "raceless nationality," Ferrer argues, allowed white revolutionaries to claim that the transcendence of race had already occurred in the revolution even as some black revolutionaries insisted that the contrary was still true and much was left for the republic to do.[11]

Alejandro de la Fuente extends Ferrer's view into the early decades of nation building and state formation. For de la Fuente, the language of raceless nationality led to an ideology of racial democracy among political elites that Cubans of African descent used to their advantage. Finding Helg's assertions of white political leaders' hypocrisy exaggerated, de la Fuente sees the combination of the republic's ideology of raceless nationality and the preexisting system of social mobility through cultural whitening as useful to blacks. In this sense, blacks used the flexibility of official discourses on nation to their advantage just as they had during the independence wars.[12]

Certainly, recent historiography on the development of race and nation building in the Cuban republic differs dramatically in the conclusions it draws. For Helg, Cubans of African descent could not advance unless they did so on hypocritical terms set up by whites. For de la Fuente and Ferrer, Cubans of African descent recognized the limitations of raceless *cubanidad* that largely white political leaders offered, but they also responded to the conditions it posed and, especially as individuals, benefited from its inclusionary features. Yet, despite their interpretive differences, these scholars elicit similar questions based on a common premise: while raceless identity served as the conceptual starting point for imagining the nation in war, Cubans held contrasting interpretations of what this would mean for state policies in the republic.

This essay explores how the inherent flexibility of discourses of raceless national identity derived from the 1895 war masked conflicting interpretations of nation as they emerged in the republic. As such, it responds to two key questions that these recent works collectively open up. First, to what degree were differing interpretations of "race" itself embedded in differing visions of nation? Second, how does privileging the concept of nation as the primary lens for an analysis of race and class help explain Cuba's political development more broadly? This study responds to these questions by finding evidence of conflicting visions of nation in political battles over the state.

CONSTRUCTING AND COUNTERING A HISPANOPHILE STATE: RACE, IDENTITY, AND THE STRUGGLE OVER THE NATION

Rather than break with the colonial laws, social mores, or authoritarian policies of the colonial past, Cuba's first national government under Estrada Palma adopted official positions and enacted measures that built on Cuba's colonial legacies. These measures repressed civil liberties, marginalized popular-class interests, and consolidated the plantation system as the basis for a foreign-dominated capitalist economy. After 1902, Estrada Palma's administration actively courted foreign investment while native planters found little government support to aid their financial recovery in the wake of war.[13] As Estrada Palma carefully put it, the role of the state was to inculcate in Cuban society the value of "work which ennobles, peace which enriches, order which secures . . . and the discreet exercise of liberty."[14] His aristocratic vice president, Luis Estévez y Romero, was even more blunt. Selectively invoking the words of José Martí in the revolution's Manifesto of Montecristi, Estévez y Romero assured that the republic would be "a tranquil home for all those Spaniards of work and honor who should like to enjoy liberty and the wealth that they might not find even . . . in their own homeland." Oddly absent from this vision were the majority of the revolution's soldiers, most of whom were still desperately poor.[15] Pronounced only days before the inauguration of the republic, these words proved prophetic. Upon taking office, Estrada Palma moved immediately to install the old civilian leadership of conservative emigrés who had organized the war effort in the United States through the Partido Revolucionario Cubano (PRC), or Cuban Revolutionary Party, as the core of his cabinet. He also reserved key cabinet positions, including the Ministries of Governance, Finance, and Justice, for the primary leaders of the pro-Spanish Autonomist Party—all former enemies of Cuban independence and proponents of a Hispanic identity for Cuba.[16] In courting Spanish loyalists, Estrada Palma confirmed a pattern of appointments and a style of government instituted by the U.S. military over the previous four years. From the earliest days of the U.S. intervention, U.S. officials had worked hard to construct what historian Louis A. Pérez calls "the Cuban absence" from their own victory over the Spanish.[17] Rather than appointing Cuban revolutionaries to positions of power in municipal governments and the judiciary, U.S. interventionists often preferred to maintain at their posts the very loyalist officials against whom they had just fought in war and whose rule they had demonized in the U.S. press. As Estrada Palma would do later, they also overlooked military officers of the Liberating Army in favor of English-speaking former emigrés, often U.S. citizens, or conservative members of the planter class, whose inclination to maintain the social status quo U.S. officials found appealing.[18]

Estrada Palma, however, was not merely imitating U.S. strategies of coopting Spanish loyalists as an ideological bulwark against the revolutionary potential of the Cuban rebel leadership. Long before the United States intervened in Cuba in 1898, Estrada Palma had already calculated the benefits of including Spaniards in state priorities. In writing a U.S. businessman with investments in Cuba in December 1895, Estrada Palma reassured him that after the war had ended, Cuba would be "the home of Cubans and Spaniards, who, as members of the same family, will live in peace and harmony, as members of the same nation. . . . Once the war ends, those dignified Spaniards should continue living in Cuba, because they, as a [social] element of hard work and order, should serve . . . to give impetus [and] the right direction to the young Republic."[19] Thus, the PRC leadership's earliest expressions of a national vision took Martí's pledge to condemn the Spanish government while embracing Spanish residents to an extreme. After 1902, Estrada Palma's inclusion of Spaniards came at the cost of excluding Cubans of African descent. Oriente representative Antonio Póveda de Ferrer made precisely this point when he wrote Estrada Palma to demand that he confine his appointments to Cubans who had favored independence. Moreover, Póveda de Ferrer insisted that the government standardize the language with which all citizens were addressed by authorities of the state in line with the policies of the 1895 revolution. Representing in practice the raceless nationality that Martí and other independence writers proposed in theory, documents produced by Cuba's Liberating Army had made no reference to soldiers' race. In dramatic contrast with Spanish colonialism's long-term practice, members of the rebel army and its government strictly prohibited racial labeling in public records or racialized forms of address. Instead, they addressed one another with the title of "citizen," a practice that undoubtedly did much to fuel black soldiers' confidence in the equality and rewards to which their service entitled them in the republic.[20] The republic's unexpected return to the Spanish colonial policy of addressing Cuban citizens by their racial identities, Póveda de Ferrer wrote, "deeply disgusts and humiliates the social classes who deserve and have a perfect right to demand that they be treated with all due respect. We are living under the command of a democratic Constitution that does not establish privileges of any kind among the diverse members of the Cuban family. Mr. President, in order to suppress this aged and undignified practice, a bottomless source of definite bitterness for mulattos and blacks, there are reasons of internal politics, of moral order and of patriotic convenience that doubtlessly, should be evident to a just and good soul as yours, Mr. President."[21]

This practice represented a key aspect of the administration's policies for building its version of an ideal Hispanic Cuban nation that paralleled similar policies of the U.S. military's interventionist government. In 1900 a delegation of Cubans had presented Governor Leonard Wood with a similar petition, asking him to decree the prohibition of racial epithets in public discourse and documents. Like Póveda de Ferrer, they proposed that the term "citizen" should be employed instead because Cuba's "colored race has already proved its value and capability." But Wood, convinced that Cuban blacks would rebel and establish another "Hayti" if encouraged to believe in their social worth and equality, ignored the petition.[22]

In both the 1900 and the 1902 cases, black veterans protested the orientation of public policy away from wartime revolutionary norms—norms they interpreted as actively subverting the legitimacy of the Spanish colonial past. That both the U.S. military and Cuba's first independent state endorsed a hierarchical structuring of Cuban society along traditional racial lines was alarming. During the war, leaders had insisted that Cuban identity was raceless. At the same time, PRC officials (like Estrada Palma) had constantly sought to downplay the mass participation of black Cubans to the U.S. government, press corps, and public.[23] With the cessation of hostilities with Spain, actions by different sets of leaders that had once seemed coordinated and motivated by the same ideological end—the inclusion and equal treatment of blacks—now acquired a wholly different ideological edge. Parallels in the policies of the U.S. and Estrada Palma administrations cast the latter's historic motivations in a new light, setting them apart from popular-class veterans' expectations.

Unlike Wood's petitioners, Póveda de Ferrer did not include in his demands the explanation that Cubans of African descent were entitled to legal equality with whites because of their service on behalf of independence. Since he was addressing a fellow revolutionary, he probably believed he did not have to. But events in 1902 quickly proved this perspective wrong. During the first year of the republic, the state coupled a discursive silence on race with blatantly discriminatory hiring policies for government positions—including the army, the Rural Guard, and the police. Because applications for government jobs required high educational qualifications and social references (both standards to which only a tiny number of black Cubans could have aspired), government posts were disproportionately allocated to Spaniards and former opponents of the revolution. Many black Cubans who worked in government offices did so as messengers and office boys. Some areas of government, such as the diplomatic corps, were entirely limited to whites. Over twice as many Spaniards worked for the Estrada Palma government as blacks.[24] Moreover, even when black Cubans were hired, their reception by employees of the same division was not necessarily tolerant. Nor, it seemed, did the state require it to be.[25]

Black veterans and conservative officials viewed continuing evidence of racial discrimination in the new republic through the ideological filter of their respective views of nation. Not surprisingly, black veterans demanded state action to correct the social disadvantages that Cuba's colonial past conferred on blacks. Conservatives justified state inaction with the inverse argument, that is, that blacks had already freed themselves of the past by securing Cuba's freedom. "In Free Cuba," the president declared, "we are now all of the same color." This meant that candidates for civil service would be evaluated on their "merits," just as Martí had promised. But "merits," as Estrada Palma defined them, meant that Cubans were employed "according to their capacity." Fulfilling the duties of civil service in a civilized government required educational training and the "higher" cultural values of white, elite society that in his view—and by default, the view of his subordinates—most black Cubans lacked.[26] To veterans, on the other hand, "merits" implied proof of prior service to the nation as a prerequisite to the ultimate employment security that working for the state offered, in contrast to the wider economy.[27] Estrada Palma's failure to honor such service and his determination to require social and educational standards beyond the reach of most veterans implied a betrayal of their interpretation of the nation even as it put into practice conservatives' own conflicting national view. Indeed, many veterans felt doubly discriminated against: first, for their African heritage and the educational differential that it necessarily implied, and second, for being forced to compete with former enemies of the revolution for jobs in a government that owed its existence to patriots like themselves.[28] By the summer of 1902, black veterans expressed their already mounting frustration with what they perceived as the state's ideological betrayal of the nation in a campaign that drew attention to the irony of their plight.

In June 1902 a group of black veterans requested an audience with the president and his new cabinet to lay out their grievances and explain the relationship between race and nation as they saw it. For this task, nine black mutual aid societies, led by a prominent veteran, General Generoso Campos Marquetti, organized a commission that eventually met with Estrada Palma for two hours. Campos Marquetti criticized the hiring process for government jobs, singling out Havana's police force as especially symbolic. Furthermore, he rejected the validity of political patronage as a means for attaining employment, which liberal opponents offered veterans as a counter to Estrada Palma's laissez-faire rule, pointing out that the only Cubans of color who held government jobs did so at the behest of Juan Gualberto Gómez (one of two mulatto congressmen). This was not a satisfying end in itself.[29]

Campos Marquetti later explained to reporters how he and Estrada Palma had come to loggerheads in the course of the meeting over what a nation founded on equality and democracy meant for state policy regarding race. While Campos Marquetti asserted that the state needed to actively champion the interests of black veterans, without whom the revolution would not have been possible, Estrada Palma countered that to make such a claim on racial grounds was to betray the raceless basis on which the revolution had been founded. "We went to the president to ask that he put the Eleventh Article of the Constitution [guaranteeing the equality of all Cubans] into practice and he tells us that our requests are inconvenient; we ask that the Republic might be established on a foundation of democracy and he responds that we are racists. We ask for access to public employment and the Chief of Police denounces as liars those who have not committed such a crime."[30] In response, Campos Marquetti concluded, "The truth is, Mr. President, this is not what we expected from the Revolution and things cannot continue like this."[31]

Three days later, a second commission of black Cubans, this time comprised entirely of veterans, met with the president. Significantly, the commission's primary representative was Colonel Evaristo Estenoz, the mulatto labor leader responsible for negotiating an end to Havana's 1899 general strike and obtaining management's consent to his union's principal demand of an eight-hour day. Estenoz articulated the frustration of veterans of color with state-sponsored racial favoritism of whites that masqueraded as nonracial, authentically "Cuban" nationalism. (Five years later, Estenoz founded a highly race-conscious political party for the same reason.) Delegates reiterated Campos Marquetti's view that a system of political patronage that admitted blacks to its ranks on the basis of convenience and tokenism was not democratic and most certainly *not* a goal for which they had fought. Such a system only used blacks while it ensured their continued lack of equal opportunity under the law.[32] The fact that Estrada Palma interpreted this policy of tokenism as ideologically true to the revolution's own tenets and practices especially angered these veterans. They wanted him to admit publicly the fitness of black Cubans for state jobs, whether or not they met the cultural standards that former colonial elites expected. As racially conscious activists who had joined the revolution to promote the interests of blacks, men like Estenoz could not understand their revolutionary experience in Estrada Palma's Hispanocentric terms. Essentially, the president's recalcitrance on racially discriminatory issues asked them to do precisely this—forsake their interpretation and their own memories of the revolution for his.

A few weeks later, the newly organized Association of Veterans of Color summoned black Cubans of various political and social persuasions to a historic meeting at Havana's Teatro Albisu. Its purpose was to discuss possible strategies of response to the state's complete inaction on racial and veterans' issues.[33] Representative Gualberto Gómez served as moderator; conspicuously absent was Martín Morúa Delgado, the only nonwhite member of the Senate, a staunch supporter (at the time) of Estrada Palma and a former factory reader among emigré tobacco workers. Having opposed the veterans' movement altogether on philosophical grounds, Morúa declared the meeting counter to the goals of the revolution and refused to attend.[34] While much spirited debate dominated the session, Gómez's concluding speech summarized the tone and course of action that he and most other national leaders of the liberal opposition—both white and black—would adopt. His message was ironic, for it combined items stipulated in the PRC's Manifesto of Montecristi with the strategy Martí had used to refute Spanish claims about black rebels that were meant to discredit the revolution by characterizing the independence struggle as nothing more than a glorified race war, meant to establish another Haitian-style "black republic."[35]

Rather than admitting that continuing feelings of racial prejudice against blacks were a problem that neither the revolution nor emerging political elites had helped to resolve, Gómez blamed U.S. influence for any displays of racial hatred against blacks.[36] He did not see that the revolution's policy of silencing race and of subsuming the historic significance of racial identities in defining the social conditions of both white and black Cubans as problematic. "If one day," he warned, "—may it never come—the black race here needs to battle with the white, whether provoked or unprovoked, you will have to look for another man to advise you and guide you. Because I represent the politics of racial fraternity, and if this were to fail, the feeling of honor, the respect which I owe my past . . . would oblige me to disappear from the political scene, with the failure of my opinions."[37]

By contrast, black activists like Campos Marquetti and Estenoz recognized that silencing race could reinforce rather than eliminate prejudice. The fundamental racelessness of *cubanidad* that had once allowed Cubans to participate in the independence struggle as ostensibly equal citizens now served to justify continuing state discrimination against blacks. Once transferred from guerrilla war to republican reality, the ideal of racial fraternity that Martí and the revolutionary leadership had championed as a substitute for claiming racial equality between whites and blacks became precisely that, a substitute.

As revolutionary caudillos in their own right, Gómez and Morúa did not simply abnegate responsibility for the black condition by ascribing to the "politics of racial fraternity." Nor did they merely accommodate to the white-generated "myth of racial equality" that Helg describes.[38] Rather, Gómez and Morúa's positions on the relationship between race and nation extended from their experience as longtime civil rights activists under Spanish colonial rule. Each interpreted their support for revolutionary options in light of that experience. Judging from their past activities on behalf of civil rights under Spanish rule, Gómez and Morúa were committed to pursuing the social transformation and unification of their society in terms of race.[39] Gómez had once been responsible, together with Spanish abolitionist Rafael María de Labra, for winning major legal victories on behalf of black civil rights in Spain's Supreme Court.[40] But in joining the independence movement, he distanced himself from such strategies, demonstrating his commitment to Martí's ideal of racial fraternity through the struggle to liberate all Cubans. Moreover, Gómez saw his work as a journalist, lawyer, and coordinator of black mutual aid societies as beneficial to blacks, because at all levels he promoted the acculturation of black Cubans away from African-derived practices and beliefs as the first step toward social advancement.

Morúa too believed in education and the cultural integration of Cubans of African descent into the racially white, literate, and European-derived culture of the elite.[41] Where he differed fundamentally from Gómez was on the issue of whether such acculturation was a prerequisite to gaining *white* approval of such measures, or simply a prerequisite to *blacks'* suitability for equality. While Gómez was a cultural chauvinist who believed that all black Cubans' "inferiority" derived from their limited access to higher, European cultures, Morúa rooted arguments about the need for acculturation in references to biological difference. For Morúa, blacks were a separate race from mulattos, meaning that mulattos stood a greater chance of self-advancement than blacks because their genetic proximity to whites gave them an advantage. In this sense, Morúa emphasized the innate nature of race, whereas Gómez, like Martí, insisted that perceived racial distinctions only attested to differences of access to levels of education that whites had preferentially enjoyed, and to the supposedly "superior" European-derived culture that they acquired as a result. Thus, Morúa viewed race as the product of biology while Gómez viewed race as the extension of historically contingent circumstances. Prior to the founding of the republic, the two men had espoused very different strategies of political action. Gómez called for the fusion of blacks' and mulattos' political forces into one struggle for mutual liberation. Morúa believed that such an alliance was artificial and ultimately counterproductive as it encouraged whites to treat all Cubans of African descent the same, regardless of relative merit and no matter how remote the ancestry.[42]

Ironically, however much their approach to defining race differed, both Gómez and Morúa championed the ideal of racial fraternity for the same reason: they thought that the promotion of meritocracy served as an antidote to racial discrimination by whites. Ultimately, their mutual contempt for what they perceived as violations of racial fraternity in the republic yielded the same result. Both rejected the legitimacy of racial discourse within the Cuban nation. Consequently, they rejected the right of black veterans to define their place in the nation for themselves and on their own terms. Championing the ideal of racial fraternity allowed Morúa to continue to harbor his own prejudicial view of mulattos' superiority over blacks. It also lent his complicity both to conservatives, whose solution to racial discrimination was self-reliance, and to liberals, who abhorred black autonomy on principle. Gómez's unshakeable faith in the power of the ideal of racial fraternity, like that of Martí in the 1890s, was conditioned by the pragmatism of patriotism. Given the recent U.S. intervention, the potential for another one, and the pretext that any semblance of racial unrest might provide for such an action, Gómez thought that black veteran activists violated the ideal of racial fraternity by claiming that it did not exist. As such, they indicted the sanctity of the revolution, and thereby the stability of the republic.

In the end, Estrada Palma adopted an opportunistic attitude toward ameliorating the appalling economic circumstances of the majority of black veterans. In practical terms, this meant that he ignored black veteran activists while making a show of his appreciation for other black veterans whose passivity he took as compliance with his own ideals. Abandoning Havana at the height of black veterans' activism in the late summer of 1902, Estrada Palma traveled to his former home in Oriente to demonstrate his goodwill and ongoing relationships with other black veterans. There he acted out his interpretation of what being a good ruler meant through symbolic gestures and speeches meant to stroke the egos of local veterans for their service to the nation, if not their participation in it as equals. During the visit, Estrada Palma rewarded with government jobs select black officers who had *not* publicly criticized his administration or lent any support to the black veterans' movement.[43] These were men who did not contradict Estrada Palma's vision of a nation led and shaped by white men like himself. As such, their attitudes of apparent submission to his leadership merited reward.[44]

Only when angry veterans threatened a revolt did Estrada Palma's administration permit the payment of black veterans' war claims, although the greatest beneficiaries were black loyalists who later repaid the president's favoritism by endorsing his conservative "Moderate" Party, founded in 1904.[45] Unfortunately, the indemnities were too little too late for the thousands of veterans who had resorted to selling their claims to speculators and now faced excessive debts.[46] Moreover, the majority of veterans in some areas were so poor and dependent on their meager wages as agricultural workers that they could not even afford to travel to municipal seats of government to submit their claims.[47]

In the early months of the republic, the treatment of black veteran activists crystallized the political intransigence for which the state under Estrada Palma would become best known. Having believed that the legitimacy of blacks' participation during the war rested on his and others' tolerance of it, the president conceded no power to them after the war unless they submitted their vision of nation to the authority and scrutiny of his own. Indeed, Estrada Palma followed his forced concession of war payments to veterans with a series of symbolic actions that publicly reinforced the commitment of his administration to re-Hispanicizing the identity of Cubans and projecting this identity as a generalized vision of the nation through the state.

On 11 November 1902, the only black member of the Secret Police guarding the Presidential Palace received a letter from Estrada Palma's office stipulating that, in light of a reception to be held at the palace the following night, "the watchman for the night be a white person." The black detective, whose superiors had judged his job performance as impeccable until then, was understandably outraged.[48] Moreover, this was the same presidential reception that mulatto Senator Martín Morúa Delgado had declined to attend since President Estrada Palma had neglected to invite his wife and daughters.[49] *La República Cubana*, Juan Gualberto Gómez's paper, responded to these latest scandals with the most heated of challenges: "Is this in accordance with the doctrines of Martí, with the creed of the Revolutionary Party, with the democratic ideas for the triumph of which white and black heroes fought side by side? . . . We appeal to all sincere and dispassionate people. Is this right? . . . Is it right that in the Cuban *patria* which we all made together, colored men may only enter the Palace of the President as servants?"[50]

In a final insult to Cubans who espoused the ideal of racial fraternity, how-

ever they interpreted it, the reception itself culminated in the honorary be-
stowal of Asturian nationality on Estrada Palma by a group of his invited guests.
Flabbergasted, editors for the liberal daily *La Lucha* sarcastically hailed him:
"Long live the grandiose bash of Don Tomás! And long live as well the honorary
Asturian!"[51] Indeed, besides the obvious affront to the suffering and honor of
those who had fought in Cuba's thirty-year struggle against Spain, Estrada
Palma's acceptance of Asturian citizenship carried a weighty message of implicit racism against people of African descent in particular: historically, Asturias was the only province of Spain never entirely conquered and governed by
the darker-skinned Moors who invaded and ruled Iberia for 700 years prior to
1492. According to tradition, the prince or princess of Asturias retained a
preferential right of accession to the national crown of Spain.[52] Apparently, it
was precisely these implications that Estrada Palma and his guests found flatter-
ing. Despite the president's Creole pedigree and the fact that he had spent most
of his adult life in the United States rather than Cuba, Spanish residents had
admitted him to their historically noble and racially "pure" ranks.

By November 1902, both conservative and liberal political elites would confront a movement of social protest unlike any they had seen before in the
republic. Led by black and white tobacco workers, many of whom had formed
the core of working-class supporters of the PRC and of the revolution from exile
in Florida, a general strike paralyzed Havana and shook the foundations of
Cuba's political economy. Notably, the strikers' demands did not center on
wages, but rather on the practical implications of a republic founded on the
ideals of racial fraternity and social unity.

CONFRONTING THE MEANING(S) OF RACIAL FRATERNITY AND SOCIAL UNITY: WORKER DEFIANCE AND POLITICAL RECALCITRANCE IN THE GENERAL STRIKE OF 1902

On the same night that Estrada Palma accepted honorary membership in the
crème de la crème of Spanish society, the Central Committee of the General
League of Workers held an organizational meeting to prepare to strike.[53] Led by
tobacco workers from factories owned by the Havana Commercial Company
(HCC), a U.S. trust, these men and women readied themselves for a protracted
struggle. Their main grievance was not pay. Rather, strikers hoped to define
national interests in working-class terms and gain the right to organize for the
protection of those interests. Specifically, strikers sought to elect factory commissions whose authority as representatives of the workers would be recog-

nized by management. Because they were paid by the piece and had a greater knowledge of the quality of the materials with which they worked than their employers did, tobacco workers also wanted to be included in the pricing process for cigars, at the time the responsibility of management. Most important, tobacco workers wanted the HCC to guarantee that Cuban children would be admitted to the factories' apprenticeship programs in the cigar trade at all levels, without distinction of race or ethnicity.

In what was emerging as a general pattern, first under the U.S. military and then under Estrada Palma's administration, Spaniards enjoyed preferential treatment over Cubans in the U.S.-dominated cigar industry. Echoing the sentiments that Estrada Palma had expressed as early as 1895 in his letter to a U.S. investor, U.S. factory owners believed the Spanish to be of purer race and therefore capable of superior, more efficient work. Whereas in other sectors of the economy white Cubans seemed unwilling to side with black Cubans over the preferential hiring of Spaniards, Cuban workers in the cigar industry operated differently. According to census figures for this period, more than half of all native tobacco workers were identified as Cubans of color.[54] Indeed, the distinctions tobacco workers made among themselves were not based so much on race (as defined by the combination of biology, phenotype, culture, education, and wealth that tended to be the case when Cubans at large made distinctions among themselves) as on nationality. Thus, what one American labor analyst called "an element of race antagonism" between Spanish and Cuban tobacco workers, both black and white, may more accurately have been understood as an ideological and historical divide. Key players in Cuba's independence struggle and members of Martí's popular base for the PRC, Cuban tobacco workers identified themselves as guardians of the revolution's ideals. In the republic they institutionalized their difference from Spaniards, former enemies of independence, by forming their own unions within the same industry and even the same factories.[55]

A great number of Havana's tobacco workers were only recently returned emigrés from Florida. Since the 1880s, these Florida emigré communities had earned a reputation as hotbeds of labor activity. Indeed, many workers had fled Cuba for Florida because of Spanish persecution of their socialist and anarchist beliefs. In the early 1890s, these same tobacco workers formed a core of support for Martí in his efforts to broaden popular support for a new independence struggle. Martí had formulated the bases for the founding of the PRC in consultation with leaders of the emigré tobacco workers, including several prominent black labor activists. And it was in his speech to tobacco workers in Tampa that Martí first launched his project for a republic "with all and for the good of all," citing racial fraternity and cross-class social unity as the means for achieving it.[56]

Martí's ideals of racial fraternity among Cubans lay at the heart of strikers' demands. Strikers requested and gained the support of individuals close to Martí such as Fermín Valdéz Domínguez, a childhood friend of Martí and prominent veteran.[57] Using the idiom of nation and the right of access to its resources, strikers cajoled, intimidated, and challenged workers of other sectors of the economy to join their strike or become "traitors." Eventually, a wave of sympathy strikes paralyzed the regional economy, encompassing such diverse sectors as the Department of Public Works, sixty tobacco factories in three cities, college students at the University of Havana, breadbakers, and typographers. Significantly, the notoriously all-black Bahía dockworkers, whose strike under U.S. occupation in December 1899 had been brutally repressed by conservative former revolutionaries serving as a police force, also lent their support. Havana's bricklayers' union, which had gained the eight-hour day in the 1899 strike led by Estenoz, also supported the strike.[58] For his part, Estrada Palma initially countered news of the strike by attending a gala dinner for Cuban consuls at the Casino Español, a formerly royalist mulatto social club that received regular funds from the Crown for its expenses. Ironically, the Casino Español was best known for Martí's denunciations of it as a testament to Spain's duplicitous instrumentalism on race issues.[59]

Eventually, however, both the Estrada Palma administration and liberal opposition leaders mobilized to deal with the strike. With 15,000 workers participating within four days of its start, the strike interrupted Havana's commerce and halted the printing of city newspapers. In response, the administration issued 30,000 bullets to city police and ordered the national armed forces, or Rural Guard, on standby for duty on the streets of Havana. By 24 November, the Rural Guard had launched an all-out assault on crowds. Although press accounts put the tallies much higher, official statistics on casualties numbered at least 114 workers wounded, 80 imprisoned, and 5 dead.[60]

At the same time, only one liberal official, Juan O'Farrill, the mayor of Havana and a longtime resident in the cigar-making emigré communities of Florida, dared to side openly with the workers. For his efforts to rein in police and free workers held on legal charges that were unconstitutional, O'Farrill, along with individual workers and editors of anarchist newspapers, was tried by the Special Court set up in Havana in December to deal with the fallout of the strike. Although originally charged with sedition, Mayor O'Farrill was eventually convicted of the contradictory crimes of abuse of power and dereliction of duty. The state's official justification for creating the Special Court in blatant violation of the Cuban constitution was that the strikers had called into question both the viability and the stability of the republic. Not only did they jeopardize Cuban independence in the context of the Platt Amendment, but more important, conservatives argued, the barbarous and anarchic course of the strike had endangered the sanctity of civilization itself. If the state had not been there to defend civilization against its would-be assailants, the republic and the nation would have fallen.[61]

Liberal politicians did not offer the strikers much of an alternative. Although they initially attempted to mediate the strike, the objective of leaders such as Juan Gualberto Gómez and General Máximo Gómez in meeting with strikers was simply to defuse the situation by convincing them to back down. Brandishing the usual warning that autonomous actions by popular-class sectors undermined the future of the fatherland by angering the United States, Máximo Gómez was particularly blunt: "Public order should be inalterable. I am against all procedures which compromise public order." Although he refocused his comments on the ideal of cross-class social unity rather than racial fraternity, Juan Gualberto Gómez echoed the same message he had sent to black veteran activists only a few months before. Dismissing the workers' accusations that the former revolutionaries did not take their interests seriously, Gómez asserted that liberal leaders' authority should be the workers' first recourse to action. "We are not bourgeois nor are we representatives of the Government. We are simple mediators. And if it is said that the Fatherland is secondary, then we have no role here."[62]

The turning point in the strike came two days before the highest surviving officer of the 1895 revolution, Máximo Gómez, joined forces with the liberal opposition to mediate it. On 24 November, evidence of the greatest "threat" to the republic arrived at Estrada Palma's doorstep. That afternoon, a group of strikers wound their way down Obispo Street toward the Plaza de Armas, site of the Presidential Palace and the center of state power in Cuba. Stopping at Mayor O'Farrill's office, the strikers were carrying the body of a black worker who had been beaten by police. Bloody and half-conscious, the black worker was near death. Infuriated, the strikers demanded the suspension of the officer responsible. Although O'Farrill would not meet with them, he ordered that the wounded striker be cared for at the closest Casa de Socorros, an emergency aid facility operated by the Catholic Church. But the strikers would not go away. Frantic, O'Farrill turned to Estrada Palma's minister of government, Diego

Tamayo, who had been consulting with him over the fate of the strikers. Fearing that the Presidential Palace might be the strikers' next destination and panicked by the possibility that the mob might assault the president, O'Farrill and Tamayo ordered an immediate dispersal of the strikers by police. The police accomplished this feat in minutes, "*alcanzando palos hasta los mirones* [even to the point of beating bystanders]." Ironically, the liberal leader who later presented himself as a friend of peasants, workers, and especially black veterans against Estrada Palma in 1906 watched the spectacle from a nearby municipal office. Afterward, this famous liberal, General José Miguel Gómez, congratulated the police who attacked the unarmed demonstrators for their fine and effective performance on behalf of the nation.[63]

Ultimately, then, the liberal opposition's love of order and commitment to maintaining strict vertical lines of authority with the "masses" undermined the very ideals they insisted the striking workers no longer espoused. Indeed, the bleeding, wounded body of the black worker poignantly symbolized workers' defiance of such views. Signaling the urgency with which they insisted that political elites confront their own hypocrisy, strikers demanded that the republic conform to the meaning of racial fraternity and social unity as popular-class revolutionaries had understood it in the revolution. Thus, the brutalized body of the black man also embodied the colonial history of Cuba and all that the revolution had once promised that it would overthrow.

SAVING CUBA: WHITE IMMIGRATION AS THE
ULTIMATE SOLUTION TO RACE-CLASS DEFIANCE

The end of the general strike of 1902 marked a pivotal moment in the history of the First Republic. After 1902, the Estrada Palma administration increasingly turned a deaf ear to complaints from below. In the early months of 1903, opposition politicians' decision to found the Liberal Party as a mass-based organization and the possibility of new elections in 1904 and 1906 offered popular-class Cubans reason to hope, at least for the time being. However, Estrada Palma's conservative project for the nation took a decidedly radical turn beginning in 1904. By the spring of 1906, the administration achieved wide congressional support for a plan to re-racialize Cuba through the immigration of European, "naturally" hardworking, agricultural laborers. The purpose was to neutralize conflicts over a past shaped by slavery and revolutionary struggle by inoculating society with new blood and new cultures that augured a prosperous united future. It was a policy whose purported benefits for the culture and economy of future generations Estrada Palma had extolled for years. This view was also repeatedly promoted in the media and accepted by the vast majority of Cubans in the upper echelons of society. Through newspaper articles, rumors, and the criminalization of African-derived popular expression in this period, conservative elites and the Cuban state culturally mystified the lower classes, depicting them as contaminated by violent instincts or perverse tendencies born of a mixed, nonwhite racial heritage.[64] Between 1903 and 1906, conservative supporters of Estrada Palma adopted a social-scientific rationale that underscored the state's promotion of white immigration.

Underlying this rationale was the idea that until independence, Cuba had gone about solving its need for cheap agricultural labor in ways detrimental to the cultural evolution and economic modernization of the country. As Dr. Juan Santos Fernández, president of the Academy of Sciences, argued in 1906, Estrada Palma's espousal of Spanish immigration represented the best, untried solution to Cuba's social and cultural stagnation vis-à-vis the rapid evolution of other countries such as Germany and the United States. As in ancient Greece, the attention of these countries to the physical characteristics of their populations had produced the kind of "vigorous people" responsible for their unsurpassed standard of progress.[65]

Because Cuba had relied on "immigration" from Africa, Yucatán, and Asia to solve its short-term labor problems in the nineteenth century, Santos Fernández contended, it had jeopardized the long-term prospects and proliferation of its people. The supposedly inferior characteristics of these races only reinforced in their descendants the "impulsive forces that produce the political crime of rebellion." The presumed effects of a tropical climate on human passions had already naturalized this condition in Cubans, he continued. Apparently as reluctant to acknowledge the horrors of the recent war as he was the use of slave labor in the past, Santos Fernández argued that the island's current low density of population was evidence of the infertility and unviability of its racially mixed people. In Latin America and the Caribbean, he claimed, racial mixing had caused the nobler features of "purer" races to mutate and reappear "as they do in animals; from there comes the regressive savage type, the cruel, thieving, hypocritical atavist."[66] Citing the famous dictum of the early-nineteenth-century Argentine statesman Juan Bautista Alberdi, "To govern is to populate," Santos Fernández confirmed the belief current among European scientists that Spanish workers were the racial group most adaptable to the unique challenges of hard labor in the tropics. To build the Panama Canal, even the United States had turned to Spain; in order to assure a prosperous future built on the foundations of large-scale agricultural production, concluded Santos Fernández, so must Cuba.[67]

Incredibly, while black leaders such as Morúa, black newspapers such as *El Nuevo Criollo*, and the labor press denounced the immigration proposal, all strategically avoided its racial and racist dimensions, ostensibly to gain broad support among the newly constituted party of Liberals.[68] Conservative proponents took the opposite tack, openly couching their arguments in favor of white immigration on explicitly racial grounds. Before the black veterans' movement and the general strike of 1902, many of the same proponents touted the project in strictly cultural terms, referring to it as an antidote to the decline of Hispanic customs and norms in the republic.[69] By 1906, however, proponents felt little need to disguise overtly biological racial arguments in a discourse that reified culture.

By the time the proposal for state-sponsored immigration made it to the floor of Congress in February 1906, the administration, conservative ex-revolutionaries, and the vast majority of former Spanish loyalists, now organized as Moderates, had constructed a vast political machine. It favored guns and terror as a means of consolidating a monopoly on local as well as national political power.[70] As a result, the bill titled "Project for an Immigration Law and National Growth" can be understood as an ideological manifesto representing the extremes to which this sector, led by Estrada Palma, would go in fulfilling its own ideal vision of the nation. Article 10 of the bill stipulated which immigrants the state favored and whose passage it agreed to sponsor. "Individuals of the Caucasian race may consider themselves sheltered under this law," the bill read, as long as such individuals demonstrate their "good conduct and laboriousness in the country or countries of prior residence." Article 17 further explained which groups were "excluded from the privileges which this law concedes." Among these were the "individuals and families of the race of color, be they black, Malaysians, Mongoloid, of the Oceanic races as well as the copper-toned and all mestizos, and the gypsies also known as *zíngaros*."[71]

Asserting that the "state of agitation and chronic turbulence" of Latin American nations since their independence had driven European immigrants north to the United States, the bill's proponents explained the logic behind their plan for national development in this way:

This constant migratory current [to the United States] has powerfully contributed to the making of the American Union, in little less than a century, into one of the richest, most civilized, progressive and powerful peoples of the earthly globe; meanwhile, the nations of Latin origin remained stationary, backward, poor, and some, because of their innumerable revolts, arrived even at the brink of barbarity. Among these peoples, fortunately, various heard the striking of the hour in time [to establish] order, work and peace—Mexico, Chile, the Republic of Argentina and Brazil, opened their doors to European immigration, which has begun to leave its benevolent influence on the progress of those peoples of our race. . . . *There are no opinions contrary to the idea of fomenting a white population; all agree on the necessity of attracting as quickly as possible the greatest number of European families who may be settled in our countryside, to contribute with their number, their example, their activity and their energy to develop production, helping us to consolidate the bases on which to set our contemporary institutions.*[72]

As supporters of the law clearly articulated, their aim was *not* to make Cuba an appendage to the United States but a leader among Latin American peoples, equally as strong, economically productive, and "racially" vibrant as the North and Latin America's leaders to the south, such as Argentina and Brazil. Representing a historical understanding of the Cuban nation that contradicted at all levels the liberals' interpretation of the nation as well as that of black veterans and workers, this document ignored and thereby defied the foundational promise of a republic built on racial fraternity and social unity. Seen through the lens of this bill, the republic's survival and progress depended on its ability to expunge the problematic, conflicting elements of its historical past. Reracializing Cuban society was the only alternative to the demise of a viable, culturally and biologically white nation.

Significantly, the bill that President Estrada Palma eventually signed into law on 11 July 1906 did not mention racial exclusions—a circumstance owed mainly to the efforts of black congressmen. With Juan Gualberto Gómez fraudulently defeated in the elections of 1905, Morúa and Rafael Serra, a onetime supporter of Estrada Palma, worked ceaselessly to impede passage of the law with these provisions in the Senate. Nonetheless, sponsors of the bill traded an explicit definition of which groups the law *excluded* for a more specific definition of which groups it *included*. Of the $1 million made available for the payment of immigrants' passage to Cuba, $800,000 was earmarked for immigrants from Europe and the Canary Islands. Apparently aimed at increasing the preponderance of "Aryan" features in Cuba's population, the law apportioned all remaining funds for the exclusive recruitment of laborers from Sweden, Norway, Denmark, and northern Italy.[73] The result was the same: denied their critical contributions to Cuba's past, blacks now had no future in the Cuban nation as conservatives imagined it. A new Cuban nation would emerge, embodied by new Cubans: white, docile, and energetic servants of their masters' republican state.

CONCLUSION

As early as the closing days of 1902, the possibilities that either the state or the political opposition could ameliorate historic conditions of discrimination and stagnation for blacks were extremely limited. Cuba's political elites perceived the propagation of race issues and identity as contradictory to the twin ideals of social unity and racial fraternity for which the independence wars had been fought and on which their visions of nation were founded. This left little room for black activists to act autonomously of the political chains of command that led either to the state or to leaders of the political opposition. Striking workers found themselves in a similar position, despite the correspondence of their demands for equal treatment vis-à-vis Spaniards with the most basic of the revolution's goals. Once again, neither the state nor the liberal opposition could tolerate the use of social protest as a means for articulating demands. Moreover, neither popular-class actions nor their ideological implications meshed with the increasingly homogeneous white nation of conservatives or the highly regimented heterogeneous nation of liberals. By contrast, black activists foregrounded their blackness in interpreting the tenet of racial fraternity as a mandate for state intervention on their behalf. Likewise, both black and white striking workers foregrounded the indecipherably mixed nature of their identity as members of a strictly Cuban racial fraternity in order to contest the continuing social privilege of Spaniards in their profession. Black veteran activists and strikers' objectives were the same: to push political elites into living up to the promises of the revolution as they had lived them in struggle and expected to implement them in the republic. However, for Estrada Palma's administration, the workers' hostility toward the Spanish undermined his project for building a nation based on the Spaniards' colonial order and an affinity for Spanish culture and identity. For the liberals, the resistance of workers to state repression signaled a revolutionary impulse for change that they could not control and therefore could not share.

By 1906, conservatives did not espouse a race-neutral identity for Cubans, but rather one in which race was defined positively in relation to the Spanish people alone. Liberals staked their reactions to the autonomous social protests of black veterans and striking workers on their view of the nation, which they defined as the bastion of sovereignty and the legitimation of their own historically in-scribed power. Inevitably, this meant that liberal leaders hid the historical significance of race in creating structures of inequality through slavery, colonial laws, and discrimination in the shadow of their own claims to state power.

Looking back on the political and ideological conflicts that defined the first four years of the republic, it is easy to see why members of the Abakuá arrested in May 1902 posed a danger. At one level, among the fifty-nine *ñáñigos* arrested were twelve cigarmakers, seven stevedores, and six bricklayers—all professions long affiliated with labor union activity in Cuba and among emigré commu-nities abroad.[74] Moreover, in a vital, practical way the Abakuá represented an alternative interpretation of social unity and racial fraternity to that endorsed by political elites. As autonomous actors, the men who danced and beat African drums in the house on Jesús Peregrino Street on the day after Cuba's indepen-dence freely embodied their right to membership in a nation they had strug-gled to build and now expected the state to implement. As such, they were already acting as equal citizens capable of choosing and expressing their beliefs without the mediation or sanction of either the state or the revolution's former leaders. Accordingly, the Abakuá threatened the authority of Cuba's new of-ficialdom because they espoused in a forthright and everyday manner the breadth of meaning that so many marginalized Cubans had long ascribed to the promise of freedom and national independence. Thus, the nature of the Abakuá's threat lay in its enactment of an alternative vision of nation.

Perhaps the greatest evidence of this lies in the ironic culmination of the case. Within days of the commencement of the defendants' prison terms in August 1902, the chancellor of the National University in Havana requested that evi-dence collected from the meeting of the *ñáñigos* and exhibited in court be transferred to the university's Museum of Anthropology for display. Within a few more days, Dr. Luis Montané, curator of the museum, arrived at the court-house to pick up the materials, including the *diablito* costumes.[75] With this act, representatives of civil society and state officials collectively conspired to per-form a ritual of their own: the cooptation and domestication of expressions, practices, and beliefs that typified an alternative vision of nation with which marginalized Cubans identified. Through such acts, political authorities in the republic repeatedly performed their own multiple meanings of the terms of social unity, racial fraternity, and citizenship that the independence struggle had inscribed in the lexicon of Cuban nationality.[76] But as the tumultuous history of Cuba's internal political development in the twentieth century clearly demonstrates, such actions rarely went uncontested.

NOTES

I offer my deepest thanks to the editors of this volume as well as to the numerous individuals who helped me to imagine, conceive, research, and eventually write this essay: Marial Iglesias, Francisco Scarano, Manuel Barcia, Oilda Hevia, Jorge Macle, Marlene Ortega, Aline Helg, Yolanda Díaz, Reinaldo Funes, Ileana Rodríguez Silva, Leo Garofalo, and Kevin Yelvington.

1. Whenever identities are racialized in documentary evidence, the categories appear as given. More often than not, the documents cited here refer to Cubans of African descent through catch-all terms such as "class of color [*clase de color*]" or "*negros*" that do not distinguish intermediate racial categories between black and white. Unless intermediate categories are used, I therefore employ the term "black."

2. See Declaración del Vigilante 410 Ygnacio Santa María y Castart and Declaración del Vigilante 436 Ulián Valdés Carrasco in records for Causa No. 285 del año 1902 del Juzgado de Instrucción del Oeste, in Archivo Nacional de Cuba (hereafter ANC), Fondo Audiencia de la Habana, Legajo 214, Expediente 5, 23 May 1902. See also Declaración de la parda Asunción Mendoza, taken 22 May 1902, and Declaración de Reconocimiento, 27 May 1902. Neither folio numbers nor consistent page enumeration are provided; I will refer to documents from this case by page headings or descriptive features.

3. Carlos Massó, Capitán de Policía, to Juez Correccional, 22 May 1902, in ibid.

4. See the Declaraciones de los Acusados, 22 May 1902, in ibid.

5. See the statement of defense attorney Alejandro Escoto y Logan on behalf of Francisco Roca Ybarra, 17 June 1902, in ibid.

6. Prosecutors cited the rumor that the Abakuá required initiates to kill someone at random and the "fact" that it derived its "ceremonies and practices from savage peoples." See the statements of Vigilante 410 and Vigilante 436 as well as the "Auto" or formal statement of charges processed, 22 May 1902, and the provisional conclusions rendered by the prosecution, 9 June 1902, under the heading "A LA SALA: EL FISCAL, en la causa número 285 del año 1902 del Juzgado de Instrucción del Oeste," in ibid. All translations are mine.

7. Article 37 of the 1901 Cuban constitution annulled preexisting laws. Article 28 guaranteed citizens' freedom of assembly. See the defense summary of Licenciado Alejandro Escoto y Logan, 13 June 1902; the appeal of bond while awaiting sentencing submitted by Licenciado Angel Fernández Larrinaga; and Apelación presentada a la Sala de lo Criminal del Tribunal Supremo de la República de Cuba by Licenciado Silverio Castro e Infante, 24 Dec. 1902, in ibid.

8. Apelación presentada a la Sala de lo Criminal del Tribunal Supremo de la República de Cuba, 24 Dec. 1902, in ibid.

9. Auto del Caso No. 285, 22 May 1902, and Apelación presentada a la Sala de lo Criminal del Tribunal Supremo de la República de Cuba, 24 Dec. 1902; Secretario del Gobierno de la Provincia de la Habana, Sección de Orden Público, to Señor Juez de Instrucción del Distrito Oeste de la Habana, 26 May 1902, in ibid.

10. Aline Helg, *Our Rightful Share: The Afro-Cuban Struggle for Equality, 1886–1912* (Chapel Hill: University of North Carolina Press, 1995), esp. 6–7, 16–17, 105–6.

11. Ada Ferrer, *Insurgent Cuba: Race, Nation, and Revolution, 1868–1898* (Chapel Hill: University of North Carolina Press, 1999), esp. 1–12, 15–70, 112–69.

12. Alejandro de la Fuente, "Myths of Racial Democracy: Cuba, 1900–1912," *Latin American Research Review* 34, no. 3 (1999): 39–73, and *A Nation for All: Race, Inequality, and Politics in Twentieth-Century Cuba* (Chapel Hill: University of North Carolina Press, 2001), esp. 1–15.

13. Louis A. Pérez Jr., *Cuba under the Platt Amendment, 1902–1934* (Pittsburgh: University of Pittsburgh Press, 1986); Oscar Zanetti, *Cautivos de la reciprocidad: La burguesía cubana y la dependencia comercial* (Havana: Ministerio de Educación Superior, 1989); and Juan Pérez de la Riva, *La república neocolonial: Anuario de estudios cubanos*, 2 vols. (Havana: Editorial de Ciencias Sociales, 1973–75).

14. Tomás Estrada Palma, 30 Apr. 1902, from aboard *Reina de los Angeles*, the ship that would bring him home to Cuba, quoted in *El Fígaro: República*, special ed., vol. 18, nos. 18–20 (20 May 1902): 207. See also the "autographs" of Gómez and Masó on the same page.

15. "Autograph" of Luis Estévez y Romero in ibid.

16. Louis A. Pérez Jr., *Cuba between Empires, 1878–1902* (Pittsburgh: University of Pittsburgh Press, 1983), 383.

17. Louis A. Pérez Jr., *The War of 1898: The United States and Cuba in History and Historiography* (Chapel Hill: University of North Carolina Press, 1998), 81–133.

18. Pérez, *Cuba between Empires*, 88–291. For an analysis of loyalists' previous demonization in the U.S. press, see Kristin L. Hoganson, *Fighting for American Manhood: How Gender Politics Provoked the Spanish-American and Philippine-American Wars* (New Haven: Yale University Press, 1998), 43–67.

19. Tomás Estrada Palma to T. E. Culmel [*sic*], 7 Dec. 1895, in Partido Revolucionario Cubano, *La revolución del 95 según la correspondencia de la delegación cubana en Nueva York*, ed. León Primelles (Havana: Editorial Habanera, 1932), 2:288–89.

20. Ada Ferrer, "The Silence of Patriots," in *José Martí's "Our America": From National to Hemispheric Cultural Studies*, ed. Jeffrey Belnap and Raúl Fernández (Durham: Duke University Press, 1998), 228–49.

21. Antonio Póveda Ferrer to Tomás Estrada Palma, 29 May 1903, in ANC, Fondo Correspondencia Secretaría de la Presidencia, Serie Felicitaciones y Muestras de Apoyo. Archivists have not yet given numerical assignation to this collection of documents.

22. Philip S. Foner, *The Spanish-Cuban-American War and the Birth of American Imperialism* (New York: Monthly Review Press, 1972), 2:464.

23. U.S. Congress, Senate, *Report of the Committee on Foreign Relations, United States Senate, Relative to Affairs in Cuba*, 55th Cong., 2d sess., S. Rept. 885 (Washington, D.C.: Government Printing Office, 1898); U.S. Congress, House, *Affairs in Cuba*, 54th Cong., 1st sess., H. Doc. 224 (Washington, D.C.: Government Printing Office, 1896); U.S. Department of State, *Papers Relating to the Foreign Relations of the United States, 1895–1898* (Washington, D.C.: Government Printing Office, 1896–1901).

24. Aline Helg, "Black Protest: The Partido Independiente de Color, 1908–1912," *Cuban Studies* 21 (1991): 105–6, and Sergio Aguirre, "El cincuentenario de un gran crimen," *Cuba Socialista* 2 (Dec. 1962): 39.

25. Thomas Tondee Orum, "Politics of Color: The Racial Dimension of Cuban Politics during the Early Republican Years, 1900–1912" (Ph.D. diss., New York University, 1975), 96.

26. Ibid., 95.

27. Helg, *Our Rightful Share*, 103.

28. Philip A. Howard, *Changing History: Afro-Cuban Cabildos and Societies of Color in the Nineteenth Century* (Baton Rouge: Louisiana State University Press, 1998), esp. 140–43.

29. Orum, "Politics of Color," 96.

30. Tomás Fernández Robaina, *El negro en Cuba, 1902–1958: Apuntes para la historia de la lucha contra la discriminación racial* (Havana: Editorial de Ciencias Sociales, 1990), 41.

31. Louis A. Pérez Jr., "Politics, Peasants, and People of Color: The 1912 'Race War' in Cuba Reconsidered," *Hispanic American Historical Review* 66, no. 3 (Aug. 1986): 528.

32. *La Lucha*, 9 June 1902, 2. For a quite different interpretation of this same article, see Orum, "Politics of Color," 97.

33. Helg, *Our Rightful Share*, 150, 156, 170, 186, 246.

34. Leopoldo Estuch Horrego, *Martín Morúa Delgado: Vida y mensaje* (Havana: Editorial Sánchez S.A., 1957), 195–96.

35. For a discussion of how the black separatist press in Cuba dealt with Spain's campaign of racial fear and refuted its charges in line with Martí, see Howard, *Changing History*, 190–205.

36. Orum, "Politics of Color," 98.

37. Fernández Robaina, *El negro en Cuba*, 43–44.

38. Compare Helg, *Our Rightful Share*, 127.

39. Howard, *Changing History*, 139–40, 145–46, 198–99.

40. Ibid., 196–202; Helg, *Our Rightful Share*, 38–40. These victories included the right to disseminate separatist propaganda in Cuba, desegregation of public schools, the prohibition of racial discrimination in public spaces, and the right of black Cubans to insert the honorific title of "Don" or "Doña" before their names.

41. Howard, *Changing History*, 138–39, 165–67, 169.

42. On Morúa and the "class of color," see Helg, *Our Rightful Share*, 39–41.

43. Orum, "Politics of Color," 99–100.

44. Ibid., 107.

45. Helg, *Our Rightful Share*, 126–27.

46. Ibid., and Orum, "Politics of Color," 108.

47. R. Sartorio B. to Máximo Gómez, 5 Dec. 1902, in ANC, Fondo Máximo Gómez, Caja 36, Exp. 4476.

48. "Nothing Has Happened," *The Lucha*, 27 Nov. 1902, 1. *The Lucha* was an English-language newspaper, not to be confused with the Spanish-language version, *La Lucha*. *The Lucha* was directed at a U.S. audience. The piece reprints in full an article from Juan Gualberto Gómez's newspaper, *La República Cubana*.

49. Ibid.

50. Ibid.

51. "¡Dios mío, qué solos se quedan los muertos!," *La Lucha*, 14 Nov. 1902, 2.

52. Personal communication by author with historian Joseph Hall, 22 Jan. 1999.

53. "La huelga general. La asamblea magna de anoche en el Teatro Cuba," *La Lucha*, 13 Nov. 1902, 2.

54. Native white cigarmakers numbered 14,922 while "colored" cigarmakers numbered 10,485. Spaniards, preferentially treated, were a minority of only 2,096. See U.S. Bureau of the Census, *Cuba: Population, History and Resources, 1907* (Washington, D.C.: Government Printing Office, 1909), 220.

55. Alejandro de la Fuente, "Two Dangers, One Solution: Immigration, Race, and Labor in Cuba, 1900–1930," *International Labor and Working-Class History*, no. 51 (Spring 1997): 39. De la Fuente notes that this practice extended into other sectors of labor as well, persisting into the 1920s.

56. Gerald E. Poyo, *"With All and for the Good of All": The Emergence of Popular Nationalism in the Cuban Communities of the United States, 1848–1898* (Durham: Duke University Press, 1989), esp. 70–97.

57. "La huelga general. La Liga General de Trabajadores Cubanos. Importante asamblea en Marte y Belona," *La Lucha*, 14 Nov. 1902, 2; "La huelga general. Numerosas fábricas secundan el movimiento y abandonan trabajo ayer por la tarde," *La Lucha*, 18 Nov. 1902, 2; "La huelga general. El Comité Central pide a sus compañeros los trabajadores de la Habana que abandonen sus trabajos el Lunes," *La Lucha*, 6 Nov. 1902, 2; and "La huelga general. Su terminación definitiva," *La Lucha*, 1 Dec. 1902, 1.

58. For an analysis of the strike process and its participants, see Lillian Guerra, "Crucibles of Liberation in Cuba: José Martí, Conflicting Nationalisms, and the Search for Social Unity, 1895–1933" (Ph.D. diss., University of Wisconsin–Madison, 2000), 274–80; for evidence of the bricklayers' and stevedores' strikes, see Foner, *Spanish-Cuban-American War*, 2:488–89, 500–501.

59. "El banquete a Mérchan en el Casino Español," *La Lucha*, 16 Nov. 1902, 2. For Martí's view of the Casino Español, see "Los cubanos de Jamaica y los revolucionarios de Haití" and "¡Basta!," in *Obras completas* (Havana: Editorial de Ciencias Sociales, 1975), 3:103–8, and 1:338–39.

60. "La huelga general. Importancia y gravedad del movimiento obrero," *La Lucha*, 26 Nov. 1902, 2, 4.

61. See court records from the case against Juan O'Farrill for usurpation of functions and dereliction of duty, titled "Primer escrito," dated 8 Dec. 1902, in ANC, Fondo Audiencia de la Habana, Caja 468, Exp. 8. See also Exp. 9 for surviving documents of the defense.

62. "Terminación de la huelga. Patriótica y oportuna intervención de los veteranos," *La Lucha*, 26 Nov. 1902, 4.

63. Ibid.

64. Helg, *Our Rightful Share*, 106–16.

65. Juan Santos Fernández, "La inmigración," in *Anales de la Academia de Ciencias Médicas, Físicas y Naturales de la Habana* (Havana: Imprenta Militar, 1907), 43:7, 13, 24–25. Santos Fernández delivered this address on 19 May 1906, the anniversary of the founding of the academy in Cuba. I am grateful to Reynaldo Funes of the Museo Carlos J. Findlay for bringing this source to my attention.

66. Ibid., 6–8.

67. Ibid., 10–11, 17–21.

68. See Guerra, "Crucibles of Liberation in Cuba," esp. 288–92.

69. See, for example, Esteban N. Robert to Tomás Estrada Palma, 10 June 1902, in ANC, Fondo Correspondencia Secretaría de la Presidencia, Serie Felicitaciones y Muestras de Apoyo.

70. Mario Priera, *Cuba política (1899–1955)* (Havana: Impresora Modelo S.A., 1955), 91–101.

71. "Proyecto de Ley de Inmigración y el Fomento Nacional. Capítulo II. De los inmigrantes," *El Economista: Revista Financiera y Comercial. El Hacendado y el Agricultor Cubanos. Gaceta Industrial de Ferrocarriles de Cuba* 5, no. 7 (18 Feb. 1906): 134–35.

72. "Proyecto de Ley de Inmigración y Fomento Nacional," *El Economista: Revista Financiera y Comercial. El Hacendado y el Agricultor Cubanos. Gaceta Industrial de Ferrocarriles de Cuba* 5, no. 6 (11 Feb. 1906): 109–11, emphasis mine.

73. *La Gaceta Oficial de la República*, 11 July 1906, in ANC, Fondo Secretaría de la Presidencia, Caja 121, Signatura 82.

74. See the initial list of prisoners with profession, race, and age, dated 27 May 1902, in Causa No. 285-1902 del Juzgado de Instrucción del Oeste, in ANC, Fondo Audiencia de la Habana, Leg. 214, Exp. 5.

75. Presidente de la Audiencia de la Habana to Presidente de la Sección Segunda de la Sala de lo Criminal, 7 Aug. 1902, in ibid. See also the certification before a notary of the transfer of goods to Dr. Luis Montané, described as "Director del Museo de Antropología de la Universidad."

76. The evidence for a 1910 case of persecution of *ñáñigos* was similarly remitted to a museological institution. See Casa de Identificación Dáctilo-Fotográfico to Presidente de la Sala Segunda de lo Criminal, 14 Dec. 1910, and list of objects for Causa No. 216-1910 transferred to Juan Francisco Steegers, 7 Mar. 1911, in ANC, Fondo Audiencia de la Habana, Leg. 205, Exp. 10.

CHAPTER SIX

INTERRACIAL COURTSHIP IN THE RIO DE JANEIRO COURTS, 1918–1940

Sueann Caulfield

Brazilians' supposed tolerance of—or even preference for—interracial sexual relations is central to two theories that have dominated studies of race in twentieth-century Brazil: the theory that the nation was a racial democracy, and the theory that Brazil's population was "improving" because of the whitening effect of miscegenation. Over the past fifty years, study after study has disproved both theories, which in itself attests to their ideological power. This chapter explains some of the ways the theories gained such power in the 1920s and 1930s, a crucial period in the development of Brazilian nationalism. First, I will outline major lines of debates among prominent social theorists about race and national character, showing how particular interpretations became part of the nationalist ideology propagated by the state. By analyzing stories of courtship between young women and men who appear in legal disputes over lost virginity, I will then evaluate the relationship between this official ideology and popular attitudes or personal choices during the same period.

THE IDEOLOGICAL CONSTRUCTION OF THE BRAZILIAN RACE

The 1920s and 1930s saw the consolidation of a remarkably homogeneous discourse of race and national identity among Brazilian intellectuals and public officials. As the disadvantages of Brazil's export-led economy, dependent on European markets, became painfully evident and as Europe was attacked as imperialistic, immoral, and barbaric by rebels in some of its colonies and by its own intellectual vanguard, Brazilian intellectuals rejected the inferiority complex that some of their predecessors had projected onto the nation. Earlier veneration of European culture and pessimism about Brazil's racial composition gave way to a faith in the eugenic improvement of the "Brazilian race" after World War I.[1]

The mainstay of most of the thinking about Brazil's "race problem" in the post–World War I period was the belief that it would be resolved through sexual selection, which would whiten the population.[2] The means by which this whitening would occur and the relative value of different ethnic groups were subjects of intense debate. Renato Kehl, the father of the Brazilian eugenics movement, energetically (but unsuccessfully) lobbied for increased immigration of "Aryan" individuals and campaigned to prevent miscegenation and reproduction among the "unfit," which he believed resulted in degeneracy, disorder, crime, and vice.[3]

Equally racist, Francisco de Oliveira Vianna took a different view—and was much more successful in shaping diverse political and intellectual projects. Vianna blended influential strains of the nationalist authoritarian, Catholic corporatist, and racist political philosophies of an earlier generation to argue that the Brazilian population was incapable of self-government and poorly adapted to republican liberal institutions. He believed that economic and geographical factors were partly to blame, but he insisted that the major problem was that the historically high proportion of "anti-eugenic," that is, inferior, African and Indian blood in Brazil's ethnic mix had hindered the European colonizers' civilizing mission. Notwithstanding this unfortunate racial heritage, however, the modern Brazilian population was rapidly "improving" as it whitened through natural selection and European immigration.[4]

Viana's optimism regarding miscegenation made his analysis more palatable than Kehl's, but his conclusions regarding African and Indian inferiority provoked intense controversy.[5] The most remarkable critique was that of Manoel Bomfim, a physician and leftist intellectual who for decades had repudiated the reigning scientific racism. Bomfim discredited Vianna and other social Darwinists by arguing that cross-racial sexual relations were the key to progressive biological evolution, and that Brazil's racial and cultural mixture was its greatest strength. The concerns of "Aryanist sociologists" such as Vianna with racial whitening were thus both ridiculous and unpatriotic.[6]

Few among Bomfim's contemporaries were so sure that there were no naturally superior or inferior races, and fewer still echoed his call for a radical
popular revolution. Nonetheless, most leading professional and intellectual
elites in the 1920s rejected the notion that a large portion of the Brazilian
population was irrevocably inferior, favoring instead the view that "racial improvement" would be achieved by reducing endemic diseases and improving
public education.[7] Unlike Bomfim, most saw no contradiction in their appreciation of African and Indian contributions to Brazilian culture and their belief
that the "Brazilian race" was improving through an evolutionary process of
both biological and cultural whitening.[8]

The nationalist desire to celebrate Brazil's diverse racial heritage without
destroying existing social and racial hierarchies was satisfied in the work of
social theorist Gilberto Freyre beginning in the early 1930s. His *Casa grande e
senzala*, published in 1933 (later published in English as *The Masters and the
Slaves*), was an immediate sensation.[9] Looking to the history of the colonial
plantation's extended household to explain Brazilian culture, Freyre reevalu-
ated the contributions of Indians, Africans, and the Portuguese. Although
Freyre agreed with Vianna that the Portuguese colonists had provided the
civilizing impulse, he argued that the other two races were crucial participants
in their mission. Cultural and biological amalgamation of the three races had
made possible the Europeans' adaptation to the new environment, and hence
the implantation of civilization in the tropics.[10]

Freyre opposed Vianna on another critical point: the history of Portuguese
conquest, slavery, and syphilis, not racial inferiority, had resulted in the moral
degeneracy and indolence that he believed characterized colonial society.
Freyre was fascinated by the "sexual irregularities" he believed were endemic to
colonial society, particularly the sexuality of colonial masters and slaves, for
here was the key to the Brazilian character and the nation's organic social and
cultural structures.[11] White men's promiscuous sexual domination of black
women not only expanded the mulatto population but also evolved into culturally institutionalized social and sexual relationships among successive generations of Brazilians.[12]

The political implications of Freyre's historical analysis were optimistic and,
ironically, strikingly similar to those of Vianna's work. Racial discrimination
and discord had been avoided through social and biological evolution, as racial
diversity was gradually erased through progressive whitening. The patron-
client relations that continued to predominate in national and local politics
could be interpreted as authentically Brazilian traditions of intimacy and social

harmony that were incompatible with the impersonal politics of capitalist liberalism. Personalism and authoritarianism could be cast as humane, if hierarchical, and preferable to the ugly results of individualistic competition and racial hatred Freyre had observed while studying in the United States.[13]

Freyre and Vianna were among the most consecrated intellectual figures of the their time, and both inspired the nationalist political regimes headed by Getúlio Vargas in the 1930s. As Vianna boasted in 1938, his call for centralized state authority, the subordination of local to national power, corporate social organization, and ethnic and moral homogenization was answered by Vargas's political organization and social policies, particularly under the dictatorial Estado Novo (1937–45); Vianna himself, as juridical consultant and cabinet minister, helped to implement these policies.[14] Freyre's more laudatory vision of Brazil's racial roots and social harmony colored state rhetoric, intellectual projects, and cultural policies, even though Freyre himself opposed the Vargas governments.[15]

Under Vargas, the state encouraged study of Brazil's African and Indian heritage as nationalist folklore while encouraging whitening and repressing ethnic diversity through immigration and educational policies. At the same time, it continued to project the image of Brazil as a socially advanced nation that had solved its "race problem" through miscegenation and had achieved racial democracy, an area where more powerful nations had failed.[16]

Studies hailing Brazil's racial democracy, often citing Freyre's thesis of relatively humane relations under slavery, multiplied in the immediate post–World War II period, with Brazil's return to political democracy. In the 1950s, in hopes of discovering solutions to ethnic discord erupting elsewhere in the world, UNESCO sponsored a cluster of research projects focused on Brazilian race relations. Unfortunately for Brazil's international image, these studies found both evidence of racial prejudice among white middle-class Brazilians and severe disparities in income, employment, education, and housing between those classified as white, black, or *pardo* (brown).[17]

A wave of revisionist scholarship followed, attacking the thesis of racial democracy as a false ideology that undermined struggles against racism. Sociologists such as Roger Bastide and Luis Costa Pinto took a new look at interracial sexual relations, concluding that these relations remained an expression of white male dominance that subjugated and humiliated women of color. Observing that most interracial sexual relations occurred outside formal marriage, Bastide argued that these relations "effectively reduce[d] a whole race to the level of prostitutes."[18] His and other studies concluded that middle- and upper-class white men saw black and especially mulatto women as sexual safety valves, an easily accessible outlet that preserved the sexual virtue of white women.[19] Revisionist scholars produced surprisingly little data on working-class views and practices but tended to imply that members of Brazil's racially mixed "popular mass" were deceived by the myth of racial democracy disseminated from above.[20]

More recent research on racial attitudes among lower-class Brazilians suggests an alternative explanation for the persistence of the myth of racial democracy, one that might help explain why Brazilians of all colors were drawn to Vargas's rhetoric of national harmony. In separate local studies, set a century apart and in different regions of Rio de Janeiro state, anthropologists Robin Sheriff and Peter Fry and historian Hebe Castro reach a similar conclusion: Brazil's racial democracy was not simply a myth disseminated from above, but also an ideal that emerged from the racially mixed lower classes.[21] Residents of an urban slum in Rio de Janeiro in the early 1990s consistently repudiated racist attitudes, explaining to Sheriff, often with ironic humor, that there are no "pure" races in Brazil.[22] As Sheriff concludes, this discourse inverts Gilberto Freyre's thesis, invoking racial mixture "not to argue that Brazilians are not or can not be racist, but to assert that this *mestiçagem* is precisely the reason why they *should* not be racist."[23] Peter Fry, citing these attitudes along with other evidence of everyday social practice in the 1990s, likewise rejects the thesis that the reality of racism proves that the ideal of racial democracy is an illusion. He insists, instead, that the two coexist in Rio de Janeiro, and that it is not always possible to predict which will prevail at any given moment.[24]

Hebe Castro's research on late-nineteenth-century Campos, a rural county of Rio de Janeiro state, suggests that an ideal of racial equality emerged among poor Brazilians alongside elite attempts to reinforce racial hierarchies. The free poor did not convert a shared history of slavery into a "black" identity. Instead, they drew upon a long history of freedom that, even before abolition, had been constructed as "essentially nonracial." Castro does not argue that persistent racial discrimination went unnoticed by its victims, but that they continued to insist that it was not legitimate.[25]

If Castro's hypothesis could be extended to urban Rio de Janeiro in the early twentieth century, the popularity of Gilberto Freyre's theory of harmonious racial mixture in the 1930s could be explained in part by its articulation with the historical demands by Brazilians of color for freedom from the mark of slavery. It is clear, as Castro points out, that the theory of racial democracy reached mythical proportions after World I, when intellectuals and politicians looked for new ways of including what they perceived as a racially mixed popular mass in their conception of the national body. Yet this does not help to answer the question of how the belief in racial democracy could coexist with widespread racist practices. In particular, how did individual state officials simultaneously disseminate the myth of racial democracy and practice discrimination? Did popular attitudes toward interracial sexual relations influence, reflect, or challenge racial and national ideologies that emphasized Brazil's unique biological mixing?

I will address these questions by analyzing 450 trials or police investigations of sexual crimes initiated in Rio de Janeiro in the 1920s and 1930s.[26] The crime of "deflowering," defined as taking the virginity of a woman between the ages of fifteen and twenty-one through seduction, deceit, or fraud, made up the overwhelming majority of these crimes. Nearly all involved working-class victims and defendants, most of whom had been sweethearts before the girl's loss of virginity prompted her parents to take her suitor to court, often with the hope that the authorities would pressure him to marry her. We can assume that in most of these cases, the young woman's family considered the accused young man an appropriate, or at least conceivable, marriage partner for her, whereas the man might not have felt the same way about his accuser.

The stories of courtship recounted in testimony of defendants, victims, and witnesses in these cases provide evidence of various ways that race or color could influence these attitudes about appropriate sexual and marriage partnerships. At the same time, the intervention of state prosecutors and judges in these relationships demonstrates that the connection between racial ideologies and the discriminatory practices of individual judicial officials was complex.

COLOR CLASSIFICATION IN RECORDS OF SEXUAL CRIME

A color label was almost always attributed to offended women in cases of sexual crime (by forensic specialists in the obligatory gynecological examination), but less systematically for defendants and almost never for witnesses. Color was recorded as black (*preto*), white (*branco*), or *pardo*, a color category considered to be between black and white.[27]

Color is a complex datum for several reasons. First, the three official categories do not reflect the variety of terms used by Brazilians. Furthermore, determination of color usually depended on the perception of judicial or medical officials and did not necessarily reflect self or peer perceptions. In several cases, the same person was assigned a different color by different people or documents. Birth certificates, which usually recorded the color stated by parents, also frequently recorded a lighter color than the deflowering examinations, in which forensic experts were expected to use their ethnological training to determine color.[28] In one case, Elvira Ferreira, who was called *preta* by forensic examiners, stated that her alleged rapist/deflowerer, who was Chinese, had referred to her as "*negra*," a popular term for black. Ferreira insisted that her assailant had impregnated her and assured the police that when the child was born, "they would see that she was not lying." After the birth of the child, a neighbor testified that "the child is not black [*preta*] like the offended woman, but light-skinned [*de cor clara*]" and had "Chinese features." Ferreira's father insisted that "the child born to his daughter is white, whereas his daughter is *parda*."[29]

The expectation that forensic experts could identify objective criteria to determine color could complicate the legal process. In a 1933 case, for instance, Ilka Fernandes was classified as *parda* in her deflowering examination and white in a separate medical examination done to determine her age.[30] Insisting that trained forensic experts could not possibly "mistake" a person's color, although laymen might do so, the defense lawyer argued that two different girls must have been examined and the medical evidence was therefore inadmissible. In a new deflowering exam performed at the order of the presiding judge, the original examiners explained their confusion: "The offended minor represents a type of *mestiçagem* [racial mixture], already very diluted, and approximates the white race. Thus, her complexion is light, her hair black and curly, lips relatively fine and nose approximating the Aryan type, while her mother represents a type of *mestiçagem*, evidenced as much by her pigmentation as by her features and hair. [H]er father is Portuguese. These data, which demonstrate that the ethnological classification of the patient can provoke much doubt, explain the discrepancy in the two documents." Still unsatisfied, the lawyer demanded a new age examination as well. This examination identified the young woman as "of light *parda* color, accompanied by her mother who is frankly *parda*." Witnesses, however, responding to the defense lawyer's questions, identified the young woman as *branquinha*. The diminutive *inho/a* was (and is) often used to soften the edges of sharp race categories, so *branquinha* may have implied "a (cute little) white girl" or "a whitish girl."

Yet the fact that "ethnological classification" was contextual and subjective does not mean that it was entirely arbitrary. In fact, the color classification of defendants and victims in deflowering cases captured some of the social differences that made race meaningful, as well as some of the common experiences that could blur racial divisions. Most notably, victims and defendants classified as black were less likely to be literate and more likely to hold lower-status jobs than their white counterparts, with the *parda* category in the middle. Slightly higher proportions of the black young women were missing one or both parents or resided far from their families, usually as live-in domestic servants. Yet female-headed households and domestic service work were common to the young women in all three categories. The families of the white, *parda*, and black young women also seemed to share common leisure activities and social values, including a preoccupation with preserving the girls' virginity.

RACIAL IDEOLOGIES IN LOVE'S EMBRACE

Nonetheless, perceptions of color difference did seem to affect young people's choice of romantic or sexual partners. In 60 percent of the cases, the offended woman and the defendant were classified in the same color category. Most strikingly, 82 percent of the white women accused white men of deflowering them. Almost all of the cases involving individuals from different color categories involved one *pardo* partner.

In contrast to the insistence of many intellectuals of the period that widespread racial mixing was a Brazilian characteristic, color endogamy in marriage for the general Brazilian population was probably higher than that of the "couples" that appear in records of sexual crime. According to demographic studies of census and household survey data, color endogamy characterized more than 80 percent of Brazilian marriages in 1980 and was probably even more prevalent in earlier decades.[31] In cases of mixed marriages, men have been more likely to marry lighter than darker women throughout the twentieth century and probably in earlier periods as well.[32] Women, however, have tended to marry men of equal or slightly higher educational levels than themselves, at least since the 1970s and probably earlier. This includes those in interracial marriages, regardless of who was the lighter partner.[33] Since, as we have seen, color categorization is determined by a complex combination of phenotype and socioeconomic factors, it is not possible to draw firm conclusions from these data. Yet they lend support to the conventional wisdom that women's appearance weighs more heavily in men's marriage choices, while men's achievement matters more to women.

Unfortunately, demographic studies of racial selection in marriages do not distinguish among types of marriage (legal or consensual), and there are no clear data on sexual relations outside marriage. The preference by white men

Color of Offended Women by Color of Accused Men

| | Offended Women's Color | | | | | | |
| | White | | Pardo | | Black | | Total |
Accused Men's Color	Number	%	Number	%	Number	%	Number
White	95	82	47	40	19	31	161
Pardo	18	16	53	45	14	23	85
Black	3	2	18	15	28	46	49
Total	116	100	118	100	61	100	295

Source: Arquivo Nacional, 450 criminal cases consulted.
Note: Excludes 155 cases in which color for either or both parties is unknown.

for women of color as sexual partners but not marriage partners, however, was commonly acknowledged not only by contemporaries of Gilberto Freyre in the 1920s and 1930s but also by the subsequent generation of social scientists who contested Freyre's theories. Sociologist Luis Costa Pinto, for example, whose 1950 study concluded that middle-class whites in Rio de Janeiro held a strong aversion to interracial marriage, confirmed that Brazilian men prized the *mulata* for her "special sexual prowess."[34] Since white middle-class women were expected to remain virgins until marriage, according to Pinto, they did not engage in interracial sexual relations.

Given the fervor of intellectual debates on miscegenation and abundant evidence that color was a significant factor in courtship and marriage, it is surprising that people involved in deflowering disputes rarely mentioned race or color at all. Even more surprising, none of the defendants mentioned the woman's color or race as a reason for resisting marriage to her. The stereotype of the *mulata* as especially sensual, and of both *mulata* and black women as easily available sexual partners, did emerge in the documents, though not always in ways that corresponded exactly to the presumptions of contemporary social scientists.

For instance, there is some evidence in court records that black and *parda* domestic servants were particularly susceptible to sexual insults—and that this kind of racism was offensive. There is one explicit example in the above-cited case of Elvira Ferreira, a sixteen-year-old domestic servant classified as black by legal-medical examiners and by one of her witnesses. When Ferreira accused her Chinese employer of raping her, she said that when his wife discovered what had happened, the employer replied "that it was not important because [the maid] was black and with money he would settle things with her father."[35] Whether or not the employer actually made this statement, Ferreira's accusation implies that this attitude was both familiar and reprehensible. The defense lawyer also recognized that the racist statement Ferreira attributed to his client was abhorrent, arguing that Ferreira's muted response to it demonstrated her lack of honor: "Elvira, hearing these words from the accused and not protesting the profound insult and his attitude toward her race, demonstrated that she was stripped of any trace of emotion and self-respect, inherent in any individual, whether cultured or not."[36]

The case of Elvira Ferreira is significant in its singularity. Perhaps as a result of a common tendency to avoid explicit expressions of racist attitudes, evidence of the specific sexual vulnerability of black or *parda* domestic servants is difficult to discern in court records. Not only did deponents seldom discuss race, but few domestic servants brought employers to court. Of the 450 cases consulted, male employers or their sons were accused in only nineteen, and only five fit the model of a white employer victimizing a black or *parda* employee.

The scarcity of cases of sexual abuse by employers in the records has a few probable explanations. First, it is possible that black women's complaints of abuse by white employers were simply not recorded by police, as Boris Fausto believes occurred in São Paulo during the period he studied (1880–1924).[37] Or maids may not have gone to the police to complain of abuse by an employer because they thought they would not stand a chance—which was probably true. In 1898 the renowned jurist Viveiros de Castro, who specialized in crimes against women's honor, instructed judges to discount domestic servants' accusations against employers in deflowering cases.[38] His observations illustrate a contradiction between legal theory and practice that would persist in subsequent generations. "In a democratic society such as ours," he insisted, "I do not consider color or class inequality to be a serious obstacle to marriage."[39] Nonetheless, he argued that it would be ludicrous for a domestic servant to believe the marriage promise of an employer "of elevated social position."[40] Since social position was determined by color as well as wealth—and most domestic servants in Rio de Janeiro were classified as *parda* or black—his observations reveal that the absence of class and racial distinctions in Brazil's democracy was a theoretical ideal, not a social reality. In a 1931 case, a police delegate recognized this reality explicitly when he argued that the white medical student accused of deflowering his family's servant "would never have courted a *parda* maid."[41]

Although in the 1930s jurists began to accept new conceptions of seduction that did not necessarily involve a marriage promise, the long-standing precedent against prosecuting employers of domestic servants for sexual offenses was rarely challenged before the 1940s. In the records consulted, none of the employers accused of sexual crimes against their employees was convicted.[42]

Given the dim prospects for an advantageous outcome for the victim in court cases of this type, it is possible that the families of many domestic servants negotiated with employers for out-of-court settlements, as was implied by the comment that Elvira Ferreira attributed to her employer. More direct evidence of this kind of negotiation appeared in a 1923 case involving Maria Almeida, a fourteen-year-old white maid who told her mother that her employer's nineteen-year-old son, Fritz Guedes, had deflowered her and gotten her pregnant. Maria's mother immediately appealed to Fritz's family for a private solution, but, as she told the police, Fritz's father "refused to straighten things out, and told her that if she thought Fritz was guilty, then she should take her complaint to the police." The fact that Fritz's father was an appeals court justice undoubtedly moved the prosecutor assigned to the case, for instead of looking for evidence of a crime, he produced an uncommonly loquacious statement that described Maria's lack of virtue and concluded that her mother was trying to exploit "one of the city's most distinguished" families. The judge did not indict Fritz but ordered the case closed.[43]

Although the drama in the Guedes household represents what was commonly considered a typical scenario, it is unique among the court documents examined. Most deflowering cases demonstrate, instead, that a great many domestic servants did not have sex with employers, even though they might have faced both employers' advances and the suspicions of their peers. In 1934, for example, Aurora de Jesus, a fifteen-year-old *parda* domestic servant, ran away from the family that employed her because of the father's sexual advances. Three years later, when she complained to police that her boyfriend, a twenty-five-year-old *pardo* soldier, had deflowered her, it was clear that the incident with the employer had left its mark. Perhaps her boyfriend blamed the employer for her loss of virginity, or perhaps she was still traumatized and defensive about the incident. Whatever the reason, she brought it up in her testimony, insisting that she had escaped from the employer "without his having abused her honesty."[44]

Yet while deflowering cases provide some evidence that the homes of "honest families" may well have been dangerous territory for working-class young

women, they also show that many black or *parda* domestic servants such as
Aurora de Jesus made their own choices about their sexuality, generally choosing men of their own color and class for sexual relationships.

Although data on the racial dynamics of sexual relationships between domestic servants and their employers are sparse, there is scattered evidence in
court testimony throughout the period that at least some men in a variety of
circumstances believed that *mulata* and black women were fit for sexual relations but not marriage. In a 1938 case, for example, in which both victim and
defendant were classified as *pardos*, a witness testified that the defendant "must
not have been Edneia's deflowerer, because she had other boyfriends, including
a white young man who couldn't marry her."[45] Jaime de Souza, a white construction worker, denied having courted the woman who accused him of deflowering her, explaining that he had always considered her an "ugly black."[46] In
a few other cases, the defense drew upon negative images of *mulatas* and black
women in attempts to portray the offended women as dishonest. One of the
witnesses Fritz Guides rounded up in 1923 accused Maria Neto of hanging out
with "a black woman, Argentina, who had a bad reputation"; in a case that
began in 1918, the white defendant, a sales clerk, testified that his accuser, a
parda domestic servant, "kept company with a black woman who led a dishonest life."[47] José Soares Gonçalves, a *pardo* fireman, went further, claiming that he
had identified his accuser as a prostitute in the street: "Taking a walk through
the garden of the Passeio Público, he encountered a *mulatinha* [little mulatto
girl] who was walking alone in the same garden," and "in view of the actions of
the *mulatinha* [these included smoking a cigarette and mentioning her lack of
money] he was convinced that she was a prostitute."[48] Finally, Virgílio Pereira
met "a *parda* girl" seated in front of him on a train from São Paulo to Rio de
Janeiro. He believed the girl was not a virgin because she was traveling alone,
dressed extravagantly, conversed first with a "fat mulatto" and then with a
soldier, both of whom got off at an earlier stop, and then accepted "without
hesitation" the defendant's invitation to sleep with him in a Rio hotel. The same
woman, classified as *parda* by legal-medical examiners, was described as black
(*preta*) in testimony of three male defense witnesses, all of whom were certain
that she was a prostitute because of her extravagant clothing and makeup and
the fact that they had seen her out after midnight with various men.[49]

What is evident in these examples is that the association between dark skin
and moral laxity was not immediate but had to be qualified. This is related to
the absence of discussion of race in testimony as a whole. The word "race," in
fact, was not ever mentioned. Color was mentioned occasionally, usually as a

descriptive device when the speaker referred to the first encounter with someone she or he did not know. This does not mean color was neutral. To the contrary, color descriptions were usually associated with moral or social characteristics and vice versa. A woman's behavior, attire, or multiple boyfriends or seatmates, and a man's social standing or employment, helped people to define both color and moral character.

These factors could be cited as the basis of elders' opposition to a young woman's suitor. Parents never admitted that they opposed their daughters' suitors because of race or color difference, but a few of the deflowered daughters and witnesses claimed that this was the case. For example, in 1939, when seventeen-year-old, white, literate Izalinda de Lourdes Carames began a romance with twenty-six-year-old, literate Lupércio de Oliveira Cahe, her father and her grandmother objected to the match because Lupércio "was of mixed [*mestiça*] color and lacked a steady job" (according to Izalinda's testimony). The grandmother's testimony omitted the reference to Lupércio's color, emphasizing only that he "did not have [a professional] position."[50] Lupércio's work booklet, which police found in the possession of his former employer and annexed to the case, confirmed his professional instability. From his photograph it is possible to detect features that might be identified as mestizo or mulatto, confirming the descriptions by Izalinda and by two different witnesses (Izalinda's neighbor and Lupércio's former employer). On the same page as the photograph, however, the work booklet described him as white.

Despite the opposition to Lupércio on racial and profession grounds, when Izalinda became pregnant and confessed to her grandmother that she had been deflowered, her grandmother and father did what they could to get Lupércio to marry Izalinda, going to the police when it became clear that he was reneging on his promise to do so. For them, it was more important for Izalinda to have support from her deflowerer than for the family to uphold its social and racial standing by rejecting the marriage.

As for the young women, they were usually influenced by other factors, in addition to socioeconomic position and color category, in their choice of a partner. The attractiveness of a young man might be affected by his color, but not absolutely determined. This was clear in a case opened in 1935 by Manoel Alves, an illiterate Portuguese factory worker.[51] Alves brought his daughter Aracy, a sixteen-year-old white textile worker, into the police station because she had run away from home, to be found five days later at her boyfriend's mother's house. Alves wanted his daughter to undergo a medical examination to verify whether she had been deflowered by the boyfriend, Antônio Sodré.

When interrogated by her father, Aracy at first denied the charge but later admitted to it. At the police station, she explained that "sometimes when Sodré brought her home from dances, at the door of her shack [*barracão*] he kissed and embraced her . . . and sought to excite her . . .; that due to these acts she felt captivated and enchanted by Antônio, in spite of the fact that he was black."

Aracy told police that she was aware that Antônio was married and separated from his wife, which meant he could not remarry. Yet, she explained, "he had always promised to live maritally with her." Aracy also told police that she had pursued Antônio by writing him a note asking him to meet her on the night of her deflowering. She knew she had won his heart when he vowed that "if the police found out about [the deflowering], he would serve the sentence that was given him and when he was freed [from prison] they would be united."

When Aracy testified before the judge three months later, she was living with Antônio. She insisted that "in September of last year, without any prompting from the accused, she sought him in order to give herself to him. On that occasion, the accused deflowered the declarant." She concluded her testimony with a deliberate affirmation of her feelings for her boyfriend: "The declarant fell in love [*ficou apaixonada*] with the accused, for whom she continues to feel love." This adamant statement stands out among the testimony, for the use of the terms "to fall in love" and "love" (*amor*) is rare. Aracy might have been expressing righteous indignation about the impediments to her union with Antônio, including his previous marriage and his color. Certainly, she placed her amorous sentiments above other, perhaps more expedient, considerations of social and economic advantages she might have enjoyed as a white woman had she married a white man.

This case is interesting for another reason. It demonstrates that people of different colors could live in very close contact, in fact, in the same tenement, where each family had separate rooms but shared a courtyard and sanitary facilities. Aracy's father described his relationship with his black neighbors (Antônio's family) as "intimate" enough that he allowed his daughter to frequent nighttime dances with them. Although the witnesses are not identified by color, Maria Santos, the one Portuguese (therefore probably considered white) witness, testified as a close friend of the black defendant. She had taken Aracy in, at Antônio's request, before Aracy moved in with Antônio.

It is also interesting that neither Aracy's father nor any of the neighbors called in to testify mentioned color when reporting on the moral character of either Aracy or Antônio. Instead, in response to the prosecutor's questions, neighbors systematically reported that they had not witnessed any "immorality" in Antônio's behavior toward Aracy, observing only that the couple courted. Apparently, they did not consider interracial courtship necessarily immoral.

Aracy and Antônio's neighbors might not have considered color a significant datum in the case. But given the favoring of color endogamy by Rio's general population, and Aracy's recognition that Antônio's blackness would have presented an obstacle to their courtship had she not felt such deep attraction to him, it is more likely that her father and neighbors felt it improper to bring up the delicate issue of color difference. The only mention of color in testimony, besides Aracy's declaration, was Maria Santos's statement that Antônio had appeared at her shack "accompanied by a white girl."

On the whole, deflowering disputes provide evidence that color prejudice was disseminated among the working-class population and that whiteness was valued positively, particularly when it came time to select a marriage partner. Yet they also reveal a correlation between ascribed color and socioeconomic position, a relatively high degree of interracial social mixing and shared moral values among working-class people, and a general reluctance on the part of witnesses to mention color when describing someone's moral character. The silence on color might be explained by a tacit recognition among deponents that color difference was not a legitimate impediment to courtship or marriage, even if it was a de facto one.

Both assumptions emerged in a deflowering dispute that made it to the police through a circuitous route in 1943. In a letter to Brazilian president Getúlio Vargas, Maria José Pinto, describing herself as "a humble Brazilian . . . an inexperienced country girl," complained that she had been deceived six years earlier by the marriage promises of Italian immigrant Luigi Procopio. "I even pointed out to him the color difference," Pinto wrote, presumably in an effort to preempt the charge that it was not credible that a white man would take a woman of a different color as his wife. "He responded," the letter continued, "that [the color difference] did not have anything to do with it, since he had taken a liking to me."[52] This attitude convinced Pinto of Procopio's good intentions, and she agreed to wait until Procopio finished building their house and paying off his new plot of land. In the meantime, she began sleeping with him regularly, "in the house she considered hers," and she "considered him her husband." When the house was finally finished and the land paid off, Luigi was forty-two years old and ready for marriage. To Maria José's desperation, he did not choose her.[53]

Interrogated at the local police station a few months after the date on the letter, Luigi Procopio confirmed the six-year sexual relationship with Maria José Pinto, whom he described as *parda*. He denied that he had ever promised her marriage but claimed instead that since she "was constantly barraging him with declarations of love," he had "invited her to live with him as though they were married." Although Luigi insisted that he never intended to marry Maria José, it seems that he did not necessarily want to give her up, either—and he may not have had to. According to Maria José, "That scoundrel tried to deceive [her] in every way," lying to her repeatedly and refusing to "let [her] see the truth." Yet Maria José also testified that even after she discovered his engage-ment to another woman and complained to President Vargas, she continued to have sex with Procopio. "I love this man very much," she explained, according to the police investigator (perhaps after the investigator threatened to rough up Luigi), "and I don't want you to do anything to hurt him."[54] She need not have worried, for her complaint was a lost cause from the start. By her own account, she was already thirty-two years old when Luigi deflowered her, well beyond the maximum age (twenty) for a deflowering victim.

It is reasonable to conjecture that Luigi Procopio saw Maria José Pinto as an appropriate partner for sex and cohabitation but not marriage because of her low status, determined by her color, her family's poverty, and her own auton-omy and assertiveness. Luigi's new fiancée, according to the police investigator, was "a neighboring girl from a very good family." She may have been an Italian immigrant like him (and thus would have been considered white); Maria José had initially believed Luigi when he told her the girl was his cousin.

Luigi Procopio's behavior toward Maria José Pinto, like several other cases mentioned above, seems to illustrate widely held assumptions about darker-skinned women. These cases help explain why men tended to be the darker-skinned partner in interracial marriages and why women seemed more likely to bring lighter-skinned than darker-skinned men to court over broken marriage promises.

The complex attitudes found in the same cases, however, might also reason-ably lead us to suppose that Procopio may indeed have declared, six years earlier, that his affection for Maria José Pinto made "the color difference" unimportant; that he may have been sincere at the time; and that either way, it would not have been at all preposterous for Pinto to have believed him. For although racist ideologies might, as Roger Bastide claims, "extend their con-flicts even into love's embrace," these conflicts were often mediated, sometimes with the help of antiracist ideologies.[55] Or, to paraphrase Peter Fry's obser-vation for the 1990s, each particular situation determined—sometimes pre-

dictably, sometimes not—what race meant, and whether racism or racial democracy would prevail.[56] Consideration of how racial categorization affected
people's experiences with the justice system provides even stronger evidence to
support this observation.

THE SIGNIFICANCE OF COLOR IN JUDGES' VERDICTS

At a time when the nation's major intellectuals and state propaganda were
broadcasting the absence of institutional racism in Brazil, perhaps it is not
surprising that legal officials rarely mentioned race or color. Yet analysis of the
outcomes of deflowering cases shows that racial discrimination could work
against the accused or, more frequently, against the victim. Elsewhere, I demonstrate that there was a statistical relationship between color and the outcome
of these cases. When both victim and defendant were in the same category,
there was no discernible difference in rates of indictment or conviction for
black, *pardo*, or white men. However, indictment and conviction were less
likely if the woman was darker than the man and more likely if she was lighter.
A white man, for instance, had about a 20 percent greater chance of escaping
indictment if the woman was black, and a 10 percent greater chance if she was
parda, than if she was white.[57]

Of course, statistical relationships do not reveal nuances or motivations, nor
do they show how prejudices creep into juridical theories that were supposed to
be neutral. Evidence from individual cases, such as the two cases of interracial
courtship discussed above, illustrate the complex and contradictory ways that
color and class prejudices could influence verdicts.

In the case of Aracy Alves and Antônio Sodré, the judge found Antônio
guilty, and the higher court denied Antônio's appeal. Antônio served two years
and four months, thus living out his declaration to Aracy that he was willing to
pay the price of a jail sentence in order to be with her. The case was closed upon
Antônio's release from prison, leaving us to wonder whether the couple was
then finally united.

The guilty verdict in this case is surprising in the light of Aracy's insistence
that she, not Antônio, had pursued their romance and her own deflowering. By
jurisprudential precedent and in the records examined, cases involving the
deflowering of assertive young women like Aracy, who gave themselves freely
without a previous promise of marriage, were usually dismissed or ended in
acquittal. Although none of the legal officials involved in the case—the police
delegate, prosecutor, and judge—mentioned race or color at any time in the

documents, it is difficult not to suspect that this verdict was influenced by a racialized conception of honor, applied to both Aracy and Antônio.

Lupércio de Oliveira Cahe's trial for the deflowering of Izalinda de Lourdes Carames demonstrates more clearly the ways judges' attitudes toward cross-color sexual relations could influence the outcome of a trial in favor of a defendant they perceived as inferior to the victim. It also provides a rare example of explicit acknowledgment by judicial officials—in this case, justices of the appeals court—of the influence of both class and color on their verdict.[58] Although the justices acknowledged that the evidence proved that Lupércio had deflowered Izalinda (and, implicitly, that he was the father of the child she bore before the trial took place), they unanimously confirmed Lupércio's acquittal, arguing the following: "The very circumstance of the difference of color and social condition, the motive of the family's opposition, serves to prove the absence of seduction, since it is incomprehensible that an honest and virtuous girl, with good intentions and proud of her family's position, against her family's will, would persist in a courtship with an individual of different color and social condition than her own. Even more frightening is that she would give herself sexually to this individual."

The attitude of the justices in this 1939 verdict seems oddly anachronistic. The colonial legislation that had allowed parents to obstruct their children's marriages in cases of "inequality" between bride and groom had been overturned by turn-of-the-century liberal legal codes, which eliminated class and racial distinctions among Brazilian citizens. But this verdict illustrates one way that the concept of sexual honor could work to preserve these distinctions. The justices were certainly aware of nationalist discourses that extolled Brazil's racial mixture and whitening. Clearly, however, they did not consider white women the appropriate vehicles for racial homogenization through miscegenation, particularly if the women chose partners of "inferior social condition."

Lupércio Cahe and Antônio Sodré's sentences also shed light on jurists' fears of the independent modern woman who had appeared with increasing frequency in juridical literature in the 1920s and 1930s. Independent women such as Izalinda de Lourdes Carames and Aracy Alves were not only subverting the legal function of sexual honor as a mechanism of gender discipline, but they were simultaneously subverting its function as a means of class and racial differentiation. This was often true symbolically, even in cases in which racial difference was not an issue, or at least not explicitly so. Because social differentiation and hierarchy were established through the category of gender in legal codes that had eliminated previous distinctions of race and class, the reconfiguration of gender norms seemed an ominous sign of social disintegration and impending chaos. Modern women, casting aside the female modesty and inhibition that, in one judge's words, "civilized the sexual instinct," were thus held responsible for cultural retrogression and racial degeneracy.

These kinds of symbolic associations between gender, class, and racial discipline were at work in Judge Eurico Cruz's imagination in 1926, when he wrote what would become the most influential deflowering verdict of his time. "What virginity is this," he asked himself, "that de-virginifies itself?" His answer was a diatribe against the erosion of moral values in modern times: "It is the virginity that rocks and sways to the indolent rhythm of the music of the slave quarters, in the dance halls—it is a virginity spent in spasms, betrayed by the dulled gaze, the wanton swaying of the body, in the contact of faces . . . and of everything else . . . beneath clothing that is carefully donned yet recklessly stripped."[59] Judge Cruz was not only concerned about the immorality of modern times and nostalgic for days past; he was also concerned about racial degeneracy, equating "the modern environment," in which (to his horror) "the sexes face one another as equals" to the barbarism of "inferior peoples."[60]

For Cruz, the erosion of male sexual dominance by women's assuming "gestures and attitudes that are peculiar only to the unashamed and innate boldness of the male" (his outrage was provoked by a young woman who sat atop her boyfriend on the occasion of her deflowering) signaled generalized moral degeneracy and the blurring of boundaries between civilized and primitive peoples.[61] Evidence from cases tried over the following fifteen years, in which Cruz's decision was frequently cited, suggests that this image continued to disturb jurists through the regime changes that institutionalized new discourses of racial pride and modernization in the 1930s.

The racial implications of Cruz's verdict are clear. In a nation whose major social theorists and politicians had long stressed the need to civilize and whiten its population, the international success and national space Brazilian culture was gaining because of its African influences could only be viewed with ambivalence, at best. Samba, probably the "music of the slave quarters" that perturbed Cruz, presented a problem similar to that of the tango in Argentina. For Cruz, this cultural universe, by producing sexual equality, corrupted women and destroyed virginity.

The discomfort of men like Cruz with broadened acceptance of black Brazilian music, considered together with jurists' tendency to look disparagingly upon interracial courtship, places many jurists alongside other public authorities in their desire to project to the world a vision of Brazil as a modern, civilized nation that had left its non-European roots behind—or had relegated those roots to the folklore of an imagined past. These modern men looked to women to uphold a moral order that would preserve traditional social hierarchies during this period of change.

CONCLUSION

Despite the elaboration in the 1920s and 1930s of official ideologies celebrating Brazil's history of cultural advancement through racial democracy and miscegenation, records of sexual crimes illustrate the ways racial attitudes could encourage color endogamy, even though these attitudes were rarely made explicit, and even though color was subjectively determined and difficult to pin down. The concept of sexual honor could be interpreted in ways that maintained color and class distinctions that had been ostensibly eliminated from republican law. Jurists interpreted honor in ways compatible with long-standing notions of appropriate racial and class divisions. Although racial attitudes could affect the outcome of the cases in opposite ways, judicial officials tended to sustain an understanding among white men that their relationships with black or mulatto women were not binding. They also placed the responsibility for the maintenance of endogamy in the hands of lighter women. This explains the stigmatization of women who chose darker partners or who, in the words of Judge Cruz, "swayed to the indolent rhythm of the music of the slave quarters," regardless of their phenotype. The enforcement of the pro-family values embodied in concepts of sexual honor gave jurists the interpretive space in which to practice this kind of discrimination, while perceiving themselves as impartial defenders of abstract cultural values, or even a natural social order. In short, sexual honor was an instrument that allowed jurists to espouse racial democracy while practicing discrimination.

Color also seems to have mattered to the common people who took their sexual conflicts to court. Although they never cited color as the sole determinant of honor or social status, they discerned color differences, and these differences influenced their choices of partners for sex or for marriage. Not everyone agreed on the significance of color differences, however, and color was only one among various attributes that made someone a desirable partner. Moreover, the general silence on color in testimony, broken in rare instances, may suggest that deponents recognized that it was not a legitimate criterion for determining moral character or social worth. These values did not contradict those of state officials such as jurists, but while everyday social contacts among common people could sometimes work to diminish racial differences, jurists' discourses seemed to accentuate them. Although it is impossible to determine whether judicial officials succeeded in influencing popular conceptions of color (or vice versa), it is likely that in many cases, working-class people's experiences with the justice system reinforced their recognition of the disadvantages of dark skin.

NOTES

I would like to thank Rebecca Scott, Barbara Weinstein, Jeffrey Needell, and João Reis for their careful readings of an earlier version of this chapter. I thank Karin Rosemblatt, Nancy Appelbaum, and Anne Macpherson for their superb editing suggestions for the present version, and John Carson for his thoughtful comments.

1. See Thomas E. Skidmore, *Black into White: Race and Nationality in Brazilian Thought* (New York: Oxford University Press, 1974; reprint, with a new preface and bibliography, Durham: Duke University Press, 1993 [page citations are to the 1974 edition]) and "Racial Ideas and Social Policy in Brazil, 1870–1940," in *The Idea of Race in Latin America, 1870–1940*, ed. Richard Graham (Austin: University of Texas Press, 1990), 7–36; Emilia Viotti da Costa, "The Myth of Racial Democracy," in *The Brazilian Empire: Myths and Histories*, rev. ed. (Chapel Hill: University of North Carolina Press, 2000), 234–46; and Nancy Leys Stepan, *"The Hour of Eugenics": Race, Gender, and Nation in Latin America* (Ithaca: Cornell University Press, 1991), for analysis of broad shifts in racial thought.

2. This idea emerged in nineteenth-century abolitionist thinking and influenced state-subsidized European immigration. Skidmore, *Black into White*, 21–27.

3. See, for example, Renato Ferraz Kehl, *Aparas eugenicas: Sexo e civilização* (Rio de Janeiro: Francisco Alves, 1933), esp. 18, 44, and *Porque eu sou eugenista: Vinte anos de campanha eugenica, 1917–1937* (Rio de Janeiro: Francisco Alves, n.d.), 24–65. For discussion of the eugenics movement in Brazil, see Stepan, *"The Hour of Eugenics,"* 46–54, 99–100, 157–59.

4. See Francisco de Oliveira Vianna, *Populações meridionais: Pequenos estudos de psicologia social* (São Paulo: Monteiro Lobato, 1921), esp. chaps. 9, 12, 14–16; *Evolução do povo brasileiro* (1923), 3d ed. (São Paulo, Editora Nacional, 1938), esp. 45–53, 160; *Raça e assimilação* (São Paulo: Editora Nacional, 1932); *O ocaso do império* (1926), 2d ed. (São Paulo: Melhoramentos, 1933); and *Problemas de política objectiva* (São Paulo: Editora Nacional, 1930), esp. 29–30, 39–40, 178–79, 242–44. For detailed analysis of the genesis of Vianna's political and racial theories, see Jeffrey D. Needell, "History, Race, and the State in the Thought of Oliveira Viana," *Hispanic American Historical Review* 75, no. 1 (Feb. 1995): 1–30.

5. See Vianna, *Raça e assimilação*, 274–85, and Needell, "History," 13–14, 13 n. 37.

6. Manoel Bomfim, *O Brasil na América: Caracterização da formação brasileira* (1929), 2d ed. (Rio de Janeiro: Topbooks, 1997), 70–174, 194, 196, 206.

7. Skidmore, *Black into White*, 145–72; Stepan, *"The Hour of Eugenics,"* 88–95.

8. Skidmore, *Black into White*, 173–218; Stepan, *"The Hour of Eugenics,"* 153–62.

9. Gilberto Freyre, *Casa grande e senzala*, 14th ed. (Recife: Imprensa Oficial, 1966).

10. See ibid., 12–18, on Portuguese civilizers' adaptation to the tropics, chap. 2 for discussion of Indians, and chaps. 4–5 on African slavery and miscegenation. Freyre's criticism of Vianna is discussed in Skidmore, *Black into White*, 203, and Jeffrey D. Needell, "Identity, Race, Gender, and Modernity in the Origins of Gilberto Freyre's Oeuvre," *American Historical Review* 100, no. 1 (Feb. 1995): 70 n. 67. For Vianna's response, see Needell, "History," 13 n. 37.

11. Freyre, *Casa grande*, 275–78, 465–66. On syphilis and the sadomasochism of master-slave relations, see ibid., 50–56, 340–46, and Dain Borges, " 'Puffy, Ugly, Slothful and Inert': Degeneration in Brazilian Social Thought, 1880–1940," *Journal of Latin American Studies* 25, no. 2 (May 1993): 253.

12. Freyre, *Casa grande*, esp. 55–56. This analysis follows Needell's in "Identity," 69–71.

13. Needell, in "Identity," 58 n. 24, 59, 63–68, analyzes the importance of Freyre's experience in the United States, where he witnessed a lynching. Freyre elaborated his conclusions regarding Brazil's "racial democracy" and whitening most explicitly in a series of lectures given in the United States and published as *Brazil: An Interpretation* (New York: Alfred A. Knopf, 1945). See Costa's summary in "The Myth of Racial Democracy," 234.

14. Vianna, *Evolução do povo*, 13. See Needell, "History," 2, for a synopsis of Vianna's political and intellectual career. For discussion of political rhetoric of the Vargas regime, see Alcir Lenharo, *Sacralização da política* (Campinas: Papirus, 1986).

15. See Needell, "Identity," 62–63, for Freyre's response to the republic's overthrow.

16. See Jeffrey Lesser, *Welcoming the Undesirables: Brazil and the Jewish Question* (Berkeley: University of California Press, 1995), 135–39, 169–70; Lenharo, *Sacralização da política*, esp. chaps. 3 and 4; Stepan, *"The Hour of Eugenics,"* 164–67; Carl N. Degler, *Neither Black nor White: Slavery and Race Relations in Brazil and the United States* (Madison: University of Wisconsin Press, 1986), 139, 193–200; Flávio Venâncio Luizetto, "Os constituintes em face da imigração" (master's thesis, Universidade de São Paulo, 1975).

17. See the syntheses of these studies in Abdias do Nascimento, *Brazil: Mixture or Massacre? Essays in the Genocide of a Black People*, 2d ed. (Dover, Mass.: Majority Press, 1989); Degler, *Neither Black nor White*; and Costa, "The Myth of Racial Democracy," 234–35, 276 n. 3.

18. Roger Bastide, "Dusky Venus, Black Apollo," *Race* 3 (Nov. 1961): 11, cited in Degler, *Neither Black nor White*, 190. See also Roger Bastide and Florestan Fernandes, *Brancos e negros em São Paulo*, 2d ed. (São Paulo: Editora Nacional, 1959), 205–10.

19. Bastide, "Dusky Venus." See also Luis A. Costa Pinto, *O negro no Rio de Janeiro:*

Relações de raça numa sociedade em mudança (São Paulo: Editora Nacional, 1960), and Degler, *Neither Black nor White*, 190.

20. See Costa, "The Myth of Racial Democracy," 236.

21. Robin E. Sheriff, " 'Negro é um apelido que os brancos deram aos pretos': Discursos sobre cor, raça e racismo num morro carioca" (Instituto de Filosofía y Ciências Sociais, Universidade Federal do Rio de Janeiro, 1995, mimeographed); Peter Fry, "O que a cinderela negra tem a dizer sobre a 'política racial' no Brasil," *Revista USP* 28 (Dec. 1995–Feb. 1996): 122–35; Hebe Maria Mattos de Castro, *Das cores do silêncio: Os significados da liberdade no sudeste escravista, Brasil, século XIX* (Rio de Janeiro: Arquivo Nacional, 1995). I thank Robin Sheriff for permission to quote her paper.

22. Sheriff, " 'Negro é um apelido,' " 23.

23. Ibid., 24.

24. Fry, "O que a cinderela negra tem a dizer," 135.

25. Castro, *Das cores do silêncio*, 404.

26. The records consulted are held at the Brazilian National Archive (hereafter AN). Citations indicate judicial division (vara), box (caixa), and number.

27. *Parda* is the feminine form of the term, *pardo* the masculine.

28. See, for example, AN, Vara 1, Caixa 1737 No. 2216 (1927), Caixa 1831 No. 2159 (1932), Caixa 1770 No. 625 (1934), Caixa 1731 No. 1057 (1935), Caixa 1813 No. 1279 (1936), Caixa 1837 No. 1534 (1937), Caixa 1840 No. 1905 (1938), Caixa 1837 No. 1534 (1937); AN, Vara 4, Caixa 2659 No. 159 (1923), Caixa 2975 No. 112 (1941); AN, Vara 5, Caixa 1746 No. 61 (1926); AN, Vara 7, Caixa 10613 No. 145 (1922), Caixa 10842 No. 40 (1930); AN, Vara 8, Caixa 2795 No. 237 (1940).

29. AN, Vara 1, Caixa 1767 No. 1969 (1927). Pseudonyms are used for deponents throughout this chapter. All translations are mine.

30. AN, Vara 1, Caixa 1731 No. 542 (1933).

31. These studies do not specify precise dates but note a decline in endogamy "in the recent past." See Elza Berquó, "Como se casam negros e brancos no Brasil?," *Desigualdade racial no Brasil*, ed. Peggy Lovell (Minas Gerais: Universidade Federal de Minas Gerais, 1991), 115–20; Nelson do Valle Silva, "Estabilidade temporal e diferenças regionais no casamento inter-racial," *Estudos Afro-Asiáticos* 21 (Dec. 1991): 49–60; Maria Celi Ramos da Cruz Scalon, "Cor e seletividade conjugal no Brasil," *Estudos Afro-Asiáticos* 23 (Dec. 1992): 17–36.

32. Degler, *Neither Black nor White*, 191; Oracy Nogueira, *Tanto preto quanto branco: Estudos de relações raciais* (São Paulo: T. A. Queiroz, 1985), 25–26; Muriel Nazzari, "Concubinage in Colonial Brazil: The Inequalities of Race, Class, and Gender," *Journal of Family History* 21, no. 2 (Apr. 1996): 107–24.

33. Berquó, "Como se casam negros e brancos no Brasil?"; Silva, "Estabilidade temporal e diferenças regionais"; Scalon, "Cor e seletividade conjugal no Brasil."

34. Pinto, *O negro no Rio de Janeiro*, 214–17.

35. AN, Vara 1, Caixa 1767 No. 1969 (1927).

36. Ibid.

37. Boris Fausto, *Crime e cotidiano: A criminalidade em São Paulo, 1880–1924* (São Paulo: Brasiliense, 1984).

38. Francisco José Viveiros de Castro, *Os delictos contra a honra da mulher*, 2d ed. (Rio de Janeiro: Freitas Bastos, 1932), 77.

39. Ibid., 195.

40. Ibid., 77.

41. AN, Vara 8, Caixa 2718 No. 84 (1931).

42. In fourteen cases, the judges decided not to indict after the police investigation. One employer was convicted in a lower court and acquitted in the appeals court. The lower courts acquitted the remaining four.

43. AN, Vara 1, Caixa 1807 No. 746 (1923).

44. AN, Vara 1, Caixa 1813 No. 1553 (1937).

45. AN, Vara 1, Caixa 1813 No. 1998 (1938).

46. AN, Vara 1, Caixa 1776 No. 262 (1930).

47. AN, Vara 1, Caixa 1807 No. 746 (1923); AN, Vara 7, Caixa 10811 No. 67 (1918).

48. AN, Vara 1, Caixa 1837 No. 1249 (1920).

49. AN, Vara 1, Caixa 1735 No. 1290 (1936).

50. AN, Vara 1, Caixa 1727 No. 2663 (1939).

51. AN, Vara 1, Caixa 1772 No. 1155 (1935).

52. AN, Gabinete Civil da Presidência da República, Código de Fundo 35, Seção de Guarda SDE, Lata 527, Doc. 5.897, 1943.

53. Ibid. Quotations are taken from Pinto's testimony in the police investigation opened as a result of her letter.

54. Ibid.

55. Bastide, "Dusky Venus," 11.

56. Fry, "O que a cinderela negra tem a dizer," 135.

57. Socioeconomic status, estimated by victims' literacy and accused men's professions, also affected the outcome of the cases, but the significance of color remained the same when controlling for these variables. See Sueann Caulfield, *In Defense of Honor: Sexual Morality, Modernity, and Nation in Early-Twentieth-Century Brazil* (Durham: Duke University Press, 2000), 173–78.

58. AN, Vara 1, Caixa 1727 No. 2663 (1939).

59. Eurico Cruz, "Sentença do juiz da 2ª vara criminal, de 8 de setembro de 1926," in Vicente Piragibe, *Diccionario de jurisprudencia penal do Brasil* (Rio de Janeiro: Freitas Bastos, 1938), 1:234–35.

60. Ibid., 235.

61. Ibid.

CHAPTER SEVEN

FROM MESTIZOPHILIA TO BIOTYPOLOGY

Racialization and
Science in Mexico,
1920–1960

Alexandra Minna Stern

LABORATORIES ON THE MOVE

In 1939 a curious entourage of urban professionals appeared at Patzcuaro Lake, located high in the mountains west of Mexico City in the state of Michoacan. Led by Dr. José Gómez Robleda, the director of the National University's recently formed Institute of Social Research (Instituto de Investigaciónes Sociales), this team of psychologists, anthropologists, and physicians came to study the region's Tarascan Indians, a majority of whom earned their livelihood in fishing or agriculture. Determined to classify the Tarascans according to the internationally recognized theory of biotypology, they literally brought their laboratory with them, carrying spirometers, stethoscopes, Rorschach inkblots, intelligence and imagination tests, blood sampling kits, ergographs, and other apparatus designed to measure the physiological and mental traits of humans.[1] Like other scientists in the Americas and Europe at the time, Gómez Robleda hoped to gather systematic statistical data about the constitution of social groups in a language that explicitly rejected racial categories. For Gómez Robleda and like-minded colleagues, biotypology offered an alternative to racial doctrines predicated on Aryan or white superiority. Indeed, he was so convinced of biotypology's methods and explanatory power that he coauthored an in-depth manual on the topic in 1947 in an attempt to encourage surveys in sites throughout the country.[2]

From the late 1930s to the early 1960s, Gómez Robleda and other biotypologists, frequently accompanied by French and Italian investigators, traveled to Mexico's coasts, mountains, and deserts with their instruments and ideas. Repudiating "races" as scientific fictions, they identified their subjects instead as omnipresent "biotypes" defined by a series of interrelated physiological, anthropometric, and cognitive variables. For close to three decades, Gómez Robleda and his colleagues analyzed, correlated, and visually graphed the biotypological determinants of hundreds of Indians, schoolchildren, athletes, and soldiers.[3] Try as they might, however, to escape the ideologies associated with Nazism and vicious patterns of de jure and de facto segregation in the United States, Mexican biotypologists did not succeed in overcoming racism. Instead, by elaborating and utilizing the seemingly more neutral statistical language of averages, deviations, and quintiles, they resignified overt racial typologies. In doing so, they revitalized older images of weak and taciturn Indians as well as related tropes of civilization and barbarism. In spite of his proclamations and stated intentions, Gómez Robleda and his mobile laboratories, rather than contracting and simplifying, expanded and complicated the terrain of racialization in Mexico. By midcentury, racial repertoires were more variegated and potent, encompassing multiple and imbricated modalities of labeling and distinguishing people.[4]

In this chapter, I trace continuities and cleavages in the process of racialization in Mexico from the late nineteenth to the mid-twentieth century by focusing on the discourses and projects of medical and scientific professionals affiliated with governmental institutions and involved in state formation.[5] Although the political architecture and orientation of the state changed markedly from the dictatorship of Porfirio Díaz (1876–1910) to the tumultuous and violent decade of the revolution (1910–20) and from the postrevolutionary era of reconstruction (1920–40) to the consolidation of the increasingly conservative Institutional Revolutionary Party (Partido Revolucionario Institucional) (1940–60s), during this entire period medical and biological models and metaphors were central to understanding and envisioning the nation and its subject-citizens. In Mexico, as in many other countries, during the nineteenth century authoritative claims for governance and rule—whether national, regional, or colonial—shifted from the religious to the scientific realm. Under the canopy of secularization and rationalization, this protracted, uneven, and perennially incomplete transition was deeply interpenetrated with the emergence of original forms of medical and biological knowledge.[6] At the zenith of the Porfiriato, the *científicos*, a coterie of mandarins who for the most part legitimized Díaz's regime and upheld its leitmotif of "order and progress," drew most of their inspiration from an amalgamation of social Darwinism and the positivism of Auguste Comte. After the revolution of 1910, an energetic cohort of professionals and leaders, emboldened by the egalitarian promises of the 1917 constitution, embarked on a plan of reconstruction and regeneration. Still residually influenced by positivism, these men and women fashioned their blueprint for national cohesion and societal fortification by inverting many of the guiding ideas of their predecessors and, furthermore, by linking these to eugenic notions of biosocial vigor and demographic optimization. By the late 1930s, when the postrevolutionary fantasy of a racially unified and harmonious country had proven to be a chimera, racialization moved in another conceptual direction toward biotypology. Mapping these three consecutive and overlapping moments demonstrates that it is difficult, if not impossible, to plot the history of racialization in twentieth-century Mexico as a narrative of progress and increasing emancipation from racialized stereotypes and resonances. In particular, it raises challenging questions about the validity of the commonplace argument that racism waned in the 1940s as "culture" gradually supplanted "science" as the predominant explanatory rubric of social difference.[7] Unraveling this history suggests that the limits of racial logics and the contours of racialization in Mexico must be comprehended in the context of transnationalism and imperialism. From the late nineteenth to the mid-twentieth century, Mexican elites—whether physicians, demographers, anthropologists, or sociologists—were consistently constrained by the contradictions of seeking "truth" and objectivity in theories and disciplinary practices that idealized a human type that, ultimately and sometimes invisibly, was urban, white, literate, and middle class.

MESTIZO NATION?: THE PARADOXES OF HYBRIDITY AND HOMOGENEITY

During the Porfiriato, Mexican *científicos* held distinct and often competing interpretations of Darwinism and positivism. Nonetheless, a large and frequently vocal segment of *científicos* accepted axioms about the backwardness of Indians as well as the degeneracy of hybrid "races" such as mestizos and mulattos. Eager to strengthen the nation by following the laws of biology and medicine, in the mid- to late 1800s prominent *científicos* promoted whitening the population through European immigration and colonization and uplifting Indians through civic assimilation and education.[8] At the close of the nineteenth century, however, some Porfirian intellectuals began to challenge these precepts. Drawing from several French and Latin American thinkers, they began to contend that rather than being a primitive and depraved product of mongrelization, mestizos were instead a virile and hearty mixture of the Indian and European.[9] This view was greatly furthered by the well-known writer Andrés Molina Enríquez, who hailed the mestizo as the beacon of national progress in his widely read *Los grandes problemas nacionales*, published in 1909.[10] After the battles of the Mexican Revolution came to a tenuous end in 1917, a new set of leaders revived this trend and seized on the mestizo as an icon of racial and social integration. Unlike the *científicos*, whose attitude toward the Indian and racial mixing was principally gloomy and pessimistic, the postrevolutionaries' perspective was one of optimism and paternalistic romanticism.

The cult of the mestizo—what one scholar has termed "mestizophilia"—has been identified as one of the most significant aspects of Mexican culture, appearing in films, theater, and murals, during the 1920s and 1930s.[11] Mestizophilia, and the dramatic racialized inversions it entailed, was facilitated by the ways in which modern science and medicine were received and elaborated in Mexico. In the United States and Germany the theories of Gregor Mendel and August Weismann predominated; these posited that hereditary material was transmitted from generation to generation with absolutely no alteration. Mexicans, however, were beholden to the neo-Lamarckian theory of the inheritance of acquired characteristics. Formulated by the French naturalist Jean Baptiste de Lamarck in the early nineteenth century, this interpretation of natural selection stated that changes to an adult organism caused by environmental factors could be transmitted to offspring and become part of a species's hereditary composition. The classic example of this phenomenon is the long neck of the giraffe, which, according to Lamarck, had grown as a result of reaching high to feed on leafy tree tops.[12] Extrapolating from animal morphology, many nineteenth-century evolutionists and physicians were convinced that other bodily conditions such as alcoholism, overwork, syphilis, and tuberculosis could permanently deform hereditary material. This cellular understanding did not distinguish clearly between germs and what would come to be called genes (in 1909). For neo-Lamarckians the two were cytologically interdependent if not identical. To a great extent, neo-Lamarckism flourished in Mexico because it implied that human actors were capable, albeit gradually, of improving the national "stock" through environmental intervention and, eventually, of generating a robust populace. Neo-Lamarckism also countered Mendelian claims that "races" and racial traits were discrete "unit characters" that should not blend biologically or, if allowed to do so, would only produce dysgenic and degenerate hybrids.

By the 1920s, neo-Lamarckian concepts of biosocial change and mestizo-philia operated as crucial facets of nationalism and state building. Proponents of the cult of the mestizo, however, confronted the paradoxes of creating a homogenous body politic out of hybrids and through the impure process of *mestizaje*. Nowhere were these fissures more evident than in the ideas formu-lated by the anthropologist Manuel Gamio and the philosopher-politician José Vasconcelos. As historians have emphasized, Gamio's version of mestizophilia revolved around the Indian, whose acculturation he saw as imperative to ensur-ing the homogenization of the country's citizenry.[13] He idolized the valiant Indian and pre-Columbian past; at the same time, he looked toward the future, insisting upon large-scale anthropological surveys of the country's many indig-enous groups. For his part, Vasconcelos charted another course, envisioning the mestizo as a spiritual beacon of Hispanic civilization. Also fixated on the concept of homogenization and convinced of the need to incorporate the Indian, Vasconcelos hoped that *mestizaje* could offset the nefarious forces of the greedy Anglo-Saxon "race" and the rapacious imperialism of the United States. Published in 1925, his classic work, *The Cosmic Race*, argued that a perfect hy-brid "race" combining the superior traits of Indians, Asians, whites, and blacks could be crafted by following a "mysterious eugenics of aesthetic taste" rather than "scientific eugenics."[14] Distancing himself from the *científicos*, whom he viewed as too wedded to Darwin and Comte, Vasconcelos proposed radically rereading the doctrines of pure "races" that had kept positivists trapped within the narrow imagination of European theories. He wrote that Mexican intellec-tuals "had been educated under the humiliating influence of a philosophy conceived by our enemies. . . . From this situation we have come to believe in the inferiority of the mestizo, in the hopelessness of the Indian, in the condem-nation of the black, and in the irreparable decadence of the oriental."[15] Spiritual eugenics could bring to life a new, fifth "race" that would transcend the other four in every way, bringing together in "a happy synthesis, the elements of beauty, that are today scattered in distinct peoples."[16]

Whereas Gamio based his mestizophilia on a celebration of both the living Indian's potential for modernization and the glories of the Aztec past, Vascon-celos was bound to the Creole or Hispanic.[17] In either case, the paradoxes between hybridity and homogeneity meant that the mestizo was a conceptually weak, if not untenable, national metonym. In an astute analysis of Gamio and Vasconcelos and the widespread idealization of the Indian in the 1920s, Alan

Knight argues that these inverted racial doctrines "tended to reproduce many of the racist assumptions" of the Western theories they patently opposed.[18]

Gamio and Vasconcelos shaped the immediate racialized landscape in which a eugenics movement emerged in Mexico. While groups with hereditarian leanings and concerns, such as the Mexican Sanitary and Moral Society for the Prophylaxis of Venereal Diseases (Sociedad Mexicana Sanitaria y Moral de Profilaxis de las Enfermedades Venéreas), had been formed as early as 1908, the formalization of Mexico's eugenics movement occurred as part of the national-ist fervor of the postrevolutionary period. In 1929, for example, the Mexican Society of Puericulture, devoted to a pronatalist agenda of maternal and infant health, was established. Two years later, the majority of its members, led by the physician Alfredo M. Saavedra, founded the Mexican Eugenics Society, which existed, at least in name, until the early 1970s.

Mexican eugenicists, like Gamio and Vasconcelos, loudly carried the banner of mestizophilia and saw homogenization as fundamental to the health of the nation. Dr. Alfredo Correa, who cofounded the Mexican Eugenics Society with Saavedra, aptly captured the eugenic perspective on *mestizaje*, writing in the mid-1930s that it "is the problem and at the same time the solution. It is the problem because we are investigating the methods to achieve it and to some extent accelerate it. It is the answer because once realized, the national race will be one, a model that we have seen in other countries whose result is growth and progress in addition to collective well-being."[19]

Eugenicists' mestizophilia seldom translated into calls for cohesion based on the exclusion of groups labeled as "undesirable" such as the Chinese, Africans, Syrians, Jews, and Gypsies. A virulent Sinophobia shot through with language drawn directly from degeneration theory was a significant aspect of Mexican nationalism's exclusionary dictates in the 1920s and 1930s, but eugenicists did not take part in anti-Chinese or anti-Semitic agitation. For instance, the Mexi-can Eugenics Society and the Pro-Race Committee of Mexico City—which drafted racist legislation and stigmatized Chinese Mexicans and, later, Jews fleeing Nazi Germany—had just one member in common, a military general and editor of the anticlerical and jingoistic journal, *La Patria*.[20]

Instead, most Mexican eugenicists echoed the vision of integration espoused by Correa and invoked the figure of the mestizo without reference to any other "race." This absence reflected their unspoken wish that the eventual outcome of racial mixing would, over time, be the disappearance of mestizos themselves from the national landscape and the concomitant ascendancy of whites or Creoles. This corollary of eugenic mestizophilia was almost always hidden within a utopian discourse of inclusion, which was more likely to extol the Indian than reveal a preference for a white(r) populace. This elision was also a strategy of official racialization and state formation. The illusion of a homogenous mestizo nation was reinforced by the enumerative categories of the 1930 census. Unlike the 1921 census, a holdover from the Porfiriato, the 1930 version did not classify inhabitants according to "race," a concept that the drafters judged to be invalid and unscientific.[21]

For the most part, the contradictions of mestizophilia remained under the surface. Sometimes, however, especially when eugenicists provided detailed explications of their ideas, these ironies became apparent. For example, in what can be read as a *lapsus linguae*, Dr. Rafael Carrillo, a tireless eugenicist involved in child welfare and clinical gynecology, divulged his predilections in a lengthy talk given before the Mexican Eugenics Society in 1932. Beginning with the declaration that "there [was] no human who [was] a racially pure descendent,"[22] Carrillo went on to outline the three problems confronting Mexican eugenicists: ethnicity and ethnology, heredity, and immigration. After emphasizing the importance of a selective immigration law, he added, "It is also certain that if *mestizaje* continues indefinitely, it will disappear over time, given that the white race, being superior, will prevail over the inferior black and Indian."[23] For the most part, however, such comments remained buried. Anxieties over the implications of the cult of the mestizo can be more readily discerned in eugenicists' repeated calls for a state-guided anthropological census of every inhabitant in the republic. By cataloguing every body within the territorial limits of the state, eugenicists hoped to gather data in order to make racial mixing a postrevolutionary mandate efficaciously guided by knowledge experts.

ENUMERATING THE NATION: CENSUSES, SURVEYS, AND DEMOGRAPHY

Taking their cue from J. Joaquín Izquierdo—one of the country's most prominent physiologists, a participant in the Second International Congress of Eugenics, and a collaborator with Gamio on a scientific treatise on the central valley—Mexican eugenicists implored the state to carry out a whole array of demographic and genealogical projects. In a lecture presented as the president of the eugenics section at the Second Mexican Congress of the Child in 1923, Izquierdo recommended that public health agencies embark on various eugenic endeavors. Most pressing was a "serious study of the distribution of the great Mexican family; to determine the characteristics of the Indian, the Creole, and the mestizo, and to precisely ascertain the results of their unions in order to finally determine how to exalt the qualities of the Mexican and discard his defects."[24] Many Mexican eugenicists also echoed the recommendation proposed by Carrillo ten years later: "Given the genuine mosaic of races which make up the inhabitants of our territory, it is necessary that the eugenicist, in order to become oriented, immediately begin to study all of the anthropometric traits which distinguish the races from one another."[25]

The criteria of state demography were influenced by eugenics in another significant way. Since the late nineteenth century, positivists had condemned Malthusian arguments about the scarcity of human resources and the implied need for population control by asserting that the issue was not the absolute quantity of those resources, but their adequate distribution. Moreover, many believed that Mexico's productivity lagged behind that of other Western countries because of underpopulation and underutilization of land. However, whereas the majority of *científicos* had encouraged growth through European colonization, eugenicists—animated by both mestizophilia and neo-Lamarckism—favored natural growth. A concern with high rates of infant mortality and myriad childhood diseases (that had been exacerbated by the revolutionary upheavals of the 1910s) had been critical to the development of the eugenics movement. Partially for these reasons, pronatalism was a constant feature of Mexican eugenics. Influenced by French eugenics, especially the field of puericulture, which focused on the evolution of the child from conception to adolescence, Mexican eugenicists linked a rhetorical aversion to theories of pure "races" to a blueprint for a qualitative and quantitative increase of population density.[26]

Proposals for achieving a demographic makeover of the country were formulated principally by the economist Gilberto Loyo. The country's first professionally trained demographer, Loyo had studied under the Italian fascist Corrado Gini at the University of Rome in the early 1930s. After returning to Mexico, he formed the Mexican Committee for the Study of Population Problems and began to work closely with the administrations of the Maximato (Plutarco Elías Calles and his handpicked successors, 1924–34) and Lázaro Cárdenas (1934–40). In 1934, for example, the Partido Nacional Revolucionario (PNR, National Revolutionary Party) published a treatise on Mexico's demographic problems that Loyo had written in Italy.[27] The nearly 500-page *Demographic Policy in Mexico*, which he had prepared at the PNR's Institute of Social, Political, and Economic Studies, appeared one year later.[28] Reiterating many of the demographic theories of Gini, which underscored the power of numbers and the need for an "optimum" population size, the tome opened with an attack on Malthus and then went on to advocate rapid but judicious natural growth guided by the revolutionary principles of the PNR.[29] Reading like a eugenicists' wish list, *Demographic Policy in Mexico* supported campaigns against infant mortality and for public health measures, prenuptial certificates, the selective immigration of "assimilable" foreigners, the repatriation of Mexican nationals from the United States, and the invigoration of the mestizo through programs aimed at modernizing the Indian. Most of the book's concluding recommendations became official dogma in 1936 when Cárdenas decreed the General Population Law (Ley General de Población). Containing stipulations regarding internal growth, migration, and naturalization, this law mandated the "fusion of all the nation's ethnic groups" and "the general protection, conservation, and improvement of the species, within the limits and through the procedures laid out in this law."[30] In 1939 Loyo's eugenic inclinations led to a joint agreement between the Mexican Committee for the Study of the Population Problem and the Mexican Eugenics Society to carry out a comprehensive demographic survey of the still extremely heterogeneous population, encourage the redistribution of peoples and lands, and enforce selective immigration restrictions.[31] A member of the Mexican Eugenics Society in the 1940s, Loyo contributed to ongoing discussions about population density and land use and continued to aver that the country needed to "rapidly increase its population and, above all, to dramatically raise the level of the quality of the life of its inhabitants, in order to fulfill Mexico's historic destiny."[32]

For the most part, these recommendations for extensive national surveys were formulated in a context dominated by neo-Lamarckian notions about the malleability of Mexico's population and, especially, the possibility of creating a vigorous mestizo nation. By the late 1930s, however, biologists and geneticists throughout the world had so discredited neo-Lamarckism that Mexican eugenicists, in order to maintain a hold on objectivity and science, began to discard some of the ideological baggage of positivism. In place of neo-Lamarckism, they began, often grudgingly, to accept Mendelism. This involved acknowledging that syphilis and tuberculosis could not be transmitted hereditarily from generation to generation through damaged cellular material, a belief that had catalyzed eugenicists' sex education and antiprostitution campaigns earlier in the decade. The results of demographic surveys abetted this fractured transition from neo-Lamarckism to Mendelism, leading to a growing preoccupation with the country's ethnic composition, which, despite twenty years of mestizomania, had failed to fulfill the aspirations laid out by Gamio and eugenicists. Throughout the 1940s, Saavedra's editorials in *Eugenesia*, the journal of the Mexican Eugenics Society (1932–35, 1939–54), increasingly called for exhaustive ethnological studies of the populace. Although still enthusiastic about eugenic goals, Saavedra erased earlier positive prognostications of racial mixing from his writings and instead began to speak about the disparate ethnic groups in the country. At the same time, he stated that environmental amelioration alone was insufficient, and that it was time to "awaken a rational concept of hereditary responsibility"[33] based on Mendelism. These views were reiterated by Alfredo L. Valle, one of Mexico's first agricultural geneticists. In 1940 he told his readers that *indigenismo* and adoration of the Indian were no longer enough to bring about national integration. According to Valle, the process of homogenization had stagnated, and a more direct action was imperative in the "short term" to "strengthen the nation."[34]

The entrenchment of the neo-Lamarckian framework of Mexican eugenics, however, made it virtually impossible for Saavedra and other physicians and biologists trained during the postrevolutionary period to accept hereditarian theories that completely undermined human intervention. Largely for this reason, Mexican eugenicists turned to biotypology, a social science then popular in the Americas and Europe that drew from anthropology, psychology, physiology, and statistics. From the 1930s to the 1960s, many scientists who wished to retain a hold on hereditarianism but avoid narrow biological determinism found in biotypology a vision of the individual and society that they could easily countenance.[35] In the process, urban and rural schoolchildren, indigenous populations, cosmopolitan middle-class men, and other conglomerates were subjected to a panoply of medical interventions for the purposes of quantification and classification. Whereas nineteenth-century anthropology had relied largely upon calipers, rulers, and several other instruments to gauge primarily physiognomy, biotypology was built upon regnant approaches to physiology that sanctified laboratory experimentation. Thus, for example, when Mexican biotypologists set out to scrutinize Zapotec Indians, athletes, or soldiers in the 1940s and 1950s, they carried their laboratory with them, arriving at their study sites with blood sampling tools, microscopes, and instruments to test basal metabolism, endocrine function, blood pressure, pulse, and visual acuity, in addition to the older anthropometric instruments. Although biotypologists claimed that their techniques for categorizing individuals and imposing social order were based upon a rejection of theories of racial superiority, the impartial and objective medicalized labels that they invented were in many ways just as laden with contradictions and tensions as the mestizophilia of the 1920s and 1930s.

CLASSIFYING BIOTYPES: FROM CLASSROOM TO COUNTRYSIDE

In Latin America, as in France and Italy, biotypology had vast appeal.[36] As devised by Nicola Pende in the climate of fascism, "the main purpose of biotypology was to ensure a knowledge and efficient development of the biotypes of the nation, since each biotype was believed to show distinctive functional aptitudes, psychic pathologies, and susceptibilities to illness and crime."[37] For Mexican eugenicists, whose earlier goals of national development, natural growth, and ethnic or racial betterment were now more consciously driven by Mendelism, biotypology offered both a new form of medicalized diagnostics and a theory of human differentiation. In a similar fashion, for many Italian, French, and U.S. physicians biotypology implied a rejection of determinist frameworks that defined individuals solely in terms of categories of "race" and nationality, since biotypes comprised a complex mixture of relational factors. First and foremost, biotypology was driven by the ostensibly transparent measurements of normal, average, and mean, instead of the racial categories associated with late-nineteenth-century evolutionism and Victorian anthropology.[38]

For example, at a time of growing medical specialization in the United States, the statistician Raymond Pearl and the physician Charles Stockard turned to constitutional medicine in order to gain a more holistic picture of the patient as a person. Working in elaborately outfitted laboratories, these practitioners measured the physiognomic, mental, and behavioral coordinates of a wide range of individuals; the indicators and correlations they obtained were used to categorize their patients into biotypes. Stockard, a renowned endocrinologist at Cornell University, devised a system of classification based on thyroid metabolism and head shape. In Italy, Pende and his disciples grouped individuals according to ratios of chest to limb size and measures of physiological functioning; in France, Henri Laughier, an honorary member of the Mexican Eugenics Society, classified schoolchildren and industrial workers by carrying out elaborate fatigue studies.[39] U.S., French, Italian, South American, and Mexican biotypologists formulated endless taxonomies during the mid-twentieth century, but what they all had in common was the goal of imposing a new social order that privileged heredity without relinquishing external factors. Stockard, for example, believed that "one's hereditary make-up, or 'type' as he called it, remained constant throughout the individual's life; but he believed that type could only be expressed to the degree allowed by the individual's environment."[40]

In Mexico, the popularization of biotypology was part of eugenicists' tempered embrace of Mendelism.[41] At the same time that Saavedra was urging the

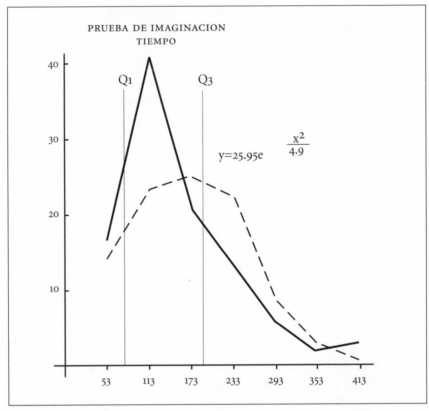

PRUEBA DE IMAGINACION
TIEMPO

$$y = 25.95e^{\frac{x^2}{4.9}}$$

Histogram of imagination test. Compared to middle-class urban Mexican men (solid line), the Otomís (broken line) were deemed normal, though weak, in response time and moderately deficient in number of responses given. From José Gómez Robleda, Estudio biotipológico de los otomíes *(Mexico City: Universidad Nacional Autónoma de México, 1961), 60.*

Mexican Eugenics Society to disabuse itself of the Lamarckian fallacy that acquired characteristics could be inherited, he was beginning to promote biotypology. In a 1940 article in *Eugenesia*, for example, Saavedra cited Pende when he asserted that "human personality is fundamentally determined by hereditary traits" but is also "seriously influenced by the environment."[42] By 1945, Saavedra had become a full-fledged advocate of biotypology and the constitutional approach to medicine. In *A Lesson in Social Work*, a manual he authored for social workers and nurses being trained at the newly established Mexican Institute of Social Security, Saavedra defined biotypology as a "humanized science, not unilateral, but universal," which would "study man not through the poor and isolated perspective of his morphology and physiology, but rather in relation to all of his problems, from his phylogenetic development through his

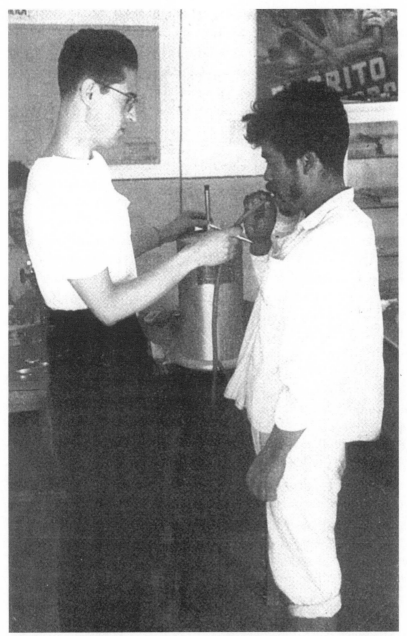

Respiration test. This test determined that the Otomís were significantly deficient types in terms of frequency and pattern of respiration, oxygen intake, and vital capacity. From José Gómez Robleda, Estudio biotipológico de los otomíes *(Mexico City: Universidad Nacional Autónoma de México, 1961), 91.*

evolution to maturity."[43] This text also contained several diagrams in which Saavedra envisioned human constitution as a series of concentric circles. In the bull's-eye was heredity, followed by ontogenetic experience, geographic environment, and social influences.[44] Essentially a training manual in biotypology, A Lesson in Social Work included in its final pages an intake form for social workers to utilize in the field.

In the 1940s and 1950s state demography, biotypology, and eugenics became intimately intertwined. While Loyo worked with other eugenicists and statisticians to divine methods for classifying and reassembling Mexico's growing and disparate population, Saavedra and other physicians began to link biotypology directly to racial hygiene and increased medical surveillance of the population at large. In 1941, for example, Saavedra recommended the establishment of a racial hygiene department attached to the central government that would be dedicated to genealogical study of the Mexican family. The first step in compiling this data would be the creation of biotypological cards to track individuals from cradle to grave, register defects and diseases, and thus provide a comprehensive picture of the country's healthiest biotypes.[45] Saavedra concluded that the "value of a nation depends on the quality of its populace and the true wealth of a country rests in the health and capacity of its inhabitants. . . . The Sanitary Authorities should concern themselves with the problems of Racial Hygiene, establishing an institution for genealogical research of the Mexican family, in order to study the application of socially beneficial measures."[46]

Saavedra's pleas for a detailed census, which echoed the urgings of Izquierdo and Gamio in the early 1920s, demonstrate that biotypology reinforced many of the previous objectives of physical anthropology and state censuses. Gamio himself endorsed biotypology in 1942 at the Eighth American Scientific Congress held in Washington, D.C. In the section of the program dedicated to indigenous issues, Gamio advocated a massive investigation of Mexican biotypes complemented by in-depth studies of cultural types.[47] Despite these continuities, however, biotypology differed from preceding attempts to classify individuals. It was designed explicitly to categorize individuals not in terms of "race"—white, mestizo, or black—but as prototypes that transcended the superficial and inflexible logic of racial differentiation. While in practice biotypologists often blurred the lines between "race" and biotype, the statistical language of this novel field both effaced and recoded the manifest racism of early-twentieth-century sciences. In addition, biotypology encouraged the intervention of diagnostic techniques into corporeal and abstract domains hitherto uncharted by medicine or biology, as well as the application of statistical quantification to every inch of the human body.

Many of the techniques of Mexican biotypologists were initially implemented in the realm of primary education, where schoolchildren had constituted subjects for anthropometric, psychometric, and physiological studies since the turn of the twentieth century. In 1925, as part of the reorganization of the Ministry of Public Education, a special unit, the Department of Psychopedagogy and Hygiene, was created. Devoted to investigating and measuring the physical and mental limits and abilities of Mexico's youngest generation, this department was responsible for introducing standardized testing in Mexican classrooms and popularizing concepts of superior and inferior intelligence. During its existence, from 1925 to 1939, many members of the Department of Psychopedagogy and Hygiene and its subdivisions belonged either to the Mexican Puericulture Society or the Mexican Eugenics Society.[48]

In the 1930s, during the height of President Cárdenas's program of socialist education, Gómez Robleda joined this department and soon found it was an ideal site from which to launch biotypology in Mexico. Trained in medicine, psychology, and biology at the National Medical School, Gómez Robleda took charge of the department's Psychological and Anthropological Research Service (Servicio de Investigacion Psicológica e Antropólogica). There he oversaw the adaptation of a new battery of I.Q. and achievement tests based more explicitly on notions of innate mental capacity. Several years later, when Cárdenas created the National Institute of Psychopedagogy (Instituto Nacional de Psicopedagogía), Gómez Robleda became the director of the Psychophysiology Service and began to manage an extensive survey aimed at categorizing all pupils according to anthropometric, physiological, and psychological constants.[49] With the assistance of the prominent biologist and eugenicist José Rulfo, Gómez Robleda undertook Mexico's first serious biotypological study in 1937. His team analyzed fingerprints, body size, visual and other sensorial capacities, muscle strength, cardiovascular function, temperature, memory, judgment, and ratiocination among 120 "proletarian" schoolboys at the Ramón López Velarde elementary school in Mexico City.[50] As was common among biotypologists, Gómez Robleda and his team discarded much of the data because it varied too widely to be statistically reliable. Nonetheless, they arrived at several conclusions. On one hand, reflecting a combination of crude materialism and environmentalism, they claimed that the ten dozen boys under investigation belonged to an oppressed social class and that this explained their weakened condition. On the other hand, influenced by human genetics, they asserted that somatic traits—such as cephalic index and other bodily correlates—were constitutional and hereditary. This principle implied that the governmental actions they recommended at the end of their report would be of little use. In the end, the researchers determined that they had identified not an ethnic group, but a universal proletarian class defined by a set of "constitutional traits" that were "almost impossible to modify."[51]

From the National Institute of Psychopedagogy, Gómez Robleda moved to the Institute of Social Research at the National University in the late 1930s and initiated a series of biotypological studies among several indigenous groups. He began by leading an investigation of Tarascan fishermen, peasants, and students at Patzcuaro Lake, then carried out a survey of Zapotecs, and finally studied the Otomís.[52] While Gómez Robleda had managed to compile an impressive array of information on schoolchildren, his conclusions were confusing and often incongruous because he lacked a clear-cut taxonomy in which to organize his data. By the time he began studying Indians, however, he had discovered the work of Italian biotypologists and was especially taken with Giacinto Viola's tripartite scheme, which consisted of short types (*braquitipos*), long types (*longitipos*), and normal types (*normotipos*). The short types were characterized by a high chest to limb ratio, the long types by the opposite, and the normal types, also known as the ideal types, fell right between the two, at the top of the bell curve.[53] Using Viola's biotypes, the categories created by Viola's disciple, Mario Barbara, and Ernst Kretschmer's system as his primary classifications of human constitution, Gómez Robleda sorted, correlated, and compared hundreds of Indians.[54]

Most of the time his results showed that Mexico's Indian groups were not normal types. The majority of Tarascans, for example, were asthenic, or akin to the long type. According to the medical examinations and statistical calculations, almost all the Tarascan men studied suffered from hypothyroidism, were inhibited, prone to neuroses, excessively effeminate, and often bisexual. The turn-of-the-century U.S. psychologist G. Stanley Hall certainly would have interpreted them as overstimulated neurasthenics. Conversely, the Otomís would have been viewed by Hall as undercivilized or primitive, while Gómez Robleda classed them as predominantly short types marked by dizziness, stupefaction, lack of imagination, asthma, myopia, manic depression, and hypersexuality. Gómez Robleda's later biotypological comparison of Indian groups showed that the Otomís were representative of most indigenous peoples, which, in general, he categorized not just as short but also as deficient (*braquitipos deficientes*).[55] These conclusions reveal a great deal about the transnational repertoire of scientific theories and methods that Mexican anthropologists and eugenicists felt compelled to utilize in the 1940s and 1950s in order to retain a hold on objectivity. No longer able to persuasively invoke neo-Lamarckian precepts and uncomfortably aware of the failures of mestizophilia, Mexican eugenicists found in biotypology a ductile and intricate version of Mendelian hereditarianism that was not blatantly offensive. One of the striking paradoxes that Mexican biotypologists faced, however, was that when they imported the taxonomies of Viola, Barbara, or Stockard, the statistical control groups and independent variables came embedded in the theoretical package. Thus, despite their admonitions about the evils of racist physical anthropology—which they defined as "anti-scientific since it is not possible to establish distinct ranks and hierarchical qualities between human groups"[56]—Gómez Robleda and his collaborators classified indigenous groups according to base types derived from working-class Italian men, U.S. soldiers, and, only secondarily, middle-class Mexican men.[57]

REVIVING THE PAST AND RECODING THE FUTURE

As Robert Buffington has shown, in the context of postwar discourses of development and modernization, biotypology catalyzed a reemergence of tropes of degeneration and criminal anthropology that had been so common during the Porfirian period and promoted the revival of the "persistent stereotype" of "the apathetic and resistant Indian."[58] The continuities between Porfirian past and revolutionary present are especially pronounced if we look at Mexican biotypological studies as attempts to gauge degree of civilization. In Gómez Robleda's study of the urban middle class, for example, he found that women were moderate and somewhat masculinized short types; men, however, were mainly long types with proclivities toward effeminacy and homosexuality.[59] In terms of civilizing discourses, this gendered distinction between the mannish, extroverted woman and the emasculated, fragile man was far from groundbreaking, being clearly rooted in nineteenth-century theories of social evolution and sexology. Conversely, biotypology was responsible for recoding racial categories into a neologistic and putatively more neutral lexicon that stressed individual heredity over racial typology. It did so, however, while simultaneously clinging to, and ushering in, an increasingly scientized language of class, gender, and ethnicity.

Saavedra and Gómez Robleda, as well as the anthropologist Juan Comas, proclaimed repeatedly that biotypology was a reaction against racist anthropology and European conceptions of biological superiority.[60] In the prologue to their 1947 manual, for example, Gómez Robleda and Ada D'Aloja averred that their hope was that biotypology would quickly become the incontrovertible canon for Mexican researchers who were "so incredibly insistent on perpetuating techniques of racist physical anthropology."[61] In his prologue to Gómez Robleda's study of Tarascans, the sociologist and editor of the *Revista Mexicana de Sociología* (Mexican Journal of Sociology) Lucio Mendieta y Nuñez applauded biotypology's ability to surpass all racial doctrines and infuse studies of ethnicity and social groups with modern science and impartiality.[62] Biotypology's introduction of technologies and methodologies of human measurement and differentiation into academic, bureaucratic, and popular domains contributed to an enlargement—not a diminution—of racialized vocabularies and practices in Mexico.

As Mexican eugenicists haltingly accepted Mendelism in the 1940s, they did so in a more complex and less reductionist manner than their Anglo-American or German counterparts. While their creative rearticulation was part and parcel of the "cultural relativism" that characterized anthropology and the social sciences in the post–World War II period, Mexican eugenicists' attitudes toward "race" had also been more fluid—if not convoluted—during the postrevolutionary decades of mestizophilia. More important, however, tracing this history suggests that biotypology may, in Mexico and elsewhere, have played an important and largely unexplored role in inventing many of the variables associated with cultural explanations of social distinction. In the particular case of Mexico, this does not mean that Saavedra and Gómez Robleda were not "racist," but that the terminology of "race" and ethnicity they fashioned and deployed was ambivalent, slippery, and prone to dissimulation. With the rise of biotypology and the entrenchment of statistical models that valorized normality above all else, the terrain of racialization in Mexico became more circuitous and multifaceted.[63] If the tensions of mestizophilia had indeed been circumnavigated by an original framework that privileged both heredity and environment, many other contradictions arose in their wake. In the end, the abstract and medicalized language of biotypologists, who spent much of their time plotting types and variables against statistical curves, was and remains much more intractable and insidious than the social Darwinian labels of the past.

NOTES

Thanks are due to numerous individuals for their constructive comments on different versions of this essay. In particular, I would like to acknowledge Paul Liffman, Robin Derby, Maria Teresa Koreck, Howard Markel, Claudio Lomnitz, and the editors of this volume. Research for this project was generously supported by a Social Science Research Council International Dissertation Research Fellowship, a Fulbright-Hays Dissertation Fellowship, and a travel grant from the Mexican Studies Program at the University of Chicago.

1. José Gómez Robleda, *Pescadores y campesinos tarascos* (Mexico City: Secretaría de Educación Pública, 1943).

2. José Gómez Robleda and Ada D'Aloja, *Biotipología* (Mexico City: Talleres Gráficos de la Nación, 1947).

3. In addition to *Pescadores*, Gómez Robleda's studies include *Características biológicas de los escolares proletarios* (Mexico City: DAPP, 1937); "Clasificación biotipológica de los grupos indígenas de México," *Revista Mexicana de Sociología* 10, no. 3 (1949): 315–31; "Estudio biotipológico," in *Los zapotecos: Monografía histórica, etnográfica y económica*, ed. Lucio Mendieta y Núñez (Mexico City: Universidad Nacional Autónoma de México, 1949), 265–415; *Estudio biotipológico de los otomíes* (Mexico City: Universidad Nacional Autónoma de México, 1961); *Imagen del mexicano* (Mexico City: n.p., 1948); José Gómez Robleda and Luis Argoytia, *Deportistas* (Mexico City: Secretaría de Educación Pública, 1940).

4. I define racialization as the process by which the signifier of "race" acquires social and historical value and is constructed, contested, and embodied through the situational interplay of culture and science. See Michael Omi and Howard Winant, *Racial Formation in the United States: From the 1960s to the 1980s*, 2d ed. (New York: Routledge, 1994), and David Theo Goldberg, *Racial Subjects: Writing on Race in America* (New York: Routledge, 1997). Unlike many theorists of racialization, however, I view biology and culture not as opposing and/or consecutive domains to which "race" is singularly attached but instead as intertwined and co-constitutive formations.

5. See Gilbert M. Joseph and Daniel Nugent, eds., *Everyday Forms of State Formation: Revolution and the Negotiation of Rule in Modern Mexico* (Durham: Duke University Press, 1994).

6. See Michel Foucault, *Ethics: Subjectivity and Truth*, ed. Paul Rabinow (New York: New Press, 1997) and *The History of Sexuality*, vol. 1, *An Introduction* (New York: Vintage Books, 1996); Sam Whimster and Scott Lash, eds., *Max Weber: Rationality and Modernity* (London: Allen and Unwin, 1987); Ann Laura Stoler, *Race and the Education of Desire: Foucault's* History of Sexuality *and the Colonial Order of Things* (Durham: Duke University Press, 1995) and "Sexual Affronts and Racial Frontiers: European Identities and the Cultural Politics of Exclusion in Colonial Southeast Asia," in *Tensions of Empire: Colo-*

nial Cultures in a Bourgeois World, ed. Frederick Cooper and Ann Laura Stoler (Berkeley: University of California Press, 1997), 198–237; Hannah Arendt, *The Origins of Totalitarianism* (New York: Harcourt Brace Jovanovich, 1973); Patrick H. Hutton, "Foucault, Freud, and the Technologies of the Self," in *Technologies of the Self*, ed. Luther H. Martin, Huck Gutman, and Patrick H. Hutton (Amherst: University of Massachusetts Press, 1988), 121–44.

7. This view is advocated by Elazar Barkan, *The Retreat of Scientific Racism: Changing Concepts of Race in Britain and the United States between the World Wars* (New York: Cambridge University Press, 1992), and creatively discussed by Marisol de la Cadena, *Indigenous Mestizos: The Politics of Race and Culture in Cuzco, Peru, 1919–1991* (Durham: Duke University Press, 2000); Verena Stolcke, "Talking Culture: New Boundaries, New Rhetorics of Exclusion in Europe," *Current Anthropology* 46, no. 1 (Feb. 1995): 1–24; and Peggy Pascoe, "Miscegenation Law, Court Cases, and Ideologies of 'Race' in Twentieth-Century America," *Journal of American History* 83, no. 1 (June 1996): 44–70.

8. See Charles A. Hale, *The Transformation of Liberalism in Late-Nineteenth-Century Mexico* (Princeton: Princeton University Press, 1989), and Rosaura Ruiz Gutiérrez, *Positivismo y evolución: Introducción del darwinismo en México* (Mexico City: Universidad Nacional Autónoma de México, 1987). On degeneration theory in Europe, see Daniel Pick, *Faces of Degeneration: A European Disorder, c. 1848–1918* (Cambridge: Cambridge University Press, 1989). For a provocative analysis of a similar phenomenon in India, see Gyan Prakash, *Another Reason: Science and the Imagining of Modern India* (Princeton: Princeton University Press, 1999).

9. See Nancy Leys Stepan, *"The Hour of Eugenics": Race, Gender, and Nation in Latin America* (Ithaca: Cornell University Press, 1991). On this pattern in other Latin American countries, see Lourdes Martínez-Echazábal, *"Mestizaje* and the Discourse of National/ Cultural Identity in Latin America, 1845–1959," *Latin American Perspectives* 25, no. 3 (May 1998): 21–42.

10. Andrés Molina Enríquez, *Los grandes problemas nacionales* (1909; reprint, with preface by Arnaldo Córdova, Mexico City: Ediciones Era, 1978).

11. I take the term "mestizophilia" from Agustín Basave Benítez, *México mestizo: Análisis del nacionalismo mexicano en torno a la mestizofilia de Andrés Molina Enríquez* (Mexico City: Fondo de Cultura Económica, 1992). See also Claudio Lomnitz-Adler, *Exits from the Labyrinth: Culture and Ideology in the Mexican National Space* (Berkeley: University of California Press, 1992), and David A. Brading, "Social Darwinism and Romantic Idealism: Andrés Molina Enríquez and José Vasconcelos in the Mexican Revolution," in *Prophecy and Myth in Mexican History* (Cambridge: Centre of Latin American Studies, 1984).

12. See Peter J. Bowler, *The Eclipse of Darwinism: Anti-Darwinian Evolution Theories in the Decades around 1900* (Baltimore: Johns Hopkins University Press, 1983).

13. See Alan Knight, "Racism, Revolution, and *Indigenismo*: Mexico, 1910–1940," in *The Idea of Race in Latin America, 1870–1940*, ed. Richard Graham (Austin: University of Texas Press, 1990), 71–113, and Alexander S. Dawson, "From Models for the Nation to Model

Citizens: *Indigenismo* and the 'Revindication' of the Mexican Indian, 1920–1940," *Journal of Latin American Studies* 30, no. 2 (May 1998): 279–308.

14. José Vasconcelos, *La raza cósmica* (1925; reprint, Mexico City: Espasa, 1943), 42. All translations are mine.

15. Ibid., 47.

16. Ibid., 42.

17. Basave Benítez, *México mestizo*, 133.

18. Knight, "Racism, Revolution, and *Indigenismo*," 87.

19. Alfredo Correa, "La eugenesia y su importancia," *Pasteur* 9, no. 4 (Oct. 1936): 73–76. Correa was optimistic about the possibilities of *mestizaje* from the outset. In a 1933 article he wrote, "[The goal is] to study if *mestizaje* is favorable and if so, which elements are most favorable. Not to have racial prejudices, [the most favorable] could be the white [race], the black or the yellow." Correa, "Importancia de la eugenesia ante el criterio del estado," *Pasteur* 6, no. 6 (Dec. 1933): 151–64.

20. General Cristóbal Rodríguez was a member of the Mexican Eugenics Society in the 1930s. He published articles by Saavedra in *La Patria* and was a founding member of the Pro-Race Committee of Mexico City upon its beginning in 1933. On Sinophobia, see Gerardo Rénique's contribution to this volume; José Jorge Gómez Izquierdo, *El movimiento antichino en México (1871–1934): Problemas del racismo y del nacionalismo durante la Revolución Mexicana* (Mexico City: Instituto Nacional de Antropología e Historia, 1991); and Ricardo Pérez Monfort, *"Por la patria y por la raza": La derecha secular en el sexenio de Lázaro Cárdenas* (Mexico City: Universidad Nacional Autónoma de México, 1993).

21. The 1921 census included the following categories: indigenous (Indian), mixed (mestizo), white, other, and foreigner (alien of any race). See Departamento de Estadística Nacional, *Resúmen del censo general de habitantes de 30 de noviembre de 1921* (Mexico City: Talleres Gráficos de la Nación, 1928). Also see Luis A. Astorga A., "La razón demográfica de estado," *Revista Mexicana de Sociología* (Jan.–Mar. 1989): 193–210, and Casey Walsh, "The Mestizo in Mexican Statistical Knowledge, 1876–1920," unpublished manuscript in possession of author. In an excellent article on Ecuador, A. Kim Clark argues that state statistics and demography were central to constructing a national ideology of the mestizo. See A. Kim Clark, "Race, 'Culture,' and Mestizaje: The Statistical Construction of the Ecuadorian Nation, 1930–1950," *Journal of Historical Sociology* 11, no. 2 (June 1998): 185–211.

22. Rafael Carrillo, "Tres problemas mexicanos de eugenesia: Etnografía y etnología, herencia e inmigración," *Revista Mexicana de Puericultura* 3, no. 25 (Nov. 1932): 1–15, quotation on 5.

23. Ibid., 9.

24. J. Joaquín Izquierdo, "Necesidad de que en México emprenda el estado estudios de eugenesia," *Medicina* 3, no. 32 (Feb. 1923): 190. This lecture was also reprinted in *Eugenesia* 21 (Feb. 1933): 4–6.

25. Carrillo, "Tres problemas mexicanos."

26. See William H. Schneider, *Quality and Quantity: The Quest for Biological Regeneration in Twentieth-Century France* (Cambridge: Cambridge University Press, 1990), esp. chap. 3, and Stepan, *"The Hour of Eugenics,"* 76–82.

27. Gilberto Loyo, *Las deficiencias cuantitativas de la población de México y una política demográfica nacional* (Mexico City: PNR, 1934).

28. Gilberto Loyo, *La política demográfica de México* (Mexico City: Ministerio de Prensa y Propaganda, 1935).

29. On Gini's politics in the context of Italian fascism, see David G. Horn, *Social Bodies: Science, Reproduction, and Italian Modernity* (Princeton: Princeton University Press, 1994).

30. *Ley general de población* (Mexico City: Ediciones Botas, 1936), 1.

31. See *Eugenesia*, 2d ser., 1, no. 1 (Nov. 1939): 2–4.

32. Gilberto Loyo, "Los problemas de la población en México," *Eugenesia* 7, no. 78 (July 1946): 12.

33. *Eugenesia* 1, no. 6 (Apr. 1940): 2.

34. Ibid., 12.

35. Sarah W. Tracy has done pathbreaking work on the history and particularities of biotypology and constitutional medicine in the United States during the interwar years. See Sarah W. Tracy, "An Evolving Science of Man: The Transformation and Demise of American Constitutional Medicine, 1920–1950," in *Greater Than the Parts: Holism in Biomedicine, 1920–1950*, ed. Christopher Lawrence and George Weisz (New York: Oxford University Press, 1998), 161–88, and "George Draper and American Constitutional Medicine, 1916–1946: Reinventing the Sick Man," *Bulletin of the History of Medicine* 66, no. 1 (Spring 1992): 53–89.

36. Stepan, *"The Hour of Eugenics,"* 116.

37. Ibid. Stepan documents biotypology's appeal to Argentine eugenicists as well as the visit of Pende to Argentina in the 1930s.

38. Alfredo M. Saavedra, "Acerca de la personalidad humana," *Eugenesia* 1, no. 13 (Nov. 1940): 16.

39. See William H. Schneider, "Henri Laughier, the Science of Work, and the Working of Science in France, 1920–1940," *Cahiers pour l'Histoire du CNRS, 1939–1989* (Paris: Editions du CNRS, 1989), 7–34.

40. Tracy, "An Evolving Science," 170, and "George Draper."

41. For an excellent introduction to biotypology, see Gonzalo Aguirre Beltrán, *Antropología médica*, vol. 8 of *Obra antropológica* (Mexico City: Fondo de Cultura Económica, 1994), 129–70.

42. Saavedra, "Acerca de la personalidad humana," 16.

43. Alfredo M. Saavedra, *Una lección de trabajo social* (Mexico City: n.p., 1945), 99.

44. Ibid., 23.

45. Alfredo M. Saavedra, "La selección de los generadores humanos," *Eugenesia* 2, no. 19 (May 1941): 12–14.

46. Ibid., 14.

47. Manuel Gamio, "El índice cultural y el biotipo," in *Proceedings of the Eighth American Scientific Congress* (Washington, D.C.: Department of State, 1942), 2:227–32. Gamio was then working as the director of the Demography Department in the Interior Ministry.

48. For a more detailed discussion of this department, see Alexandra Minna Stern, "Responsible Mothers and Normal Children: Eugenics, Welfare, and Nationalism in Post-Revolutionary Mexico, 1900–1940," *Journal of Historical Sociology* 12, no. 4 (Fall 1999): 369–97.

49. See Archivo Histórico de la Secretaría de Educación Pública, Departamento de Psicopedagogía e Higiene, Box 5158, Folder 8; *Memoria de la Secretaría de Educación Pública, 1936–1937* (Mexico City: Secretaría de Educación Pública, 1937), 221–59.

50. Gómez Robleda, *Características biológicas*.

51. Ibid., 279.

52. Gómez Robleda, "Estudio biotipológico" and *Estudio biotipológico de los otomíes*.

53. Gómez Robleda, *Pescadores*.

54. On Barbara, see Gómez Robleda and D'Aloja, *Biotipología*. Although he concentrated on Viola, Barbara, and also Pende, Gómez Robleda drew upon biotypological taxonomies devised by dozens of physicians and anthropologists in the United States, Germany, France, and Latin America. For an excellent discussion of Kretschmer's studies of ectomorphs, endomorphs, and mesomorphs, see Heather Munro Prescott, "I Was a Teenage Dwarf: The Social Construction of 'Normal' Adolescent Growth and Development in the United States," in *Formative Years: Children's Health in the United States, 1880–2000*, ed. Alexandra Minna Stern and Howard Markel (Ann Arbor: University of Michigan Press, 2002), 200–235.

55. Gómez Robleda, "Clasificación biotipológica," 331.

56. Gómez Robleda, *Pescadores*, xxvii.

57. Calculations for the Mexican normal type—determined by comparing 1,500 urban middle-class men to Viola's Italian group—actually categorized the former as a moderate long type (and male adolescents as mixed types). The Mexican group was nonetheless used as a point of comparison and reference in many of his other studies. See Gómez Robleda, *Imagen del mexicano*. U.S. soldiers were used as control groups to study Mexican men in the military and should figure into any study of perceptions and embodiments of Mexican masculinity in the twentieth century. See, for example, Javier Romero Molina, "Los cadetes del H. Colegio Militar: Estudio biométrico," *Anales del Instituto Nacional de Antropología e Historia* 3 (1951): 113–49. In this particular study, Romero relies on independent variables drawn from men in the U.S. army and at Harvard University. For other uses of biotypology, see Enrique Solis Cervantes, "Ensayo de biotipología mexicana" (thesis, Universidad Nacional Autonóma de México, Escuela Nacional de Medicina, 1952), and

Antonio Galicia Ciprés, "La biotipología y el psicoanálisis aplicados al estudio del delincuente" (thesis, Universidad Nacional Autónoma de México, Facultad de Derecho y Ciencas Sociales, 1946).

58. For his incisive analysis, see Robert M. Buffington, *Criminal and Citizen in Modern Mexico* (Lincoln: University of Nebraska Press, 2000), 162.

59. See Gómez Robleda, *Imagen del mexicano*.

60. See Juan Comas, *Conferencia de antropología y biotipología* (Monterrey, Nuevo Léon: n.p., 1944).

61. Gómez Robleda and D'Aloja, *Biotipología*, unpaginated prologue.

62. See Lucio Mendieta y Núñez, prologue to Gómez Robleda, *Pescadores*, xiii–xviii.

63. For a provocative discussion of the complexity and recursiveness of racial regimes, see Ann Laura Stoler, "Racial Histories and Their Regimes of Truth," *Political Power and Social Theory* 11 (1997): 183–206.

CHAPTER EIGHT

RACE, REGION, AND NATION

Sonora's Anti-Chinese
Racism and Mexico's
Postrevolutionary
Nationalism,
1920s–1930s

Gerardo Rénique

Despite their minority status and historians' neglect, the Chinese—as well as other nonwhite, non-Indian, and nonblack communities—have played an important role in the reconstruction of Latin American nationalisms.[1] Because of their demographic importance or their historical consideration as original inhabitants of the national territory, the belonging of Indians and blacks to the nation is relatively less ambiguous than that of the Chinese. This chapter will argue that the Chinese presence in postrevolutionary Mexico played a crucial role in shaping both regional and national identities. Anti-Chinese attitudes provided a safe outlet for the otherwise denied or muted racialism inscribed in the official *indigenista* racial orthodoxy. Anti-Chinese racism also acted as one catalyst for the territorialized construction of racial difference. Similar to the case of São Paulo, Brazil, examined by Barbara Weinstein in the next chapter, Sonora—and the northern (*norteño*) states in general—became identified in Mexico's racial/national imagination as a repository of whiteness and political progressivism. Examined from the perspective of anti-Chinese racism, the racial (and racist) base of Mexico's postrevolutionary nationalism appears crystal clear. Through an emphasis on the northern border state of Sonora, home of the largest Chinese community in Mexico and place of origin of the dominant revolutionary faction, this chapter will also argue for a reconsideration of regional racial formations in the construction of national identity and state formation.

From a Mexico City–centered historiographical perspective—in which regional histories and cultures were regarded as "fragments adverse to integration"—the *norteño* states were considered marginal to the formation of a national consciousness. Because of the region's supposed domination by the cultural values of the United States, Sonorans have usually been disregarded as "semi-American" or "semi-Mexican."[2] In this long-held and well-entrenched centralist view, Sonorans' identities and loyalties were regarded with suspicion and skepticism. At the same time, because of their crucial military role in defending the nation from the "barbarian" Apaches and Yaquis, Sonorans were also regarded as the paradigmatic model of "civilized people [*gente de razón*]."[3] Moreover, in Porfirian racial understanding, Sonorans were placed in a prominent niche in Mexico's racial/cultural hierarchy. The Porfirian intellectual and educator Justo Sierra attributed Sonorans' "progressive character" to their habitual consumption of wheat and meat. On the other hand, the influential Francisco Bulnes blamed the "lack of phosphorus" in the corn-based diet of the indigenous peoples of central and southern Mexico for their allegedly "dull and brutish" nature.[4] Following the revolutionary decade of 1910–20 these ideas formed part of a broad racial common sense sustained by revolutionary orthodoxy's reassessment of the historical and cultural importance of the popular classes, the recognition of these classes as quintessential representatives of the national identity, and the identification of the mestizo as the national/racial prototype.

The case of Sonora, however, raises questions about the importance of other non-Indian and nonblack groups in the construction of a national identity grounded in the paradigm of the centrality of the mestizo. In Sonora and the other northern frontier states the social and political upheaval unleashed by the revolutionary conditions of the 1910s was accompanied by an unprecedented wave of racially motivated anti-Chinese attacks. These actions marked a radical turn from the "quiescent animosity" that had governed Sonoran behavior and attitudes toward the Chinese during the almost three decades of the Porfirio Díaz regime.[5] A few years later Sonora was home to a full-fledged anti-Chinese political movement. The expansion of this racial movement to national prominence was galvanized by the cultural and intellectual debates of the 1920s and 1930s, which redefined Mexican national identity.

In this chapter I trace the origins of this racial common sense to the anti-Chinese racism of the 1920s and 1930s. I argue that Mexico's postrevolutionary national identity was a product of the mutual articulation of regional, racial, and gender identities, mediated by the political and cultural mobilization sponsored by the state and by the campaigns of the anti-Chinese movement. I discuss this complex genealogy through the analysis of (1) Sonora's frontier culture and ideology, and the transnational formation of its itinerant working class; (2) the racialization of the revolutionary war by which the Sonorans, as "*blanco-criollos* [white Creoles]," emerged victorious over the mostly peasant and/or indigenous armies of Francisco Villa and Emiliano Zapata; (3) the role of gender in Sonora's patriotic regionalist traditions; and (4) the epistemological and political coalescence between anti-Chinese racism and postrevolutionary nationalist orthodoxy.

FRONTIER IDEOLOGY AND POPULAR ANTI-CHINESE RACISM

Because of its extreme aridity, its location far from the center of New Spain, and, most important, its enduring Indian resistance to colonial rule, Sonora was one of the last regions to be incorporated into the colonial domain. Until the late Porfiriato, Sonoran entrepreneurs and landowners did not have easy access to labor and land. A direct railroad to Mexico City was not established until 1927, more than four decades after the establishment of the first railway connection between Sonora and the United States. During the rule of Porfirio Díaz (1884–1911), American investors found fertile ground in Sonora for the development of mining, the construction of railroads, cattle raising, and colonization and irrigation projects. Attracted by job openings in railway construction and mining, as well as by the expansion of Sonora's internal market, large numbers of Chinese immigrants also settled in the state.[6]

In the harsh Sonoran environment, people depended for their very survival on mutual cooperation. Apparently isolated ranches and settlements formed part of an extensive web of familial, political, and communal relations that spanned the international border separating Mexico from the United States. The social networks and identities of the people living in these areas were, in turn, mobilized around shared labor experiences and memories of armed resistance from the region's several indigenous groups, defense against foreign invasions, and a commonly expressed resentment of central state intervention.[7]

Perhaps the most important factor shaping the ideology and culture of

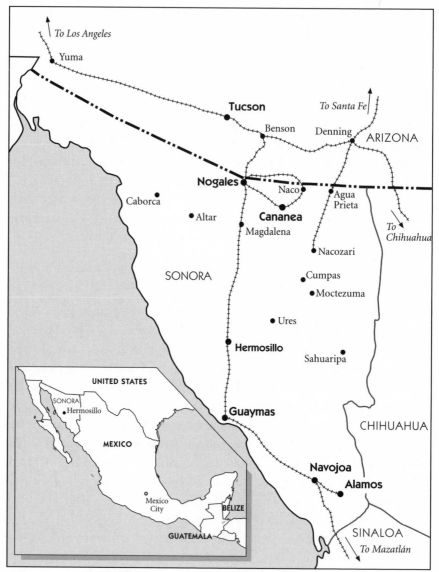

MAP 4. *State of Sonora, Mexico, 1920s*

Sonoran frontier society, however, was the gulf separating the aspirations and desires of the region's Spanish, and later Mexican, colonists from the indigenous native inhabitants. As in the frontier ideology described by nineteenth-century Argentinean statesman Domingo F. Sarmiento, this opposition was frequently interpreted as a struggle between the racially and culturally differentiated forces of civilization and barbarism. In Sonora, the racial distinctions inherent to this discourse of progress and civilization were heightened by a gendered code of honor in which manliness was defined in terms of the personal valor and fighting skills that were most often realized in the Indian campaigns.[8]

The racial underpinnings of Sonora's frontier code of honor were refined, codified, and popularized during the Porfiriato in an influential series of articles written in 1885 and 1886 by the prominent Sonoran politician Ramón Corral.[9] In this work—published in the official gazette of the state government—Corral argued that the degree of civilization of a particular group of indigenous peoples depended, in the first place, on the nature of their military cooperation with the colonialist forces and their acceptance of Mexican state law, and, in the second place, on their degree of adaptation to capitalism as either individual private producers or waged workers. Corral's prescriptions for Sonoran society conformed to the neo-Lamarckian traditions dominant in nineteenth-century Mexican racial theory.[10] Thus, Corral believed that the Opatas, Pimas, and Pápagos had improved their "race" by virtue of their closer relations with Spanish and Mexican colonists and, most important, through their cooperation in the colonists' war against the (hopelessly "barbarous") Apaches. While this historical experience laid the ground for racial improvement, the Opatas' and Pimas' final incorporation into civilization would be determined by their transformation into farmers or wageworkers, and by their adoption of the language, dress, and customs of the "white race."

In fact, since the mid-nineteenth century *blanco-criollo* Sonorans had come to form the "majority" population in the state.[11] As a result, the "average" or "prototypical" Sonoran came to be represented in Mexican literature and the popular imagination as a tall, "white" male with a racial identity and phenotype that differed from those of the mestizo and Indian populations of central and southern Mexico. The Sonoran newspaper *El Tráfico* attributed this physical and racial distinctiveness to "the [Sonoran] climate and the patriarchal lifestyle of our ancestors that imprinted [in the Sonorans] the seal of their pristine vigor."[12] Informed by this particular cultural landscape, Sonoran perspectives on *mestizaje* broke from commonsensical understandings of a racial mixture and cultural synthesis to propose instead the exclusionary incorporation of the Indians into a Sonoran population that was considered locally—and by most of the rest of Mexico—as *blanco-criollo*.[13]

Another important formative aspect of Sonora's frontier ideology was closely related to the intermittent movement of Sonoran male labor across the new international border established in the aftermath of the U.S.-Mexican War of 1846–48. The massive participation of Sonoran men in the 1849 California gold rush and the subsequent formation of a California working class were crucial factors in shaping popular anti-Chinese attitudes. The concentration of a large multinational and multiracial international labor force around the California gold deposits created the conditions for a sequence of violent, racially motivated confrontations. During the first stage, white supremacist groups in California targeted Mexicans, Chileans, Peruvians, and other South Americans. Later, resentment toward the massive influx of Chinese and other Asian immigrants led Mexicans in California to form a common front with their former attackers.[14] Culturalist perceptions of the Chinese's "unexplainable" or "bizarre" religious, ethical, and moral attributes and practices further reinforced a dominant, and largely shared, racial ideology, according to which Africans, Chinese, and Native Americans occupied the lowest echelon of racial acceptance. Mexicans, by comparison, were commonly considered to occupy a position slightly superior to the Chinese.[15] This racial hierarchy was replicated in the rigid occupational structure and racially segmented pay scales of the mining, construction, smelting, and railroad industries of California, where nonwhites were relegated to the lower ranks. Under these circumstances, the real and just concerns of non-Chinese workers regarding low salaries, poor labor conditions, and lack of employment were attributed to competition from cheap and supposedly servile Chinese workers.[16]

By the end of the nineteenth century these attitudes and perceptions constituted a complex and diffuse, but mostly rhetorical, anti-Chinese feeling expressed through jokes, insults, and prejudiced behavior. However, both the United States Exclusion Act of 1882, proscribing Chinese immigration, and Mexico's own debates on the conveniences—or inconveniences—of introducing Chinese labor galvanized these rather understated and personal feelings. Frustrated by their successive failures in transforming the Yaqui Indians into wage laborers, a fraction of the Sonoran elite developed a dislike for immigrants who were deemed unfit to be hardworking, civilized, clean, nice-looking, and law-abiding laborers. These circumstances coalesced by the turn of the century in the first important anti-Chinese impulse in Mexican territory.

Between 1895 and 1905 the leading voice promoting this view was *El Tráfico*, the editorial line of which was shaped by the Sonoran commercial elite's vision of progress and development. This strategy was grounded on three central pillars: an export economy, a male-dominated patriarchal family, and a social hierarchy and racial order dominated by Sonora's *blanco-criollo* men.[17]

Reflecting the dominant opinion among planters and entrepreneurs in Mexico's southeastern tropical regions, *El Tráfico* also considered Chinese immigration a "necessary evil" for the "material development" of Mexico's export economy. Another article, however, suggested restricting Chinese immigration to southern regions such as Yucatán or Tehuantepec, where "unhealthy weather" had deterred European immigration.[18] These attitudes also reflected the belief that Sonora was destined, because of its location and racial composition, to play a central role in Mexico's progress. Because of Sonora's strategic position in the Pacific basin, it was expected that the U.S.-led "opening of the Orient" would bring an advantageous expansion to the national economy.[19] However, *El Tráfico* stipulated that to take advantage of this historic opportunity, Mexico had to find a solution to its "national problem"—a "problem" that was primarily and simultaneously understood as "a problem of racial evolution" and a lack of "civilization."[20] This "morally diseased mestizo race," suggested *El Tráfico*, was responsible for the "psychological and physiological descent" that allegedly marked Mexico's racial degeneration. Because of their racial makeup, this condition was only of marginal importance in the frontier states.[21]

Under these circumstances, according to *El Tráfico*, the preferred solution to Mexico's "national problem" was the immigration of the "strong races"—above all, the "Germanic or Teutonic"—whose "great capacity of assimilation" would eventually absorb the best qualities and traits of the so-called *blanco-criollo* racial prototype.[22] To complement its ideal racial order, the Sonoran elite also considered the forced repatriation of Yaquis and the prohibition of Chinese immigration. Unions between Chinese men and Mexican women of the "lowest classes" were believed to produce individuals of "a new racial type still more degenerated than [Mexico's] naturally abject indigenous castes." As inheritor of the worst "vices and degeneration" of both races, the "product of these filthy unions" would ultimately lead to the disappearance of "the inherent patriotism of the Mexican people."[23]

Initially, *El Tráfico*'s early (1899) call to organize a "crusade against the Chinese" gained only marginal acceptance within Sonoran society. The low prices and convenient credit offered by Chinese businessmen in the import-export trade benefited consumers and local entrepreneurs as well as the state treasury.

Under these circumstances *El Tráfico*'s demands for anti-Chinese legislation and a boycott of Chinese businesses were rejected both by the state legislature and the population at large.[24]

THE *BLANCO-CRIOLLO* RACIAL TYPE IN REVOLUTIONARY MEXICO

The decade of revolutionary turmoil and disorder served as background for a reconsideration of the Sonoran's place in Mexico's politics, culture, and racial order. Commonly referred to by the Mexico City press as the "Attila of the South," revolutionary leader Emiliano Zapata was considered to display an "oriental imagination" in the torturing of prisoners and dissidents, while, by contrast, Sonoran military caudillo Alvaro Obregón was described as the "white savior" and compared to Hernán Cortés.[25] The northern general Obregón proudly proclaimed himself "to be superior to five *calzonudos*," a pejorative term often used by northerners and city dwellers to refer to those who wore the *calzones*, or breeches, used by indigenous men.[26]

Contemporary intellectual and cultural debates on national identity, popular expressions, and cultural types consolidated Sonoran predominance in Mexico's postrevolutionary racial formation. At the center of these debates was the concept of *mestizaje*. Since the precursor text of the eighteenth-century Jesuit writer Francisco Javier Clavijero, the concept has stood as one of Mexico's more enduring cultural and political traditions.[27] As discussed by Alexandra Minna Stern in the previous chapter, during the postrevolutionary years *mestizaje* became the dominant paradigm of national and racial formation, while the mestizo was consecrated as the unquestioned symbol of Mexican national culture.

In the idiosyncratic intellectual paradigm of Andrés Molina Enríquez, "the uneven distribution of the racial mixtures [*mestizajes*]," together with environmental and regional variations in national culture, were at the foundation of Mexican "geo-ethnic" diversity. Molina Enríquez described Mexico's territory as divided into a "Creole North," an "indigenous South," and a "central [mestizo] region" subjected to a "perpetual race struggle." Following this logic, he suggested that the racial and cultural characteristics of northerners made them more prone to politics, whereas southerners were more interested in agrarian problems.[28] On the other hand, Manuel Gamio's homogenizing strategy contemplated an "intermediary race" modeled after the white-Creole northerners. This stage in the development of the "Mexican race" would pave the way for the formation of an authentic nation-state. As the next step, Gamio envisioned the "precipitation of *mestizaje*" by increasing the white population "to the point that its numbers will match those of the Indians." This was to be accomplished through the settlement of "millions of selected immigrants lacking racial prejudices." In this fashion Gamio expected to resolve the "serious problem of the heterogeneity" of the Mexican population by creating a syncretic product that would have more resemblance to the northern *blanco-criollo* than to the rustic, undernourished, and pre-modern individuals of "backward indigenous civilization."[29]

Northern racial characteristics also occupied a prominent place in the image of a "cosmic race" popularized by the Oaxacan intellectual José Vasconcelos. Vasconcelos—who served at different points in his career as president of the National University, secretary of education (under President Obregón), and enthusiastic supporter of nationalist art—was generally contemptuous of Sonorans (and *norteños* in general), whom he reviled for their reputed "barbarism" and "*apochamiento*" (Americanization). His staunch political opposition to the "barbarous" Sonoran caudillos, however, did not prevent him from admiring their racial makeup. Thus, Vasconcelos described Obregón as, on the one hand, an individual "without any culture," and, on the other, a man whose legendary political acumen and military capabilities could be accounted for by the "robust appearance, high forehead, white complexion, light-colored eyes and above-average height" that signaled his "Creole type of Spanish descent."[30]

SONORAN PATRIOTIC REGIONALISM, "MALE SHORTAGE," AND ANTI-CHINESE MOBILIZATION

In 1913 the young Martín Luis Guzmán arrived in the Villa de Magdalena in Sonora to organize a dinner dance to honor Venustiano Carranza, chief of the Constitutionalist forces. Taken aback by the beauty of the town's women, Guzmán also noticed that "without taking into consideration the Chinese," there were hardly any "marrying-age adult men." At the time, other neighboring municipalities were also experiencing a severe reduction of their male populations. This problem—known locally as the "shortage of men"—figured among the considerations that, three years later, inspired a group of approximately twenty shopkeepers, schoolteachers, small entrepreneurs, and public functionaries to found a Commercial Association of Businessmen in Magdalena.[31] Under the leadership of José María Arana, former schoolteacher, commercial agent, journalist, and newspaper editor, the association established as its goal the defense of the Mexican merchant and the "extinction of the Asiatic merchant." Members considered the presence of such "Asiatics" harmful because Mexican youths "are forced upon graduation to emigrate [to the United States] in search of jobs denied to them [in Mexico] by the Chinese."[32]

Arana outlined the nature, principles, ideological foundations, and strategic goals of his proposed anti-Chinese movement in a speech delivered in the mining center of Cananea on 29 April 1916. In his opening remarks he praised the victory of "the [Constitutionalist] revolution" and Governor Plutarco Elías Calles's determination to find a solution to Sonora's "intellectual and material progress." These tasks, continued Arana, demanded, in the first place, a solution to the problems associated with the Chinese presence. Prominent in Arana's long and detailed inventory of what he considered to be the negative consequences of the "insatiable yellow hydra" was his concern with the "corrosive effect" that the "weak, feeble, sick, and unpatriotic" offspring of Chinese men and "bad Mexican women" would have upon the "national spirit." This eugenic threat was worsened, Arana claimed, by the supposedly dishonest business practices of the Chinese, their alleged avoidance of tax payments, and their practice of paying bribes to functionaries and political authorities. In addition, he argued, their "terrible contagious diseases, their unhealthy life style, and their consumption of opium and alcohol" posed a danger to both public health and morality.[33]

By ascribing racial meaning to class and gender issues, Arana's simple and rhetorically dramatic explanations for the source of Sonorans' recent woes also served to anchor his brand of anti-Chinese racism in the political and social imaginations of broad sectors of Sonora's population. In his speeches, Arana referred constantly to the "*chinización*" of Sonoran women due to their relationships with Chinese men, whose work (in stores and laundries) he devalued by describing it as the work of women and male prostitutes. This conflation of economic, sanitary, and moral arguments in Arana's speeches reveals a racializing logic that helped to cement capitalist hegemony by reinscribing class relations in terms of the popular, moral, and biological languages of gender and race.

Finally, in the last part of his speech, Arana made a rhetorical effort to establish affinities between his proposed anti-Chinese movement and popular Mexican liberal traditions, the principles of the Constitutionalist revolution, and Sonoran regional patriotism. His invocations to Benito Juárez, Miguel Hidalgo, and Francisco Madero aimed to inscribe his anti-Chinese racism within the political traditions of Mexican liberalism, particularly that of anticlericalism, one of its most popular expressions. Taking revolutionary France as example and inspiration he suggested that, from a Sonoran perspective, "*el amarillismo chino*" appeared to threaten the autonomy of the new revolutionary state, much as had the Church in revolutionary France. In Arana's rhetoric, the liberal emphasis on the retrograde role of the Church in the creation of modern, literate, and rational subjects found a parallel in his consideration of the "nefarious effect" of the "dammed race" on Mexico's state formation. He concluded by demanding a "solution to the Chinese problem" as the prerequisite for the "salvation of the [Mexican] State." Similarly, he inscribed his proposed anti-Chinese campaign within Sonora's patriotic traditions, shaped by the resistance to the United States and French invasions and the private filibustering expeditions that had plagued the state during the nineteenth century.[34]

An examination of the letters sent to Arana by sympathizers and supporters offers interesting insights into the ways certain sectors of the population perceived race—and specifically anti-Chinese racism—as a component of a comprehensive patriotic strategy of progress and national regeneration. This project grew out of a liberal tradition supposedly embodied in the Constitutionalist regime, and particularly in Sonora's Governor Calles. Therefore for Alfredo Salazar, author of the popular "Anti-Chinese Anthem," Arana's anti-Chinese campaign was as patriotic as the temperance campaigns initiated by Governor Calles in 1916. Moreover, it was a central part of Calles's "intellectual war," aimed to unveil the "obscurantism" implanted in people's minds by the Porfirian dictatorship in partnership with the "criminal clergy." The anthem called on the nation to "firmly raise the principles of Hidalgo and Juárez" against the Chinese, who represented "a nuisance and an obstacle to the happiness of the motherland."[35]

National/racial anxiety found forceful expression in the gendered, sexist, and class-biased understandings of anti-Chinese discourse and popular common sense, depicting working-class Mexican women as the vehicle for the penetration and contamination of the national organism. A recurrent theme in most of the letters sent to Arana by supporters and sympathizers was their rejection of unions between Chinese men and Mexican women. Each issue of *Pro-Patria*—the anti-Chinese newspaper published by Arana starting in July 1917—featured letters from readers denouncing these "traitorous" relationships and associations. In these letters, Arana's correspondents, both men and women, expressed the "regret and shame" and "disgust and anger" they felt after witnessing public displays of friendship and intimacy between Chinese men and Mexican women, whom they derided as "*chineras*."[36]

Arana galvanized and mobilized these racial fears and anxieties in the Sonoran population through his speeches and propaganda. By the end of 1916 he had managed to create sixteen "patriotic or nationalist" committees. Under the slogan *"por la patria y por la raza* [for the Motherland and the Race]," these committees established as their main goals "the defense of the Motherland," "the protection of the Mexican race," and "the promotion of national industry."[37] The committees' actions were mostly concentrated in urban and semi-urban centers in the mining districts and settlements of southern Sonora's large agricultural valleys, where Porfirian capitalist expansion had attracted businessmen and workers from abroad as well as from other parts of Mexico. Most of the readers, correspondents, organizers, supporters, and "organic intellectuals" of the anti-Chinese movement belonged to the middle and working classes. They included schoolteachers, professionals, mine workers, medium and small businessmen, journalists, housewives, and public functionaries.

The anti-Chinese movement led by Arana climaxed in 1919, during the successful electoral campaign of Adolfo de la Huerta for the office of governor of Sonora. During the campaign, de la Huerta declared himself in favor of the nullification of Mexico's diplomatic treaties with China and the expulsion of Chinese nationals and their descendants from Sonoran territory. Arana and his anti-Chinese committees were also incorporated within the ranks of Calles's and de la Huerta's Partido Revolucionario Sonorense. Once in office, Governor de la Huerta, following a practice established by his predecessor, Calles, offered his support for Arana's *Pro-Patria* newspaper and the organization of more anti-Chinese committees.[38] More important, de la Huerta's Labor Law (Law 67) of March 1919 included an article requiring foreign-owned enterprises to offer 80 percent of their jobs to Mexican nationals (defined both racially and in terms of citizenship). Although it did not explicitly refer to the Chinese, the "80 percent law," coming as it did on the heels of de la Huerta's and Arana's well-known anti-Chinese initiatives, bore clear, though implicit, reference to the Chinese as the most important foreign community involved in Sonoran commerce and manufacturing.

As an ideological and cultural force, Arana's anti-Chinese racism left a disturbing legacy in the convergence of anti-Chinese racism and the anticentralist traditions that had historically shaped Sonora's regional cultural identity. Sonoran anti-Chinese legislation, promoted by Arana and de la Huerta, was opposed by the national government of President Venustiano Carranza as unconstitutional and in violation of the letter and spirit of an 1899 treaty between China and Mexico. Far from dispelling the popular bases of Sonoran anti-Chinese racism, however, the central government's opposition was instead widely seen as a form of interventionism and, as such, as a threat to Sonoran autonomy.[39]

Antigovernment sentiments culminated in the Agua Prieta rebellion of April 1920. Taking advantage of President Carranza's conflictive relationship with other states, his conservative stance toward land reform and other social issues, his appointment to public office of individuals linked to the bureaucratic and professional circles of the old regime, and his opposition to Obregón's highly popular bid for the presidency in the 1920 elections, the Sonoran government, with the support of most of the revolutionary military, headed this brief but effective rebellion against the Carranza government. In a few days, the rebels had the country under their control and installed Sonoran governor de la Huerta as provisional president. This revolt (named for the Sonoran border town of Agua Prieta, where the rebels issued their proclamation) marked the initial institutionalization of the military and political forces that had emerged victorious from a decade of violence and disorder. Over the next fourteen years, the "Sonoran faction" led by Calles and Obregón laid the ideological and institutional base of Mexico's new state.[40]

SONORAN ANTI-CHINESE RACISM AND POSTREVOLUTIONARY NATIONALISM

During the 1920s anti-Chinese sentiments resonated within both the intellectual debates on Mexican identity and nationalist popular cultural representations. A popular song significantly titled "Viva México" closed its long celebratory recitation of cultural and material products representative of the country's regional diversity with a warning against the Chinese. The lyrics warned to "firmly disregard the Chinese," implying that their presence not only was at odds with Mexico's diverse culture but was also offensive to Mexican manliness. Another popular tune from the state of Jalisco considered Mexican women married to Chinese men to be "shameless" and "filthy."[41] In the words of José María Dávila, the Baja California Norte representative to the national congress, the Chinese had to be excluded from the national community because "they do not represent a step forward in the ideal *mestizaje* . . . but rather signify a step backward in the anthropological search for the prototypical [Mexican] man." Despite the existence of a small number of "Chinese-Mexican products," continued Dávila, these few individuals offered incontrovertible evidence of the "weak and ugly types undesirable to the *mestizaje* that is more convenient for our ethnic future."[42]

Such statements suggest that the obsessive preoccupation with the "Chinese problem" expressed a deeper concern with the future of the nation, its racial makeup, and its progress. That was, for example, the case with *El Intruso* (a newspaper published in the mining town of Cananea), which upheld "the defective Mexican race" as the sole cause of Mexico's backwardness. The reputed Mexican "laziness," together with the Mexican "ineptitude for analysis, and active and persistent labor," was considered responsible for the foreigners' control of business in Sonora and the rest of the country.[43] This "Mexican indolence," continued the newspaper, was behind the "misery and degeneration" of the country and was also to blame for the lack of resolve in solving "the Chinese problem." By comparison, the defects of the Chinese were seen as more dangerous and serious for the integrity of the motherland.[44] Besides their perceived threat to the "purity of Aztec blood," the virtual monopoly of trade maintained by the Chinese was cited as a cause of the economic crisis that "had sunk Sonora in a terrible misery." The crisis was particularly grave in the once-dynamic mining districts, whose towns included large number of Chinese shop owners, street vendors, artisans, and laborers. Cananea, for example, was home to both the largest mining company in Sonora and its largest Chinese community.[45]

The Chinese were also thought to endanger Sonoran masculine honor. "Decent ladies" or "married women," commented *El Intruso*, were "easily seduced by the depraved sons of Confucius" with a mere "kilogram of coffee or a bunch of legumes."[46] The fact that many homemakers patronized Chinese businesses was attributed not to their convenient credit system and low prices, but to the women's alleged "improvidence, indolence and lack of nationalism."[47] Sexual relations with Chinese men were regarded as a permanent "stain of dishonor" visible in the offspring of individuals of a "degenerate race." This intimate association between gender, race, and nationalism lay at the heart of the anti-Chinese movement's popular appeal. In his recollections of the anti-Chinese campaigns of the 1920s and 1930s, Felipe Cortés claimed that "improper relations" between Chinese men and Mexican women had "strongly contributed to the creation of the masculine determination to expel the Chinese out of the country."[48]

Whereas previous anti-Chinese impulses had been largely restricted to Sonora and the northern frontier states, during the second half of the 1920s an unstable political situation, national identity debates, and nationalist campaigns and propaganda created conditions for its expansion into the rest of the country. Indeed, the racial and patriotic discourse of anti-Chinese racism was fully compatible with Calles's and the other revolutionaries' eclectic mixture of "progress and Puritanism, anticlericalism, abstinence, statism, and secular edu-

Anti-Chinese illustration, "La Mestización." "Twelve-year-old Indo-Latin mestizo" and "fourteen-year-old product of Chinese-Mexican mixture." From José Angel Espinoza, El ejemplo de Sonora *(Mexico City: n.p., 1932), 56. Courtesy of General Research Division, New York Public Library, Astor, Lenox, and Tilden Foundations.*

cation."[49] It was precisely during the Calles administration and the subsequent six-year period known as the Maximato, when Calles still ran the government, that the anti-Chinese movement thrived as an integral part of the complex and dynamic constellation of forces that shaped Mexico's state, politics, and culture. Unlike his presidential predecessor, political enemy and fellow Sonoran

Alvaro Obregón, who had maintained a cautious stance toward anti-Chinese demands, Calles enthusiastically embraced anti-Chinese racism. His affinity for the highly racist language of popular anti-Chinese discourse was clearly expressed in his July 1924 response, a few months after taking office as president, to the Chinese diplomatic envoy's queries about abuses against the Chinese in Sonora. After deriding the Chinese in moral, sanitary, and racial terms, Calles stated clearly that, although the Mexican constitution did not explicitly recognize racial difference, he nonetheless saw no inconvenience in "restraining the increase of the Chinese population." To achieve this goal, Calles continued, "it matters little what method is used."[50]

In these circumstances, anti-Chinese racism formed a natural synergy with the overtly nationalist and racial agenda of Calles's new revolutionary orthodoxy. Moreover, the anti-Chinese movement quickly emerged as a natural base for the "mass political groups" upon which Calles erected the alliance that would enable him to consolidate his grasp on power, to reconstruct the "revolutionary family," and to lay the foundations for the institutionalization of the postrevolutionary state.[51]

"YELLOW PERIL," REGIONALISM, AND DECENTERED STATE FORMATION

The cultural practices of race, gender, and ethnicity embedded in the migratory, sanitary, and moral stances of the anti-Chinese movement had an effect on postrevolutionary forms of power both locally and nationally. Ignited by the violent confrontations carried out by antagonistic Chinese nationalist groups, anti-Chinese press and propaganda disseminated its racist and essentialist perspective of this conflict as a "criminal war of mafias," motivated by "Asian ferocity, slyness and perfidy," for control of the opium trade and gambling in Mexico's Chinese communities.[52] A reflection of the contentious power struggle between revolutionary fractions in post-imperial China, the confrontation between partisans of the Kuo Ming Tong and the Chee Kung Tong became a customary event in the overseas Chinese communities during the second half of the 1920s. Depicted by Mexico City newspapers as a "tong" or "mafia war," this conflict acted as an incentive for popularization of stereotyped images and perceptions of Chinese history, culture, and racial nature. At the same time it fed into broader public debates on postrevolutionary immigration policies, the nature of the Chinese presence in Mexico, and its impact on Mexican racial and national identity. These regional stimuli to anti-Chinese rhetoric were reinforced by political and intellectual debates on Mexico's national identity and popular culture; by the government's "social prophylaxis" and temperance campaigns against prostitution, alcohol, and drug consumption; by prohibitions against Syrian, Lebanese, Armenian, Palestinian, Arab, Turkish, Russian, Polish, and black or African immigration; and, finally, by Calles's initiative to unite the fractious "revolutionary family."

The complex trajectory of anti-Chinese attitudes, policies, and practices through the different layers and sectors of Mexico's state and society offers valuable insights into the "decentered" nature of the postrevolutionary state and regime suggested by Jeffrey Rubin.[53] Thus, a common anti-Chinese thread—made up of shared anti-Chinese racialized perceptions, knowledge, and practices— ostensibly linked the central state's immigration and sanitation policies, Sonoran regional and patriotic rhetoric, and the everyday actions and public performances of the local anti-Chinese committees. In this shifting and multilayered political and cultural configuration, it became difficult—if not impossible—to disentangle "*norteño*" and "national" perceptions, understandings, and stances. From a regional and cultural nation-view, as opposed to a centralist and statist one, the emergence of an official anti-Chinese racism blurred the otherwise neat divide between the center and its periphery, or between Mexico City and the provinces. In other words, the creation of the official party and the launching of its "nationalist campaign" indicated the centrality of the otherwise marginal northern states for postrevolutionary state formation.

A common ground for the concerted efforts and cooperation between the national and regional states was given by the generalized fears and anxieties regarding the spread of disease and the upkeep of good sanitary conditions. The country, particularly the northern states, had suffered recurring epidemics of influenza, smallpox, measles, and meningitis since 1918, which were easily blamed on the alleged negative sanitary conditions of the Chinese. The press promptly and dramatically attributed epidemic diseases to the "Yellow Peril."[54] One of the first tasks of the central government's newly created Dirección de Salud Pública (Directorate of Public Health) was to devise and execute an "anti-Chinese hygiene campaign," prohibiting the Chinese from selling "products that could serve as vehicles of infection." Entrusted with the periodical medical supervision and control of the Chinese, the government created local committees of public health, in many cases packed with anti-Chinese activists. In the hands of the postrevolutionary elites, public health and hygiene became important instruments of modernization, state construction, and national formation.[55]

Sanitary concerns also informed the two proposals presented by Congressman Alejandro Villaseñor to the Sonoran state legislature in mid-December 1923. The first proposed to create "Chinatowns"; the other called for the prohibition of marriage between Chinese men and Mexican women. In his presentation, Villaseñor cited the need to protect the population from infectious diseases (such as "beriberi, trachoma, leprosy, small pox and Asiatic bubonic plague") that he considered to be "proper to the Asian race." Villaseñor's proposals, which were unanimously passed, became Law 27 and Law 31 respectively.[56]

With the financial support of the government, an anti-Chinese press and racist organizations flourished in many parts of Mexican territory. Early in 1925, an Anti-Chinese Convention held in Hermosillo approved the creation of the Liga Nacionalista Pro-Raza (Nationalist Pro-Race League) as an umbrella organization for anti-Chinese committees around the country.[57] A few weeks later, Sonoran and Sinaloan representatives in Congress constituted an anti-Chinese block that, together with the recently created Liga, sponsored anti-Chinese legislation in state legislatures and the creation of regional anti-Chinese organizations. Thus, by the second half of the 1920s, anti-Chinese racism, although still strongest in the northwest states of Sonora and Sinaloa, had emerged as a nationally organized political movement with broad political appeal among popular classes and middle sectors of Mexican society.

These increasingly vocal public demonstrations and political organizations launched by the anti-Chinese movement in early 1925 must be understood within the broader context of Calles's multifaceted political offensive against the Church, the expansion of the popular armed resistance to Calles's closing of churches and Catholic schools, the renewed tensions with American oil interests, and a number of workers' conflicts. In order to keep his regime afloat, Calles established as his primary goal the political elimination of his adversaries and opponents. While government-supported workers' organizations demolished independent unions and labor federations, the anti-Chinese movement flourished without problems, and with Calles's approval, as a site from which the unifying flames of nationalist and racial sentiment could be usefully—and safely—fanned.

Norteño leaders of the anti-Chinese movements played an important role in the political organization foreseen by Calles as the unifying factor of the "revolutionary family."[58] The committee charged with the formation of the Partido Nacional Revolucionario (PNR, National Revolutionary Party) in Sonora, for example, was led by José Angel Espinoza, Mexico's most prominent anti-Chinese leader and organic intellectual, and included among its members other important anti-Chinese leaders. Taking full advantage of his position as congressional representative, Espinoza formed the Steering Committee of the Anti-Chinese Campaign as a branch of the recently created PNR. In concert with the Bloque Nacional Revolucionario, made up of PNR legislators and senators, and the Chambers of Commerce, the committee also organized the so-called "nationalist campaigns" for "the defense of national commerce . . . national sovereignty . . . and the integrity of the race."[59] With the support of the state and its official party, anti-Chinese rhetoric gained greater authority, legitimacy, and reach within both the state and civil society. The incorporation of the anti-Chinese movement into the ranks of the PNR also marked the beginning of an official or state anti-Chinese racism. As part of Calles's state formation, the creation of the official party played an important role in the reorganization of the relationship between the states and the capital, and the refurbishing of the latter as a "new center." The anti-Chinese movement became an arena for the negotiations and accommodations that marked the emergence of this new spatial configuration of power.

More important, the anti-Chinese movement became a catalyst for the consolidation of Mexico's postrevolutionary racial formation. A myriad of social and political forces within both the state and civil society envisioned a racially and culturally homogeneous nation. The racial/national goals of the anti-Chinese movement overlapped, first, with the eugenicist strategies espoused by state functionaries, demographers, anthropologists, public health specialists, and revolutionary ideologues (discussed by Stern in the preceding chapter), and, second, with a number of organizations, within and outside the official party, whose nationalism was shaped both by eugenicists and by sanitary concerns. That was the case of the Unión Nacionalista Mexicana Pro-Raza y Salud Pública (Mexican Nationalist Pro-Race and Public Health Union). Made up of revolutionary doctors, health specialists, functionaries, and politicians, it preached the need for a "national prophylaxis of social, ethnic, and racial character."[60] Needless to say, its actions and rhetoric were mainly aimed against the Chinese. This scientific strategy of national/racial formation interfaced with state-sponsored prophylactic, anti-alcoholic, and sex education programs. These campaigns, in turn, included (or implied) assertions made by the Sociedad Eugénica Mexicana para el Mejoramiento de la Raza (Mexican Eugenic Society for the Improvement of the Race) concerning the negative eugenic value of the Chinese population.[61]

The anti-Chinese movement found fertile ground for launching its campaign to expel the Chinese from Mexico during the general economic crisis and political turmoil of the early 1930s. Inaugurated in Sonora during the summer of 1931, the illegal deportations continued into 1933. Not surprisingly, this campaign was more successful in states such as Sonora and Sinaloa, where anti-Chinese actions were conducted in a coordinated manner between central state institutions, anti-Chinese authorities, and local anti-Chinese committees. Between 1927 and 1940 the Chinese population—racially defined—was reduced at the national level from 24,218 to 4,856. In the northwestern frontier states the Chinese population was virtually wiped out. By 1940, only 92 and 165 Chinese individuals were respectively accounted for in Sonora and Sinaloa.

In the 1930s, moral demonization of the Chinese acted as an "ideological vehicle," articulating the many crises disturbing Mexico at the moment. For the Maximato regimes, whose central feature was their lack of consensus, the national/racial appeal of anti-Chinese rhetoric provided a language of consensus within the highly conflictive projects of state and nation building, the contentious relationship between the central state and the regions and, more important, between frustrated popular demands and the postrevolutionary capitalist strategy of development. At the same time, as part of the broader "nationalist campaigns" waged by the state and its official party, the anti-Chinese movement also became a factor contributing to the legitimization of the racial nature of both the postrevolutionary state and its emergent orthodoxy.[62] From a Sonoran perspective in the crucial decades of the 1920s and 1930s, anti-Chinese racism materialized as a factor of integration between the northern frontier and a central state immersed in the redefinition of both its own process of state formation and Mexico's national identity. Through the optic of anti-Chinese racism, the *blanco-criollo* racial type of Sonora (and the *norteño* states more generally) reinforced northern predominance over the regions identified by the theories of *mestizaje* with the indigenous and mestizo types. According to the 1930 national census, "Being physically better developed . . . the northern population has somatic conditions and spiritual expressions" that determine "its greater capacity for civic ceremonies . . . and lesser fanaticism." Six decades later, the guerrilla leader known as "Subcomandante Marcos" suggested that such racialized attitudes have not changed. He noted that the indifference and contempt of certain sectors of Mexican society toward the indigenous conflict in Chiapas was informed by their racialized assumption that "the North works, the South sleeps, and the Center eats what is produced by the North."[63]

NOTES

An Eisner Scholar Research Award from the Simon H. Rifkind Center for the Humanities and the Arts at City College of New York and a Professional Staff Council—City University of New York Research Award made possible the research for this chapter. I would like to thank Deborah Poole and the editors and readers of this volume for their comments and suggestions.

1. Jeffrey Lesser, *Negotiating National Identity: Immigrants, Minorities, and the Struggle for Ethnicity in Brazil* (Durham: Duke University Press, 1999), and José Jorge Gómez Izquierdo, *El movimiento antichino en México (1871–1934): Problemas del racismo y del nacionalismo durante la Revolución Mexicana* (Mexico City: Instituto Nacional de Antropología e Historia, 1991).

2. See Carlos Monsiváis, "'Just over That Hill': Notes on Centralism and Regional Cultures," in *Mexico's Regions: Comparative History and Development*, ed. Eric Van Young (San Diego: University of California, Center for U.S.-Mexican Studies, 1992), 247–59, quotation on 247. For anti-*norteño* perceptions, see Federico Gamboa, *Diario, 1892–1899* (Mexico City: Siglo XXI, 1977). See also Agustín Yánez, *Al filo del agua* (Mexico City: Fondo de Cultura Económica, 1996), and Elena Garro, *Los recuerdos del porvenir* (Mexico City: Joaquín Mortíz, 1997).

3. For Sonoran political and military traditions, see Barry Carr, "Las peculiaridades del norte mexicano, 1880–1927: Ensayo de interpretación," *Historia Mexicana* 22 (1973): 32–46, and Héctor Aguilar Camín, *La frontera nómada: Sonora y la Revolución Mexicana* (Mexico City: Siglo XXI, 1977).

4. Justo Sierra, *Evolución política del pueblo mexicano* (Caracas: Biblioteca Ayacucho, 1977), 295–99, and Francisco Bulnes, *El porvenir de las naciones hispanoamericanas* (Mexico City: Mariano Nava, 1988), 273–74.

5. Charles C. Cumberland, "The Sonora Chinese and the Mexican Revolution," *Hispanic American Historical Review* 40, no. 2 (May 1960): 191–211.

6. Gerardo Rénique, "Frontier Capitalism and Revolution in Northwest Mexico: Sonora, 1830–1910" (Ph.D. diss., Columbia University, 1990), 42–47, 254–66; Evelyn Hu-DeHart, *La comunidad china en el desarrollo de Sonora*, vol. 4 of *Historia General de Sonora* (Hermosillo: Gobierno del Estado de Sonora, 1985), 195–211.

7. See Miguel Tinker Salas, *In the Shadow of the Eagles: Sonora and the Transformation of the Border during the Porfiriato* (Berkeley: University of California Press, 1997).

8. For the ideology of honor in a frontier context, see Ana María Alonso, *Thread of Blood: Colonialism, Revolution, and Gender on Mexico's Northern Frontier* (Tucson: University of Arizona Press, 1995). See also Domingo Faustino Sarmiento, *Life in the Argentine Republic in the Days of the Tyrants; or, Civilization and Barbarism*, 1st American ed. from the 3d Spanish ed. (1868; reprint, New York: Free Press, 1970), 5–55.

9. Born in Sonora, Corral served as governor of the state between 1887 and 1891, as

governor of Mexico City between 1900 and 1903, and, from 1904 to 1911, as vice president of Mexico. Ramón Corral, "Las razas indígenas de Sonora," in *Obras históricas* (Hermosillo: Gobierno del Estado de Sonora, 1959), 195–260.

10. For a discussion of Lamarckian and neo-Lamarckian concepts in Mexico, see Alexandra Minna Stern's contribution to this volume. See also Nancy Leys Stepan, *"The Hour of Eugenics": Race, Gender, and Nation in Latin America* (Ithaca: Cornell University Press, 1991), 128–33, and Roberto Moreno, *La polémica del darwinismo en México* (Mexico City: Universidad Nacional Autónoma de México, 1989).

11. "*Blanco-criollo*" refers to native-born white individuals of Hispanic descent.

12. *El Tráfico* (hereafter *ET*), "Raza e inmigración," 6 Jan. 1899. See also Stern's essay in this volume. *El Tráfico* was a Sonoran newspaper published in the port of Guaymas between 1889 and 1896 and in the border town of Nogales between 1896 and 1905. This and all subsequent translations are mine.

13. Corral, "Las razas indígenas de Sonora."

14. Jack Chen, *The Chinese of America* (New York: Harper and Row, 1980), 40–47, and Alexander Saxton, *The Indispensable Enemy: Labor and the Anti-Chinese Movement in California* (Berkeley: University of California, 1971), 258.

15. Turn-of-the-century poll in Rose Hum Lee, *The Chinese in the United States of America* (Hong Kong: Hong Kong University Press, 1960), 335–36.

16. For the centrality of anti-Chinese racism in the formation of California's working class, see Alexander Saxton, *The Rise and Fall of the White Republic: Class Politics and Mass Culture in Nineteenth-Century America* (London: Verso, 1990), 293–320, and *The Indispensable Enemy*. On racism and working-class formation, see David R. Roediger, *The Wages of Whiteness: Race and the Making of the American Working Class* (London: Verso, 1991).

17. José Jorge Gómez Izquierdo, "El nacimiento del prejuicio antichino en México, 1877–1932," *Antropología* 12 (Jan.–Feb. 1987): 21–25. For elitist visions of progress, see Stuart F. Voss, *On the Periphery of Nineteenth-Century Mexico: Sonora and Sinaloa, 1810–1877* (Tucson: University of Arizona Press, 1982).

18. *ET*, "Los chinos en México," 8 Feb. 1899, and "A propósito de los chinos," 11 Feb. 1899.

19. *ET*, "Sonora en el siglo XX," 5 Jan. 1900.

20. *ET*, "El problema nacional," 29 Sept. 1895.

21. *ET*, "La peste amarilla," 7 Dec. 1900.

22. *ET*, "La maldición de México," 7 Jan. 1901. See also "Razas fuertes," 14 Nov. 1898, and "Sajones y latinos," 19 Feb. 1900.

23. *ET*, "Los chinos y sus matrimonios con las mexicanas," 18 Jan. 1900, and "La inmigración asiática, la cuestión racial y nuestras relaciones con China," 5 Mar. 1900.

24. *ET*, "Cruzada contra los chinos," 9 Mar. 1899; see also "Un grito de alarma," 1 Mar. 1899; "ProBono público," 7 Mar. 1899; "No más chinos," 8 Mar. 1899; "Contra los chinos," 11 Mar. 1889.

25. Descriptions of southerners and northerners in Agustín Casasola and Gustavo Casola, *Historia gráfica de la Revolución Mexicana* (Mexico City: Casasola Ediciones, 1940), 2:878–81; John Womack, *Zapata and the Mexican Revolution* (New York: Alfred A. Knopf, 1960), 100, 142. For the comparison of Obregón with Cortés, see Enrique Krauze, *Alvaro Obregón: El vértigo de la victoria* (Mexico City: Fondo de Cultura Económica, 1995), 33. See also Alan Knight, *The Mexican Revolution* (Lincoln: University of Nebraska Press, 1990), 1:367–68.

26. See José María Maytorena, *Algunas verdades sobre el general Alvaro Obregón* (Los Angeles: El Heraldo, 1919), 78.

27. See Francesco Saverio Clavigero, *Historia antigua de México*, 4th ed. (Mexico City: Editorial Porrúa, 1974), 503–6, and José E. Pacheco, "La patria perdida: Notas sobre Clavijero y la cultura nacional," in *En torno a la cultura nacional*, ed. Héctor Aguilar Camín (Mexico City: CONACULTA/Instituto Nacional Indigenista, 1983), 15–50.

28. Andrés Molina Enríquez, *La revolución agraria en México* (Mexico City: Instituto Nacional de Estudios Históricos de la Revolución Mexicana, 1985), 91–99. See also Andrés Molina Enríquez, "Aspectos de la cuestión agraria" (speech, Apr. 1924), quoted in Agustín Basave Benítez, *México mestizo: Análisis del nacionalismo mexicano en torno a la mestizofilia de Andrés Molina Enríquez* (Mexico City: Fondo de Cultura Económica, 1992), 73.

29. Manuel Gamio, *Hacia un México nuevo* (Mexico City: Instituto Nacional Indigenista, 1987), 228–29, and *La población de Teotihuacán* (1919; reprint, Mexico City: Instituto Nacional Indigenista, 1979), 1:xix–xx. See also his *Forjando patria*, 4th ed. (Mexico City: Editorial Porrúa, 1992).

30. José Vasconcelos, "Barbarie adentro," in *Ulises criollo*, ed. Claude Fell (Madrid: ALLCA, XX, 2000), 345–53, and *Breve historia de México* (Mexico City: Trillas, 1987), 355. In contrast to Obregón, Calles—whom he described as arbitrary and violent—was considered to be of "Syrian-Lebanese type." See Vasconcelos, *Ulises*, 36.

31. Martín Luis Guzmán, *El águila y la serpiente* (Mexico City: Editorial Porrúa, 1995), 66–67, and Archivo Histórico General del Estado de Sonora (hereafter AHGES) T. 3072 (2ª parte) (1916), "Informes relativos a la situación en el estado."

32. Flyer announcing the creation of the committee in José María Arana Archive (hereafter AJMA) kept at the Special Collections Library of the University of Arizona, Tucson. See also AHGES T. 3083 (1916), "Campaña anti-china," and J. M. Arana, "Borrador y notas al margen del informe del Gobernador Cesáreo Soriano," 4 Apr. 1918, in AJMA.

33. Broadsheet, "Discurso de José María Arana en Cananea, 29 de abril de 1916," in AHGES T. 3083 (1916), "Campaña anti-china."

34. Ibid.

35. A. B. Salazar to J. M. Arana, Cananea, 16 Aug. 1917, AJMA; Reinaldo Villalobos to J. M. Arana, Culiacán, 4 May 1919, "Correspondencia 1917–1919," AJMA. The anthem appears in *Pro-Patria*, 26 Aug. 1917.

36. See, for example, A. García, "Es peligroso el roce de chinos y mexicanas" (un-

published manuscript), and letters from Micaela Dorado, Magdalena, 22 Oct. 1917, Francisco Ibáñez, Nacozari, 20 Oct. 1917, Manuela Santa Cruz, Tepache, 9 Nov. 1917, all in AJMA. Also see "Carta de un urense anónimo," in *Pro-Patria*, 5 Sept. 1917.

37. J. M. Arana, "Borrador y notas al margen del informe del Gobernador Cesáreo Soriano," 4 Apr. 1918, AJMA.

38. See letters between Calles, his right-hand man Luis L. León, and Arana in "Correspondencia con autoridades políticas, 1918" and "Correspondencia, 1919," AJMA.

39. Antonio G. Rivera, *La revolución en Sonora*, 2d ed. (Hermosillo: Gobierno del Estado de Sonora, 1981), 450–58; Clodoveo Valenzuela, ed., *Sonora y Carranza* (Hermosillo: n.p., n.d.), 338–39, 357–59, 385–86, 442–44.

40. After the Agua Prieta rebellion Sonoran governor Adolfo de la Huerta served as interim president between June and December 1920. Obregón ruled as constitutional president during the period 1921–24, followed by Calles between 1925 and 1928. The assassination of Obregón before he took office for a second term (1928–32) cleared the path for the emergence of his rival Calles as the "Jefe Máximo" of the revolution. The six-year period of the puppet administrations of Emilio Portes Gil (1928–30), Pascual Ortiz Rubio (1930–32), and Abelardo Rodríguez (1932–34) is known in Mexican history as the Maximato, or the "Rule of the Jefe Máximo."

41. Lyrics for "Viva México" in Ricardo Pérez Monfort, *Estampas de nacionalismo popular mexicano: Ensayos sobre cultura popular y nacionalismo* (Mexico City: CIESAS, 1994), 113, 118–19, and for "Las mujeres que se casan con los chinos" in Vicente T. Mendoza, *Panorama de la música tradicional de México* (Mexico City: Universidad Nacional Autónoma de México, 1984), 249. I owe this information to the anthropologist Raúl García from Chihuahua.

42. José María Dávila quoted in José Angel Espinoza, *El problema chino en México* (Mexico City: Porrúa, 1931), 16–17.

43. "Defectos de nuestra raza. Así nos estamos muriendo," *El Intruso* (hereafter *EI*), 14 Aug. 1923.

44. "Creación de barrios chinos. Primer paso para resolver el problema chino," *EI*, 4 Jan. 1923.

45. "Es aflictiva la situación en Cananea," *EI*, 17 Mar. 1922, and "El peligro chino," *EI*, 12 June 1923.

46. "Chinos depravados," *EI*, 6 Mar. 1921.

47. Espinoza, *El problema*, 220.

48. Felipe Cortés, *Sonora y Sinaloa recogen los frutos de la campaña anti-china iniciada por José María Arana y consumada por Felipe Cortés G. de 1919 a 1930: Reseña* (Hermosillo: Felipe Cortés, 1943), 18.

49. Knight, *Mexican Revolution*, 2:503. For a discussion of postrevolutionary nationalism and anti-Chinese racism, see Alan Knight, "Racism, Revolution, and *Indigenismo*: Mexico, 1910–1940," in *The Idea of Race in Latin America, 1870–1940*, ed. Richard Graham

(Austin: University of Texas Press, 1990), 71–114; see also Gómez Izquierdo, *El movimiento antichino*, and Gerardo Rénique, "Anti-Chinese Racism, Nationalism, and State Formation in Post-Revolutionary Mexico, 1920s–1930s," *Political Power and Social Theory* 14 (2001): 89–137.

50. "Informe rendido por Plutarco Elías Calles ante el Sr. Secretario de Gobernación con motivo de las quejas del embajador chino," *EI*, 29 July 1924. See also Espinoza, *El problema*, 268–85.

51. Arnaldo Córdova, *La ideología de la Revolución Mexicana: La formación del nuevo régimen* (Mexico City: Ediciones Era, 1973), 309–10. For Catholics as scapegoats, see Jean Meyer and Enrique Krauze, *Estado y sociedad con Calles* (Mexico City: El Colegio de México, 1981), 280–81.

52. José Angel Espinoza, *El ejemplo de Sonora* (Mexico City: n.p., 1932), 227–32, 241–44.

53. Jeffrey W. Rubin, *Decentering the Regime: Ethnicity, Radicalism, and Democracy in Juchitán, Mexico* (Durham: Duke University Press, 1997).

54. Regarding the Chinese and public health, see "Envenenadores públicos," *EI*, 12 May 1921; "La tracoma en las escuelas públicas," *EI*, 22 May 1921; "Piden clausura de panaderías," *EI*, 26 Jan. 1922; "El enemigo está en la casa," *EI*, 16 Mar. 1922; "Los chinos se están apoderando de las panaderías," *EI*, 7 Sept. 1922. On epidemics in Sonora, see "Grippe, influenza española y viruela amenazan a esta población," *EI*, 21 Nov. 1922, and AHGES T. 3534, "Salubridad Pública–Expediente General."

55. AHGES T. 3654 Bis (1924), "Cuestión china," and *EI*, 23 Mar. 1924. For a discussion of the relevance of public health and hygiene for nation formation, see Donna Guy, *Sex and Danger in Buenos Aires: Prostitution, Family, and Nation in Argentina* (Lincoln: University of Nebraska Press, 1991).

56. See *EI*, 13 and 29 Dec. 1923, 4 Jan. 1924. The Villaseñor article is in *EI*, 24 Jan. 1924.

57. AHGES T. 3645 Bis (1924), "Cuestión china," and Archivo General de la Nación—Fondo Obregón y Calles 104-Ch-1, 104-Ch-16. See also Moisés González Navarro, *Población y sociedad en México* (Mexico City: Universidad Nacional Autónoma de México, 1974), 2:71–72.

58. See Comité Organizador, *Como estamos organizando un gran partido de principios en el estado* (Hermosillo: Comité Organizador, 1930); see also *EI*, 25 Dec. 1929; 4 Jan., 27 Feb., 30 Mar., and 30 Apr. 1930.

59. Ricardo Sánchez Lira, *Iluminación nacionalista* (Mexico City: Ediciones Luz, 1956), 33. See also José Manuel López Victoria, *La campaña nacionalista* (Mexico City: Botas, 1965).

60. Secretaría de Salubridad Pública—Archivo Histórico, Fondo Salubridad Publica C.29, e.6, and C.21, e.3. See also articles in *El Nacional Revolucionario*, 1, 2, 18, and 29 Oct. 1930.

61. "Informe anual de las labores de la Sociedad Eugénica Mexicana durante su primer año de trabajo, 1931–1932," *Boletín de la Sociedad Eugénica Mexicana*, no. 10 (21 Sept. 1932).

62. Espinoza, *El Ejemplo*, 120. For a discussion of the lack of consensus, see Arnaldo

Córdova, *La Revolución en crisis: La aventura del Maximato* (Mexico City: Cal y Arena, 1995), 201–16. For moral panics and hegemony, see Stuart Hall et al., *Policing the Crisis: Mugging, the State, and Law and Order* (New York: Holmes and Meier, 1978), vii–viii.

63. Quoted in Ignacio Almada Bay, "Maytorenismo, rebelión indígena y violencia social," in *Memoria XVII Simposio de Historia y Antropología de Sonora* (Hermosillo: Universidad de Sonora, 1992), 2:29–78; Aurelio Hernández, "La globalización no tira las fronteras, las crea: Marcos," *La Jornada*, 2 Jan. 2001.

CHAPTER NINE

RACIALIZING REGIONAL DIFFERENCE

São Paulo versus
Brazil, 1932

Barbara Weinstein

The Paulistas constituted a blatant aberration within the race and the nation. São Paulo had become too great for Brazil. . . . Brazil had not yet become a civilization, [whereas] São Paulo was a European Christian civilization, with the mentality, the climate, the cosmopolitanism, the resources of a European Christian civilization.

MÁRIO DE ANDRADE, "Guerra de São Paulo"

The standard narrative of postcolonial Brazilian history portrays the consolidation of the centralizing state under Getúlio Vargas in the 1930s as effectively suppressing the robust regional identities that were salient features of Brazilian politics and culture during the first century of independence. According to this chronicle of nation-state formation, under the new, postfederalist order, regional political oligarchies subordinated themselves to the hegemony of the central state and local economic elites gradually articulated their interests to a project for national economic integration.[1] And Brazilians of every region and social class adopted racial democracy as the hegemonic discourse on national identity, in place of the ideology of whitening that had dominated racial thinking during the Old Republic (1889–1930). The concept of racial democracy, as defined by its main intellectual architect, Gilberto Freyre, imagined a nation based on the harmonious fusion of European, African, and Indian cultures in a single nationality that, despite the "principal" role played by Brazilians of European descent, rejected racial discrimination and valorized non-European cultural traditions.[2] In short, according to this view, the Vargas regime not only managed to centralize the political and economic systems but also promoted a homogeneous national identity that transcended regional variation and custom.

In recent decades there has been a flood of books and articles excoriating the concept of racial democracy as a myth that obscures the continuing discrimination suffered by people of color in Brazil, or as an official discourse that has been a major impediment to movements in favor of racial equality and social justice.[3] Such studies have been tremendously valuable for contemporary Brazilian political struggles but often have the defect of shading into a functionalist fallacy that treats racial democracy as a concept that emerges for the sole purpose of obscuring racial discrimination and absolving elites of any guilt for racial inequality.[4] To be sure, this aspect of the discourse certainly helps to explain its enduring popularity among powerful segments of Brazilian society, but it hardly addresses how and why racial democracy emerged as a compelling element of national identity in the first place (with an appeal that went well beyond self-serving elites), and it does not consider the historical circumstances (and competing racial discourses) that produced Freyre's work and allowed his ideas to flourish.[5]

Again, the assumption has long been that the discourse of racial democracy, whatever its flaws and limitations, superseded and displaced previous discourses on race and served to further homogenize national identity. In this essay, however, I will argue that there continued to be a plurality of discourses about race and its place in Brazilian national identity, and that these were intimately connected to regional identities that persisted well beyond the Vargas years. Crucial to the continued deployment of regional (cum national) identity was the construction of racial difference on the basis of regional origins, with images of modernity and economic progress, tradition and backwardness being tightly interwoven with representations of race. Indeed, in a "racially democratic" nation where explicit discussion of race was increasingly frowned upon, regional identity could conveniently stand in for notions of blackness and whiteness. More specifically, I contend that regional identity in the state of São Paulo—Paulista identity—became associated in Brazilian culture not only with industry, modernity, and economic progress, but also with whiteness and a particular narrative of Brazilian history that marginalized the role of Afro-Brazilians in the construction of the nation. Furthermore, this identity has continued to inform debates over citizenship and political inclusion into the twenty-first century.

There are many different ways to explore the relationship between race and regionalism in Brazil, but no moment seems more fortuitous for this purpose than the period from 1931 to 1932, which saw escalating tension between São Paulo and the newly installed Vargas regime, culminating in a three-month, full-scale civil war between an insurgent state government and federal forces.[6] The Constitutionalist Revolution of 1932 was a crucial moment for considering what it meant to be Paulista, how this related to being Brazilian, and what this implied for other regional identities. Though São Paulo's defeat sounded the death knell for the regionally based political machines of the Old Republic, its enduring position as the dominant economic center of the Brazilian nation allowed a particular, racialized construction of Paulista identity to survive and thrive long after the Constitutionalist forces laid down their arms.

In the case of São Paulo, the variety of regionalism in question is a version that emerges together with the very uneven spread of modernity and capitalist development, a process that is particularly conspicuous in Brazil.[7] The discursive basis for regionalism in this version is the aggressive assertion of regional distinctiveness as equivalent to superiority, usually accompanied by the claim that the region in question is disproportionately responsible for the greatness and sustenance of the nation.[8] Such movements may couch their resentments and demands in fiscal and political terms, but their critique of the status quo usually rests on the implicit claim that the region's (and by extension, the nation's) prosperity is a consequence of its population's superior cultural attributes, an argument that can easily lend itself to racialist ideologies. Unlike the more familiar regional discourses that position their cause as a movement of the excluded or the oppressed,[9] those writers, intellectuals, and politicians who constructed the identity of São Paulo within the Brazilian nation typically regarded their home region as culturally and economically superior, as the vanguard of progress and civilization, while the rest of the nation served as the "other," in a cultural relationship reminiscent of that between colonizer and colonized.[10]

In crafting this discourse of regional superiority, Paulistas drew upon racialized assumptions about modernity and civilization shared by elites throughout Brazilian society—after all, Brazil had the dubious distinction of being the very last slaveholding power in the hemisphere, only abolishing slavery in 1888. The postemancipation decades coincided with the global heyday of scientific racism and saw considerable concern among a wide variety of Brazilian intellectuals and statesmen to promote their nation as modern and honorable through a process of whitening.[11] But such notions gained particular currency in São Paulo. There, burgeoning state revenues from the coffee boom allowed the government to subsidize massive European immigration and foster favorable conditions for industrialization. These same policies consigned former slaves, whose backbreaking toil had made the state's prosperity possible, to an increasingly marginal position in Paulista social and economic life and cast aspersions on the capabilities of Brazilians from other regions.[12] Despite the declining prestige of biological or scientific racism by the 1920s, certain "immutable" characteristics would continue to be attributed to Brazilians according to their region of origin, both in elite and popular culture. Even as discourses of civilization, modernity, and progress replaced earlier preoccupations with race mixture and degeneration, notions of difference based on race (broadly construed), far from fading, flourished in new discursive contexts.

REGIONAL INEQUALITIES AND THE STRUGGLE FOR POLITICAL HEGEMONY

Historians have traditionally assumed that regionalism and nationalism are antithetical tendencies, but Brazil's Old Republic provides a compelling historical example of a period that witnessed both resurgent regionalism and emergent nationalism. Prasenjit Duara, writing about turn-of-the-century China, does contend that regionalism and nationalism flourished in tandem, but he is primarily concerned with regions struggling to retain an autonomous identity against the threat of marginalization or homogenization represented by the dominant centralizing forces.[13] In the case of São Paulo, we are discussing regional elites who exercised considerable political dominance at the federal level—a dominance they energetically sought to "naturalize" through a set of discursive and narrative strategies, especially once Vargas's ascendance threatened to disturb the existing configuration of power.

Nevertheless, Paulista politicians (and the state's formidable armed guard, the Força Pública) did not immediately respond to Vargas's 1930 seizure of power with alarm. Given rising nationalist sentiment, intensifying criticism of the republican system, and the various crises of the 1920s (including military revolts and the stock market crash), Paulista responses to Vargas's "Revolution of 1930" ranged from cautious neutrality to enthusiastic support.[14] In return they expected him to reaffirm São Paulo's special position within the Brazil federation by appointing a civilian Paulista as *interventor* (interim governor) and speedily calling a new constituent assembly. Instead Vargas appointed the northeastern-born "lieutenant" (*tenente*) João Alberto Lins de Barros as *interventor* and designated Miguel Costa, an even more radical *tenente*, as head of the state police. These appointments immediately provoked manifestations of discontent within the Paulista political elites, but factionalism within the regional political leadership hobbled initial attempts to defy the Vargas regime. Increasingly incensed by the dictatorship's "humiliation" of São Paulo, in early 1932 the two major state political factions unified against Vargas, and the movement began to assume broader dimensions, including mass protests in favor of a return to constitutional order. In hopes of avoiding a direct confrontation, Vargas finally appointed a civilian Paulista, Pedro de Toledo, as *interventor* but failed to remove the widely despised Miguel Costa and refused to allow Toledo to appoint a Paulista cabinet. The Paulista Constitutionalists (so named due to their demand for a constituent assembly) responded with the seizure of the state government on 23 May, though not yet a full-fledged armed revolt. Meanwhile, disgruntled (anti-*tenente*) military officials sided with São Paulo, as did the state's Força Pública. This led, on 9 July, to a declaration of war against the central government. For the next eighty-three days "loyal" state troops and a handful of regular army soldiers, as well as a large number of poorly trained and ill-equipped Paulista volunteers, engaged in a lopsided struggle with federal troops. In early October, officials of the Força Pública, regarding the situation as hopeless, negotiated a settlement with the central government, forcing an end to the conflict.[15]

The official (*getulista*) interpretation of the uprising dismissed the revolution of 1932 as nothing more than a rearguard or restorationist action by the Paulista oligarchy to recover the power and privileges it lost with the rise of Getúlio Vargas (whose regime represented the inevitable march of the nation toward centralization and unification).[16] By and large, historians have reproduced this official story, even though it does not even coincide with the basic empirical evidence in several respects. For example, among the key instigators of the revolt were members of the Partido Democrático—a party that had been intensely critical of the state machine and strongly supportive of Vargas when he first seized power.[17] Furthermore, far from positioning themselves as the bulwark of tradition against the tide of radical change, the Paulistas based their claims to national leadership on the modernity of São Paulo compared to the rest of Brazil. It was precisely the alleged "backwardness" of the pro-Vargas regions that the Paulista leadership publicly decried.

Finally, the notion of the revolution as a rearguard action engineered by the Paulista oligarchy explains neither the enormous outpouring of regionalist enthusiasm in the course of the Constitutionalist campaign nor the massive popular support for the movement at various moments in the struggle. I am also assuming, in the vein of the "new political history," that political language and action are what give meaning to a particular movement—in contrast to an older, Marxian approach that seeks to uncover the "real" class or sectoral interests underlying a political conflict. To be sure, there were elite factions that sought to advance their economic interests by promoting rebellion, but that hardly explains why or, more important, *how* the uprising occurred, and the meaning it had for those who participated.[18]

As one would expect, the Constitutionalist campaign and the revolution of 1932 produced a torrent of literature, polemics, poetry, posters, music, and artifacts as Paulistas sought to delineate and clarify their regional (cum national) identity and justify their claims to national dominance. Regional struggle against the central government provided a hothouse environment for the cultivation of representations and discourses of regional identity. But these narratives and images of Paulista superiority did not spring full-blown into the political arena with the onset of the Constitutionalist campaign (just as they did not disappear once the revolt suffered defeat). Rather, leaders and supporters of the movement could draw upon nearly six decades of speeches, essays, and iconography to advance their claims to regional greatness.[19]

The material bases for these claims have been thoroughly elaborated in the Brazilian historiography and will only be briefly reviewed here. By the 1870s, with coffee prices booming, the major center of export production (and slave labor) shifted to the province of São Paulo, which, during the final decade of the Empire (1879–89), made a transition from an economic backwater, with a sleepy capital city, to the wealthiest province in Brazil, crisscrossed by railroads and thriving plantations and home to Latin America's fastest-growing urban center. During the 1890s hundreds of thousands of European immigrants streamed into São Paulo to replace the emancipated slaves on the coffee *fazendas*, and by the early decades of the twentieth century, São Paulo had begun the transition to an industrial economy.[20] Indeed, by the 1930s São Paulo was an aspirant to the title of the most important manufacturing center in all of Latin America.[21] Moreover, by then São Paulo no longer lagged far behind Rio de Janeiro as a center of erudite culture. The 1920s saw the flamboyant debut of the Paulista modernists—an audacious assortment of avant-garde writers and artists who touted their home region as the apotheosis of Brazilian modernity, even as they raised critical questions about contemporary urban life.[22] In light of these multiple developments, it required little ideological work for Paulista intellectuals to portray their native province as fortune's favorite. By the 1920s elites throughout Brazil grudgingly recognized São Paulo as the home of the nation's most prosperous industrial and agrarian economies and its most innovative cultural trends.[23]

Since Paulista regionalism would later be equated with separatism by many of its opponents, it is important to note that the foregoing conception of Paulista superiority was, in a sense, the very opposite of separatism—it conflated the Brazilian nation as a whole with São Paulo.[24] At the same time, the Paulista construction of Brazilian national identity, which attributed virtually all historical agency and all national progress and modernity to São Paulo, was hardly more inclusive than a separatist program. Not only was this a regional cum national identity, it was one that relegated most of the other regions of Brazil to the status of pre-modern or insufficiently civilized "other."[25] Thus, even a self-proclaimed antiracist nationalist like Antonio Baptista Pereira declared that São Paulo would always be in the "forefront" of Brazil's march to modernity, and that his home region was "the Apostle of the Peoples. . . . It is São Paulo that takes up the burden of the long crusades, to teach Brazil the meaning of Brazilianness [brasilidade], to show Brazil the path to a Greater Brazil [Brasil-Maior]."[26] As Tânia de Luca aptly notes, the Paulistas spoke of national greatness in entirely regional terms.[27] During the 1932 revolution, a popular slogan—"Tudo por São Paulo! Tudo pelo Brasil! [Everything for São Paulo! Everything for Brazil!]"—neatly encapsulated this inclination.

Both São Paulo's political dominance under the federalist Old Republic and its dramatic economic growth during those years contributed to the metonymic image of São Paulo as "o Brasil que deu certo"—the successful Brazil. But neither political power nor economic success can be treated as self-evident bases for identity formation; they do not, in and of themselves, provide the raw materials for the construction of a regional identity with widespread popular appeal. Indeed, compared to other regionalisms, Paulista identity is relatively thin in the cultural domain, in part because a regionalist movement inspired by rapid economic progress and claims to modernity is unlikely to boast of a rich lode of folklore or traditions (invented or otherwise).[28] São Paulo would seem to be, on the whole, remarkably poor in those performative aspects of regionalism that Pierre Bourdieu cites as crucial to the cultivation of regional loyalties.[29] There is one exception: Paulista intellectuals, principally historians, can be credited with the successful construction of a foundational myth of origin— one that positioned São Paulo not only as crucial to the formation of the Brazilian nation, but also as qualitatively different from the rest of that nation.

In this historical narrative, the Brazil beyond São Paulo's borders appears as fundamentally backward, weighed down by a colonial legacy of declining Portuguese power, unenlightened monarchy, and plantation slavery. In contrast, São Paulo's idiosyncratic colonial past supposedly explained the region's singular aptitude for, and receptivity to, modernity. The foundational myth for this cultural representation was the saga of the *bandeirante*.

Briefly, the *bandeiras* were bands of men who had their home base in São Paulo, from which they organized long-distance expeditions to explore the Brazilian interior during the seventeenth and early eighteenth centuries, mainly in search of precious minerals to mine and Indians to enslave. In the "Black Legend" writings of Spanish missionaries, the *bandeirante* is a cruel and unsavory character, but in the hands of early-twentieth-century Paulista publicists, he is recast as a proto-capitalist entrepreneur. In contrast to the parasitical, decadent, and tradition-bound sugar planter of the colonial Northeast, the *bandeirante* is enterprising and risk-taking. Moreover, it was the *bandeirantes*, by intrepidly exploring the farthest reaches of the Brazilian interior, who guaranteed the capacious boundaries of the future Brazilian nation (and thereby established its one unimpeachable claim to greatness).[30]

What these self-congratulatory paeans to São Paulo's exceptionalism routinely suppressed was the rather crucial "interlude" of plantation slavery. Indeed, one could read popular and scholarly accounts of São Paulo's history and entirely miss the fact that the region, for several decades in the second half of the nineteenth century, had been the home of Brazil's most important slave-plantation economy. When acknowledged at all, this inconvenient fact was trumped with the claim that Paulista planters displayed a progressive disposition that made them reluctant to rely on slaves and eager to adopt new technologies. Not only was the Paulista planter *not* a typical slavocrat, but he even played a crucial role in abolishing slavery and modernizing agriculture.[31] As for slavery's "stain" on São Paulo's population, noted folklorist Dalmo Belfort de Mattos consoled his readers with the assurance that people of color only briefly and temporarily became a majority during the first phase of the coffee boom. "This soon passed. Mortality and mixture gradually eliminated the African *excess*."[32]

The success of the *bandeirante* saga, and its role in the construction of regional identity, could hardly be exaggerated. Virtually every piece of poetry or polemic from the period of the Constitutionalist campaign makes some reference to the Paulistas' *bandeirante* forebears. Portraits of Fernão Dias, Domingos Jorge Velho, and other historic *bandeirantes* graced the banknotes issued by the short-lived revolutionary government, and *bandeirantes* hovered in the background on recruitment posters issued by the volunteer militias. And beginning in the 1930s, the *povo bandeirante* became a widely accepted synonym for the *povo paulista* (Paulista populace). In short, the *bandeirologistas* had created a highly successful "fictive ethnicity," based on a "master narrative of *discent*," to use Prasenjit Duara's apt phrase.[33]

THE DISCOURSE OF PAULISTA SUPERIORITY AND THE 1932 REVOLUTION

The remainder of this article will focus primarily on the 1932 Constitutionalist campaign and civil war. During this historical episode, regional leaders forged particularly heated defenses of Paulista superiority and unusually derogatory depictions of Brazilians from other regions, making explicit the assumptions that might remain implicit in "normal times." Drawing liberally on social Darwinist theories about the suitability of different races for progress and modernity, as well as on apparently contradictory historical theories about stages of civilization, Paulista journalists and intellectuals celebrated the civic virtues of the regional population, which they routinely attributed to its more "civilized" character. In speech after speech and essay after essay, Paulistas extolled the civic and moral fiber of the *povo bandeirante*, the civilized and cultured character of the Paulista people, and the direct association between their region's "stage of civilization" and their concern for the rule of law.

What of the rest of Brazil? How did Paulista regionalist discourse construct its "other" within the Brazilian nation? This typically varied according to the political proposals of the individual or group, though certain assumptions informed political discourse across the spectrum of political factions. The handful of Paulistas who openly advocated separatism in 1932 did not hesitate to construct every other region of Brazil as vastly inferior to the state of São Paulo, and in the most derogatory of terms. Conversely, most of the Constitutionalist leadership maintained hopes of receiving support from anti-Vargas factions in Rio de Janeiro, Minas Gerais, Paraná, and Rio Grande do Sul and therefore had to represent these regions in a more favorable light; they might be inferior to São Paulo, but the tendency among "moderates" was to emphasize their shared concern for the rule of law and the maintenance of order.[34] What, then, was the common nemesis? It was the North/Northeast of Brazil, which would be consistently portrayed as a backward land populated mainly by primitive or degenerate peoples.

Indeed, one of the most striking features of Paulista discourse during this period is the increasing identification of Vargas's regime with the impoverished and largely nonwhite regions of northern/northeastern Brazil—despite the fact that Vargas and many of his closest advisors were from the far south of Brazil. The bases for this identification varied, but several prominent writers claimed that only peoples who had reached the "industrial" stage of civilization felt the need for the rule of law; agrarian/pastoral societies such as those of the Northeast had a natural affinity for arbitrary, authoritarian rule.[35] And the federal troops that "invaded" São Paulo were consistently described as having been recruited from among the semisavage inhabitants of the northeastern backlands. Through this process of representation, the Paulistas heightened the cultured, civilized character of their own campaign while situating Vargas's forces in the camp of the backward, the uncivilized, and the "darker" elements of Brazilian society—according to Mário de Andrade, during the 1932 campaign Paulistas would jokingly refer to the Vargas regime as the "*dictanegra*."[36] Perhaps no account expresses this process of "othering" better than Vivaldo Coaracy's description of the "occupying forces" that entered São Paulo city upon the state's surrender: "They were soldiers of a strange sort, who seemed to belong to another race, short, yellow-skinned, with prominent cheekbones and slanted eyes. Many of them had teeth filed to a point. All carried in their dark eyes, mixed together with astonishment at the sight of the superb city, a glint of menace and provocation."[37] Another striking expression of the Paulistas' contempt for the "intruders" in their midst is the comment by Paulo Duarte, a leader of the Democratic Party, that *nordestinos* "act the same role as those Negroes in Dakar, top hat on their heads and [bare] feet on the floor, who are convinced that they hold the high position of 'French citizen.' "[38]

Some contemporary accounts of the war even contained eerie echoes of Euclides da Cunha's *Os sertões*, his renowned chronicle of the 1896 conflict between members of a millenarian community in the backlands of Bahia and republican troops. It is the quintessential examination of the struggle between the "two Brazils": the civilized and increasingly Europeanized nation of the littoral and the backward, racially mixed, and religion-soaked society of the interior. During the brief phase of armed struggle in 1932, Paulista war correspondents and combatants were reluctant to admit that the Constitutionalist forces were at a severe technical and material disadvantage, since such an admission would have belied the notion of São Paulo as by far the most technologically advanced and materially prosperous region of Brazil. Instead, they preferred to lay the blame upon the thousands of *nortistas* who "fanatically" hurled their bodies against Paulista troops and overwhelmed the Constitutionalist forces with their sheer numbers. This scenario of rational, modern soldiers pitted against mindless barbarians is very much the struggle that da Cunha chronicled in his account of Canudos, but this time it was the self-anointed "forces of civilization" that suffered defeat.[39]

WHITENESS, MODERNITY, AND THE CONSTRUCTION OF PAULISTA IDENTITY

In the section below, I will offer some specific examples of the different ways in which Paulista identity was explicitly or implicitly racialized in the context of regionally based political struggles for national power.[40] Before I begin this discussion of racialized imaginings of Paulista (and Brazilian) identity, however, I should clarify what I mean by this. By no means am I arguing that the participants in the Constitutionalist Revolution were exclusively white and middle class. The Paulista forces included a sizable Legião Negra (Black Legion), and many of the municipal battalions, judging from photographs, included men of color. Rather, I am arguing at the level of representation, and there, I would contend, the Paulista is unimpeachably white and middle class. As C. R. Cameron, the U.S. Consul-General to São Paulo during the 1932 rebellion, observed: "São Paulo . . . has an extraordinary morale engendered by twenty months of humiliation and the realization that it is fighting for its political position, *its white man's culture*, and the wealth, the lives, and the homes of its citizens."[41]

The key point I want to make about the material that follows is that, despite the variation in degrees of explicitness about racial difference, all leading participants in the Constitutionalist Revolution justified their rebellion against the federal government with allusions to São Paulo's superiority—a position that could only be sustained with reference to racialized understandings of the evolution of the Brazilian nation. There were, to be sure, variations in language and rhetoric, as well as adjustments for reasons of political expediency, but it is far more striking to see the considerable overlap in the arguments tendered by a leading member of the supposedly "progressive" Democratic Party, Paulo Duarte, and an openly racist stalwart of the Paulista Republican Party, Alfredo Ellis Júnior, when they compared Paulistas to other Brazilians. I should also stress that the examples cited below come almost entirely from elite or intellectual sources with privileged access to the press and publication. Among the "rank and file," views on race and regional identity did not always echo those of the leadership. However, I would argue that those who engaged in this struggle had to adopt a certain "script" about Paulista superiority (and non-Paulista

Gold Campaign poster. This poster by the popular artist Belmonte celebrates the campaign in which Paulistas were urged to donate their valuables to finance the war. The nonphotographic representation of an Afro-Paulista is unusual, but he is elderly and frail and appears to be a relic of the past. From José Barros Martins, Álbum da Família *(São Paulo: Livraria Martins Editora, 1954), unpaginated.*

inferiority) that severely circumscribed the discursive positions that could be publicly expressed on issues of race, class, or gender.[42]

The small but noisy group of Paulistas who openly advocated separatism—what we might call nation building by other means—could, for obvious reasons, employ the most nakedly racist imagery. Predictably, the separatists expressed their strongest animus toward northerners or northeasterners; again, given the severe poverty and economic decadence (now dubbed "backwardness") of that region, as well as its largely nonwhite population, it provided the perfect foil for claims about São Paulo's vast superiority.[43] In their short-lived newspaper, *O Separatista*, the separatists often resorted to degrading caricature and racist humor to lampoon Brazilians of northeastern origin (for example, "playfully" claiming that the Paulistas were planning to erect a monument to the murderous northeastern bandit, Lampião, in gratitude for his role in reducing the number of *nordestinos*). But in their moments of greatest despair, the separatists dropped the tattered veil of cordiality altogether and resorted to the most explicit forms of racial demagoguery, as they did in a manifesto issued after the October defeat that urged Paulistas to pursue secession and seek to be a "small nation" rather than continue as "mere associates of an unviable homeland, dominated by mestizos who have the souls of slaves, and who are but one step removed from their ancestors whose bodies were enslaved both here and in Africa." The manifesto went on to describe these rapacious invaders as "sons of the slave quarters and misery, victims of destructive climates, encrusted with the grossest ignorance, a people who are losing human form, such is the physical degeneration that ravages them." And it ends by denouncing the "mestizos born of slaves, the foul offspring of the slave quarters, who now wish to enslave you."[44]

Despite their explicit use of racist imagery, even the separatists did not adhere exclusively to classic notions of "scientific" racism. They, too, drew upon widely held views about stages of civilization, arguing that the Amazon was still at the hunting and gathering stage and the Northeast was still pastoral or agricultural, while only São Paulo had entered the "industrial age," which set it apart from the rest of Brazil.[45] Even the scurrilous manifesto cited above, with its references to the effects of slavery, climate, disease, and misery, did not wholly rely upon the conventional tenets of biological racism to denigrate Brazilians of other regional origins.[46] Unencumbered by the need to curry favor with potential allies from other regions, the small separatist faction could produce the most extreme version of a racialized discourse, but I would maintain that there was considerable overlap (in both directions) between the rhetoric of this group and other, ostensibly more moderate factions supporting the 1932 revolution. Even those Paulistas who seemingly rejected racially determinist ideologies, preferring cultural or economic explanations of São Paulo's "difference," often employed the discourse of civilization and progress in such a way as to implicitly racialize the conflict between São Paulo and the central government.[47]

Many Paulistas who advocated regional autonomy and a loose confederation of Brazilian states—self-rule stopping just short of actual secession—proffered arguments that amounted to a more discreet version of separatist discourse. Most prominent within the autonomist faction was Alfredo Ellis Júnior, a well-known historian and Republican politician. In his *Confederação ou separação?*, published in early 1932, Ellis emphasized two themes: the ethnic "divergence" of the various regions of Brazil, and the extremely uneven development of these regions. Both features, he argued, had become much more pronounced since the abolition of slavery and the transition from monarchy to republic, as immigration further whitened São Paulo, and his home state emerged as by far the wealthiest in the nation.

Ellis, unlike some of his more temperate colleagues in the movement, never shrank from deploying explicitly racialized "evidence" and arguments. For example, while acknowledging that all Brazilian regions had some mixture of races, he claimed that São Paulo was 85 percent "pure white," while Bahia was only 33 percent. He then claimed that such racial "divergences" automatically translated into weak national ties: "It would be pure sentimental lyricism if we were to regard as brothers of a *dolico-louro* from Rio Grande do Sul, of a *brachy-moreno* from S. Paulo, or of a *dolico-moreno* from Minas, a *platycephalo amongoilado* from Sergipe or Ceará, or a *negro* from Pernambuco."[48]

None of the above is especially surprising, given Ellis's intellectual background as a historian whose work on the *bandeirantes* helped construct the legend of a "race of giants" on the Paulista plateau. However, most of Ellis's arguments are not directly derived from racial categories but instead rely on much more "mainstream" notions of São Paulo as culturally, civically, and economically superior. Indeed, the majority of the book cited consists of economic arguments in favor of Paulista autonomy in the face of Vargas's centralizing thrust, with particular emphasis (amply illustrated by dozens of tables) on São Paulo's massive contribution to the federal treasury. Thus, as his argument unfolds, the *explicitly* racialist elements fade, but they reemerge in the context of a language of stages of civilization, a concept that Ellis imbues with a range of cultural and political implications. Thus, in *A nossa guerra*, Ellis contends that the *nortistas* support the Vargas dictatorship because their stage of civilization/economic development makes a "constitutional regime" unnecessary: "These small states, that have a much more backward level of civilization, much less economic development, etc., do not have the same needs [as São Paulo]."[49]

The modernist poet Menotti del Picchia, in his *A Revolução Paulista*, played a similar refrain. A prominent nationalist figure among modernist writers in São Paulo during the 1920s (most of whom eagerly supported the Paulista revolt), Menotti insisted that the 1932 movement was an expression of the "cultural revolution" that began with Modern Art Week in 1922.[50] Despite, or perhaps because of, his nationalist sympathies, Menotti argued for federalism and regional autonomy, offering as his justification "the ethnic heterogeneity of the Brazilian populations, their historical experiences as a people, and the differences in their economic and industrial levels."[51] And he goes on to argue, in the same vein as Ellis, that "there is no nation [on earth] as unequal as the Brazilian nation." Consistently linking levels of economic development with political culture, Menotti claims that São Paulo's stage of economic progress makes its inhabitants especially fearful of a dictatorship that can disturb order and industry. Moreover, among Brazilians, only the Paulistas are sufficiently "*cultos*" (cultured) to object to dictatorship. Again echoing Ellis, he contends that most other regions of Brazil, being predominantly rural and pre-industrial, are perfectly content with a dictatorial regime: the rule of law is only attractive to societies (such as São Paulo) that are "cultured and policed."[52]

On this same theme, Vivaldo Coaracy argued that São Paulo, because of its unique character, "based on a robust and hardy individualism," was alone among the regions of Brazil in denouncing the dictatorship: "What has made São Paulo exceptional within the Union was its economic determination . . . the spirit of initiative it aroused in reaction against the compulsory routinism of the colonial era, the accumulation of traditions, that entire web [of habits] that constitutes the living foundation of History. São Paulo became different. And because it is different, it is misunderstood. This is why São Paulo stands alone!"[53] Elsewhere Coaracy (like Ellis) emphasized the geography of Brazilian racial diversity as a major explanatory factor of the nation's uneven evolution.[54] In other words, Paulista intellectuals and politicians did not necessarily forsake a racialist discourse when they shifted to the language of "stages of civilization."[55] Even Mário de Andrade, today celebrated as one of the most critical and insightful of the modernist writers with respect to racism, claimed that São Paulo was "too great for Brazil" and derided the federal troops who came to "kill Paulistas" as akin to primitive Indian tribes.[56]

Again, these types of arguments and this sort of language were by no means confined to the writings of a handful of Paulista intellectuals. In virtually every daily newspaper, in popular magazines, in radio addresses, in leaflets and flyers, even in private letters and diaries, one encounters not only claims to São Paulo's superiority and grandeur, but also assertions about the inferiority and

Recruiting poster. "They Await You to Complete the Battalion. Enlist." The initials "MMDC" refer to the first four Paulista men killed in conflict. With the São Paulo state and Brazilian flags in the background, these volunteers represent the São Paulo ethnic "type" and imply a homogeneity not reflected in the actual ranks. From Arquivo do Estado de São Paulo, São Paulo, 1932 (facsimile collection, organized by Ana Maria de Almeida Camargo, 1982).

barbarity of Brazilians from other regions. An excellent example is the description from the newspaper *O Estado de São Paulo* of the Vargas government's efforts to crush the Constitutionalist Revolution: "Against the youth of São Paulo, against the students, the doctors, the lawyers, the engineers, the merchants, the landowners, the men of industry and intelligence, [the government is] throwing a band of thugs [*jagunçada*] gathered and herded together in the backlands. . . . Against a civilized people, they hurl battalions of hoodlums."[57] Similarly, a headline in *A Gazeta* informed São Paulo's citizenry that "The Dictatorship Makes Use of Fanatical Jagunços against the Conscious Army of Liberty."[58]

Perhaps even more telling is a secondhand narrative of an unusual encounter between Paulista soldiers and federal forces. During an impromptu cease-fire, according to the Paulista soldier's account, he and his companions engaged in a poignant conversation with their fellow Brazilians from Rio Grande do Sul in which both sides expressed regret at having to "fight against brothers." But the idyll ended when an "ungainly mulatto northerner [*um nortista mulato e desengonçado*]" intruded himself into the conversation and began threatening the Paulistas.[59] In other words, despite the war there was a natural solidarity between white, middle-class Brazilians from two different states, but the fly in the ointment was the nonwhite northerner whose backwardness and ignorance translated into irrational hostility and envy toward the Paulistas.

Paulistas eager to enlist support from other regions and to combat the opposition's "lies" about São Paulo's separatist ambitions insisted that Constitutionalism was a self-sacrificing movement "formed in the spirit of *brasilidade*" to redeem Brazil from an oppressive dictatorship. Accordingly, the "revolutionary" *Jornal das Trincheiras* (Journal of the Trenches) initially portrayed Paulista identity as transcending regional boundaries. Due to the uprising the meaning of the term "Paulista" "had broadened, expanded, widened and extended to include in its purview more than just a simple designation of an accident of birth"; rather, it had become a category that included all those who "think like São Paulo."[60]

This message of transcendent *paulistinidade* did find some resonance among groups beyond the boundaries of São Paulo—particularly aspiring middle-class professionals in the law and medical schools of Brazil's urban centers. But the charges of separatism proved difficult to shake precisely because even those factions of the Paulista movement that claimed the greatest devotion to *brasilidade* could not convey a sense of horizontal solidarity with the rest of the nation.[61] Despite some earnest efforts, the *Jornal das Trincheiras* could not sustain this pose: as defeats piled up and the war neared its conclusion, the newspaper resorted to more inflammatory rhetoric, including a front-page article that defined the war as a struggle between two different ideas of civilization, "not to say between civilization and barbarism."[62]

RACE, REGIONAL IDENTITIES, AND DISCOURSES OF DEMOCRACY

The limited resonance of Constitutionalist discourse beyond state lines is hardly surprising given its emphasis on how superior and how distinctive São Paulo was compared to the rest of Brazil (indicating the limits of an *overtly* regionalist effort to reimagine the nation). Thus Paulistas could deride as ridiculous anti-Constitutionalist claims that São Paulo was trying to turn the other regions of Brazil into its economic colonies, but there was nevertheless something distinctly "colonial" about the way São Paulo positioned the rest of Brazil, especially the poorer areas of the Northeast, depicted as politically immature, economically underdeveloped, and culturally backward.

This set of attitudes helps to explain an initially puzzling silence in Constitutionalist discourse. One might expect a movement that was rallying people against a dictatorship to make extensive use of the term "democracy," a word that even in the early 1930s was widely regarded as expressing the antithesis of dictatorship. And yet there were remarkably few references to the need for democratization in the writings and speeches of the movement. There were uncountable references to the need for a constitution, for the restoration of order and the rule of law, but for the most part the Paulistas were silent on the matter of democracy. On the rare occasions when the issue did appear, it was likely to be called into question. Thus we have the unusually blunt assertion by Vivaldo Coaracy, who, in *O caso de São Paulo*, wrote: "The difference in their evolutionary rhythms unavoidably establishes a hierarchy among the Brazilian States. . . . Democracy proclaims civil equality for all citizens and tends to concede them political equality. But it is incapable of creating natural equality."[63]

From this perspective, we can appreciate more fully the political vacuum that existed in Brazil during the early 1930s as far as democracy is concerned, with Vargas edging toward an authoritarian/populist appeal to the popular classes and the supposedly liberal Paulista middle class identifying with a hierarchical and noninclusive notion of political rights. Ironically, under these circumstances, it was the dictator Vargas and his allies, not the "liberal constitutionalists" of São Paulo, who were more likely to favor an eventual transition to a broad-based democratic politics. Paulista regionalism cum nationalism, so intensely identified with the white middle and upper classes in São Paulo, had little capacity for sustained popular mobilization, making democratization an implicit challenge to Paulista dominance. Both before and during the Constitutionalist campaign, the Paulista elites cited the inhabitants of Brazil's less "advanced" regions as impediments to the formation of a coherent and progressive national culture. But I would argue that it was precisely the Paulistas' insistence on a *hierarchy* (rather than a diversity) of regional identities that formed the greatest impediment to a more progressive and democratic national culture in the early 1930s.

This hierarchical structure, moreover, rested on racialized concepts. While most of the exponents and chroniclers of the 1932 revolution did not resort to explicitly racist ideas in defining regional character, key elements in the construction of Paulista identity—the tropes of civilization and modernity—easily lent themselves to a racialized discourse without requiring explicit reference to race or color. In every context São Paulo was presented not only as the most prosperous, but also the most civilized, the most cultured, and the most modern. And this mode of representation depended upon a sharp contrast with other regions of Brazil, especially the Northeast, with its largely nonwhite and impoverished population figured as backward, illiterate, and semicivilized.

As Paul Gilroy argues in *The Black Atlantic*, in a world where modernity is so routinely linked with European culture, to whiteness, it is difficult to deploy this concept in racially neutral terms.[64] Some scholars of racial ideologies have tended to draw a sharp distinction between biological and cultural racism, with the latter typically seen as less pernicious than the "true" racism based on notions of biological difference. But I think this particular historical episode in São Paulo provides us with abundant examples of the considerable slippage from one racist language to another, and the way in which a racist discourse based on historical processes and cultural inclinations can be both more flexible and more durable.[65]

Paulista claims of superiority, of course, would not go unanswered. Given the considerable competition for national power unleashed by the revolution of 1930, the moment became an auspicious one for competing regional interests to construct a national identity that was an overt challenge to the Paulistas' racial exclusivism. Again, without ignoring the flaws and defects of the notion of racial democracy, it is worth recognizing that, in this particular historical context, the discourse of racial democracy imagined a much more inclusive version of the Brazilian national community than the one offered by Paulista intellectuals.[66] It may have been a nationalist discourse that occluded ongoing racial discrimination and discouraged militancy around identities of color but, in contrast to the Paulista vision of the nation, it did not expunge non-European ethnicities from Brazil's colonial or postcolonial history or imagine a nation where whiteness was the only guarantor of modernity and progress.

It is also significant that Gilberto Freyre, the main architect of the concept of racial democracy, was writing not from some abstract supraregional space, but from the immediate context of northeastern regionalism, and with the conscious objective of rehabilitating his home region's cultural position in the Brazilian nation.[67] For Freyre, as for the Paulista intellectuals, imagining national identity did not require rejecting regional loyalties; rather, regional identities provided the raw materials to craft national identities. The difference is that Freyre's regionalism produced a vision of the nation that would resonate with both elite and popular aspirations in a way that the Paulistas' explicitly racist, exclusionary, and hierarchical vision could not.[68]

NOTES

I have discussed the issue of race and regional identity with so many colleagues, both in the United States and in Brazil, that it would be impossible to recognize everyone whose ideas are somehow reflected in this article. But I would like to thank the editors of this volume for their particularly constructive criticisms. I am also grateful for the comments I received from the students and faculty at the Latin American Studies Centers at Princeton University and the University of Michigan, where I presented an earlier version of this article.

1. Typically, studies of regional politics end in 1937 with Vargas's declaration of an "Estado Novo," a more authoritarian and centralized version of his regime. See, for example, Joseph L. Love, *São Paulo in the Brazilian Federation, 1889–1937* (Stanford: Stanford University Press, 1980), and John D. Wirth, *Minas Gerais in the Brazilian Federation, 1889–1937* (Stanford: Stanford University Press, 1977). Love correctly argues that federalism and regionalism are not synonymous, but the fact that regionally based political studies virtually never go beyond 1937 certainly reinforces the notion that Vargas effectively centralized Brazilian politics. See Joseph L. Love, "A república brasileira: Federalismo e regionalismo (1889–1937)," in *Viagem incompleta*, ed. Carlos G. Mota (São Paulo: Editora SENAC, 2000), 121–60.

2. For a standard account of Freyre's impact on conceptualizations of Brazilian national identity, see E. Bradford Burns, *A History of Brazil*, 3d ed. (New York: Columbia University Press, 1993), 329–31; see also Peter Fry, "Politics, Nationality, and the Meanings of 'Race' in Brazil," *Daedalus* 129, no. 2 (Spring 2000): 83–118, esp. 86–90. On *mestiçagem*

and Brazilian identity, see Renato Ortiz, *Cultura brasileira e identidade nacional* (São Paulo: Brasiliense, 1985). On the ideology of whitening, see Thomas E. Skidmore, *Black into White: Race and Nationality in Brazilian Thought* (New York: Oxford University Press, 1974; reprint, with a new preface and bibliography, Durham: Duke University Press, 1993 [page citations are to the 1974 edition]). The line between Freyre's thought and the idea of whitening is sometimes blurry (see Skidmore, *Black into White*, 192). Freyre himself argued that the African was "disappearing" from Brazilian society, but as in discourses of *mestizaje*, his emphasis was on "amalgamation," not marginalization or dilution through immigration, and he did not eagerly promote the extinction of all Africanisms from Brazilian culture. Gilberto Freyre, *Brazil: An Interpretation* (New York: Alfred A. Knopf, 1945).

3. Of particular note is the important essay by Emilia Viotti da Costa, "The Myth of Racial Democracy: A Legacy of the Empire," in *The Brazilian Empire: Myths and Histories*, rev. ed. (Chapel Hill: University of North Carolina Press, 2000), 234–46, which actually historicizes the concept of racial democracy. See also Frances Winddance Twine, *Racism in a Racial Democracy: The Maintenance of White Supremacy in Brazil* (New Brunswick: Rutgers University Press, 1998).

4. According to Carlos Hasenbalg (cited in Twine, *Racism in a Racial Democracy*, 6), "Freyre created the most formidable ideological weapon against anti-racist activists." Was this Freyre's intent? That seems unlikely given the minor role of antiracist activists in Brazil when his work first appeared in the 1930s. But he made little subsequent effort to prevent his work from being used by apologists for Portuguese colonialism or Brazilian authoritarianism.

5. We are starting to see a shift toward less denunciatory and more nuanced approaches to racial democracy, including works that emphasize its multiple discursive uses (rather than dismissing it as a "myth"). See Howard Winant, "Rethinking Race in Brazil," *Journal of Latin American Studies* 24, no. 1 (Feb. 1992): 173–92, and Sueann Caulfield's essay in this volume.

6. The best short history of the revolution of 1932 is Maria Helena Capelato, *O movimento de 1932: A causa paulista* (São Paulo: Brasiliense, 1982).

7. Barbara Weinstein, "Brazilian Regionalism," *Latin American Research Review* 17, no. 2 (Summer 1982): 262–76; Ruben George Oliven, *A parte e o todo: A diversidade cultural no Brasil-nação* (Petrópolis: Vozes, 1992), chap. 2; Vera Alice Cardoso Silva, "O enfoque metodológico e a concepção histórica," in *República em migalhas*, coord. Marcos A. da Silva (São Paulo: Marco Zero, 1990), 42–47.

8. For the comparable northern Italian case, see Antonio Gramsci, *Selections from the Prison Notebooks*, ed. and trans. Quintin Hoare and Geoffrey Nowell Smith (New York: International Publishers, 1971), 70–71, 94.

9. See, for example, Pierre Vallieres, *White Niggers of America: The Precocious Autobiography of a Quebec "Terrorist"* (New York: Monthly Review Press, 1971). On regional-

isms in the European context, see Celia Applegate, "A Europe of Regions: Reflections on the Historiography of Sub-National Places in Modern Times," *American Historical Review* 104, no. 4 (Oct. 1999): 1157–82.

10. On Antioqueño regionalism, see Nancy Appelbaum, "Whitening the Region: Caucano Mediation and 'Antioqueño Colonization' in Nineteenth-Century Colombia," *Hispanic American Historical Review* 79, no. 4 (Nov. 1999): 631–67.

11. Skidmore, *Black into White*, chaps. 2–3.

12. George Reid Andrews, *Blacks and Whites in São Paulo, Brazil, 1888–1988* (Madison: University of Wisconsin Press, 1991), chap. 3. Andrews notes that enthusiasm for immigration declined in the 1920s, as nationalism and distaste for anarchist agitation intensified. Accompanying this decline in enthusiasm was a campaign to valorize the "national" worker, but the latter was still constructed in highly racialized and often demeaning terms.

13. Prasenjit Duara, *Rescuing History from the Nation: Questioning Narratives of Modern China* (Chicago: University of Chicago Press, 1995), 177–204.

14. Maria Lígia Coelho Prado, *A democracia ilustrada: O Partido Democrático de São Paulo, 1926–1934* (São Paulo: Editora Ática, 1986), 97–114.

15. Love, *São Paulo in the Brazilian Federation*, 119–21.

16. Burns's account of the revolt (*A History of Brazil*, 352) is a textbook example of this interpretation: "The significance of the revolt was readily discernible in its limited geographic and popular appeal. . . . More than anything else, the rebellion seemed to be a rearguard action by the Paulista oligarchy who looked to the past and desired a restoration of their former privileges and power, and the government treated it as such. Federal forces converged on the capital of São Paulo, and after three months of siege and desultory fighting, the revolt collapsed."

17. Prado, *A democracia ilustrada*, 97–99.

18. On industrialists' support for the uprising against Vargas, see Barbara Weinstein, *For Social Peace in Brazil: Industrialists and the Remaking of the Working Class in São Paulo, 1920–1964* (Chapel Hill: University of North Carolina Press, 1996), 62–66.

19. As early as the 1880s, Paulista chauvinism had produced a small but influential separatist movement. See Cássia Chrispiniano Adduci, "A 'pátria paulista': O separatismo como resposta à crise final do império brasileiro" (master's thesis, Pontifícia Universidade Católica–São Paulo, 1998).

20. Again, the literature on this subject is vast. A few outstanding works are Emilia Viotti da Costa, *Da senzala à colônia*, 2d ed. (São Paulo: Ciências Humanas, 1982); Warren Dean, *The Industrialization of São Paulo, 1880–1945* (Austin: University of Texas Press, 1969); and Wilson Cano, *Raízes da concentração industrial em São Paulo* (São Paulo: Difel, 1977).

21. Heightening the sense of São Paulo's singular trajectory was the stagnation or decline of such regions as Minas Gerais, the interior of Rio de Janeiro, and the Northeast. The diffusion of record-keeping and statistical methods also created a representational context within which one could quickly and dramatically visualize São Paulo's "superi-

ority" over other regions. See Alfredo Ellis Júnior, *Confederação ou separação?* (São Paulo: Paulista, 1934), and T. de Souza Lobo, *O Brasil confederado* (São Paulo: Escolas Coração do Jesus, 1933).

22. Nicolau Sevcenko, *Orfeu extático na metrópole: São Paulo, sociedade e cultura nos frementes anos 20* (São Paulo: Companhia das Letras, 1992).

23. For a particularly compelling discussion of this tendency, see Tânia Regina de Luca, *A Revista do Brasil: Um diagnóstico para a (n)ação* (São Paulo: Editora Universidade Estadual de São Paulo Fundação, 1999), 108. Nicolau Sevcenko claims that at the turn of the century, Rio native Euclides da Cunha "treated as established, valid and stimulating facts English hegemony over the world and Paulista hegemony over Brazil." Nicolau Sevcenko, *Literatura como missão* (São Paulo: Brasiliense, 1983), 124.

24. Luca, *A Revista do Brasil*, 78.

25. In other words, these regions would always be at a more distant (and therefore inferior) point in history than São Paulo. For a provocative discussion of what she calls both "the imperial idea of linear time" and "panoptical time," see Anne McClintock, *Imperial Leather: Race, Gender, and Sexuality in the Colonial Contest* (New York: Routledge, 1995), 9–11, 36–42.

26. Baptista Pereira, *Pelo Brasil maior* (São Paulo: n.p., 1934), 347. This and all subsequent translations are mine.

27. Luca, *A Revista do Brasil*, chap. 1.

28. For example, as part of its 1954 quatricentennial celebrations, the city of São Paulo staged what a magazine based in Rio called "the biggest folkloric procession ever held in Latin America," but almost all of the presentations were "imported" from other regions of Brazil. Indeed, according to this magazine, "the majority of that highly varied presentation constituted a complete novelty for the Paulista." *O Mundo Ilustrado*, no. 84 (8 Sept. 1954): 25.

29. Pierre Bourdieu, "Identity and Representation: Elements for a Critical Reflection on the Idea of Region," in *Language and Symbolic Power*, ed. and with an introduction by John B. Thompson, trans. Gino Raymond and Matthew Adamson (Cambridge, Mass.: Harvard University Press, 1991), 221–23.

30. For examples of the *bandeirante* myth in the making, see Paulo Prado, *Paulística: História de São Paulo* (São Paulo: n.p., 1925), and Alfredo Ellis Júnior, *Raça de gigantes* (São Paulo: Novíssima, 1926). The best historical study of the construction of the *bandeirante* myth is Kátia Maria Abud, "O sangue intimorato e as nobilíssimas tradições: A construçáo de um símbolo paulista—o bandeirante" (Ph.D. diss., Universidade de São Paulo, 1985).

31. I discuss this persistent theme in the slavery historiography in "The Decline of the Progressive Planter and the Rise of Subaltern Agency: Shifting Narratives of Slave Emancipation in Brazil," in *Reclaiming the Political in Latin American History: Essays from the North*, ed. Gilbert Joseph (Durham: Duke University Press, 2001), 81–101.

32. Dalmo Belfort de Mattos, "A influência negra na alma paulista," *Paulistânia*, no. 3

(Oct. 1939), unpaginated, emphasis mine. He also claimed that São Paulo's white to nonwhite ratio during the colonial period was 3 to 1, a statistic that seems little more than a racist's wishful thinking.

33. Prasenjit Duara, "Historicizing National Identity, or Who Imagines What and When," in *Becoming National: A Reader*, ed. Geoff Eley and Ronald Grigor Suny (New York: Oxford University Press, 1996), 151–74, emphasis in original. Duara invents the word "discent" to express both descent and dissent. The phrase "fictive ethnicity" comes from Etienne Balibar, "The Nation Form: History and Ideology," in Eley and Suny, *Becoming National*, 132–49.

34. Some important Paulista political figures, however, found it difficult to suppress their contempt for other regions. See Paulo Duarte, *Que é que há?* (São Paulo: n.p., 1931), 38–39.

35. *A Gazeta*, 24 Aug. 1932, 1.

36. Mário de Andrade, "Guerra de São Paulo," unpublished manuscript, Coleção Mário de Andrade, Caixa 1, Instituto de Estudos Brasileiros, Universidade de São Paulo.

37. Vivaldo Coaracy, *A sala da capela* (São Paulo: Livraria José Olympio, 1933), 14. The images Coaracy evokes here are an interesting pastiche: teeth sharpening was a practice associated with *sertanejos* of African descent, but the other features (short, yellow, oblique eyes) seem more reminiscent of the derogatory stereotypes associated with the Japanese troops that had recently (1931–32) occupied Manchuria.

38. Duarte, *Que é que há?*, 257–58.

39. By the end of *Os sertões*, da Cunha himself exhibited little certainty on the question of who the forces of civilization might be, but that aspect of his masterwork tended to get lost in the remembering. (The English-language version is titled *Rebellion in the Backlands* [Chicago: University of Chicago Press, 1944]). Some Paulista writers in 1932 echoed da Cunha's grudging admiration for the *sertanejo* but always depicted the backlander's courage as the mindless bravery of a semiprimitive man. See "Viva o sertão!," *Folha da Noite*, 15 Sept. 1932, 2. Some journalists actually claimed that federal troops had been recruited from the Canudos region, as well as from the Contestado, site of another major millenarian rebellion—in other words, the government was deliberately recruiting "mindless fanatics" to fight against São Paulo. See *A Gazeta*, 7 Aug. 1932, 3, 24 Aug. 1932, 1.

40. In an intriguing article on the depreciation of citizenship in a "relational universe," Roberto da Matta argues that no Brazilian aspires to be a mere citizen, since this implies equality devoid of privileged treatment. Roberto da Matta, "The Quest for Citizenship in a Relational Universe," in *State and Society in Brazil: Continuity and Change*, ed. John D. Wirth, Edson de Oliveira Nunes, and Thomas E. Bogenschild (Boulder, Colo.: Westview Press, 1987), 307–35. His argument considers only individual behavior structured by relations of patronage and clientele. I would argue that there are, simultaneously, notions of hierarchy that situate certain collectivities within the Brazilian nation as more privileged than others—more deserving of *full* citizenship.

41. C. R. Cameron to Walter C. Thurston [Chargé, Rio de Janeiro], São Paulo Political

Report no. 49, 9 Aug. 1932, Record Group 59, "Records of the Department of State Relating to the Internal Affairs of Brazil, 1930–1939," National Archives, Washington, D.C., emphasis mine. My thanks to James Woodard for this citation.

42. I explore the discursive limits of women's emancipation during this campaign in "Inventing *A Mulher Paulista*: Politics and the Gendering of Brazilian Regional Identities in the 1932 São Paulo Revolution" (unpublished manuscript). Peter Wade's Afterword in this volume correctly notes that constructions of Paulista whiteness would be considerably "nuanced by the everyday realities of Paulista life," but I chose to focus on the level of representation because I believe that this is where the terms of debate were set (though not fixed), and that nobody escaped these discursive boundaries; having agreed to kill and die for the "*causa paulista*," participants had little room to contest its dominant representations. For a discussion of "civilization" as a trope that structured hegemonic and oppositional discourses, see Gail Bederman, *Manliness and Civilization: A Cultural History of Gender and Race in the United States, 1880–1917* (Chicago: University of Chicago Press, 1995).

43. Duarte, *Que é que há?*, 257–58.

44. "Paulista, não te desanimes," Arquivo do Estado de São Paulo (hereafter AESP), Coleção Rev. de 1932, Pasta 357, Doc. 673.

45. *São Paulo, 1932,* AESP, facsimile collection. This was a variation of the well-known image of São Paulo as the "*locomotiva*" pulling a dilapidated train of empty boxcars.

46. For a discussion of the way discourses of cultural racism and scientific racism inform each other, see Ann Laura Stoler, "Sexual Affronts and Racial Frontiers: European Identities and the Cultural Politics of Exclusion in Colonial Southeast Asia," in *Tensions of Empire: Colonial Cultures in a Bourgeois World,* ed. Frederick Cooper and Ann Laura Stoler (Berkeley: University of California Press, 1997), 198–237.

47. Baptista Pereira, *Pelo Brasil maior,* 347.

48. Ellis, *Confederação ou separação?,* 20.

49. Alfredo Ellis Júnior, *A nossa guerra* (São Paulo: Editora Piratininga, 1933), 128.

50. Menotti del Picchia, *A revolução paulista,* 4th ed. (São Paulo: n.p., 1932), vii–viii.

51. Ibid., x.

52. Ibid., 26–27.

53. Vivaldo Coaracy, *O caso de São Paulo* (São Paulo: Editora Ferraz, 1932), 135. Interestingly enough, Coaracy was not a native Paulista.

54. See the chapter "Os dois brasis," in Vivaldo Coaracy, *Problemas nacionaes* (São Paulo: n.p., 1930).

55. I agree with Ann Stoler ("Sexual Affronts," 214) that even at the height of scientific racism's influence, racial ideologies tended to blur the lines of culture and biology. See also Sidney Chalhoub, "The Politics of Disease Control: Yellow Fever and Race in Nineteenth-Century Rio de Janeiro," *Journal of Latin American Studies* 23, no. 3 (Oct. 1993): 441–63.

56. Andrade, "Guerra de São Paulo." This is all the more striking since Andrade himself was of mixed-race background.

57. *O Estado de São Paulo*, 19 July 1932.

58. *A Gazeta*, 7 Aug. 1932, 3.

59. AESP, Col. Rev. de 1932, Pasta 378, Doc. 1587, 9–10. Note that the "racial" identity of the *nordestino* in the Paulista gaze was quite unstable. The "racial type" deprecatingly referred to as "*cabeça chata*" could be vaguely described as a mixture of Portuguese, Indian, and African, whereas in other contexts *nortistas* are referred to as "*negro*" or "*mulato.*"

60. "Paulistas," *Jornal das Trincheiras*, no. 5 (28 Aug. 1932): 1.

61. On horizontal solidarity as a key aspect of national identity, see Benedict Anderson, *Imagined Communities: Reflections on the Origin and Spread of Nationalism*, rev. ed. (London: Verso, 1991), 7.

62. "'Paulistas,'" *Jornal das Trincheiras*, no. 5 (28 Aug. 1932): 1.

63. Coaracy, *O caso de São Paulo*, 18.

64. Paul Gilroy, *The Black Atlantic: Modernity and Double Consciousness* (Cambridge, Mass.: Harvard University Press, 1993), 2.

65. On the way cultural identity allows race and nation to fuse, see Paul Gilroy, "One Nation under a Groove," in Eley and Suny, *Becoming National*, 357.

66. For a thoughtful discussion of the relationship between Gilberto Freyre's regionalism and his ideas about modernity and national identity, see Ruben George Oliven, "O nacional e a regional na construção da identidade brasileira," in *A parte e o todo*, 31–45. On regionalist efforts to whiten the "Man of the Northeast," see Stanley E. Blake, "The Invention of the Nordestino: Race, Region, and Identity in Northeastern Brazil, 1889–1945" (Ph.D. diss., State University of New York at Stony Brook, 2001).

67. Oliven, "O nacional e a regional na construção." To be sure, Vargas himself (locked in battle with regional interests in São Paulo and Rio Grande do Sul) presented this as an "either-or" question, as symbolized by the ceremonial burning of the state flags in 1937. On Vargas and regionalism, see his *Diário*, esp. vol. 2, *1937–1942* (Rio de Janeiro: Siciliano/Fundação Getúlio Vargas, 1995), 9–101.

68. Again, we no longer need to focus all our energies on debunking the "myth" of racial democracy; we can now consider the meanings and circulation of this discourse, both among elites and the popular classes. For a stimulating discussion along these lines, see Sueann Caulfield, *In Defense of Honor: Sexual Morality, Modernity, and Nation in Early-Twentieth-Century Brazil* (Durham: Duke University Press, 2000), chap. 5, and her essay in this volume. On Gilberto Freyre, regionalism, and national identity, see Hermano Vianna, *The Mystery of Samba: Popular Music and National Identity in Brazil*, ed. and trans. John Charles Chasteen (Chapel Hill: University of North Carolina Press, 1999), 40–42.

RACE AND NATION
IN LATIN AMERICA
An Anthropological View

Peter Wade

SAMENESS AND DIFFERENCE

Homogeneity and diversity exist in tension with each other in discourses and practices of *mestizaje*. I highlight this in an attempt to nuance the opposition between, on the one hand, the nationalist glorification of *mestizaje* as a democratic process leading to and symbolic of racial harmony and, on the other, *mestizaje* as a rhetorical flourish that hides racist and even ethnocidal practices of whitening. In my book *Blackness and Race Mixture*, I argued that Colombia was characterized by a racial order in which black people (always an ambiguous category) were both included and excluded: included as ordinary citizens, participating in the overarching process of *mestizaje*, and simultaneously excluded as inferior citizens, or even as people who only marginally participated in "national society," and as individuals with whom whiter people might not want to actually practice *mestizaje*, especially in the most intimate sense of forming links not just of sex but of kinship.[1] Other scholars, such as Whitten and Stutzman, have noted something similar for Ecuador, but a good deal of their emphasis has been on the real exclusion underlying the apparent inclusion.[2] This remains a vital argument and my own work has been strongly influenced by it. In Brazil, much of the revisionist literature on race that appeared from the

1950s onward made a similar argument: that racial democracy was a myth that disguised the harsh realities of racism and racial inequality. The disguise was nevertheless recognized to be effective in that in countries such as Colombia and Brazil many people of varied racial identities denied that racism existed, while black social movements intent on revealing and contesting racism did not seem to resonate with many black people.[3]

More recently, some scholars have highlighted a more nuanced approach to the issue of racial democracy in Brazil. In the present volume, Sueann Caulfield and Barbara Weinstein both emphasize that racial democracy was not simply an illusion or an effectively created element of false consciousness for working-class Brazilians in the decades before the Second World War. John Burdick, Peter Fry, and Denise Ferreira da Silva have made similar arguments for present-day Brazil.[4] That is, there are aspects of living life as a dark- or brown-skinned person in Brazil—or Colombia—that resonate strongly with the idea that racism there is a minor anachronism, that people of different racial identities can get along harmoniously, and that black people can be respected and valued and can rise up the social hierarchy. There are, of course, other aspects of the same life or different lives that suggest exactly the opposite: that racism is an integral and flourishing element in daily existence and that black people are devalued and have to fight harder than their lighter-skinned peers to rise in the social hierarchy, only to be refused the symbolic attributes of material success.

The idea that *mestizaje* evokes both sameness and hierarchical difference is related to this: the trope allows both equality and inequality to be imagined and experienced. *Mestizaje* inherently involves both a symbolics of future homogeneity and a symbolics of original, primordial differences: both are continuously re-created, never entirely superseded. This is so in the texts of intellectuals who from the mid-nineteenth century onward have discussed the nature of nationhood and their country's diversity, including its racial diversity. At the level of the individual body, such origins are reiterated in religious practices that involve the possession of people by racialized spirits—whether they be the *pretos velhos* of Umbanda, the *orixás* of Candomblé, or spirits such as El Negro Felipe and El Indio Guaicaipuro who possess devotees of the Venezuelan cult of María Lionza.[5] In my work on popular music in twentieth-century Colombia, I argued that when people talk about music they also constantly break it down into notionally racial components, harking back to the classic triad on which the nation was reputedly founded—Africans, indigenous peoples, and Europeans.[6] The drums are generally linked to Africa, the language and often the melody are linked to Europe, while different aspects (individual instruments, perhaps a certain emotion such as melancholy) are associated with indigenous origins. I also argued—somewhat speculatively—that people experience popular music and dance in an embodied way that evokes racialized elements inside. The "blackness" they may feel themselves to have inside by virtue of their mixed heritage may "come out" when certain music plays. In this sense, the nation is not only imagined as a collectivity of people doing the same things in a shared space and time but is also lived as a shared experience of embodiment.

Various chapters in this collection refer to this tension between sameness and difference. The remarks by Caulfield and Weinstein about the nonillusory quality of ideas of racial democracy in Brazil are one example. Race was rarely mentioned in the court cases Caulfield examines: people were tacitly expressing a belief in racial sameness. Yet when the actual outcomes of the cases are examined, it is clear that perceived racial identity influenced judgments in ways that discriminated against darker-skinned people in terms of their supposed moral and sexual qualities. Weinstein's chapter brings out the same tension, via the frequent association of race with region. The strongly racist regionalism of the Paulistas (or some of them, at least) fit broadly with notions of Brazilian nationalism in that blackness was disparaged and relegated to the lower eche-lons of the nation. On the other hand, regionalism went too far by seeming to exclude blacks altogether—and by arrogating all the virtues of national identity to one region alone. Weinstein tends to contrast Paulista racism to the "more inclusive" and racially democratic nation associated with Vargas, but it bears emphasizing that, as her material shows, the ideologies of racial democracy also included a very hierarchized notion of race, mediated through ideas about the modernity and the backwardness of the nation's regions. The contrast Wein-stein makes is also nuanced by the everyday realities of Paulista life, which, as she observes, included the presence of many dark-skinned people. At the level of representation, on which Weinstein chooses to focus, the racial exclusivity of Paulista regionalism is more evident than it perhaps would be if other, more experiential dimensions were to be considered.

The chapters by Gerardo Rénique and Alexandra Minna Stern also touch upon issues of homogeneity and heterogeneity. Rénique's piece shows how Sonoran regionalism, based in part on mythologies of nonblackness (and non-indigenousness), gave rise to quite a virulent anti-Chinese racism that func-tioned as a point of consensus in a nation-building project.[7] In Sonora, and more widely in Mexico, there seemed to be very little idea of Chinese people as "the same" as other Mexicans; it appears they were perceived as more radically "other," as originating from beyond the original triad of African-European-

Amerindian, and as unsuitable candidates for becoming mestizos. Yet Ré-nique's treatment also focuses above all on representations of race and region. He tells us that some concern surrounded relationships between Chinese men and Mexican women, but the very existence of such relationships hints that exclusion was not as complete as it might seem.

Stern's work demonstrates the energy that was dedicated by the literate elite to recording the huge diversity of the nation, while images of the mestizo were being held up as a standard. I was struck by her observation that the scientists she studied had to discard much of the data they collected as it "varied too widely to be statistically reliable." This is surely a testament to the active con-struction by such scientists and other literate people of the diversity they re-corded. It indicates that such commentators were not just *acknowledging* the diversity in their nations but actively *elaborating* it. I believe such elaborations were a necessary and functional aspect of elite nationalist discourse because, within the nation, it was a means by which the differences between the elites and the darker-skinned, more "backward," more peripheral people could be recorded and reinforced.[8]

APPROPRIATION

The elaboration of diversity feeds into the dynamic of appropriation, in which middle and upper classes include in their cultural repertoires elements that they identify as originating from the lower and/or darker-skinned classes, often resignifying such elements, mystifying their origins, and repositioning them in value hierarchies. This process, I think, has not been explored fully by the chapters in this volume. In their periodization of ideas about race and nation, the editors do not mention that it was during the "third period" of twentieth-century populist politics that, in many places, music and other expressive forms associated directly with black people became nationalized: *son*, tango, and *cumbia* are just three examples.[9] Such musical forms were associated with lower-class blackness, and they encountered resistance from middle classes and elites when they began to become popular in the burgeoning mass media. Yet they were also accepted, usually in a "cleaned up" form that also toned down the perceived "blackness" of the music without, however, erasing it.

Vital to this process was the primitivism that was fashionable in European and North American circles.[10] This indicated to Latin American elites that blackness might be construed as modern—even if it was for what many of them saw as all the wrong reasons: the image of sexual adventure, sensuality, emotion, and so on. However, it was more than just a question of Latin Americans imitating European models: as Aims McGuinness argues in his chapter, Latin Americans were participating in the construction of these models, in two ways.

First, there had long existed the idea that black (or indigenous) culture harbored certain powers and values that, although primitive and therefore to be despised, might also, in certain contexts, be useful, beneficial, and stimulating. Black and indigenous peoples were reputed to have curing and magical powers.[11] Ideas about the sexual availability of and licentiousness of black women (and of course the sexual prowess of black men) also have a long history—although such supposed characteristics were often seen as morally reprehensible.[12] In many areas of Latin America, there was a long-standing pattern of lighter-skinned men of a certain class maintaining sexual relationships with darker-skinned women of a lower class than themselves.[13] Social contexts in which lower-class black music filtered into middle-class (male) experiences were often related to male encounters with lower-class and often darker-skinned women: for Cuba, Robin Moore mentions beer gardens, brothels, and private parties of a slightly orgiastic nature; this mirrors what I found for Colombia.[14] Thus middle-class and elite men were quite prepared to see blackness (in women, in music) as exciting and powerful. This was not the same as fashionable and modern—which is what primitivism was suggesting— but there were clear overlaps, which meant that Latin Americans were not just accepting foreign models of primitivism but engaging them with their own ideas about the exciting nature of blackness. Second, the black musical forms that Latin American middle classes and elites eventually accepted as national styles were often exported to North America and Europe, where they were accepted with enthusiasm—tango and rumba, for example—thence to be reexported back to Latin America in recordings and films. This was a transnational dialogue that formed part of the process of appropriation.

Appropriation is a key dynamic in understanding race and nation in Latin America. In this volume, it is touched upon by Lillian Guerra and Anne Macpherson. Guerra notes how, after the trial of the *ñáñigos* that she describes, the University of Havana's museum curator arrived at the courthouse to collect the ritual paraphernalia that had been confiscated from the *ñáñigos* by the police. She interprets the "museumification" of the *ñáñigos* as a ritual of "cooptation and domestication." Yet the bulk of her chapter describes discrimination against Afro-Cubans. One cannot dispute this description, yet I was struck by the fact that the *ñáñigos*' Abakuá society also "attracted many prominent whites from Cuba's privileged classes," at least prior to the period that is Guerra's main concern. She does not discuss what the motives of such prominent people (men, I imagine) might have been in participating in the Abakuá society, nor does she reveal whether they continued to do so in the early twentieth century. I recall that Fernando Ortiz, writing in 1906, deplored that "rich women of elevated lineage" engaged in ceremonies conducted by "*brujos*" (sorcerers), despite the fact that these ritual specialists were also persecuted by the authorities.[15] This suggests that the acts of the museum curator might have been part of a larger set of complex interactions of mutual appropriation and incorporation. Appropriation can be, however, a misleading term insofar as it suggests a simple taking-up by the middle classes of a lower class form. In fact, some of the key figures in the nationalization of black musical styles were themselves black and mulatto, just as it must have been Afro-Cuban Abakuá members who allowed white men into their circles and black *brujos* who allowed wealthy white women to participate in—and perhaps fund—their rituals.

The image of black powers of healing, sexual energy, or musical talent is a common one in these processes of appropriation, but it does not exhaust the possibilities. Macpherson shows that nation-building Belizean Creoles embraced blackness in the image of self-sacrificing fraternity: black men were portrayed as partners in racial harmony, not resentful of their slave status and loyal to their masters. I am reminded here of the image of the *preto velho*, the old black slave who possesses Umbanda mediums in Brazil. Lindsay Hale argues that a key trope for these figures is that of redemption: these old slaves suffered during life, but through their suffering and often through their self-sacrificing help to others (even including their former tormentors), they achieved a spiritual blessedness.[16] Redemption through suffering is the keystone of Judeo-Christian religion, and it would be interesting to enquire into the religious dimensions of what was going on in Belize in the 1890s. Was the fraternity that the slaves apparently displayed also a religious one? Was there some sense in which the slaves in 1798 were included, albeit mythically and in retrospect, in a religious brotherhood with their masters? How did the Creole nation-builders, mostly Protestants of one denomination or another, think about the connection between slavery, abolition, and religion both in the 1890s and as they looked back to the key event in their national myth, the 1798 battle against the (Catholic) Spanish, which took place at a time when Protestant-inspired abolitionism was an important force.

I pose this speculative question in part inspired by the work of John Pulis on the so-called black loyalists—slaves and freed blacks who helped the British against the American patriots in North America in the 1770s. Pulis describes a black loyalist who had been encouraged to follow Baptism by his master in North America, becoming an itinerant preacher in Georgia and, as a freed man, helping to lay the foundations of "native Baptism" in his new home in Jamaica.[17] The intersections of religious thought with ideas of freedom and emancipation are intriguing and open up questions about how religion could provide elements for the narratives about national, cross-racial loyalties of the kind the Creole nationalists in Belize were constructing.

KINSHIP, NATION, RACE, AND GENDER

Metaphors of the family are frequently encountered in images of the nation. These metaphors suggest unity and loyalty, but also hierarchy and patriarchy, and they draw in their wake the struggles and differences that divide families. The intersection of gender, race, and nation is also invoked in such familial metaphors. In anthropological terms, this all implies the category of kinship, which, as various authors have pointed out, is intertwined with ideas about nation, race, sex, and gender.[18]

Take the common Latin American trope, "*¿Y dónde está tu abuela?* [Where's your grandmother then?]." Perhaps a person has made deprecating remarks about black (or indigenous) people, or has implicitly claimed to be white or near-white. The challenge implies that the person has not-so-distant black or indigenous ancestry and is dishonoring his/her own relatives by denying them or disparaging them. Note that the trope commonly uses *abuela*. This is a person distant enough to allow the grandchild to look very different from her. The person is also a female, and this invokes the image of a black woman having a relationship, perhaps not a formal one, with a lighter-skinned man and thus "whitening" her children, but also perhaps dishonoring herself by the informality of her union (which, in this narrative, may have been with a man who already had an "official," white family). The trope is redolent of national progress: in Western ideas of kinship, at least, genealogical time is progressive and unilinear; the children are "further on" in time than the parents.[19] It fits with ideas about race and place, in which blacks and indigenous people are associated with places perceived to be rural and backward. It fits too with ideas about moral progress: for a white or near-white grandchild, there is less likelihood of the morally dubious informal union with a lighter man and more likelihood of the official formal union. Thus the black grandmother is located out of sight and out of time; the grandchild has progressed in genealogical, racial, national, and moral terms.

Yet the progression cannot sever the link, because that link is one of substance and nurture, each confounded with the other. The link of kinship is not just one of "blood," but also one of nurture, especially as grandmothers are frequently key figures in the upbringing of children in the African diaspora in the Americas. Through "blood" and through feeding and caring, the link between grandmother and grandchild is made strong, strong enough to resist the "progressions" of urbanization, vertical mobility, whitening, and nationalization. Hence the power of the trope, as it recalls that link and brings the grandmother into view and into time.

From this simple trope emerge many of the intimate intersections of kinship, race, nation, sex, and gender. Macpherson shows how the Belizean Creole men who invoked the collective fraternal loyalty of the male slaves in the formation of the nation at the same time erased any reference to their own darker-skinned mothers and grandmothers, who were linked to them by personal genealogical connections of substance and nurture. The fraternal embrace of the slaves, distant in time, evokes a harmonious cordiality; the maternal embrace of grandmother and mother, not so distant in time, threatens discord. The racial identity of the individual, however manipulable, is still tied stubbornly to family—family familiar to audiences who "quite likely knew that these [Creole nationalist] speakers' backgrounds included free colored slaveowners and women" (Macpherson, this volume). In contrast to these vertical links of motherhood that constitute individual persons, the identity of the nation is imagined in the horizontal time of fraternity—not the sibling kinship born of common descent, but rather the ritual kinship of blood brotherhood that makes sense of the narrative in which blacks and whites together "produced" the nation through the battle of 1798, in which they shed blood together. Genealogical mothers are thus banished in favor of ritual brothers, but the banishment cannot be fully effective because kinship, at least in Western idioms, always involves both blood and ritual: the mothers are connected through caring as well as "blood"; the ritual brothers have shared "blood," and kinship is exactly what is being constructed through these ritual performances. Thus to invoke the fraternal embrace of the nation, even if it is of a ritual nature, one must invoke the maternal embrace of (black) mothers and grandmothers.

In its implication of possibly dishonorable unions between whiter men and darker women, the trope of the *abuela* also recalls Caulfield's chapter in this volume. Caulfield demonstrates that the ideas of honor that saw whiter women as guardians of a virtuous and proper morality constituted a set of gender/sex values that permitted a dissimulated racial discrimination that did not overtly disturb ideas of racial harmony. Ideas of a racially homogeneous nation entailed the image of male-female relationships in which, whatever other proprieties had to be observed, racial identifications had no relevance. But her material makes it clear that the "other proprieties" were themselves subtly racialized. Not only was there a clear hierarchy of good and bad unions, in terms of the relative class status and moral qualities of the partners, but the hierarchy also carried racial connotations. All the unions in Caulfield's data were potentially "bad" unions in that they were alleged to have involved a crime, but some of these unions were ratified as officially bad (i.e., someone was found guilty), while others were not. And those classed as officially bad tended to involve darker-skinned people. Even where a man was not found guilty, the woman was left with question marks over her honor, and such women tended to be darker skinned.

That racism operates through ideas about the need to protect and control women's virtue has been noted before.[20] The related idea that racism can effectively be disguised in ideas about gender and sexual morality is an interesting one.[21] The problem with seeing this as a mechanism allowing the existence of dissimulated racism in Latin America—and this is part of Caulfield's argument—is that the same kind of intertwining of ideas about sex/gender values and race (and nation) are evident in cases where racism is far from dissimulated—for example, the United States and the United Kingdom.

RACE, NATURE, CULTURE

I agree that "systems of racial classifications have drawn as often on cultural as biological criteria" (Appelbaum, Macpherson, and Rosemblatt, this volume). To argue otherwise would be to define as nonracial most of the racial identifications that take place in Latin America, which rarely depend on biological criteria alone. David Theo Goldberg disputes the argument that "ideas about race are inherently committed to claims about biological inheritance, whether of physical or intellectual or moral characteristics," and although he is making a general statement, it is particularly appropriate to Latin America.[22] This is made clear in the chapters by Sarah Chambers, McGuinness, Stern, and Weinstein.

Cultural racism, to use the label commonly applied to this phenomenon, implies at least two problems, however. First, it assumes that there is something called biological racism that is somehow its polar opposite. This form of racism is usually assumed to have its concrete expression in nineteenth-century and early twentieth-century "scientific racism" and eugenics, and also in the United States's "one-drop" rule, according to which "one drop" of "black blood" defined a person as black. Second, it leaves rather open the question of what a "racial" classification is. If such a classification is not limited to a discursive reference to biology and can depend also on references to culture, then what defines it as a *racial* classification, as opposed to an ethnic, class, or simply "cultural" classification?

My reaction here is to take a step away from "biology" and look at it as a cultural artifact. As soon as we do this, the apparently obvious distinction between culture and biology becomes blurred, as does a clear distinction between cultural racism and biological racism. This is partly to say, as does Weinstein, that there may be "considerable slippage from one [biological] racist language to another [cultural one]," but it is also to say that the biological language is itself cultural (and, by implication, the opposite may also be true). In other words, I question the common assumption that racial thought took on a purely "biological" form during the heyday of racial science and racial typologies and that, since then, it has acquired more cultural forms, gradually losing its biological discourse—especially since the Second World War and the demise of racial science—until it has become a mainly cultural discourse, albeit one that suggests cultural attributes that are almost naturally ingrained.[23] I do not deny that a biological discourse has taken a lesser role and that culture has become a more important referent, but I would like to nuance the narrative of a straightforward switch from one to the other. Classic Western oppositions between nature and culture make such a switch too easy in our conceptual arguments. I suspect that racial thought in its typological heyday, while it certainly invoked a biological—and biologically determinist—discourse, also included what today would be called cultural influences within its very conception of biology. I also think that modern cultural racism has not abandoned a sort of biological thought—although it might not be counted as such by biologists—which underwrites its naturalizing tendencies. I am not referring here so much to realms of public political discourse where references to biology are risky, but rather to less public realms of life in which people are talking and thinking about everyday social relationships and about how people come to be as they are as a complex result of their families and their surroundings.[24]

In concrete terms, if we look at the racial science of the late nineteenth century, the science based on ideas about biology, in which racial classifications were elaborated on the basis of comparative anatomy, we find that the racial types that were being established were admitted to be conceptual abstractions, unobservable empirically. What scientists were dealing with were individuals who, due to the influence of environment, climate, and intermixture, showed aspects of the notional, original racial types. Nancy Leys Stepan notes that the notion of racial type was explicitly understood as something not directly observable. It was an underlying essence, subject to all kinds of variation in its observable manifestations. The U.S. sociologist William Z. Ripley, who based his book *Races of Europe* (1899) on European research into physical anthropology, used maps of trait distributions to infer underlying racial types. These types, three originally, had been confused over time by "chance, variation, migration, intermixture and changing environments."[25] It was the job of the analyst to get behind these confusions and establish the underlying type. Ripley had, in the end, to be both an environmentalist and a racial typologist; he believed in permanent, hereditary racial types, but also in the shaping influence of the environment. He also held to the doctrine of the inheritance of acquired characteristics, as did most scientists of his day, and this inevitably introduced an environmentalist and even a culturalist dynamic into his racial thought. Ripley was not alone in this way of thinking. Louis Agassiz, the U.S. antievolutionist who believed that differences between "races" were like species differences, claimed that it was part of the potential of the essence to respond to the environment.[26] Tzvetan Todorov notes how the French historian Hippolyte Taine considered races to be innate and immutable: "There is one [fixed element], a character and a spirit proper to the race, transmitted from generation to generation, remaining the same through cultural change."[27] Yet Taine also held that the same fixed element was an adaptation to the environment. Todorov comments: "The inside that was supposed to be opposed to the outside is only a slightly older outside."[28]

Ann Stoler's work in the Dutch and French colonies of southeast Asia also demonstrates that, while colonial authorities and colonists might have thought in essentialist ways that used a biological discourse, the essences they conceived were actually "protean."[29] They were, for example, open to environmental influence. Specifically, Europeans could be made degenerate by the tropical climate and even more by consorting with native partners, while their children could be badly affected by being brought up by native nursemaids, especially if they were breast-fed by them. A person's very nature was formed by these processes and was thus subject to change. Stoler concludes that "a notion of essence does not necessarily rest on immovable parts but on the strategic inclusion of different attributes, of a changing constellation of features and a changing weighting of them."[30]

Studies of the eugenics movement also suggest a nuancing of simple opposi-tions between biology and culture. Stepan argues that the eugenics movement was received in Latin America in a characteristically environmentalist way. Thinkers there, especially medics, preferred to eschew the most strictly biologi-cally determinist ideas, associated with Anglo-Saxon theorists, and to adopt a program in which "social hygiene" was important. Taking a cue from Conti-nental European thinkers, it was argued in neo-Lamarckian fashion that, by improving the environment, a permanent improvement could be made to "the race."[31] Yet this was by no means only a Latin American response. Diane Paul shows that in the United States, too, eugenics was a program of social hygiene and that advocates believed—as did many people, even at the beginning of the twentieth century—in the inheritance of acquired characteristics.[32]

At the other end of the spectrum, Marisol de la Cadena argues that, in Peru, biological idioms dropped out of intellectuals' discourse about race and nation from about the 1920s, when the whole edifice of scientific racism was only just beginning to be dismantled. Such determinist idioms were rejected by Peruvian intellectuals, clashing as they did with ideologies of *indigenismo*. Yet, especially when considering the indigenous population, these thinkers continued to con-ceive of culture—or "soul" or "spirit," to use their terms—as more or less innate and immanent. Thus a silent racism persisted in culturalist guise. There were "racialized notions of culture" at work which acted to "naturalize social differ-ences."[33] This argument points toward the kind of approach I am taking here: when culture is thought of as innate and heritable, and considered as funda-mental as a soul or spirit, one wonders where the difference lies between it and something called biology. Yet de la Cadena does not really pursue this question and retains a clear divide between biological idioms of race, as purveyed by most of the scientific community of the time, and cultural idioms, as adopted by these Peruvian intellectuals. It seems to me that such a distinction breaks down under the weight of her own material. While these thinkers were clearly rejecting a specific version of racial theory that condemned the indigenous population to permanent inferiority, I am less convinced that they simply switched from "nature" to "culture" as social scientists might understand those terms after, say, the Second World War. Instead they seem to have thought in a mode that, while it could be seen as simply combining elements of culture and biology in ways that are familiar to us now—"We're all a bit of both"—also blurred the very distinction between culture and biology by attributing to the former some of the traits we might expect to belong to biology, such as innate-ness, essence, and heritability through descent.

These are all matters that are not a major theme of the chapters in this volume. Yet it is an underlying concern and the editors rightly state that "racial categorization has not operated exclusively through biologically determinist scientific discourses" and that such a realization is especially important for an appreciation of race and nation in Latin America. My comment is, first, that biologically determinist discourses need to be examined very carefully to analyze the "biology" that is actually being invoked, and, second, that apparently cultural discourses of race need to be examined to see how ideas about "blood," heritage, environment, and bodies are dealt with, rather than assuming that such ideas belong only to a realm called "biology"—itself over-narrowly conceived as a matter of essentialist determinisms[34]—seen as relevant primarily to the history of North American and European race relations.

NAMING RACE

In the Latin American context, the issue of whether or not to be explicit about race and racial identity has been a problematic one in public debates. Traditionally, the ideas of *mestizaje* and racial democracy have enjoined silence when it comes to linking racial identity to citizenship and rights, even if the specificity of racial identity is maintained and may be reinforced on other planes—from discrimination in the job market to the objectification and even commodification of black and indigenous identities in literary, musical, ritual, and other expressive dimensions. In general, it has been hard to argue that racial minorities deserve specific rights or treatment. In this respect, the situation for indigenous peoples has been significantly different from that for blacks. In many nations, a specific place has long been carved out for indigenous minorities, ideologically and in some cases legally (as, for example, Chambers's chapter indicates for Peru). This has been despite widespread attempts, in the aftermath of independence and under the influence of European liberalism, to eliminate any special categories of citizen. Elsewhere, I have argued that this difference between blacks and indigenous peoples derives in part from the different ways that, from the earliest colonial times, they have been inserted into the "structures of alterity," and I will not review this argument here.[35]

The chapters in this volume do not compare the place of indigenous peoples with that of blacks in much detail, but James Sanders's chapter does present some interesting material. He shows how indigenous people in the Cauca region of Colombia managed to combine ideas about universalist republican citizenship with particularist claims about rights to land and identity. Basing their case partly on prejudicial stereotypes of "Indians" as weak, stupid, and defenseless—and therefore in need of special treatment—these indigenous communities managed to get support for their claims from the Conservative Party and even to play off the Liberals and Conservatives against each another. Meanwhile, although black people in the region allied more with Liberals than Conservatives, they did not identity themselves as *negros* or *mulatos*, although Sanders found cases of people identifying themselves as slaves or ex-slaves in legal petitions. This shows a basic difference in the way black and indigenous identities fit into structures of alterity that was a result both of how these people chose to represent themselves as "others" and—something that Sanders considers less—of the extent to which such claims might be recognized as appropriate or even possible by mestizos and whites. In addition to this general difference, the Cauca material indicates that quite specific regional factors mediate the way identities related to structures of alterity. In this case, indigenous identities acquired a particular solidity due to the political power struggles going on at the time, the fact that indigenous communities constituted a significant electorate, and the way patron-client relationships had built up in the area. This is a salutary lesson in the need to pay attention to local and historical context in making broad comparisons between the place of black and indigenous people in Latin America.

Guerra's chapter shows something of the opposite trend. In Cuba, blackness was more of a topic of public debate, in the sense that there was a struggle over whether race was to be explicitly named or not. Liberal circles among the elite insisted on ideas of racial democracy: their society was to be a raceless one, in which racial identities had no place by fiat. Conservative elites adhered rather to a Hispanophile image of the nation in a way that implicitly, if not explicitly, named race and valued whiter over blacker people. The independence war veterans and the black working classes in general demanded a raceless society too, but for them this meant one in which race really did have no place; that is, racial identity should have no influence on life chances, rather than being an absent presence. The Liberal view was superficial: a society that did not mention race was supposed to be, de facto, a society in which racism did not exist. Black Cubans' experiences told them otherwise. The Liberal view is not confined to Cuba, of course, but has been identified too in the United States—despite this being a society in which race has long been very clearly named.[36]

These kinds of processes and debates have remained current and indeed have become especially salient in the last few decades. The question of whether to name racial (or "ethnic")[37] difference in Latin American nations and, even more, whether to attach specific legal or political rights to such names has become more pressing since the 1960s with the widespread organization of indigenous peoples and, later, Afro-Latins into movements participating in what we would now call identity or recognition politics. The recent passage of various constitutional and legal reforms in a number of countries has given official legitimacy to some of the demands voiced by these movements. One of the most developed legislative frameworks in this respect is in Colombia, where both indigenous people and black people (or, more accurately, some "black communities") have access to special land rights, special political representation in the Congress, and representation in a number of state organs.[38]

The chapters by Sanders and Guerra indicate that these kinds of debates are far from new, even if the context for them is now rather different and the possibility of combining universalist citizenship with particularist rights is now given more official space. From my arguments, above, about the long-standing tension between sameness and difference, I also draw the conclusion that the new official multiculturalism is less of a break with the past than it might at first appear to observers who see the past as having been characterized by ideologies of *mestizaje* that simply erased difference and who now see those ideologies as having been somewhat dislodged, if by no means entirely displaced, by black and indigenous social movements. I think it is clear that blackness and indigenousness have long been objectified aspects of the dominant national perspective. I grant that such objectification—which must perforce include some type of recognition—has been limited to specific realms (such as music, dance, curing, and so on) and has generally been highly paternalist, romanticizing, and often straightforwardly racist in character. But understanding this also forces us to ask to what extent the new multiculturalisms suffer from some of the same defects and constrict indigenous and black minorities into defined ideological, legal, and political spaces.[39] This is a fairly standard critique of official multiculturalism.[40] The advantage of a historical perspective is that it indicates that these debates are not new but rather are the latest twist in a long-established dynamic. This gives added weight to arguments that critique the problems of official multiculturalism, to those that indicate that universalist citizenship can be combined with particularist rights, and to those that challenge the idea that an insistence on silence about race translates into a society in which race does not matter to people's life chances.

NOTES

1. Peter Wade, *Blackness and Race Mixture: The Dynamics of Racial Identity in Colombia* (Baltimore: Johns Hopkins University Press, 1993).

2. Norman E. Whitten Jr., *Black Frontiersmen: A South American Case*, 2d ed. (Prospect Heights, Ill.: Waveland Press, 1986); Ronald Stutzman, "*El Mestizaje*: An All-Inclusive Ideology of Exclusion," in *Cultural Transformations and Ethnicity in Modern Ecuador*, ed. Norman E. Whitten Jr. (Urbana: University of Illinois Press, 1981), 45–94.

3. See, for example, France Winddance Twine, *Racism in a Racial Democracy: The Maintenance of White Supremacy in Brazil* (New Brunswick: Rutgers University Press, 1998); Michael George Hanchard, *Orpheus and Power: The* Movimento Negro *of Rio de Janeiro and São Paulo, Brazil, 1945–1988* (Princeton: Princeton University Press, 1994); Howard Winant, "Rethinking Race in Brazil," *Journal of Latin American Studies* 24, no. 1 (Feb. 1992): 173–92.

4. John Burdick, *Blessed Anastácia: Women, Race, and Popular Christianity in Brazil* (New York: Routledge, 1998); Peter Fry, "Politics, Nationality, and the Meanings of 'Race' in Brazil," *Daedalus* 129, no. 2 (Spring 2000): 83–118; Denise Ferreira da Silva, "Facts of Blackness: Brazil Is Not (Quite) the United States . . . and Racial Politics in Brazil?," *Social Identities* 4, no. 2 (June 1998): 201–34. See also, on Colombia, Wade, *Blackness and Race Mixture*, chap. 16.

5. On María Lionza, see Barbara Placido, " 'It's All to Do with Words': An Analysis of Spirit Possession in the Venezuelan Cult of María Lionza," *Journal of the Royal Anthropological Institute* 7, no. 2 (June 2001): 207–24; Michael Taussig, *The Magic of the State* (New York: Routledge, 1997). On Umbanda, see Lindsay L. Hale, "*Preto Velho*: Resistance, Redemption, and Engendered Representations of Slavery in a Brazilian Possession-Trance Religion," *American Ethnologist* 24, no. 2 (May 1997): 392–414.

6. Peter Wade, *Music, Race, and Nation: Música Tropical in Colombia* (Chicago: University of Chicago Press, 2000).

7. For a similar argument in other contexts, see Paul Gilroy, "*There Ain't No Black in the Union Jack": The Cultural Politics of Race and Nation* (London: Hutchinson, 1987), and Anthony W. Marx, *Making Race and Nation: A Comparison of South Africa, the United States, and Brazil* (Cambridge: Cambridge University Press, 1998).

8. See Wade, *Music, Race, and Nation*, 5.

9. See Robin D. Moore, *Nationalizing Blackness: Afrocubanismo and Artistic Revolution in Havana, 1920–1940* (Pittsburgh: University of Pittsburgh Press, 1997); Marta E. Savigliano, *Tango and the Political Economy of Passion* (Boulder, Colo.: Westview Press, 1995); Wade, *Music, Race, and Nation*.

10. Elazar Barkan and Ronald Bush, eds., *Prehistories of the Future: The Primitivist Project and the Culture of Modernism* (Stanford: Stanford University Press, 1995).

11. Michael Taussig, *Shamanism, Colonialism, and the Wild Man: A Study in Terror and Healing* (Chicago: University of Chicago Press, 1987).

12. Jan Nederveen Pieterse, *White on Black: Images of Africa and Blacks in Western Popular Culture* (New Haven: Yale University Press, 1992); Winthrop D. Jordan, *White over Black: American Attitudes toward the Negro, 1550–1812* (New York: Norton, 1977).

13. Verena Martínez-Alier, *Marriage, Class, and Colour in Nineteenth-Century Cuba: A Study of Racial Attitudes and Sexual Values in a Slave Society*, 2d ed. (Ann Arbor: University of Michigan Press, 1989).

14. Moore, *Nationalizing Blackness*, chap. 4; Wade, *Music, Race, and Nation*, chaps. 4 and 5.

15. Fernando Ortiz, *Hampa afro-cubana: Los negros brujos* (1906; reprint, Madrid: Editorial América, 1917), 257.

16. Hale, "*Preto Velho*"; see also Burdick, *Blessed Anastácia*.

17. John W. Pulis, "The Jamaican Diaspora: Moses Baker, George Liele, and the African American Migration to Jamaica" (paper presented to the School of American Research Advanced Seminar "From Africa to the Americas: New Directions in Afro-American Anthropology," Santa Fe, N.M., 11–15 Apr. 1999). See also John W. Pulis, ed., *Moving On: Black Loyalists in the Afro-Atlantic World* (New York: Garland, 1999).

18. Benedict Anderson, *Imagined Communities: Reflections on the Origin and Spread of Nationalism*, rev. ed. (London: Verso, 1991), 5; Brackette F. Williams, "Classification Systems Revisited: Kinship, Caste, Race, and Nationality as the Flow of Blood and the Spread of Rights," in *Naturalizing Power: Essays in Feminist Cultural Analysis*, ed. Sylvia Yanagisako and Carol Delaney (New York: Routledge, 1995), 201–36.

19. Marilyn Strathern, *After Nature: English Kinship in the Late Twentieth Century* (Cambridge: Cambridge University Press, 1992), 21, 80.

20. Martínez-Alier, *Marriage, Class, and Colour*; Ann Laura Stoler, *Race and the Education of Desire: Foucault's* History of Sexuality *and the Colonial Order of Things* (Durham: Duke University Press, 1995); Brackette F. Williams, ed., *Women Out of Place: The Gender of Agency and the Race of Nationality* (New York: Routledge, 1996).

21. See Joel Streicker, "Policing Boundaries: Race, Class, and Gender in Cartagena, Colombia," *American Ethnologist* 22, no. 1 (Feb. 1995): 54–74.

22. David Theo Goldberg, *Racist Culture: Philosophy and the Politics of Meaning* (Oxford: Blackwell, 1993), 72.

23. Gilroy, *"There Ain't No Black in the Union Jack,"* chap. 2; for Peru, Marisol de la Cadena, *Indigenous Mestizos: The Politics of Race and Culture in Cuzco, Peru, 1919–1991* (Durham: Duke University Press, 2000). See also Etienne Balibar, "Is There a 'Neo-Racism'?," in *Race, Nation, Class: Ambiguous Identities*, by Etienne Balibar and Immanuel Wallerstein (London: Verso, 1991), 17–28.

24. I develop these arguments in much greater depth in Peter Wade, *Race, Nature, and Culture: An Anthropological Perspective* (London: Pluto Press, 2002).

25. Ripley, cited in Nancy Leys Stepan, *The Idea of Race in Science: Great Britain, 1800–1960* (London: Macmillan and St. Antony's College, Oxford, 1982), 94.

26. Ernst E. Mayr, *The Growth of Biological Thought: Diversity, Evolution, and Inheritance* (Cambridge, Mass.: The Belknap Press of Harvard University Press, 1982), 688.

27. Taine, cited in Tzvetan Todorov, *On Human Diversity: Nationalism, Racism, and Exoticism in French Thought* (Cambridge, Mass.: Harvard University Press, 1993), 155.

28. Todorov, *On Human Diversity*, 155.

29. Stoler, *Race and the Education of Desire*, 205; see also Ann Laura Stoler, "Sexual Affronts and Racial Frontiers: European Identities and the Cultural Politics of Exclusion in Colonial Southeast Asia," in *Tensions of Empire: Colonial Cultures in a Bourgeois World*, ed. Frederick Cooper and Ann Laura Stoler (Berkeley: University of California Press, 1997), 198–237.

30. Ann Laura Stoler, "Racial Histories and Their Regimes of Truth," *Political Power and Social Theory* 11 (1997): 183–206, quotation on 200.

31. Nancy Leys Stepan, *"The Hour of Eugenics": Race, Gender, and Nation in Latin America* (Ithaca: Cornell University Press, 1991).

32. Diane B. Paul, *Controlling Human Heredity: 1865 to the Present* (Atlantic Highlands, N.J.: Humanities Press, 1995). Michelle Condit shows that Lamarckian theories of the inheritance of acquired characteristics were being publicly touted in 1919. Celeste Michelle Condit, *The Meanings of the Gene: Public Debates about Human Heredity* (Madison: University of Wisconsin Press, 1999), 50.

33. De la Cadena, *Indigenous Mestizos*, 140–41.

34. For an attempt to outline processual forms of biological thinking, see Alan H. Goodman and Thomas L. Leatherman, eds., *Building a New Biocultural Synthesis: Political-Economic Perspectives on Human Biology* (Ann Arbor: University of Michigan Press, 1998).

35. Peter Wade, *Race and Ethnicity in Latin America* (London: Pluto Press, 1997), chap. 2.

36. Ruth Frankenberg comments on what she calls the color- and power-evasive discursive repertoire used by some white women in the United States, which seeks to avoid recognizing difference and asserts equality between everyone, underplaying the real inequalities and discriminations that do exist; see Ruth Frankenberg, *White Women, Race Matters: The Social Construction of Whiteness* (London: Routledge, 1993). Howard Winant also identifies what he labels a neoconservative position in the United States that demands a raceless society in much the same terms as Cuban Liberals did; see Howard Winant, "Difference and Inequality: Postmodern Racial Politics in the United States," in *Racism, the City and the State*, ed. Malcolm Cross and Michael Keith (London: Routledge, 1993), 108–27.

37. I prefer not to link blacks to "race" and indigenous people to "ethnicity" and instead to see both "black" and "Indian" as basically terms of racial identification. See Wade, *Race and Ethnicity*, 19–21, 37–39.

38. See Jaime Arocha, "Inclusion of Afro-Colombians: An Unreachable Goal?," *Latin American Perspectives* 25, no. 3 (May 1998): 70–89; Jaime Arocha and Nina S. de Friedemann, "Colombia," in *No Longer Invisible: Afro–Latin Americans Today*, ed. Minority Rights Group (London: Minority Rights Publications, 1995), 47–75; Juana Camacho and

Eduardo Restrepo, eds., *De montes, ríos y ciudades: Territorios e identidades de la gente negra en Colombia* (Bogotá: Natura-Ecofondo and Instituto Colombiano de Antropología Nacional, 1999); Mauricio Pardo, "Movimientos sociales y actores no gubernamentales," in *Antropología en la modernidad: Identidades, etnicidades y movimientos sociales en Colombia*, ed. María Victoria Uribe and Eduardo Restrepo (Bogotá: Instituto Colombiano de Antropología Nacional, 1997), 207–52; Mauricio Pardo, ed., *Acción colectiva, estado y etnicidad en el Pacífico Colombiano* (Bogotá: Colciencias/Instituto Nacional de Antropología e Historia, 2000); Peter Wade, "The Cultural Politics of Blackness in Colombia," *American Ethnologist* 22, no. 2 (May 1995): 342–58. Black community representation in the House of Representatives, as allowed by Law 70 of 1993, was later declared unconstitutional, but there are signs that it will be reinstated in the near future.

39. This is an argument that I and others have made about Colombia, even while recognizing the groundbreaking changes made by recent legislative actions. See Arocha, "Inclusion of Afro-Colombians"; Pardo, *Acción colectiva, estado y etnicidad*; Mieke Wouters, "Ethnic Rights under Threat: The Black Peasant Movement against Armed Groups' Pressure in Chocó, Colombia," *Bulletin of Latin American Research* 20, no. 4 (Oct. 2001): 498–519; Wade, "The Cultural Politics of Blackness"; Peter Wade, "The Guardians of Power: Biodiversity and Multiculturality in Colombia," in *The Anthropology of Power: Empowerment and Disempowerment in Changing Structures*, ed. Angela Cheater (London: Routledge, 1999), 73–87; Peter Wade, "La population noire en Amérique latine: Multiculturalisme, législation et situation territoriale," *Problèmes d'Amérique Latine*, no. 32 (1999): 3–16.

40. See Tariq Modood and Pnina Werbner, eds., *The Politics of Multiculturalism in the New Europe: Racism, Identity, and Community* (London: Zed Books, 1997).

SELECT BIBLIOGRAPHY

Abud, Kátia Maria. "O sangue intimorato e as nobilíssimas tradições: A construção de um símbolo paulista—o bandeirante." Ph.D. diss., Universidade de São Paulo, 1985.

Adduci, Cássia Chrispiniano. "A 'pátria paulista': O separatismo como resposta à crise final do império brasileiro." Master's thesis, Pontifícia Universidade Católica—São Paulo, 1998.

Aguilar Camín, Héctor. *La frontera nómada: Sonora y la Revolución Mexicana*. Mexico City: Siglo XXI, 1977.

Aguirre Beltrán, Gonzalo. *Antropología médica*. Vol. 8 of *Obra antropológica*. Mexico City: Fondo de Cultura Económica, 1994.

——. *Obra polémica*. Mexico City: Instituto Nacional de Antropología e Historia, 1976.

Almada Bay, Ignacio. "Maytorenismo, rebelión indígena y violencia social." In *Memoria XVII Simposio de Historia y Antropología de Sonora*. Vol. 2. Hermosillo: Universidad de Sonora, 1992.

Alonso, Ana María. *Thread of Blood: Colonialism, Revolution, and Gender on Mexico's Northern Frontier*. Tucson: University of Arizona Press, 1995.

Anderson, Benedict. *Imagined Communities: Reflections on the Origin and Spread of Nationalism*. Rev. ed. London: Verso, 1991.

Anderson, Rodney D. "Race and Social Stratification: A Comparison of Working-Class Spaniards, Indians, and Castas in Guadalajara, Mexico, in 1821." *Hispanic American Historical Review* 68, no. 2 (May 1988): 209–43.

Andrews, George Reid. *The Afro-Argentines of Buenos Aires, 1800–1900*. Madison: University of Wisconsin Press, 1980.

——. *Blacks and Whites in São Paulo, Brazil, 1888–1988*. Madison: University of Wisconsin Press, 1991.

Appelbaum, Nancy P. *Muddied Waters: Race, Region, and Local History in Colombia, 1846–1948*. Durham: Duke University Press, forthcoming.

——. "Remembering Riosucio: Race, Region, and Community in Colombia, 1850–1950." Ph.D. diss., University of Wisconsin–Madison, 1997.

——. "Whitening the Region: Caucano Mediation and 'Antioqueño Colonization' in Nineteenth-Century Colombia." *Hispanic American Historical Review* 79, no. 4 (Nov. 1999): 631–67.

Applegate, Celia. "A Europe of Regions: Reflections on the Historiography of Sub-National Places in Modern Times." *American Historical Review* 104, no. 4 (Oct. 1999): 1157–82.

Arboleda, Gustavo. *Historia contemporánea de Colombia*. Vol. 4, *1851–1853*. Bogotá: Banco Central Hipotecario, 1990.

Ardao, Arturo. *América Latina y la latinidad*. Mexico City: Universidad Nacional Autónoma de México, 1993.

——. *Génesis de la idea y el nombre de América Latina*. Caracas: Centro de Estudios Latinoamericanos Rómulo Gallegos, 1980.

Arendt, Hannah. *The Origins of Totalitarianism*. New York: Harcourt Brace Jovanovich, 1973.

Arocha, Jaime. "Inclusion of Afro-Colombians: An Unreachable Goal?" *Latin American Perspectives* 25, no. 3 (May 1998): 70–89.

Arocha, Jaime, and Nina S. de Friedemann. "Colombia." In *No Longer Invisible: Afro–Latin Americans Today*, edited by the Minority Rights Group. London: Minority Rights Publications, 1995.

Astorga A., Luis A. "La razón demográfica de estado." *Revista Mexicana de Sociología* (Jan.–Mar. 1989): 193–210.

Avirama, Jesús, and Rayda Márquez. "The Indigenous Movement in Colombia." In *Indigenous Peoples and Democracy in Latin America*, edited by Donna Lee Van Cott. New York: St. Martin's Press, 1994.

Baker, Lee D. *From Savage to Negro: Anthropology and the Construction of Race, 1896–1954*. Berkeley: University of California Press, 1998.

Balibar, Etienne. "Is There a 'Neo-Racism'?" In *Race, Nation, Class: Ambiguous Identities*, by Etienne Balibar and Immanuel Wallerstein. London: Verso, 1991.

——. "The Nation Form: History and Ideology." In *Becoming National: A Reader*, edited by Geoff Eley and Ronald Grigor Suny. New York: Oxford University Press, 1996.

——. "Racism and Nationalism." In *Race, Nation, and Class: Ambiguous Identities*, by Etienne Balibar and Immanuel Wallerstein. London: Verso, 1991.

Banton, Michael. *Racial Theories*. Cambridge: Cambridge University Press, 1987.

Barkan, Elazar. *The Retreat of Scientific Racism: Changing Concepts of Race in Britain and the United States between the World Wars*. New York: Cambridge University Press, 1992.

Barkan, Elazar, and Ronald Bush, eds. *Prehistories of the Future: The Primitivist Project and the Culture of Modernism*. Stanford: Stanford University Press, 1995.

Basave Benítez, Agustín. *México mestizo: Análisis del nacionalismo mexicano en torno a la mestizofilia de Andrés Molina Enríquez*. Mexico City: Fondo de Cultura Económica, 1992.

Bastide, Roger, and Florestan Fernandes. *Brancos e negros em São Paulo*. 2d ed. São Paulo: Editora Nacional, 1959.

Bean, Annemarie, James V. Hatch, and Brooks McNamara, eds. *Inside the Minstrel Mask: Readings in Nineteenth-Century Blackface Minstrelsy*. Hanover, N.H.: Wesleyan University Press, 1996.

Bederman, Gail. *Manliness and Civilization: A Cultural History of Gender and Race in the United States, 1880–1917*. Chicago: University of Chicago Press, 1995.

Behar, Ruth. *Translated Woman: Crossing the Border with Esperanza's Story*. Boston: Beacon Press, 1993.

Belnap, Jeffrey, and Raúl Fernández, eds. *José Martí's "Our America": From National to Hemispheric Cultural Studies*. Durham: Duke University Press, 1998.

Berquó, Elza. "Como se casam negros e brancos no Brasil?" In *Desigualdade racial no Brasil*, edited by Peggy Lovell. Minas Gerais: Universidade Federal de Minas Gerais, 1991.

Besse, Susan K. *Restructuring Patriarchy: The Modernization of Gender Inequality in Brazil, 1914–1940*. Chapel Hill: University of North Carolina Press, 1996.

Betalleluz, Betford. "Fiscalidad, tierras y mercado: Las comunidades indígenas de Arequipa, 1825–1850." In *Tradición y modernidad en los Andes*, edited by Henrique Urbano. Cuzco: Centro de Estudios Andinos Bartolomé de las Casas, 1992.

Blake, Stanley E. "The Invention of the Nordestino: Race, Region, and Identity in Northeastern Brazil, 1889–1945." Ph.D. diss., State University of New York at Stony Brook, 2001.

Bolland, O. Nigel. *The Formation of a Colonial Society: Belize, from Conquest to Crown Colony*. Baltimore: Johns Hopkins University Press, 1977.

——. "Slavery in Belize." In *Colonialism and Resistance in Belize: Essays in Historical Sociology*. Belize: Cubola/ISER/SPEAR, 1988.

Bolland, O. Nigel, and Assad Shoman. *Land in Belize, 1765–1871*. Mona, Jamaica: Institute of Social and Economic Research, University of the West Indies, 1977.

Borges, Dain. " 'Puffy, Ugly, Slothful and Inert': Degeneration in Brazilian Social Thought, 1880–1940." *Journal of Latin American Studies* 25, no. 2 (May 1993): 235–56.

Bourdieu, Pierre. "Identity and Representation: Elements for a Critical Reflection on the Idea of Region." In *Language and Symbolic Power*, edited and with an introduction by John B. Thompson; translated by Gino Raymond and Matthew Adamson. Cambridge, Mass.: Harvard University Press, 1991.

Bourdieu, Pierre, and Loïc Wacquant. "On the Cunning of Imperialist Reason." *Theory, Culture, and Society* 16, no. 1 (1999): 41–58.

Bourgois, Philippe. *Ethnicity at Work: Divided Labor on a Central American Banana Plantation*. Baltimore: Johns Hopkins University Press, 1989.

Bowler, Peter J. *The Eclipse of Darwinism: Anti-Darwinian Evolution Theories in the Decades around 1900*. Baltimore: Johns Hopkins University Press, 1983.

Brading, David A. "Manuel Gamio and Official Indigenismo in Mexico." *Bulletin of Latin American Research* 7, no. 1 (1988): 75–89.

——. "Social Darwinism and Romantic Idealism: Andrés Molina Enríquez and José Vasconcelos in the Mexican Revolution." In *Prophecy and Myth in Mexican History*. Cambridge: Centre of Latin American Studies, 1984.

Brock, Lisa, and Digna Castañeda Fuentes. *Between Race and Empire: African-Americans and Cubans before the Cuban Revolution*. Philadelphia: Temple University Press, 1998.

Bronfman, Alejandra. "Reforming Race in Cuba, 1902–1940." Ph.D. diss., Princeton University, 2000.

Brown, Kendall W. *Bourbons and Brandy: Imperial Reform in Eighteenth-Century Arequipa*. Albuquerque: University of New Mexico Press, 1986.

Bryan, Patrick E. *The Jamaican People, 1880–1902: Race, Class, and Social Control*. London: Macmillan, 1991.

Buffington, Robert M. *Criminal and Citizen in Modern Mexico*. Lincoln: University of Nebraska Press, 2000.

Bulnes, Francisco. *El porvenir de las naciones hispanoamericanas*. Mexico City: Mariano Nava, 1988.

Burdick, John. *Blessed Anastácia: Women, Race, and Popular Christianity in Brazil*. New York: Routledge, 1998.

Burns, E. Bradford. *A History of Brazil*. 3d ed. New York: Columbia University Press, 1993.

——. *Patriarch and Folk: The Emergence of Nicaragua, 1798–1858*. Cambridge, Mass.: Harvard University Press, 1991.

Bushnell, David. *The Making of Modern Colombia: A Nation in Spite of Itself*. Berkeley: University of California Press, 1993.

Butler, Kim D. *Freedoms Given, Freedoms Won: Afro-Brazilians in Post-Abolition São Paulo and Salvador*. New Brunswick: Rutgers University Press, 1998.

Cahill, David. "Colour by Numbers: Racial and Ethnic Categories in the Viceroyalty of Peru, 1532–1824." *Journal of Latin American Studies* 26, no. 2 (May 1994): 325–46.

Camacho, Juana, and Eduardo Restrepo, eds. *De montes, ríos y ciudades: Territorios e identidades de la gente negra en Colombia*. Bogotá: Natura-Ecofondo and Instituto Colombiano de Antropología Nacional, 1999.

Camiscioli, Elisa. "Producing Citizens, Reproducing the 'French Race': Immigration, Demography, and Pronatalism in Early Twentieth-Century France." *Gender and History* 13, no. 3 (Fall 2001): 503–621.

Cañizares-Esguerra, Jorge. *How to Write the History of the New World: Histories, Epistemologies, and Identities in the Eighteenth-Century Atlantic World*. Stanford: Stanford University Press, 2001.

Cano, Wilson. *Raízes da concentração industrial em São Paulo*. São Paulo: Difel, 1977.

Capelato, Maria Helena. *O movimento de 1932: A causa paulista*. São Paulo: Brasiliense, 1982.

Carpentier, Alejo. *El reino de este mundo*. Mexico City: Edición y Distribución Ibero Americana de Publicaciones, 1949.

Carr, Barry. "Las peculiaridades del norte mexicano, 1880–1927: Ensayo de interpretación." *Historia Mexicana* 22 (1973): 32–46.

Castillero Calvo, Alfredo. *Los negros y mulatos libres en la historia social panameña*. Panama City: n.p., 1969.

——. *La vivienda colonial en Panamá: Arquitectura, urbanismo y sociedad: Historia de un sueño*. Panama City: Biblioteca Cultural Shell, 1994.

Castillo Cárdenas, Gonzalo. *Liberation Theology from Below: The Life and Thought of Manuel Quintín Lame*. Maryknoll, N.Y.: Orbis Books, 1987.

Castro, Hebe Maria Mattos de. *Das cores do silêncio: Os significados da liberdade no sudeste escravista, Brasil, século XIX*. Rio de Janeiro: Arquivo Nacional, 1995.

——. *Escravidão e cidadania no Brasil monárquico*. Rio de Janeiro: Jorge Zahar, 2000.

Caulfield, Sueann. *In Defense of Honor: Sexual Morality, Modernity, and Nation in Early-Twentieth-Century Brazil*. Durham: Duke University Press, 2000.

Chakrabarty, Dipesh. "Postcoloniality and the Artifice of History: Who Speaks for the 'Indian' Pasts?" *Representations*, no. 37 (Winter 1992): 1–26.

Chalhoub, Sidney. "The Politics of Disease Control: Yellow Fever and Race in Nineteenth-Century Rio de Janeiro." *Journal of Latin American Studies* 23, no. 3 (Oct. 1993): 441–63.

Chambers, Sarah C. *From Subjects to Citizens: Honor, Gender, and Politics in Arequipa, Peru, 1780–1854*. University Park: Pennsylvania State University Press, 1999.

Chance, John K. *Race and Class in Colonial Oaxaca*. Stanford: Stanford University Press, 1978.

Chasteen, John Charles. "Black Kings, Blackface Carnival, and Nineteenth-Century Origins of the Tango." In *Latin American Popular Culture: An Introduction*, edited by William H. Beezley and Linda A. Curcio-Nagy. Wilmington, Del.: Scholarly Resources, 2000.

Chatterjee, Partha. *The Nation and Its Fragments: Colonial and Postcolonial Histories*. Princeton: Princeton University Press, 1993.

Chen, Jack. *The Chinese of America*. New York: Harper and Row, 1980.

Chomsky, Aviva. *West Indian Workers and the United Fruit Company in Costa Rica*. Baton Rouge: Louisiana State University Press, 1996.

Clark, A. Kim. "Race, 'Culture,' and Mestizaje: The Statistical Construction of the Ecuadorian Nation, 1930–1950." *Journal of Historical Sociology* 11, no. 2 (June 1998): 185–211.

Colmenares, Germán. *Historia económica y social de Colombia*. Vol. 2, *Popayán: Una sociedad esclavista, 1680–1800*. Bogotá: Tercer Mundo, 1997.

Condit, Celeste Michelle. *The Meanings of the Gene: Public Debates about Human Heredity*. Madison: University of Wisconsin Press, 1999.

Cooper, Frederick, Thomas C. Holt, and Rebecca J. Scott. *Beyond Slavery: Explorations of Race, Labor, and Citizenship in Postemancipation Societies*. Chapel Hill: University of North Carolina Press, 2000.

Cooper, Frederick, and Ann Laura Stoler. *Tensions of Empire: Colonial Cultures in a Bourgeois World*. Berkeley: University of California Press, 1997.

Cope, R. Douglas. *The Limits of Racial Domination: Plebeian Society in Colonial Mexico City, 1660–1720*. Madison: University of Wisconsin Press, 1994.

Córdova, Arnaldo. *La ideología de la Revolución Mexicana: La formación del nuevo régimen*. Mexico City: Ediciones Era, 1973.

——. *La Revolución en crisis: La aventura del Maximato*. Mexico City: Cal y Arena, 1995.

Coronil, Fernando. "Beyond Occidentalism: Toward Nonimperial Geohistorical Categories." *Cultural Anthropology* 11, no. 1 (Feb. 1996): 51–87.

Costa, Emilia Viotti da. *The Brazilian Empire: Myths and Histories*. Rev. ed. Chapel Hill: University of North Carolina Press, 2000.

——. *Da senzala à colônia*. 2d ed. São Paulo: Ciências Humanas, 1982.

Cripps, Thomas. *Slow Fade to Black: The Negro in American Film, 1900–1942*. New York: Oxford University Press, 1977.

Cumberland, Charles C. "The Sonora Chinese and the Mexican Revolution." *Hispanic American Historical Review* 40, no. 2 (May 1960): 191–211.

Curry, Glenn Thomas. "The Disappearance of the Resguardos Indígenas of Cundinamarca, Colombia, 1800–1863." Ph.D. diss., Vanderbilt University, 1981.

Da Cunha, Euclides. *Rebellion in the Backlands*. Chicago: University of Chicago Press, 1944.

Daley, Mercedes Chen. "The Watermelon Riot: Cultural Encounters in Panama City, 15 April 1856." *Hispanic American Historical Review* 70, no. 1 (Feb. 1990): 85–108.

Da Matta, Roberto. "The Quest for Citizenship in a Relational Universe." In *State and Society in Brazil: Continuity and Change*, edited by John D. Wirth, Edson de Oliveira Nunes, and Thomas E. Bogenschild. Boulder, Colo.: Westview Press, 1987.

Dawson, Alexander S. "From Models for the Nation to Model Citizens: *Indigenismo* and the 'Revindication' of the Mexican Indian, 1920–1940." *Journal of Latin American Studies* 30, no. 2 (May 1998): 279–308.

——. "Our Noble Race: Remaking the Indian in Revolutionary Mexico." Unpublished manuscript.

Dean, Warren. *The Industrialization of São Paulo, 1880–1945*. Austin: University of Texas Press, 1969.

Degler, Carl N. *Neither Black nor White: Slavery and Race Relations in Brazil and the United States*. Madison: University of Wisconsin Press, 1986.

De la Cadena, Marisol. *Indigenous Mestizos: The Politics of Race and Culture in Cuzco, Peru, 1919–1991*. Durham: Duke University Press, 2000.

De la Fuente, Alejandro. "Myths of Racial Democracy: Cuba, 1900–1912." *Latin American Research Review* 34, no. 3 (1999): 39–73.

——. *A Nation for All: Race, Inequality, and Politics in Twentieth-Century Cuba*. Chapel Hill: University of North Carolina Press, 2001.

——. "Two Dangers, One Solution: Immigration, Race, and Labor in Cuba, 1900–1930." *International Labor and Working-Class History*, no. 51 (Spring 1997): 30–49.

Delpar, Helen. *Red against Blue: The Liberal Party in Colombian Politics, 1863–1899*. University: University of Alabama Press, 1981.

Derby, Lauren. "Haitians, Magic, and Money: *Raza* and Society in the Haitian-Dominican Borderlands, 1900 to 1937." *Comparative Studies in Society and History* 36, no. 3 (July 1994): 488–526.

Deutsch, Sandra McGee. "Gender and Sociopolitical Change in Twentieth-Century Latin America." *Hispanic American Historical Review* 71, no. 2 (May 1991): 259–306.

Díaz Rementería, Carlos J. *El cacique en el Virreinato del Perú: Estudio histórico-jurídico*. Sevilla: Universidad de Sevilla, 1977.

Dore, Elizabeth. "One Step Forward, Two Steps Back: Gender and the State in the Long Nineteenth Century." In *Hidden Histories of Gender and the State in Latin America*, edited by Elizabeth Dore and Maxine Molyneux. Durham: Duke University Press, 2000.

Duara, Prasenjit. "Historicizing National Identity, or Who Imagines What and When." In *Becoming National: A Reader*, edited by Geoff Eley and Ronald Grigor Suny. New York: Oxford University Press, 1996.

———. *Rescuing History from the Nation: Questioning Narratives of Modern China*. Chicago: University of Chicago Press, 1995.

Edison, Paul N. "Latinizing America: The French Scientific Study of México, 1830–1930." Ph.D. diss., Columbia University, 1999.

Eley, Geoff, and Ronald Grigor Suny, eds. *Becoming National: A Reader*. New York: Oxford University Press, 1996.

Estrade, Paul. "Del invento de 'América Latina' en París por latinoamericanos (1856–1889)." In *París y el mundo ibérico e iberoamericano*, compiled by Jacques Maurice and Marie-Claire Zimmerman. Paris: Université Paris X-Nanterre, 1998.

Estuch Horrego, Leopoldo. *Martín Morúa Delgado: Vida y mensaje*. Havana: Editorial Sánchez S.A., 1957.

Euraque, Darío A. "The Banana Enclave, Nationalism, and Mestizaje in Honduras, 1910s–1930s." In *Identity and Struggle at the Margins of the Nation-State: Laboring Peoples of Central America and the Hispanic Caribbean*, edited by Aviva Chomsky and Aldo Lauria-Santiago. Durham: Duke University Press, 1998.

Fausto, Boris. *Crime e cotidiano: A criminalidade em São Paulo, 1880–1924*. São Paulo: Brasiliense, 1984.

Fernandes, Florestan. *The Negro in Brazilian Society*. New York: Columbia University Press, 1969.

Fernández Robaina, Tomás. *El negro en Cuba, 1902–1958: Apuntes para la historia de la lucha contra la discriminación racial*. Havana: Editorial de Ciencias Sociales, 1990.

Ferrer, Ada. *Insurgent Cuba: Race, Nation, and Revolution, 1868–1898*. Chapel Hill: University of North Carolina Press, 1999.

———. "The Silence of Patriots." In *José Martí's "Our America": From National to Hemispheric Cultural Studies*, edited by Jeffrey Belnap and Raúl Fernández. Durham: Duke University Press, 1998.

Field, Les W. "State, Anti-State, and Indigenous Entities: Reflections upon a Páez Resguardo and the New Colombian Constitution." *Journal of Latin American Anthropology* 1, no. 2 (1996): 98–119.

Figueroa Navarro, Alfredo. *Dominio y sociedad en el Panamá colombiano (1821–1903)*. Panama City: Editorial Universitaria, 1982.

Findji, María Teresa. "From Resistance to Social Movement: The Indigenous Authorities Movement in Colombia." In *The Making of Social Movements in Latin America: Identity, Strategy, and Democracy*, edited by Arturo Escobar and Sonia E. Alvarez. Boulder, Colo.: Westview Press, 1992.

Findji, María Teresa, and José María Rojas. *Territorio, economía y sociedad Páez*. Cali, Colombia: Universidad del Valle, 1985.

Findlay, Eileen Suárez. *Imposing Decency: Race and Sexuality in Puerto Rico, 1870–1920*. Durham: Duke University Press, 1999.

Foner, Philip S. *The Spanish-Cuban-American War and the Birth of American Imperialism*. Vol. 2. New York: Monthly Review Press, 1972.

Foucault, Michel. *Ethics: Subjectivity and Truth*. Edited by Paul Rabinow. New York: New Press, 1997.

——. *The History of Sexuality*. Vol. 1, *An Introduction*. New York: Vintage Books, 1996.

Frankenberg, Ruth. *White Women, Race Matters: The Social Construction of Whiteness*. London: Routledge, 1993.

French, John D. *The Brazilian Workers' ABC: Class Conflict and Alliances in Modern São Paulo*. Chapel Hill: University of North Carolina Press, 1992.

——. "The Missteps of Anti-Imperialist Reason: Bourdieu, Wacquant, and Hanchard's *Orpheus and Power*." *Theory, Culture, and Society* 17, no. 1 (2000): 107–28.

Freyre, Gilberto. *Brazil: An Interpretation*. New York: Alfred A. Knopf, 1945.

——. *Casa grande e senzala*. 14th ed. Recife: Imprensa Oficial, 1966.

Friede, Juan. *El indio en lucha por la tierra*. Bogotá: Editorial Espiral, 1944.

Friedemann, Nina S. de. "Niveles comtemporáneos de indigenismo en Colombia." In *Indigenismo y aniquilamiento de indígenas en Colombia*, edited by Juan Friede, Nina S. de Friedemann, and Darío Fajardo. Bogotá: Universidad Nacional de Colombia, 1975.

Fry, Peter. "O que cinderela negra tem a dizer sobre a 'política racial' no Brasil." *Revista USP* 28 (Dec. 1995–Feb. 1996): 122–35.

——. "Politics, Nationality, and the Meanings of 'Race' in Brazil." *Daedalus* 129, no. 2 (Spring 2000): 83–118.

Gamio, Manuel. *Forjando patria*. 4th ed. Mexico City: Editorial Porrúa, 1992.

——. *Hacia un México nuevo*. Mexico City: Instituto Nacional Indigenista, 1987.

——. *La población de Teotihuacán*. 1919. Reprint, Mexico City: Instituto Nacional Indigenista, 1979.

Garrido, Margarita. *Reclamos y representaciones: Variaciones sobre la política en el Nuevo Reino de Granada, 1770–1815*. Bogotá: Banco de la República, 1993.

Gerstle, Gary. "Theodore Roosevelt and the Divided Character of American Nationalism." *Journal of American History* 86, no. 3 (Dec. 1999): 1280–1307.

Gilroy, Paul. *The Black Atlantic: Modernity and Double Consciousness*. Cambridge, Mass.: Harvard University Press, 1993.

——. "One Nation under a Groove." In *Becoming National: A Reader*, edited by Geoff Eley and Ronald Grigor Suny. New York: Oxford University Press, 1996.

——. *"There Ain't No Black in the Union Jack": The Cultural Politics of Race and Nation*. London: Hutchinson, 1987.

Goldberg, David Theo. *Racial Subjects: Writing on Race in America*. New York: Routledge, 1997.

——. *Racist Culture: Philosophy and the Politics of Meaning*. Oxford: Blackwell, 1993.

Gómez Izquierdo, José Jorge. *El movimiento antichino en México (1871–1934): Problemas del racismo y del nacionalismo durante la Revolución Mexicana*. Mexico City: Instituto Nacional de Antropología e Historia, 1991.

——. "El nacimiento del prejuicio antichino en México, 1877–1932." *Antropología* 12 (Jan.–Feb. 1987): 21–25.

González Navarro, Moisés. *Población y sociedad en México*. Vol. 2. Mexico City: Universidad Nacional Autónoma de México, 1974.

Goodman, Alan H., and Thomas L. Leatherman, eds. *Building a New Biocultural Synthesis:*

Political-Economic Perspectives on Human Biology. Ann Arbor: University of Michigan Press, 1998.

Gootenberg, Paul. "Population and Ethnicity in Early Republican Peru: Some Revisions." *Latin American Research Review* 26, no. 3 (Summer 1991): 109–57.

Gordon, Edmund T. *Disparate Diasporas: Identity and Politics in an African-Nicaraguan Community*. Austin: University of Texas Press, 1998.

Gotkowitz, Laura. "Commemorating the Heroínas: Gender and Civic Ritual in Early-Twentieth-Century Bolivia." In *Hidden Histories of Gender and the State in Latin America*, edited by Elizabeth Dore and Maxine Molyneux. Durham: Duke University Press, 2000.

Gould, Jeffrey L. *To Die in This Way: Nicaraguan Indians and the Myth of Mestizaje, 1880–1965*. Durham: Duke University Press, 1998.

Graham, Richard, ed. *The Idea of Race in Latin America, 1870–1940*. Austin: University of Texas Press, 1990.

Gramsci, Antonio. *Selections from the Prison Notebooks*. Edited and translated by Quintin Hoare and Geoffrey Nowell Smith. London: International Publishers, 1971.

Grandin, Greg. *The Blood of Guatemala: A History of Race and Nation*. Durham: Duke University Press, 2000.

Grieshaber, Erwin P. "Survival of Indian Communities in Nineteenth-Century Bolivia: A Regional Comparison." *Journal of Latin American Studies* 12, no. 2 (Nov. 1980): 223–69.

Gruesz, Kirsten Silva. *Ambassadors of Culture: The Transamerican Origins of Latino Writing*. Princeton: Princeton University Press, 2001.

Guardino, Peter F. *Peasants, Politics, and the Formation of Mexico's National State: Guerrero, 1800–1857*. Stanford: Stanford University Press, 1996.

Gudmundson, Lowell, and Héctor Lindo-Fuentes. *Central America, 1821–1871: Liberalism before Liberal Reform*. Tuscaloosa: University of Alabama Press, 1995.

Guerra, Lillian. "Crucibles of Liberation in Cuba: José Martí, Conflicting Nationalisms, and the Search for Social Unity, 1895–1933." Ph.D. diss., University of Wisconsin–Madison, 2000.

Gutiérrez, Ramón A. *When Jesus Came, the Corn Mothers Went Away: Marriage, Sexuality, and Power in New Mexico*. Stanford: Stanford University Press, 1991.

Guy, Donna. *Sex and Danger in Buenos Aires: Prostitution, Family, and Nation in Argentina*. Lincoln: University of Nebraska Press, 1991.

Hale, Charles A. "Political and Social Ideas in Latin America, 1870–1930." In *The Cambridge History of Latin America*. Vol. 4, *C. 1870–1930*. Cambridge: Cambridge University Press, 1986.

———. *The Transformation of Liberalism in Late-Nineteenth-Century Mexico*. Princeton: Princeton University Press, 1989.

Hale, Charles R. *Resistance and Contradiction: Miskitu Indians and the Nicaraguan State, 1894–1987*. Stanford: Stanford University Press, 1994.

Hale, Lindsay L. "*Preto Velho*: Resistance, Redemption, and Engendered Representations of Slavery in a Brazilian Possession-Trance Religion." *American Ethnologist* 24, no. 2 (May 1997): 392–414.

Hall, Catherine. "Gender Politics and Imperial Politics: Rethinking the Histories of

Empire." In *Engendering History: Caribbean Women in Historical Perspective*, edited by Verene Shepherd, Bridget Brereton, and Barbara Bailey. New York: St. Martin's Press, 1995.

Hall, Stuart, Chas Critcher, Tony Jefferson, John Clarke, and Brian Roberts. *Policing the Crisis: Mugging, the State, and Law and Order*. New York: Holmes and Meier, 1978.

Halperín Donghi, Tulio. *El espejo de la historia: Problemas argentinos y perspectivas hispanoamericanas*. Buenos Aires: Editorial Sudamericana, 1987.

Halperín Donghi, Tulio, Iván Jaksic, Gwen Kirkpatrick, and Francine Masiello. *Sarmiento, Author of a Nation*. Berkeley: University of California Press, 1994.

Hanchard, Michael George. *Orpheus and Power: The* Movimento Negro *of Rio de Janeiro and São Paulo, Brazil, 1945–1988*. Princeton: Princeton University Press, 1994.

Harris, Marvin, ed. *Patterns of Race in the Americas*. New York: Walker Press, 1964.

Harris, Olivia. "Ethnic Identity and Market Relations: Indians and Mestizos in the Andes." In *Ethnicity, Markets, and Migration in the Andes: At the Crossroads of History and Anthropology*, edited by Brooke Larson and Olivia Harris with Enrique Tandeter. Durham: Duke University Press, 1995.

Helg, Aline. "Black Protest: The Partido Independiente de Color, 1908–1912." *Cuban Studies* 21 (1991): 101–21.

———. *Our Rightful Share: The Afro-Cuban Struggle for Equality, 1886–1912*. Chapel Hill: University of North Carolina Press, 1995.

———. "Race in Argentina and Cuba, 1880–1930: Theory, Policies, and Popular Reaction." In *The Idea of Race in Latin America, 1870–1940*, edited by Richard Graham. Austin: University of Texas Press, 1990.

Helguera, J. León. *Indigenismo in Colombia: A Facet of the National Identity Search, 1821–1973*. Buffalo: Council on International Studies, 1974.

Heuman, Gad J. *The Killing Time: The Morant Bay Rebellion in Jamaica*. Knoxville: University of Tennessee Press, 1994.

Hoganson, Kristin L. *Fighting for American Manhood: How Gender Politics Provoked the Spanish-American and Philippine-American Wars*. New Haven: Yale University Press, 1998.

Holt, Thomas C. "Markings: Race, Race-making, and the Writing of History." *American Historical Review* 100, no. 1 (Feb. 1995): 1–20

———. *The Problem of Freedom: Race, Labor, and Politics in Jamaica and Britain, 1832–1938*. Baltimore: Johns Hopkins University Press, 1992.

Horn, David G. *Social Bodies: Science, Reproduction, and Italian Modernity*. Princeton: Princeton University Press, 1994.

Horsman, Reginald. *Race and Manifest Destiny: The Origins of American Racial Anglo-Saxonism*. Cambridge, Mass.: Harvard University Press, 1981.

Howard, Philip A. *Changing History: Afro-Cuban Cabildos and Societies of Color in the Nineteenth Century*. Baton Rouge: Louisiana State University Press, 1998.

Hu-DeHart, Evelyn. *La comunidad china en el desarrollo de Sonora*. Vol. 4 of *Historia General de Sonora*. Hermosillo: Gobierno del Estado de Sonora, 1985.

———. *Yaqui Resistance and Survival: The Struggle for Land and Autonomy, 1821–1910*. Madison: University of Wisconsin Press, 1984.

Huggins, Nathan I. *The Harlem Renaissance*. New York: Oxford University Press, 1971.

Hurtado, Albert L. "Crossing the Borders: Sex, Gender, and the Journey to California." In *Intimate Frontiers: Sex, Gender, and Culture in Old California*. Albuquerque: University of New Mexico Press, 1999.

Hutton, Patrick H. "Foucault, Freud, and the Technologies of the Self." In *Technologies of the Self*, edited by Luther H. Martin, Huck Gutman, and Patrick H. Hutton. Amherst: University of Massachusetts Press, 1988.

Ianni, Octavio. "Research on Race Relations in Brazil." In *Race and Class in Latin America*, edited by Magnus Mörner. New York: Columbia University Press, 1970.

Jackson, Robert H. "Race/Caste and the Creation and Meaning of Identity in Colonial Spanish America." *Revista de Indias* 55, no. 203 (Jan.–Apr. 1995): 149–73.

Jacobsen, Nils. *Mirages of Transition: The Peruvian Altiplano, 1780–1930*. Berkeley: University of California Press, 1993.

Jacobson, Matthew Frye. *Whiteness of a Different Color: European Immigrants and the Alchemy of Race*. Cambridge, Mass.: Harvard University Press, 1998.

James, Daniel. *Resistance and Integration: Peronism and the Argentine Working Class, 1946–1976*. Cambridge: Cambridge University Press, 1988.

Jaramillo Uribe, Jaime. "Mestizaje y diferenciación social en el Nuevo Reino de Granada en la segunda mitad del siglo XVIII." *Anuario Colombiano de Historia Social y de la Cultura* 2, no. 3 (1965): 21–48.

Jimeno, Myriam, and Adolfo Triana, eds. *Estado y minorías étnicas en Colombia*. Bogotá: Cuadernos del Jaguar, 1985.

Jimeno Santoyo, Myriam. "Pueblos indios, democracia y políticas estatales en Colombia." In *Democracia y estado multiétnico en América Latina*, edited by Pablo González Casanova and Marcos Roitman Rosenmann. Mexico City: La Jornada Ediciones, 1996.

Johnson, Lyman L., and Sonya Lipsett-Rivera, eds. *The Faces of Honor: Sex, Shame, and Violence in Colonial Latin America*. Albuquerque: University of New Mexico Press, 1998.

Johnson, Susan Lee. *Roaring Camp: The Social World of the California Gold Rush*. New York: Norton, 2000.

Jordan, Winthrop D. *White over Black: American Attitudes toward the Negro, 1550–1812*. New York: Norton, 1977.

Joseph, Gilbert M. *Revolution from Without: Yucatán, Mexico, and the United States, 1880–1924*. Durham: Duke University Press, 1988.

Joseph, Gilbert M., Catherine C. LeGrand, and Ricardo D. Salvatore, eds. *Close Encounters of Empire: Writing the Cultural History of U.S.–Latin American Relations*. Durham: Duke University Press, 1998.

Joseph, Gilbert M., and Daniel Nugent, eds. *Everyday Forms of State Formation: Revolution and the Negotiation of Rule in Modern Mexico*. Durham: Duke University Press, 1994.

Judd, Karen H. "Elite Reproduction and Ethnic Identity in Belize." Ph.D. diss., City University of New York, 1992.

Katz, Leslie S. " 'Julius the Snoozer': Independence Day in Blackface." *Theatre History Studies* 13 (1993): 17–32.

Kemble, John Haskell. *The Panama Route, 1848–1869*. 1943. Reprint, Columbia: University of South Carolina Press, 1990.

Klubock, Thomas Miller. *Contested Communities: Class, Gender, and Politics in Chile's El Teniente Copper Mine, 1904–1951*. Durham: Duke University Press, 1998.

——. "Nationalism, Race, and the Politics of Imperialism: Workers and North American Capital in the Chilean Copper Industry." In *Reclaiming the Political in Latin American History: Essays from the North*, edited by Gilbert M. Joseph. Durham: Duke University Press, 2001.

Knight, Alan. *The Mexican Revolution*. 2 vols. Lincoln: University of Nebraska Press, 1990.

——. "Racism, Revolution, and *Indigenismo*: Mexico, 1910–1940." In *The Idea of Race in Latin America, 1870–1940*, edited by Richard Graham. Austin: University of Texas Press, 1990.

Krauze, Enrique. *Alvaro Obregón: El vértigo de la victoria*. Mexico City: Fondo de Cultura Económica, 1995.

Lame, Manuel Quintín. *En defensa de mi raza*. Edited by Gonzalo Castillo Cárdenas. Bogotá: Comité de Defensa del Indio, 1971.

Lancaster, Roger. *Life Is Hard: Machismo, Danger, and the Intimacy of Power in Nicaragua*. Berkeley: University of California Press, 1992.

Larson, Brooke. *Cochabamba, 1550–1900: Colonialism and Agrarian Transformation in Bolivia*. Exp. ed. Durham: Duke University Press, 1998.

Lauria-Santiago, Aldo A. *An Agrarian Republic: Commercial Agriculture and the Politics of Peasant Communities in El Salvador, 1823–1914*. Pittsburgh: University of Pittsburgh Press, 1999.

Lavrin, Asunción. *Women, Feminism, and Social Change in Argentina, Chile, and Uruguay, 1890–1940*. Lincoln: University of Nebraska Press, 1995.

Lecuña, Vicente, and H. A. Bierck Jr. *Selected Writings of Bolívar*. New York: Colonial Press, 1951.

Lee, Rose Hum. *The Chinese in the United States of America*. Hong Kong: Hong Kong University Press, 1960.

Lenharo, Alcir. *Sacralização da política*. Campinas: Papirus, 1986.

Lesser, Jeffrey. *Negotiating National Identity: Immigrants, Minorities, and the Struggle for Ethnicity in Brazil*. Durham: Duke University Press, 1999.

——. *Welcoming the Undesirables: Brazil and the Jewish Question*. Berkeley: University of California Press, 1995.

Levy, Jo Ann. *They Saw the Elephant: Women in the California Gold Rush*. Hamden, Conn.: Archon Books, 1990.

Lewis, Martin W., and Kären Wigen. *The Myth of Continents: A Critique of Metageography*. Berkeley: University of California Press, 1997.

Linebaugh, Peter, and Marcus Buford Rediker. *The Many-Headed Hydra: Sailors, Slaves, Commoners, and the Hidden History of the Revolutionary Atlantic*. Boston: Beacon Press, 2000.

Lomnitz-Adler, Claudio. *Exits from the Labyrinth: Culture and Ideology in the Mexican National Space*. Berkeley: University of California Press, 1992.

——. "Nationalism as a Practical System: Benedict Anderson's Theory of Nationalism from the Vantage Point of Spanish America." In *The Other Mirror: Grand Theory through the*

Lens of Latin America, edited by Miguel Angel Centeno and Fernando López-Alves. Princeton: Princeton University Press, 2001.

López Victoria, José Manuel. *La campaña nacionalista*. Mexico City: Botas, 1965.

Lott, Eric. *Love and Theft: Blackface Minstrelsy and the American Working Class*. Oxford: Oxford University Press, 1993.

Love, Joseph L. "A república brasileira: Federalismo e regionalismo (1889–1937)." In *Viagem incompleta*, edited by Carlos G. Mota. São Paulo: Editora SENAC, 2000.

——. *São Paulo in the Brazilian Federation, 1889–1937*. Stanford: Stanford University Press, 1980.

Luca, Tânia Regina de. *A Revista do Brasil: Um diagnóstico para a (n)ação*. São Paulo: Editora Universidade Estadual de São Paulo Fundação, 1999.

Luizetto, Flávio Venâncio. "Os constituintes em face da imigração." Master's thesis, Universidade de São Paulo, 1975.

Lynch, John. *The Spanish American Revolutions, 1808–1826*. 2d ed. New York: W. W. Norton, 1986.

Macpherson, Anne S. " 'Those Men Were So Coward': The Gender Politics of Social Movements and State Formation in Belize, 1912–1982." Ph.D. diss., University of Wisconsin–Madison, 1998.

——. "Viragoes, Victims, and Volunteers: Female Political Cultures in Nineteenth-Century Belize." In *Belize: Selected Proceedings from the Second Interdisciplinary Conference*, edited by Michael Phillips. Lanham, Md.: University Press of America, 1996.

Mallon, Florencia E. *Peasant and Nation: The Making of Postcolonial Mexico and Peru*. Berkeley: University of California Press, 1995.

Martí, José. *Obras completas*. Havana: Editorial de Ciencias Sociales, 1975.

——. *Our America: Writings on Latin America and the Struggle for Cuban Independence*. Edited by Philip S. Foner. New York: Monthly Review Press, 1977.

Martínez-Alier, Verena. *Marriage, Class, and Colour in Nineteenth-Century Cuba: A Study of Racial Attitudes and Sexual Values in a Slave Society*. 2d ed. Ann Arbor: University of Michigan Press, 1989.

Martínez-Echazábal, Lourdes. "*Mestizaje* and the Discourse of National/Cultural Identity in Latin America, 1845–1959." *Latin American Perspectives* 25, no. 3 (May 1998): 21–42.

Marx, Anthony W. *Making Race and Nation: A Comparison of South Africa, the United States, and Brazil*. Cambridge: Cambridge University Press, 1998.

Masiello, Francine. *Between Civilization and Barbarism: Women, Nation, and Literary Culture in Modern Argentina*. Lincoln: University of Nebraska Press, 1992.

Mayr, Ernst E. *The Growth of Biological Thought: Diversity, Evolution, and Inheritance*. Cambridge, Mass.: The Belknap Press of Harvard University Press, 1982.

McCaa, Robert. "*Calidad, Clase*, and Marriage in Colonial Mexico: The Case of Parral, 1788–90." *Hispanic American Historical Review* 64, no. 3 (Aug. 1984): 477–501.

McClintock, Anne. *Imperial Leather: Race, Gender, and Sexuality in the Colonial Contest*. New York: Routledge, 1995.

——. "No Longer in a Future Heaven: Gender, Racism, and Nationalism." In *Dangerous Liaisons: Gender, Nation, and Postcolonial Perspectives*, edited by Anne McClintock, Aamir Mufti, and Ella Shohat. Minneapolis: University of Minnesota Press, 1997.

McGuinness, Aims. "In the Path of Empire: Land, Labor, and Liberty in Panamá during the California Gold Rush, 1848–1860." Ph.D. diss., University of Michigan, 2001.

McNamara, Patrick J. "Sons of the Sierra: Memory, Patriarchy, and Rural Political Culture in Mexico, 1851–1911." Ph.D. diss., University of Wisconsin–Madison, 1999.

Mehta, Uday Singh. *Liberalism and Empire: A Study of Nineteenth-Century British Liberal Thought*. Chicago: University of Chicago Press, 1999.

Méndez, Cecilia. "Los campesinos, la Independencia y la iniciación de la República." In *Poder y violencia en los Andes*, edited by Henrique Urbano. Cuzco: Centro de Estudios Andinos Bartolomé de las Casas, 1991.

——. "República sin indios: La comunidad imaginada del Perú." In *Tradición y modernidad en los Andes*, edited by Henrique Urbano. Cuzco: Centro de Estudios Andinos Bartolomé de las Casas, 1992.

Mendoza, Vicente T. *Panorama de la música tradicional de México*. Mexico City: Universidad Nacional Autónoma de México, 1984.

Meyer, Jean, and Enrique Krauze. *Estado y sociedad con Calles*. Mexico City: El Colegio de México, 1981.

Minchom, Martin. "The Making of a White Province: Demographic Movement and Ethnic Transformation in the South of the Audiencia de Quito (1670–1830)." *Bulletin de l'Institut Français d'Etudes Andines* 12, nos. 3–4 (1983): 23–39.

——. *The People of Quito, 1690–1810: Change and Unrest in the Underclass*. Boulder, Colo.: Westview Press, 1994.

Modood, Tariq, and Pnina Werbner, eds. *The Politics of Multiculturalism in the New Europe: Racism, Identity, and Community*. London: Zed Books, 1997.

Monsiváis, Carlos. " 'Just over That Hill': Notes on Centralism and Regional Cultures." In *Mexico's Regions: Comparative History and Development*, edited by Eric Van Young. San Diego: University of California, Center for U.S.-Mexican Studies, 1992.

Moore, Robin D. *Nationalizing Blackness: Afrocubanismo and Artistic Revolution in Havana, 1920–1940*. Pittsburgh: University of Pittsburgh Press, 1997.

Moreno, Roberto. *La polémica del darwinismo en México*. Mexico City: Universidad Nacional Autónoma de México, 1989.

Mörner, Magnus. *Race Mixture in the History of Latin America*. Boston: Little, Brown, 1967.

Mosse, George L. *Toward the Final Solution: A History of European Racism*. New York: Howard Fertig, 1978.

Muratorio, Blanca. "Images of Indians in the Construction of Ecuadorian Identity at the End of the Nineteenth Century." In *Latin American Popular Culture: An Introduction*, edited by William H. Beezley and Linda A. Curcio-Nagy. Wilmington, Del.: Scholarly Resources, 2000.

Nascimiento, Abdias do. *Brazil: Mixture or Massacre? Essays in the Genocide of a Black People*. 2d ed. Dover, Mass.: Majority Press, 1989.

Nazzari, Muriel. "Concubinage in Colonial Brazil: The Inequalities of Race, Class, and Gender." *Journal of Family History* 21, no. 2 (Apr. 1996): 107–24.

Needell, Jeffrey D. "History, Race, and the State in the Thought of Oliveira Viana." *Hispanic American Historical Review* 75, no. 1 (Feb. 1995): 1–30.

——. "Identity, Race, Gender, and Modernity in the Origins of Gilberto Freyre's Oeuvre." *American Historical Review* 100, no. 1 (Feb. 1995): 51–77.

Nogeira, Oracy. *Tanto preto quanto blanco: Estudos de relações raciais*. São Paulo: T. A. Queiroz, 1985.

Ocampo, José Antonio. *Colombia y la economía mundial, 1830–1910*. Bogotá: Tercer Mundo, 1998.

Offutt, Leslie S. *Saltillo, 1770–1810: Town and Region in the Mexican North*. Tucson: University of Arizona Press, 2001.

Oliven, Ruben George. *A parte e o todo: A diversidade cultural no Brasil-nação*. Petrópolis: Vozes, 1992.

Omi, Michael, and Howard Winant. *Racial Formation in the United States: From the 1960s to the 1980s*. 2d ed. New York: Routledge, 1994.

Orlove, Benjamin S. "Putting Race in Its Place: Order in Colonial and Postcolonial Peruvian Geography." *Social Research* 60, no. 2 (Summer 1993): 301–36.

Ortiz, Fernando. *Hampa afro-cubana: Los negros brujos*. 1906. Reprint, Madrid: Editorial América, 1917.

Ortiz, Renato. *Cultura brasileira e identidade nacional*. São Paulo: Brasiliense, 1985.

Orum, Thomas Tondee. "Politics of Color: The Racial Dimension of Cuban Politics during the Early Republican Years, 1900–1912." Ph.D. diss., New York University, 1975.

Pacheco, José E. "La patria perdida: Notas sobre Clavijero y la cultura nacional." In *En torno a la cultura nacional*, edited by Héctor Aguilar Camín. Mexico City: CONACULTA/Instituto Nacional Indigenista, 1983.

Palmer, Steven Paul. "Racismo intelectual en Costa Rica y Guatemala, 1870–1920." *Mesoamerica* 17, no. 31 (June 1996): 99–121.

Pardo, Mauricio. "Movimientos sociales y actores no gubernamentales." In *Antropología en la modernidad: Identidades, etnicidades y movimientos sociales en Colombia*, edited by María Victoria Uribe and Eduardo Restrepo. Bogotá: Instituto Colombiano de Antropología Nacional, 1997.

——, ed. *Acción colectiva, estado y etnicidad en el Pacífico Colombiano*. Bogotá: Colciencias/Instituto Nacional de Antropología e Historia, 2000.

Pascoe, Peggy. "Miscegenation Law, Court Cases, and Ideologies of Race in Twentieth-Century America." *Journal of American History* 83, no. 1 (June 1996): 44–70.

Pateman, Carole. *The Disorder of Women: Democracy, Feminism, and Political Theory*. Stanford: Stanford University Press, 1989.

Paul, Diane B. *Controlling Human Heredity: 1865 to the Present*. Atlantic Highlands, N.J.: Humanities Press, 1995.

Peard, Julyan G. *Race, Place, and Medicine: The Idea of the Tropics in Nineteenth-Century Brazilian Medicine*. Durham: Duke University Press, 1999.

Peralta Ruíz, Víctor. *En pos del tributo: Burocracia estatal, elite regional y comunidades indígenas en el Cusco rural, 1826–1854*. Cuzco: Centro de Estudios Andinos Bartolomé de las Casas, 1991.

Pérez, Louis A., Jr. *Cuba between Empires, 1878–1902*. Pittsburgh: University of Pittsburgh Press, 1983.

——. *Cuba under the Platt Amendment, 1902–1934*. Pittsburgh: University of Pittsburgh Press, 1986.

——. *On Becoming Cuban: Identity, Nationality, and Culture*. Chapel Hill: University of North Carolina Press, 1999.

——. "Politics, Peasants, and People of Color: The 1912 'Race War' in Cuba Reconsidered." *Hispanic American Historical Review* 66, no. 3 (Aug. 1986): 509–39.

——. *The War of 1898: The United States and Cuba in History and Historiography*. Chapel Hill: University of North Carolina Press, 1998.

Pérez de la Riva, Juan. *Los culíes chinos en Cuba, 1847–1880: Contribución al estudio de la inmigración contratada en el Caribe*. Havana: Editorial de Ciencias Sociales, 2000.

——. *La república neocolonial: Anuario de estudios cubanos*. 2 vols. Havana: Editorial de Ciencias Sociales, 1973–75.

Pérez Monfort, Ricardo. *Estampas de nacionalismo popular mexicano: Ensayos sobre cultura popular y nacionalismo*. Mexico City: CIESAS, 1994.

——. *"Por la patria y por la raza": La derecha secular en el sexenio de Lázaro Cárdenas*. Mexico City: Universidad Nacional Autónoma de México, 1993.

Phelan, John L. "Pan-Latinism, French Intervention in Mexico (1861–1867), and the Genesis of the Idea of Latin America." In *Conciencia y autenticidad históricas*, edited by Juan A. Ortega y Medina. Mexico City: Universidad Nacional Autónoma de México, 1968.

Pick, Daniel. *Faces of Degeneration: A European Disorder, c. 1848–1918*. Cambridge: Cambridge University Press, 1989.

Pieterse, Jan Nederveen. *White on Black: Images of Africa and Blacks in Western Popular Culture*. New Haven: Yale University Press, 1992.

Pineda Camacho, Roberto. "La reivindicación del indio en el pensamiento social colombiano (1850–1950)." In *Un siglo de investigación social: Antropología en Colombia*, edited by Jaime Arocha and Nina S. de Friedemann. Bogotá: ETNO, 1984.

Pinto, Luis A. Costa. *O negro no Rio de Janeiro: Relações de raça numa sociedade em mudança*. São Paulo: Editora Nacional, 1960.

Placido, Barbara. " 'It's All to Do with Words': An Analysis of Spirit Possession in the Venezuelan Cult of María Lionza." *Journal of the Royal Anthropological Institute* 7, no. 2 (June 2001): 207–24.

Platt, Tristan. *Estado boliviano y ayllu andino*. Lima: Instituto de Estudios Peruanos, 1982.

——. "Liberalism and Ethnocide in the Southern Andes." *History Workshop Journal* 17 (1984): 3–18.

Ponce, Fernando. "Social Structure of Arequipa, 1840–1879." Ph.D. diss., University of Texas at Austin, 1980.

Poole, Deborah. "Cultural Diversity and Racial Unity in Oaxaca: Rethinking Hybridity and the State in Post-Revolutionary Mexico." Paper presented to the New York City Latin American History Workshop, New York University, 26 Jan. 2001.

Poyo, Gerald E. *"With All and for the Good of All": The Emergence of Popular Nationalism in the Cuban Communities of the United States, 1848–1898*. Durham: Duke University Press, 1989.

Prado, Maria Lígia Coelho. *A democracia ilustrada: O Partido Democrático de São Paulo, 1926–1934*. São Paulo: Editora Ática, 1986.

Prakash, Gyan. *Another Reason: Science and the Imagining of Modern India*. Princeton: Princeton University Press, 1999.

Prescott, Heather Munro. "I Was a Teenage Dwarf: The Social Construction of 'Normal' Adolescent Growth and Development in the United States." In *Formative Years: Children's Health in the United States, 1880–2000*, edited by Alexandra Minna Stern and Howard Markel. Ann Arbor: University of Michigan Press, 2002.

Priera, Mario. *Cuba política (1899–1955)*. Havana: Impresora Modelo S.A., 1955.

Pulis, John W. "The Jamaican Diaspora: Moses Baker, George Liele, and the African American Migration to Jamaica." Paper presented to the School of American Research Advanced Seminar "From Africa to the Americas: New Directions in Afro-American Anthropology," Santa Fe, New Mexico, 11–15 Apr. 1999.

——, ed. *Moving On: Black Loyalists in the Afro-Atlantic World*. New York: Garland, 1999.

Purnell, Jennie. *Popular Movements and State Formation in Revolutionary Mexico: The Agraristas and Cristeros of Michoacán*. Durham: Duke University Press, 1999.

Quijada, Mónica. "Sobre el origen y difusión del nombre 'América Latina': O una variación heterodoxa en torno al tema de la construcción social de la verdad." *Revista de Indias* 58, no. 214 (Sept.–Dec. 1998): 595–616.

Rappaport, Joanne. *Cumbe Reborn: An Andean Ethnography of History*. Chicago: University of Chicago Press, 1994.

——. *The Politics of Memory: Native Historical Interpretation in the Colombian Andes*. Cambridge: Cambridge University Press, 1990.

Rappaport, Joanne, and Robert V. H. Dover. "The Construction of Difference by Native Legislators: Assessing the Impact of the Colombian Constitution of 1991." *Journal of Latin American Anthropology* 1, no. 2 (1996): 22–45.

Reeves, René Rethier. "Liberals, Conservatives, and Indigenous Peoples: The Subaltern Roots of National Politics in Nineteenth-Century Guatemala." Ph.D. diss., University of Wisconsin–Madison, 1999.

Remy, María Isabel. "La sociedad local al inicio de la República: Cusco, 1824–1850." *Revista Andina* 6, no. 2 (1988): 451–84.

Rénique, Gerardo. "Anti-Chinese Racism, Nationalism, and State Formation in Post-Revolutionary Mexico, 1920s–1930s." *Political Power and Social Theory* 14 (2001): 89–137.

——. "Frontier Capitalism and Revolution in Northwest Mexico: Sonora, 1830–1910." Ph.D. diss., Columbia University, 1990.

Rivera, Antonio G. *La revolución en Sonora*. 2d ed. Hermosillo: Gobierno del Estado de Sonora, 1981.

Roberts, Brian. *American Alchemy: The California Gold Rush and Middle-Class Culture*. Chapel Hill: University of North Carolina Press, 2000.

Roberts, Bryan. "The Place of Regions in Mexico." In *Mexico's Regions: Comparative History and Development*, edited by Eric Van Young. San Diego: Center for U.S.-Mexican Studies, 1992.

Roediger, David R. *The Wages of Whiteness: Race and the Making of the American Working Class*. London: Verso, 1991.

Rojas Mix, Miguel A. "Bilbao y el hallazgo de América latina: Unión continental, socialista y libertaria." *Cahiers du Monde Hispanique et Luso-Brasilien—Caravelle* 46 (1986): 35–47.

Roldán, Mary. *Blood and Fire:* La Violencia *in Antioquia, Colombia, 1946–1953*. Durham: Duke University Press, 2002.

Rosemblatt, Karin Alejandra. *Gendered Compromises: Political Cultures and the State in Chile, 1920–1950*. Chapel Hill: University of North Carolina Press, 2000.

——. "Sexuality and Biopower in Chile and Latin America." *Political Power and Social Theory* 15 (2002): 229–62.

Rubin, Jeffrey W. *Decentering the Regime: Ethnicity, Radicalism, and Democracy in Juchitán, Mexico*. Durham: Duke University Press, 1997.

Ruiz Gutiérrez, Rosaura. *Positivismo y evolución: Introducción del darwinismo en México*. Mexico City: Universidad Nacional Autónoma de México, 1987.

Safford, Frank. "Race, Integration, and Progress: Elite Attitudes and the Indian in Colombia, 1750–1870." *Hispanic American Historical Review* 71, no. 1 (Feb. 1991): 1–33.

Safford, Frank, and Marco Palacios. *Colombia: Fragmented Land, Divided Society*. Oxford: Oxford University Press, 2002.

Sala i Vila, Núria. *Y se armó el Tole Tole: Tributo indígena y movimientos sociales en el Virreinato del Perú, 1790–1814*. Huamanga: Instituto de Estudios Regionales José María Arguedas, 1996.

Sánchez Lira, Ricardo. *Iluminación nacionalista*. Mexico City: Ediciones Luz, 1956.

Sanders, James. "Contentious Republicans: Popular Politics, Race and Class in Nineteenth-Century Southwestern Colombia." Ph.D. diss., University of Pittsburgh, 2000.

Sarmiento, Domingo. *Facundo: Civilización y barbarie: Vida de Juan Facundo Quiroga*. Edited by Raimundo Lazo. Mexico City: Editorial Porrúa, 1977.

Savigliano, Marta E. *Tango and the Political Economy of Passion*. Boulder, Colo.: Westview Press, 1995.

Saxton, Alexander. *The Indispensable Enemy: Labor and the Anti-Chinese Movement in California*. Berkeley: University of California Press, 1971.

——. *The Rise and Fall of the White Republic: Class Politics and Mass Culture in Nineteenth-Century America*. London: Verso, 1990.

Scalon, Maria Celi Ramos da Cruz. "Cor e seletividade conjugal no Brasil." *Estudos Afro-Asiáticos* 23 (Dec. 1992): 17–36.

Scarano, Francisco A. *Sugar and Slavery in Puerto Rico: The Plantation Economy of Ponce, 1800–1850*. Madison: University of Wisconsin Press, 1984.

Schneider, William H. "Henri Laughier, the Science of Work, and the Working of Science in France, 1920–1940." *Cahiers pour l'histoire du CNRS, 1939–1989*. Paris: Editions du CNRS, 1989.

——. *Quality and Quantity: The Quest for Biological Regeneration in Twentieth-Century France*. Cambridge: Cambridge University Press, 1990.

Schwarcz, Lilia Moritz. *O espetáculo das raças: Cientistas instituições e questão racial no Brasil, 1870–1930*. São Paulo: Companhia das Letras, 1993.

Schwartz, Stuart B. *Sugar Plantations in the Formation of Brazilian Society: Bahia, 1500–1835*. Cambridge: Cambridge University Press, 1985.

Schwartz, Stuart B., and Frank Salomon. "New Peoples and New Kinds of People: Adaptation, Readjustment, and Ethnogenesis in South American Indigenous Societies (Colonial Era)." In *South America*. Vol. 3 of *The Cambridge History of Native Peoples of the Americas*, edited by Stuart B. Schwartz and Frank Salomon. Cambridge: Cambridge University Press, 1999.

Scott, James C. *Domination and the Arts of Resistance: Hidden Transcripts*. New Haven: Yale University Press, 1990.

Scott, Rebecca J. *Slave Emancipation in Cuba: The Transition to Free Labor, 1860–1899*. Princeton: Princeton University Press, 1985.

Seed, Patricia. "Social Dimensions of Race: Mexico City, 1753." *Hispanic American Historical Review* 62, no. 4 (Nov. 1982): 569–606.

———. *To Love, Honor, and Obey in Colonial Mexico: Conflicts over Marriage Choice, 1524– 1821*. Stanford: Stanford University Press, 1998.

Sevcenko, Nicolau. *Literatura como missão*. São Paulo: Brasiliense, 1983.

———. *Orfeu extático na metrópole: São Paulo, sociedade e cultura nos frementes anos 20*. São Paulo: Companhia das Letras, 1992.

Sewell, William H., Jr. *Work and Revolution in France: The Language of Labor from the Old Regime to 1848*. Cambridge: Cambridge University Press, 1989.

Sheriff, Robin E. " 'Negro é um apelido que os brancos deram aos pretos': Discursos sobre cor, raça e racismo num morro carioca." Instituto de Filosofía y Ciências Sociais, Universidade Federal do Rio de Janeiro, 1995. Mimeographed.

Shoman, Assad. *13 Chapters of a History of Belize*. Edited by Anne S. Macpherson. Belize: Angelus Press, 1995.

Silva, Denise Ferreira da. "Facts of Blackness: Brazil Is Not (Quite) the United States . . . and Racial Politics in Brazil?" *Social Identities* 4, no. 2 (June 1998): 201–34.

Silva, Nelson do Valle. "Estabilidade temporal e diferenças regionais no casamento inter-racial." *Estudos Afro-Asiáticos* 21 (Dec. 1991): 49–60.

Silva, Vera Alice Cardoso. "O enfoque metodológico e a concepção histórica." In *República em migalhas*, coordinated by Marcos A. da Silva. São Paulo: Marco Zero, 1990.

Skidmore, Thomas E. *Black into White: Race and Nationality in Brazilian Thought*. New York: Oxford University Press, 1974. Reprint, with a new preface and bibliography, Durham: Duke University Press, 1993.

———. "Racial Ideas and Social Policy in Brazil, 1870–1940." In *The Idea of Race in Latin America, 1870–1940*, edited by Richard Graham. Austin: University of Texas Press, 1990.

Smith, Gavin. *Livelihood and Resistance: Peasants and the Politics of Land in Peru*. Berkeley: University of California Press, 1989.

Sociedad Bolivariana de Venezuela. *Decretos del Libertador*. Vol. 1. Caracas: Imprenta Nacional, 1961.

Soler, Ricaurte, ed. *Panamá y nuestra América*. Mexico City: Universidad Nacional Autónoma de México/Biblioteca del Estudiante Universitario, 1981.

Sommer, Doris. *Foundational Fictions: The National Romances of Latin America*. Berkeley: University of California Press, 1991.

Spivak, Gayatri Chakravorty. "Can the Subaltern Speak?" In *Marxism and the Interpretation of Culture*, edited by Cary Nelson and Lawrence Grossberg. Urbana: University of Illinois Press, 1988.

Stepan, Nancy Leys. *"The Hour of Eugenics": Race, Gender, and Nation in Latin America*. Ithaca: Cornell University Press, 1991.

——. *The Idea of Race in Science: Great Britain, 1800–1960*. London: Macmillan and St. Antony's College, Oxford, 1982.

Stern, Alexandra Minna. "Responsible Mothers and Normal Children: Eugenics, Welfare, and Nationalism in Post-Revolutionary Mexico, 1900–1940." *Journal of Historical Sociology* 12, no. 4 (Fall 1999): 369–97.

Stern, Steve J. "The Age of Andean Insurrection, 1742–1782: A Reappraisal." In *Resistance, Rebellion, and Consciousness in the Andean Peasant World, Eighteenth to Twentieth Centuries*, edited by Steve J. Stern. Madison: University of Wisconsin Press, 1987.

——. *The Secret History of Gender: Women, Men, and Power in Late Colonial Mexico*. Chapel Hill: University of North Carolina Press, 1995.

Stocking, George W., Jr. *Race, Culture, and Evolution: Essays in the History of Anthropology*. New York: Free Press, 1968.

Stolcke, Verena. "Talking Culture: New Boundaries, New Rhetorics of Exclusion in Europe." *Current Anthropology* 46, no. 1 (Feb. 1995): 1–24.

Stoler, Ann Laura. *Race and the Education of Desire: Foucault's* History of Sexuality *and the Colonial Order of Things*. Durham: Duke University Press, 1995.

——. "Racial Histories and Their Regimes of Truth." *Political Power and Social Theory* 11 (1997): 183–206.

——. "Sexual Affronts and Racial Frontiers: European Identities and the Cultural Politics of Exclusion in Colonial Southeast Asia." In *Tensions of Empire: Colonial Cultures in a Bourgeois World*, edited by Frederick Cooper and Ann Laura Stoler (Berkeley: University of California Press, 1997).

Stovall, Tyler. *Paris Noir: African Americans in the City of Light*. Boston: Houghton Mifflin, 1996.

Strathern, Marilyn. *After Nature: English Kinship in the Late Twentieth Century*. Cambridge: Cambridge University Press, 1992.

Streicker, Joel. "Policing Boundaries: Race, Class, and Gender in Cartagena, Colombia." *American Ethnologist* 22, no. 1 (Feb. 1995): 54–74.

Stubbs, Jean. "Social and Political Motherhood of Cuba: Mariana Grajales Cuello." In *Engendering History: Caribbean Women in Historical Perspective*, edited by Verene Shepherd, Bridget Brereton, and Barbara Bailey. New York: St. Martin's Press, 1995.

Stutzman, Ronald. "*El Mestizaje*: An All-Inclusive Ideology of Exclusion." In *Cultural Transformations and Ethnicity in Modern Ecuador*, edited by Norman E. Whitten Jr. Urbana: University of Illinois Press, 1981.

Szuchman, Mark D., and Jonathan C. Brown, eds. *Revolution and Restoration: The Rearrangement of Power in Argentina, 1776–1860*. Lincoln: University of Nebraska Press, 1994.

Tannenbaum, Frank. *Slave and Citizen: The Negro in the Americas*. New York: Random House, 1946.

Taracena Arriola, Arturo. *Invención criolla, sueño ladino, pesadilla indígena: Los Altos de Guatemala: De región a estado, 1740–1850*. Antigua, Guatemala: Centro de Investigaciones Regionales de Mesoamérica, 1997.

Taussig, Michael. *The Magic of the State*. New York: Routledge, 1997.

——. *Shamanism, Colonialism, and the Wild Man: A Study in Terror and Healing*. Chicago: University of Chicago Press, 1987.

Tenorio-Trillo, Mauricio. *Mexico at the World's Fairs: Crafting a Modern Nation*. Berkeley: University of California Press, 1996.

Tepaske, John J., and Herbert S. Klein. *Peru*. Vol. 1 of *The Royal Treasuries of the Spanish Empire in America*. Durham: Duke University Press, 1982.

Thurner, Mark. *From Two Republics to One Divided: Contradictions of Postcolonial Nationmaking in Andean Peru*. Durham: Duke University Press, 1997.

Tinker Salas, Miguel. *In the Shadow of the Eagles: Sonora and the Transformation of the Border during the Porfiriato*. Berkeley: University of California Press, 1997.

Todorov, Tzvetan. *On Human Diversity: Nationalism, Racism, and Exoticism in French Thought*. Cambridge, Mass.: Harvard University Press, 1993.

Torres-Saillant, Silvio. "The Tribulations of Blackness: Stages in Dominican Racial Identity." *Callaloo* 23, no. 3 (Summer 2000): 1086–111.

Tracy, Sarah W. "An Evolving Science of Man: The Transformation and Demise of American Constitutional Medicine, 1920–1950." In *Greater Than the Parts: Holism in Biomedicine, 1920–1950*, edited by Christopher Lawrence and George Weisz. New York: Oxford University Press, 1998.

——. "George Draper and American Constitutional Medicine, 1916–1946: Reinventing the Sick Man." *Bulletin of the History of Medicine* 66, no. 1 (Spring 1992): 53–89.

Troyan, Brett. "The Indigenous Rural Folk's Discourses and Identities in the '30s and '40s of the Twentieth Century in Cauca, Colombia." Paper presented at the Conference on Latin American History, Boston, 4–7 Jan. 2001.

Turits, Richard Lee. "A World Destroyed, a Nation Imposed: The 1937 Haitian Massacre in the Dominican Republic." *Hispanic American Historical Review* 82, no. 3 (Aug. 2002): 585–630.

Twinam, Ann. *Public Lives, Private Secrets: Gender, Honor, Sexuality, and Illegitimacy in Colonial Spanish America*. Stanford: Stanford University Press, 1999.

Twine, France Winddance. *Racism in a Racial Democracy: The Maintenance of White Supremacy in Brazil*. New Brunswick: Rutgers University Press, 1998.

UNESCO. *The Race Concept: Results of an Inquiry*. Paris: UNESCO, 1951.

Urban, Greg, and Joel Sherzer, eds. *Nation-States and Indians in Latin America*. Austin: University of Texas Press, 1991.

Valencia Llano, Alonso. *Estado soberano del Cauca: Federalismo y regeneración*. Bogotá: Banco de la República, 1988.

Vallieres, Pierre. *White Niggers of America: The Precocious Autobiography of a Quebec "Terrorist."* New York: Monthly Review Press, 1971.

Van Cott, Donna Lee. *The Friendly Liquidation of the Past: The Politics of Diversity in Latin America*. Pittsburgh: University of Pittsburgh Press, 2000.

Van Young, Eric. "The New Cultural History Comes to Old Mexico." *Hispanic American Historical Review* 79, no. 2 (May 1999): 211–47.

Vargas, Getúlio. *Diário*. Vol. 2, *1937–1942*. Rio de Janiero: Siciliano/Fundação Getúlio Vargas, 1995.

Vasconcelos, José. *Breve historia de México*. Mexico City: Trillas, 1987.

——. *The Cosmic Race/La raza cósmica*. Translated and with an introduction by Didier T. Jaén. Baltimore: Johns Hopkins University Press, 1997.

——. *Ulises criollo*. Edited by Claude Fell. Madrid: ALLCA, XX, 2000.

Vaughan, Mary Kay. *Cultural Politics in Revolution: Teachers, Peasants, and Schools in Mexico, 1930–1940*. Tucson: University of Arizona Press, 1997.

Vianna, Hermano. *The Mystery of Samba: Popular Music and National Identity in Brazil*. Edited and translated by John Charles Chasteen. Chapel Hill: University of North Carolina Press, 1999.

Villegas, Jorge, and Antonio Restrepo. *Resguardos de indígenas, 1820–1890*. Medellín: Universidad de Antioquia, 1977.

Vollmer, Günter. *Bevölkerungspolitik und Bevölkerungsstruktur im Vizekonigreich Peru zu Ende der Kolonialzeit (1741–1821)*. Bad Homburg: Gehlen, 1967.

Voss, Stuart F. *On the Periphery of Nineteenth-Century Mexico: Sonora and Sinaloa, 1810–1877*. Tucson: University of Arizona Press, 1982.

Wade, Peter. *Blackness and Race Mixture: The Dynamics of Racial Identity in Colombia*. Baltimore: Johns Hopkins University Press, 1993.

——. "The Cultural Politics of Blackness in Colombia." *American Ethnologist* 22, no. 2 (May 1995): 342–58.

——. "The Guardians of Power: Biodiversity and Multiculturality in Colombia." In *The Anthropology of Power: Empowerment and Disempowerment in Changing Structures*, edited by Angela Cheater. London: Routledge, 1999.

——. *Music, Race, and Nation: Música Tropical in Colombia*. Chicago: University of Chicago Press, 2000.

——. "Negros, indígenas e identidad nacional en Colombia." In *Imaginar la nación*, edited by François-Xavier Guerra and Mónica Quijada. Münster: Lit, 1994.

——. "La population noire en Amérique latine: Multiculturalisme, législation et situation territoriale." *Problèmes d'Amérique Latine*, no. 32 (1999): 3–16.

——. *Race, Nature, and Culture: An Anthropological Perspective*. London: Pluto Press, 2002.

——. *Race and Ethnicity in Latin America*. London: Pluto Press, 1997.

Walker, Charles F. "Los indios en la transición de colonia a república." In *Tradición y modernidad en los Andes*, edited by Henrique Urbano. Cuzco: Centro de Estudios Andinos Bartolomé de las Casas, 1992.

——. *Smoldering Ashes: Cuzco and the Creation of Republican Peru, 1780–1840*. Durham: Duke University Press, 1999.

Weinstein, Barbara. "Brazilian Regionalism." *Latin American Research Review* 17, no. 2 (Summer 1982): 262–76.

——. "The Decline of the Progressive Planter and the Rise of Subaltern Agency: Shifting Narratives of Slave Emancipation in Brazil." In *Reclaiming the Political in Latin American History: Essays from the North*, edited by Gilbert M. Joseph. Durham: Duke University Press, 2001.

——. *For Social Peace in Brazil: Industrialists and the Remaking of the Working Class in São Paulo, 1920–1964*. Chapel Hill: University of North Carolina Press, 1996.

——. "Unskilled Worker, Skilled Housewife: Constructing the Working-Class Housewife in São Paulo, Brazil, 1900–1950." In *The Gendered Worlds of Latin American Women Workers: From the Household and Factory to the Union Hall and Ballot Box*, edited by John D. French and Daniel James. Durham: Duke University Press, 1997.

Weismantle, Mary, and Stephen F. Eisenman. "Race in the Andes: Global Movements and Popular Ontologies." *Bulletin of American Research* 17, no. 2 (May 1998): 121–42.

Whimster, Sam, and Scott Lash, eds. *Max Weber: Rationality and Modernity*. London: Allen and Unwin, 1987.

Whitten, Norman, Jr. *Black Frontiersmen: A South American Case*. 2d ed. Prospect Heights, Ill.: Waveland Press, 1986.

Whitten, Norman, and Rachel Corr. "Contesting the Images of Oppression: Indigenous Views of Blackness in the Americas." *NACLA Report on the Americas* 34, no. 6 (May–June 2001): 24–28.

Williams, Brackette F. "Classification Systems Revisited: Kinship, Caste, Race, and Nationality as the Flow of Blood and the Spread of Rights." In *Naturalizing Power: Essays in Feminist Cultural Analysis*, edited by Sylvia Yanagisako and Carol Delaney. New York: Routledge, 1995.

———, ed. *Women Out of Place: The Gender of Agency and the Race of Nationality*. New York: Routledge, 1996.

Williams, Derek. "Indians on the Verge: The 'Otavalo Indian' and the Regional Dynamics of the Ecuadorian 'Indian Problem,' 1830–1940." Paper presented at the Conference on Latin American History, Boston, 4–7 Jan. 2001.

Winant, Howard. "Difference and Inequality: Postmodern Racial Politics in the United States." In *Racism, the City and the State*, edited by Malcolm Cross and Michael Keith. London: Routledge, 1993.

———. "Rethinking Race in Brazil." *Journal of Latin American Studies* 24, no. 1 (Feb. 1992): 173–92.

Wirth, John D. *Minas Gerais in the Brazilian Federation, 1889–1937*. Stanford: Stanford University Press, 1977.

Womack, John. *Zapata and the Mexican Revolution*. New York: Alfred A. Knopf, 1960.

Wood, Peter, and Karen C. C. Dalton. *Winslow Homer's Images of Blacks: The Civil War and Reconstruction Years*. Austin: University of Texas Press, 1988.

Wouters, Mieke. "Ethnic Rights under Threat: The Black Peasant Movement against Armed Groups' Pressure in Chocó, Colombia." *Bulletin of Latin American Research* 20, no. 4 (Oct. 2001): 498–519.

Young, Robert J. C. *Colonial Desire: Hybridity in Theory, Culture, and Race*. London: Routledge, 1995.

Zanetti, Oscar. *Cautivos de la reciprocidad: La burguesía cubana y la dependencia comercial*. Havana: Ministerio de Educación Superior, 1989.

Zimmerman, Eduardo A. "Racial Ideas and Social Reform: Argentina, 1890–1916." *Hispanic American Historical Review* 72, no. 1 (Feb. 1992): 23–46.

CONTRIBUTORS

NANCY P. APPELBAUM is Assistant Professor of History and Latin American Studies at the State University of New York at Binghamton. She is the author of *Muddied Waters: Race, Region, and Local History in Colombia, 1846–1948*.

SUEANN CAULFIELD is Associate Professor of History at the University of Michigan. Her publications include *In Defense of Honor: Morality, Modernity, and Nation in Early-Twentieth-Century Brazil* and a number of articles on gender and social history in Brazil and Latin America. Her current research focuses on family history and illegitimacy in twentieth-century Bahia, Brazil.

SARAH C. CHAMBERS is Associate Professor of History at the University of Minnesota. She has published *From Subjects to Citizens: Honor, Gender, and Politics in Arequipa, Peru, 1780–1854*. Her current research focuses on gender during the transition from the colonial to republican periods in Spanish South America.

LILLIAN GUERRA is Assistant Professor of Latin American and Caribbean History at Bates College. Specializing in twentieth-century Puerto Rico and Cuba, she is the author of *Popular Expression and National Identity in Puerto Rico* and a forthcoming book on conflicting nationalisms and revolutionary politics in the Cuban republic. Her current research focuses on gender and sexuality in the regional history of Trinidad, Cuba.

THOMAS C. HOLT is the James Westfall Thompson Professor of American and African-American History at the University of Chicago and a past president of the American Historical Association. Among his recent publications are *The Problem of Freedom: Race, Labor, and Politics in Jamaica and Britain, 1832–1938*, which won the Elsa Goveia Prize from the Association of Caribbean Historians, and *Beyond Slavery: Explorations of Race, Labor, and Citizenship in Postemancipation Societies*, coauthored with Frederick Cooper and Rebecca J. Scott.

ANNE S. MACPHERSON is Associate Professor of Latin American and Caribbean History at SUNY College at Brockport. She is editor of *Backtalking Belize: Selected Writings*, a compilation of works by radical nationalist Assad Shoman, and has written essays on women and politics in Belize and on comparative colonial reform in Puerto Rico and Belize. She is completing a book on gender, colonialism, and nationalism in twentieth-century Belize.

AIMS MCGUINNESS is Assistant Professor of History at the University of Wisconsin–Milwaukee. He received his Ph.D. from the University of Michigan and is currently completing a book on U.S. empire in Panama in the mid-nineteenth century.

GERARDO RÉNIQUE is Associate Professor of History at the City College of the City University of New York. He is the coauthor (with Deborah Poole) of *Peru: Time of Fear* and has written articles on Peru and Mexico. He is completing a manuscript on the anti-Chinese movement and the racial and nationalist projects of the Sonoran revolutionary faction that laid the foundations of Mexico's postrevolutionary state.

KARIN ALEJANDRA ROSEMBLATT is Associate Professor of History and Senior Research Associate in the Moynihan Institute of Global Affairs at Syracuse University. Her book *Gendered Compromises: Political Cultures and the State in Chile, 1920–1950* was cowinner of the 2000 Berkshire Prize. She is currently conducting research on the transnational politics of class, race, and urban poverty.

JAMES SANDERS is Assistant Professor of History at Utah State University. His book on the social history of politics of Indians, Afro-Colombians, and Antioqueño migrants, *Contentious Republicans: Popular Politics, Race, and Class in Nineteenth-Century Colombia*, was recently published.

ALEXANDRA MINNA STERN is Associate Director of the Center for the History of Medicine and Assistant Professor in the Program in American Culture at the University of Michigan. Her book, *Eugenic Nation: Faults and Frontiers of Better Breeding in Modern America*, is forthcoming from the University of California Press.

PETER WADE is Professor of Social Anthropology at the University of Manchester. His publications include *Blackness and Race Mixture: The Dynamics of Racial Identity in Colombia*; *Race and Ethnicity in Latin America*; *Music, Race, and Nation: Música Tropical in Colombia*; and *Race, Nation, and Culture: An Anthropological Perspective*.

BARBARA WEINSTEIN is Professor of History at the University of Maryland and coeditor of the *Hispanic American Historical Review.* Her most recent book is *For Social Peace in Brazil: Industrialists and the Remaking of the Working Class in São Paulo, 1920–1964.* She is currently working on a study of race, gender, and the construction of regional and national identities in Brazil.

INDEX

Italic page numbers refer to illustrations.